# The IDG Books *Creating Cool*™ Series Advantage

We at IDG Books Worldwide created *Creating Cool™ Web Pages with Perl* to meet your growing need for quick access to the most complete and accurate computer information available. Our books work the way you do: They focus on accomplishing specific tasks — not learning random functions. Our books are not long-winded manuals or dry reference tomes. In each book, expert authors tell you exactly what you can do and how to do it. Easy to follow, step-by-step sections; comprehensive coverage; and convenient access in language and design — it's all here.

The authors of IDG books are uniquely qualified to give you expert advice as well as to provide insightful tips and techniques not found anywhere else. Our authors maintain close contact with end users through feedback from articles, training sessions, e-mail exchanges, user group participation, and consulting work. Because our authors know the realities of daily computer use and are directly tied to the reader, our books have a strategic advantage.

Our authors have the experience to approach a topic in the most efficient manner, and we know that you, the reader, will benefit from a "one-on-one" relationship with the author. Our research shows that readers make computer book purchases because they want expert advice. Because readers want to benefit from the author's experience, the author's voice is always present in an IDG book.

In addition, the author is free to include or recommend useful software in an IDG book. The software that accompanies each book is not intended to be casual filler but is linked to the content, theme, or procedures of the book. We know that you will benefit from the included software.

You will find what you need in this book whether you read it from cover to cover, section by section, or simply one topic at a time. As a computer user, you deserve a comprehensive resource of answers. We at IDG Books Worldwide are proud to deliver that resource with *Creating Cool™ Web Pages with Perl.*

Brenda McLaughlin
Senior Vice President and Group Publisher

Internet: YouTellUs@idgbooks.com

# CREATING COOL™ WEB PAGES WITH PERL

Jerry Muelver

IDG Books Worldwide, Inc.
An International Data Group Company

Foster City, CA ♦ Chicago, IL ♦ Indianapolis, IN ♦ Dallas, TX

**Creating Cool™ Web Pages with Perl**

Published by
**IDG Books Worldwide, Inc.**
An International Data Group Company
919 E. Hillsdale Blvd.
Suite 400
Foster City, CA 94404



Library of Congress Catalog Card No.: 96-77080

ISBN: 0-7645-3018-6

Printed in the United States of America

10 9 8 7 6 5 4 3 2 1

1E/RS/QY/ZW/IN

Distributed in the United States by IDG Books Worldwide, Inc.

Distributed by Macmillan Canada for Canada; by Contemporanea de Ediciones for Venezuela; by Distribuidora Cuspide for Argentina; by CITEC for Brazil; by Ediciones ZETA S.C.R. Ltda. for Peru; by Editorial Limusa SA for Mexico; by Transworld Publishers Limited in the United Kingdom and Europe; by Academic Bookshop for Egypt; by Levant Distributors S.A.R.L. for Lebanon; by Al Jassim for Saudi Arabia; by Simron Pty. Ltd. for South Africa; by Pustak Mahal for India; by The Computer Bookshop for India; by Toppan Company Ltd. for Japan; by Addison Wesley Publishing Company for Korea; by Longman Singapore Publishers Ltd. for Singapore, Malaysia, Thailand, and Indonesia; by Unalis Corporation for Taiwan; by WS Computer Publishing Company, Inc. for the Philippines; by WoodsLane Pty. Ltd. for Australia; by WoodsLane Enterprises Ltd. for New Zealand. Authorized Sales Agent: Anthony Rudkin Associates for the Middle East and North Africa.

For general information on IDG Books Worldwide's books in the U.S., please call our Consumer Customer Service department at 800-762-2974. For reseller information, including discounts and premium sales, please call our Reseller Customer Service department at 800-434-3422.

For information on where to purchase IDG Books Worldwide's books outside the U.S., contact IDG Books Worldwide's International Sales department at 415-655-3172 or fax 415-655-3295.

For information on foreign language translations, contact IDG Books Worldwide's Foreign & Subsidiary Rights department at 415-655-3021 or fax 415-655-3281.

For sales inquiries and special prices for bulk quantities, contact IDG Books Worldwide's Sales department at 415-655-3200 or write to the address above.

For information on using IDG Books Worldwide's books in the classroom or for ordering examination copies, contact IDG Books Worldwide's Educational Sales department at 800-434-2086 or fax 817-251-8174.

# About the Author

Jerry Muelver has been freelancing in technical writing and its associated fields (photography, programming, desktop publishing) since 1966. He considers computer languages, karate, and the vibraphone to be high sport and pursues them all with roughly the same enthusiasm and technique, somewhat to the dismay of his betters in those fields.

"My saving grace," says Jerry, "is a knack for explaining. New concepts and techniques are challenging and fun to learn, but the real kick comes in simplifying the complicated and explaining it to people. I like to see them light up when an explanation clicks." He lives in the southern Wisconsin lake country near Oconomowoc. When he is not online (home page at `http://www.hytext.com`), Jerry is in the oak woods off the back deck, battling the invading buckthorn over the issue of property rights.

# ABOUT IDG BOOKS WORLDWIDE

Welcome to the world of IDG Books Worldwide.

IDG Books Worldwide, Inc., is a subsidiary of International Data Group, the world's largest publisher of computer-related information and the leading global provider of information services on information technology. IDG was founded more than 25 years ago and now employs more than 8,500 people worldwide. IDG publishes more than 270 computer publications in over 75 countries (see listing below). More than 90 million people read one or more IDG publications each month.

Launched in 1990, IDG Books Worldwide is today the #1 publisher of best-selling computer books in the United States. We are proud to have received eight awards from the Computer Press Association in recognition of editorial excellence and three from *Computer Currents*' First Annual Readers' Choice Awards, and our best-selling . . .*For Dummies*® series has more than 25 million copies in print with translations in 28 languages. IDG Books Worldwide, through a joint venture with IDG's Hi-Tech Beijing, became the first U.S. publisher to publish a computer book in the People's Republic of China. In record time, IDG Books Worldwide has become the first choice for millions of readers around the world who want to learn how to better manage their businesses.

Our mission is simple: Every one of our books is designed to bring extra value and skill-building instructions to the reader. Our books are written by experts who understand and care about our readers. The knowledge base of our editorial staff comes from years of experience in publishing, education, and journalism — experience which we use to produce books for the '90s. In short, we care about books, so we attract the best people. We devote special attention to details such as audience, interior design, use of icons, and illustrations. And because we use an efficient process of authoring, editing, and desktop publishing our books electronically, we can spend more time ensuring superior content and spend less time on the technicalities of making books.

You can count on our commitment to deliver high-quality books at competitive prices on topics you want to read about. At IDG Books Worldwide, we continue in the IDG tradition of delivering quality for more than 25 years. You'll find no better book on a subject than one from IDG Books Worldwide.

John Kilcullen
President and CEO
IDG Books Worldwide, Inc.

IDG Books Worldwide, Inc., is a subsidiary of International Data Group, the world's largest publisher of computer-related information and the leading global provider of information services on information technology. International Data Group publishes over 270 computer publications in over 75 countries. Ninety million people read one or more International Data Group publications each month. International Data Group's publications include: **ARGENTINA:** Annuario de Informatica, Computerworld Argentina, Infoworld, PC World Argentina; **AUSTRALIA:** Australian Macworld, au.World, Client/Server Journal, Computer Living, Computerworld, Computerworld 100, Digital News, Network World, PC World, Publishing Essentials, Reseller, WebMaster; **AUSTRIA:** Computerwelt Osterreich, Networks Austria, PC Tip; **BELARUS:** PC World Belarus; **BELGIUM:** Data News; **BRAZIL:** Annuário de Informática, Computerworld Brazil, Connections, Super Game Power, Macworld, PC World Brazil, Publish Brazil, SUPERGAME; **BULGARIA:** Computerworld Bulgaria, Networkworld/Bulgaria, PC & MacWorld Bulgaria; **CANADA:** CIO Canada, Client/Server World, ComputerWorld Canada, InfoCanada, Network World Canada; **CHILE:** Computerworld Chile, PC World Chile; **COLOMBIA:** Computerworld Colombia, PC World Colombia; **COSTA RICA:** PC World Costa Rica/Nicaragua; **THE CZECH AND SLOVAK REPUBLICS:** Computerworld Czechoslovakia, Elektronika Czechoslovakia, PC World Czechoslovakia; **DENMARK:** Communications World, Computerworld Danmark, Macworld Danmark, PC Privat Danmark, PC World Danmark, PC World Danmark Supplements, TECH World; **DOMINICAN REPUBLIC:** PC World Republica Dominicana; **ECUADOR:** PC World Ecuador; **EGYPT:** Computerworld Middle East, PC World Middle East; **EL SALVADOR:** PC World Centro America; **FINLAND:** MikroPC, Tietoverkko, Tietoviikko; **FRANCE:** Distributique, Golden, Hebdo-Distributique, Info PC, Le Guide du Monde Informatique, Le Monde Informatique, Reseaux & Telecoms; **GERMANY:** Computer Partner, Computerwoche, Computerwoche Extra, Computerwoche Focus, Electronic Entertainment, GamePro, I/M Information Management, Macwelt, PC Welt; **GREECE:** GamePro, Multimedia World; **GUATEMALA:** PC World Centro America; **HONDURAS:** PC World Centro America; **HONG KONG:** Computerworld Hong Kong, PCWorld Hong Kong, Publish in Asia; **HUNGARY:** ABCD CD-ROM, Computerworld Szamitastechnika, PC & Mac World Hungary, PC-X Magazine; **ICELAND:** Tolvuheimur/PC World Island; **INDIA:** Computerworld India, PC World India, Publish in Asia; **INDONESIA:** InfoKomputer PC World, Komputek Computerworld, Publish in Asia; **IRELAND:** ComputerScope, PC Live!; **ISRAEL:** People & Computers; **ITALY:** Computerworld Italia, Computerworld Italia Special Editions, Macworld Italia, Networking Italia, PC Shopping, PC World Italia, PC World/Walt Disney; **JAPAN:** Macworld Japan, Nikkei Personal Computing, SunWorld Japan, Windows World Japan; **KENYA:** East African Computer News; **KOREA:** Hi-Tech Information/Computerworld, Macworld Korea, PC World Korea; **MACEDONIA:** PC World Macedonia; **MALAYSIA:** Computerworld Malaysia, PC World Malaysia, Publish in Asia; **MEXICO:** Computerworld Mexico, Macworld, PC World Mexico; **MYANMAR:** PC World Myanmar; **NETHERLANDS:** Computable, Computer! Totaal, LAN Magazine, LanWorld Buyers Guide, Macworld, Net Magazine, Totaal! Beurskrant; **NEW ZEALAND:** Absolute Beginner's Guide, Computer Buyer, Computer Industry Directory, Computerworld New Zealand, Electronic Entertainment, MTB, Network World, PC World New Zealand; **NICARAGUA:** PC World Costa Rica/Nicaragua; **NIGERIA:** PC World Nigeria; **NORWAY:** CAD/CAM World Norge, Computerworld Norge, Computerworld Privat (Datamagasinet), CW Rapport Norge, IDG's KURSGUIDE, Macworld Norge, Multimediaworld, PC World Ekspress, PC World Nettverk, PC World Norge, PC World's Produktguide; **PAKISTAN:** Computerworld Pakistan, PC World Pakistan; **PANAMA:** PC World Panama; **P. R. OF CHINA:** China Computer Users, China Computerworld, China Infoworld, Computer & Communication, Electronic Design China, Electronics Today, Electronics Weekly, Game Camp, PC World China, Popular Computer Weekly, Software Weekly, Software World, Telecom World; **PERU:** Computerworld Peru, PC World Profesional Peru, PC World Peru; **PHILIPPINES:** Computerworld Philippines, PC World Philippines, Publish in Asia; **POLAND:** Computerworld Poland, Computerworld Special Report, Macworld, Networld, PC World Komputer; **PORTUGAL:** Cerebro/PC World, Computerworld/Correio Informático, MacIn/PCIn, Multimedia World Portugal; **PUERTO RICO:** PC World Puerto Rico; **ROMANIA:** Computerworld Romania, PC World Romania, Telecom Romania; **RUSSIA:** Computerworld Russia, Mir PK, Sety; **SINGAPORE:** Computerworld Singapore, PC World Singapore, Publish in Asia; **SLOVENIA:** MONITOR; **SOUTH AFRICA:** Computing S.A., InfoWorld S.A., Network World S.A., Software World; **SPAIN:** Computerworld España, COMUNICACIONES WORLD, Dealer World, Macworld España, PC World España; **SWEDEN:** CAP&Design, Computer Sweden, Corporate Computing, MacWorld, Maxi Data, MikroDatorn, Nätverk & Kommunikation, PC/Aktiv, PC World, Windows World; **SWITZERLAND:** Computerworld Schweiz, Macworld Schweiz, PCtip; **TAIWAN:** Computerworld Taiwan, Macworld Taiwan, PC World Taiwan, Publish Taiwan, Windows World; **THAILAND:** Thai Computerworld, PC World Thailand, Publish in Asia; **TURKEY:** Computerworld Monitör, MACWORLD Turkiye, PC Games, PC WORLD Turkiye; **UKRAINE:** Computerworld Kiev, Computers & Software, Multimedia World Ukraine, PC World Ukraine; **UNITED KINGDOM:** Acorn User, Amiga Action, Amiga Computing, Appletalk, CD-ROM Now, Computing, GamePro, Macaction, Macworld, Network News, Parents and Computers, PC Home, PSX Pro UK, The WEB; **UNITED STATES:** Cable in the Classroom, CD Review, CIO Magazine, Computerworld, Computerworld Client/Server Journal, Digital Video Magazine, DOS World, Electronic Entertainment, Federal Computer Week, GamePro, InfoWorld, I+Way, JavaWorld, Macworld, Maximize, Multimedia World, Netscape World, Network World, PC World, Publish, SunWorld Online, SWATPro Magazine, Video Event, WebMaster; **URUGUAY:** PC World Uruguay; **VENEZUELA:** Computerworld Venezuela, PC World Venezuela; and **VIETNAM:** PC World Vietnam.

6/24/96

# Dedication

This book is dedicated to my wife, Susan Stacy, who expects me to have the right answer for any question on any topic, and to the crowd of friends and acquaintances on CompuServe who know better than to hold such high expectations.

# Acknowledgments

I owe these people, and many more like them:

My wife, Susan Stacy, pushed me for years to get my writing out of client-bound corporate anonymity so that the public at large could assume some of the reading burden. My parents, Emil and Goldie Muelver, built for me and my talented siblings a nurturing environment where wit and a facility for language were always more important than the jingle of coins in a pocket. Ron Wodaski got me into writing this book and, superb agent that he is, cajoled me successfully through the entire process. Pat O'Brien, Kerrie Klein, Greg Croy, and the rest of the staff at IDG Books showed such faith in their budding author that they conspired to bend the rules now and then to let me have my way. Technical editor Gary Johnson extracted the marrow from the bones of Perl and shined a light into nooks and crannies where few had dared to look. My understanding karate buddies and teacher Roger Salick, and long-suffering vibraphone instructor Carl Storniolo, helped me juggle conflicting priorities and maintain my internal harmonies throughout this book's gestation and final birth.

My fond appreciation goes to the CompuServe gang on the Internet Publishing Forum and the Technical Writing section of the Writers Forum for putting up with my jabs and jibes this winter and spring. The daily injection of advice, counsel, and buffoonery kept my creative juices flowing and my typing fingers nimble. Special thanks go to the helpful group of volunteer manuscript readers and code testers — you delighted me with your questions and amazed me with your ability to actually learn Perl from my draft manuscripts.

A note of thanks to Randal Schwartz, author of *Learning Perl* (the LlamaBook), whose prompt, incisive repines to a question of mine on the `comp.lang.perl.misc` newsgroup unlocked a key mystery for me.

Finally, my deep gratitude and awe to Larry Wall, author of Perl the language and *Programming Perl* (the Camel Book), for creating and supporting Perl, the language I might have invented if I were 50 times smarter than I am. What a piece of work!

*(The publisher would like to give special thanks to Patrick J. McGovern, without whom this book would not have been published.)*

# Credits

**Senior Vice President and Group Publisher**
Brenda McLaughlin

**Acquisitions Manager**
Gregory S. Croy

**Acquisitions Editor**
Ellen L. Camm

**Software Acquisitions Editor**
Tracy Lehman Cramer

**Brand Manager**
Melisa M. Duffy

**Managing Editor**
Andy Cummings

**Administrative Assistant**
Laura J. Moss

**Editorial Assistant**
Timothy J. Borek

**Production Director**
Beth Jenkins

**Supervisor of Project Coordination**
Cindy L. Phipps

**Supervisor of Page Layout**
Kathie S. Schutte

**Supervisor of Graphics and Design**
Shelley Lea

**Production Systems Specialist**
Debbie J. Gates

**Development Editor**
Pat O'Brien

**Copy Editor**
Kerrie Klein

**Technical Editor**
Gary Johnson

**Project Coordinator**
Regina Snyder

**Layout and Graphics**
E. Shawn Aylsworth
Brett Black
Elizabeth Cárdenas-Nelson
J. Tyler Connor
Dominique DeFelice
Maridee V. Ennis
Angela F. Hunckler
Jane Martin
Brent Savage
Gina Scott
Michael Sullivan

**Proofreaders**
Joel Draper
Michelle Shaw
Robert Springer
Carrie Voorhis
Karen York

**Indexer**
David Heiret

**Production Administration**
Tony Augsburger
Todd Klemme
Jason Marcuson
Jacalyn L. Pennywell
Leslie Popplewell
Patricia R. Reynolds
Theresa Sánchez-Baker
Melissa Stauffer
Bryan Stephenson

**Book Design**
three 8 Creative Group

Contents
at a
Glance

Table
of
Contents

# Foreword

The rise in popularity of the Internet has dubbed the 1990s "The Information Age." Competition between Internet Service Providers means that more and more of the world's population is surfing the World Wide Web, all of them searching for that "perfect wave" of information that fulfills their needs.

For users, finding the information they need has become increasingly difficult as the sheer volume of data on the Internet continues to grow. Search engines and other Internet agents are fast becoming a popular way to locate the required data quickly and efficiently.

For business, the need to provide information to attract consumers is combined with the need to gather information about those consumers and their responses to the products or services being offered. Online feedback surveys and other interactive forms enable businesses to gather statistical data on their customer base, which enables the business to tailor their efforts to best meet the desires of the consumer. Of course, the ability to provide a sales outlet on a Web page gives the consumer a painless method of shopping and provides the business with an opportunity to increase sales from "impulse buying."

Jerry Muelver's extensive background in technical writing, his facility for programming, and his quick wit have allowed him to eliminate from this text the dry and verbose style of writing so often found in programming manuals. There's certainly no techno-babble here! His style makes *Creating Cool Web Pages with Perl* both fun to read and easy to follow, even for those with very little exposure to programming concepts.

*Creating Cool Web Pages with Perl* will take you step-by-step through the Perl programming language. Using Perl, you will be able to write programs that enable users to search the contents of your Web pages and allow you to collect data from your users that you can use to enhance your business. Perl programs can also be constructed as great time-saving devices for managing large Web sites with hundreds of files or for non-Internet projects like a telephone directory.

Best of all, you can improve your social life, fight disease, and cure baldness now that you're "cool."

**Dave Navarro**
**Director of Technical Support, PowerBASIC, Inc.**

# Instant Perl for the Internet

**Skill Targets**

- Setting up Perl for your computer
- Issuing Perl instructions on the command line
- Writing and running basic Perl scripts
- Writing a Perl program to find a specific text pattern in any file

This chapter begins with a gentle jostle to get you up and running with Perl and then turns serious and preachy toward the end. I start with the command `perl -v` on a bare command line and finish with how to program a useful, file-searching tool. That is a long way to go in one short chapter.

To get started in Perl, you need a firm grasp of some simple concepts and principles. Because these unfamiliar topics are interlinked, I explain them by skipping lightly from stone to stone to get you safely across the stream. We'll have plenty of time later to turn over those stones and see all the wonders they hide.

You may feel a moment or two of disorientation when getting started. Have no fear — that feeling will pass before you are halfway through Chapter 2. So, press on and have confidence in your eventual success.

# How Perl Works

Perl (*P*rogram *E*xtraction and *R*eport *L*anguage), which started out as a UNIX system administration tool, grew from an enhancement of some of the text processing and formatting tools available on UNIX installations into a language all its own. Perl processes data. In the simplest scenario, you enter raw data and files at one end (standard input, called `STDIN`) and get organized, formatted, useful information from the other end (standard output, called `STDOUT`). The process is flexible, fast, and relatively painless.

Perl is a computer language interpreter that works like QBasic or any other interpreter. It needs an instruction or a script full of instructions to know what to do. Programming in Perl consists of writing instructions — no more, no less. In case you skipped the Introduction, I'll repeat the (obligatory for all programming books) instruction for printing "Hello, World!":

```
print "Hello, World!"
```

Some Perl instructions can run right on the command line. I show you how to create Perl programs like "Hello, World!" on the command line after I talk about installing Perl.

Computer language compilers start by reading a script, but instead of just following the instructions, they translate the script into an executable program. For example, instead of running a script to say "Hello," a compiled language produces a stand-alone program (probably called `hello.exe`). (See Figure 1-1.) The EXE program runs on its own and doesn't need the compiler's help anymore. You cannot directly read `hello.exe` and understand it because it is no longer a script. What's worse, from the programmer standpoint, is that an EXE for Windows won't run on a UNIX computer or a Mac. That problem spells trouble if you want to develop programs on a DOS machine and then run them on a UNIX Internet server.

The key advantage of an interpreted language such as Perl for CGI programming is that Perl scripts are platform-independent. The interpreter on each machine can read the script you wrote and convert it to machine instructions for its own CPU. As a result, you can program and test scripts in Windows, transfer the scripts to a UNIX machine, and know that they will run correctly.

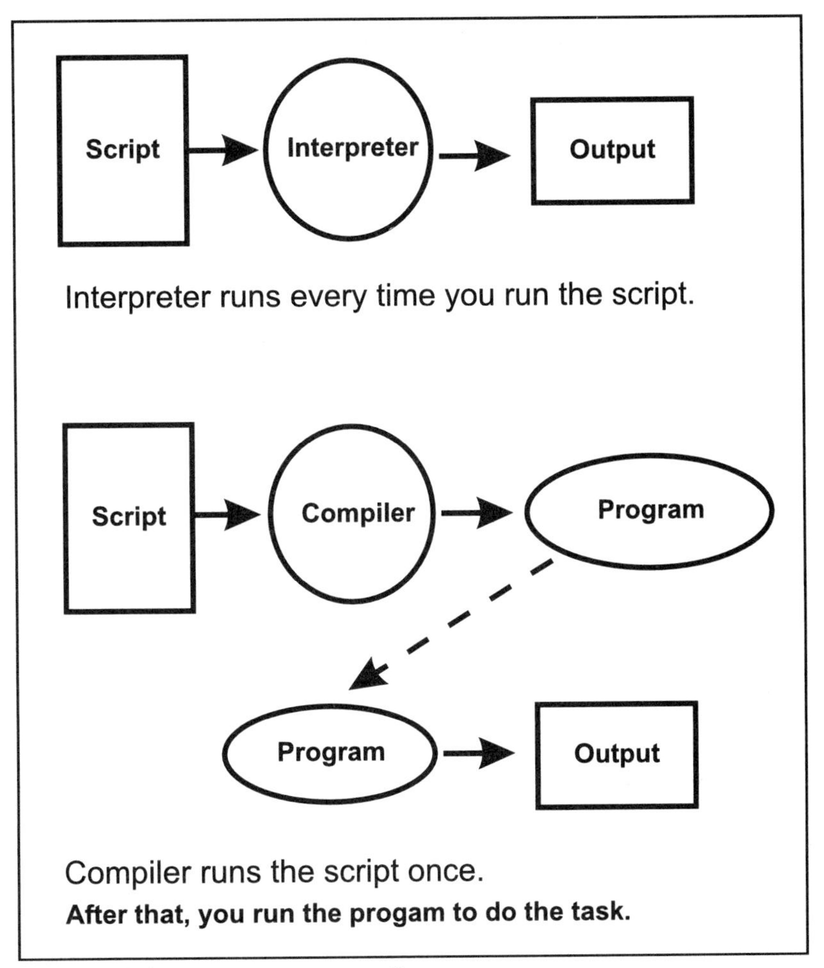


**Figure 1-1:** Interpreters versus compilers.

# Installing Perl

Perl 4 consists of two programs on most operating systems:

- **PERL.EXE** — The Perl interpreter
- **PERLGLOB.EXE** — The Perl helper for file and directory handling

Both programs must be in a directory on your system's search path. I put them in C:\DOS on my computer.

## Installing from the CD-ROM

To install Perl from the CD-ROM included with this book, do one of the following:

- For DOS or Windows 3.11, go to the \PERLDOS directory on the CD-ROM and from there copy `perl.exe` and `perlglob.exe` to a directory in your PATH (for instance, C:\DOS).
- For Windows 95, go to the \PERL5 directory on the CD-ROM and run `setup.bat` from there.

## Upgrading from Internet sources

You can find the latest versions of Perl 5 for Windows 95 and NT at

```
http://info.hip.com/info/
```

# Hands-On Perl Tutorial

Learning a computer language is like learning to play a musical instrument. You cannot just read a book about the topic and then go out and do it. You have to practice, study, and then practice some more. For learning Perl, that means you have to write programs and make them work.

### The Hard Way is the Easiest

You can learn Perl any way that you want, but, as the author, I have to tell you the method that I know works best. Typing the Perl code found in this book into your computer is the fastest, most effective way to learn Perl. I know it looks like useless drudgery — after all, every program and exercise from this book is already on the CD-ROM, so you can just copy and paste and be done with it.

A mysterious link exists between the fingers and the brain, however, that kicks in and solidifies your widening circle of knowledge if you do the typing yourself. I wish it were different, but it's not. To learn Perl, you have to practice.

## Setting up: Welcome to the command line!

Everything in Perl happens on the command line. Perl doesn't care about GUIs (Graphical User Interfaces) and formatted input screens. Rather, you only need a DOS prompt and command line to do basic Perl. If you add a text editor in another DOS window, you've got a complete programming environment. The best thing about Windows, from a Perl programmer's command-line view, is the ease of producing multiple DOS windows to get more command lines, which you can then use simultaneously (Figure 1-2).

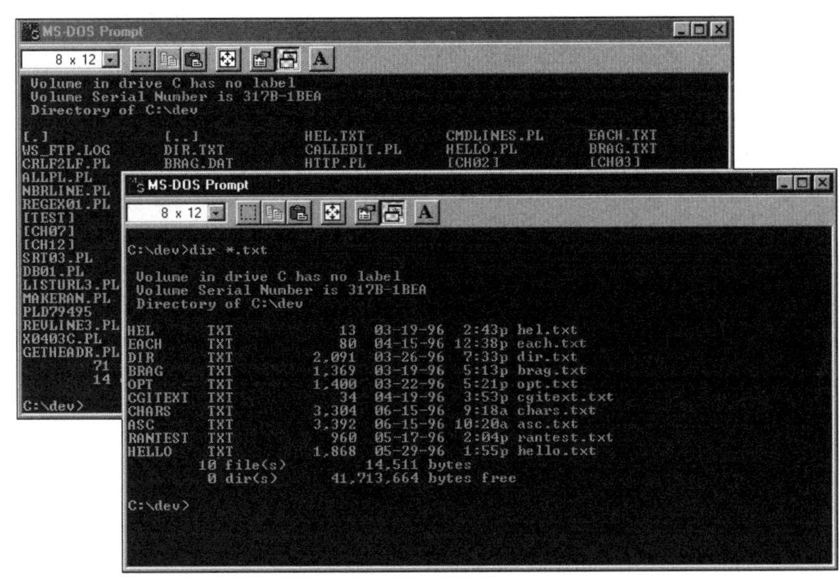


**Figure 1-2:** Multiple command lines in action.

## Command line versus script

In the same way that `command.com` does with file instructions such as Copy and Delete, Perl can grab an instruction from the command line and run with it. But life on the command line is very temporary. You type in the command, such as the print "Hello World!" instruction, run it, and that's it. The next time you want to greet the world, you have to invent the same wheel all over again.

Scripts have a permanence to them that is so gratifying that I even put one-liners such as "Hello World!" into scripts. That way, the next time I need the greeting, my script is there. And best of all, I know in advance that the tiny program will work because I've already polished, shined, and debugged it. In a short time, I can amass an entire directory of these little gems.

I know people who can call up the command line, bang out a Perl instruction, and have it work correctly the first time they run it. These people are called *programmers.* Those users who fall into the *ordinary people* category, like me, are much better off writing their Perl programs in scripts, because scripts allow for creative tinkering and adjusting and convenient re-use.

## One-liners: command-line action

Once you install Perl, you will be ready to start testing it. Perl tells you about itself if you enter the command `perl -v` to check for the version number:

```
C:\dev>perl -v

This is perl, version 5.001

        Unofficial patchlevel 1m.

Copyright 1987-1994, Larry Wall
Win32 port Copyright (c) 1995 Microsoft Corporation. All rights
reserved.
        Developed by hip communications inc., http://
info.hip.com/info/

        Perl for Win32 Build 105
        Built Jan 31 1996@12:17:54
Perl may be copied only under the terms of either the Artistic
License or the GNU General Public License, which may be found in
the Perl 5.0 source kit.
```

### Where am I?

I use C:\DEV> in my sample command-line exercises in this book to show you that I am dealing directly with the DOS prompt on the C: drive, in a directory called DEV, and not working inside a script. Your command-line prompt will be different, depending on how you set up your programming environment. I suggest putting `perl.exe` and `perlglob.exe` in the \DOS directory so that they appear in your path. Then create a programming directory for your experiments. I usually call mine DEV, so I do my work in C:\DEV, as you can see in the example code.

That is quite a screenful for one version number! Some versions of Perl add a long list of command explanations when you run them with the `-v` option. If Perl's response to your command scrolled off your screen, try piping the text through the DOS `more` command:

```
C:\dev> perl -v | more
```

If the screen is full of text and you can't see your DOS prompt, press Spacebar to see the rest of the output. My screen looks like Figure 1-3.

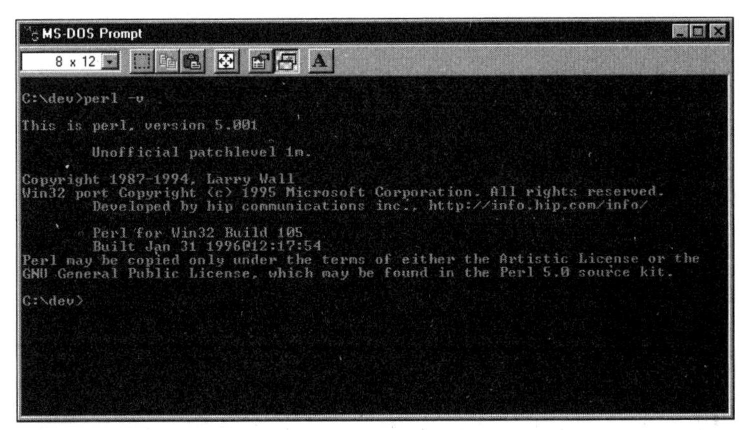


**Figure 1-3:** Perl confesses to command-line options.

UNIX programs typically reply with usage information similar to the previous example if you invoke them without any command-line options or with a special flag such as `-v` or `-?` (which ask for help). In that case, Perl lists its command-line options, each with a brief, sometimes cryptic, description. The following table shows some of the available command-line options. I'll explain what the relevant options do when we reach the point where you use them. For now, be content knowing that you can find a great deal of power and flexibility in Perl if you know where to look.

| Command-Line Option | What It Does |
|---|---|
| `filename` | Run script in filename: `perl hello.pl` |
| `-e` | Run following expression as a one-line program: `perl -e "print 'Hello';"` |
| `-n` | Run following expression as repeating loop program: `perl -n -e "print if /Chicago/;"` |

## Hello, World!

Perl can read a script to get instructions or can take them right off the command line. To tell Perl to use a single command-line instruction, use the `-e` option: `perl -e "something"`. For example, you saw the `print` function in the "Hello, World!" program in the Introduction. To show you how to instruct Perl to use a command-line instruction, I supplied that program here for you to try. On your DOS command line, type everything that appears from `perl` through the last quote and then press Enter (the backslash `-n` is Perl for newline or carriage return; it's needed here because Perl does not automatically go to the next line after printing):

```
C:\dev> perl -e "print 'Hello, World!'\n;"
Hello, World!
```

Why does it work? The `-e` option tells Perl that "Program follows next." The program is the statement `print 'Hello, World!'`. As a result, Perl prints `Hello, World!`

Think of the `-e` option as saying "Evaluate the next expression and execute as a program." When you use this option, type the program (or expression) in double quotes on the command line right after `-e` so that Perl can find it. Notice that the string (sequence of characters) you want Perl to print is enclosed in single quotes to keep Perl from confusing the instruction with what you want printed.

### Warning — Exercise Ahead!

Here comes the work. The fun and games are over. The first of a projected 7,000 (or maybe fewer — actually, a lot fewer) exercises follows immediately after this warning. The exercises are in this book to give you an opportunity to mull the concepts and procedures over in your mind, push them around with your fingers on the keyboard, and stretch them into a shape that fits into your growing knowledge about programming with Perl. Each exercise is doable with the information you've studied up to that point in the book. If you want to experience the thrill of being right, check your answers with the ones I worked out for Appendix A. Matching files are available on the CD-ROM, just in case some tiny, little typing glitch sidetracks your best intentions.

**Exercise 1-1**

You can experiment with replacing single and double quotes in this Hello program to find out what works and what doesn't when you run the command. Type the line a few times with a variety of mistakes to get them out of your system early. You won't break anything, and this method enables you to see how Perl reports errors.

## Redirection

Perl's `print` function just prints — it doesn't care where the data goes. The default target location is called `STDOUT`, or standard output, which usually is the computer monitor (unless you get more specific in your instructions, as I explain later). To aim the output of a command-line program into a file instead of the monitor use the DOS *send to* redirection symbol (>), which traps the data stream and creates a file to hold the captured output:

```
C:\dev> perl -e "print 'Hello, World!';" > hello.txt
```

When you run this command, it looks like nothing happens — Perl just pops up and goes away. In that short time, however, it created `hello.txt` and redirected the `print` output into the file. You can take a peek at the new file by using the DOS `type` command, as in the following example:

```
C:\dev> type hello.txt
Hello, World!
```

The single bracket (>) creates a new file or overwrites a file with the same name. Use the double bracket *append-to* DOS redirection symbol (>>) to append the output to an existing file or to create a new file (if a file with the target filename does not already exist):

```
C:\dev> perl -e "print 'Hello, Anybody!';" >> hello.txt
```

You then can test for success by looking at the contents of the `hello.txt` file, as follows:

```
C:\dev> type hello.txt
Hello, World!
Hello, Anybody!
```

The new message is added to the end of the `hello.txt` file (Figure 1-4).

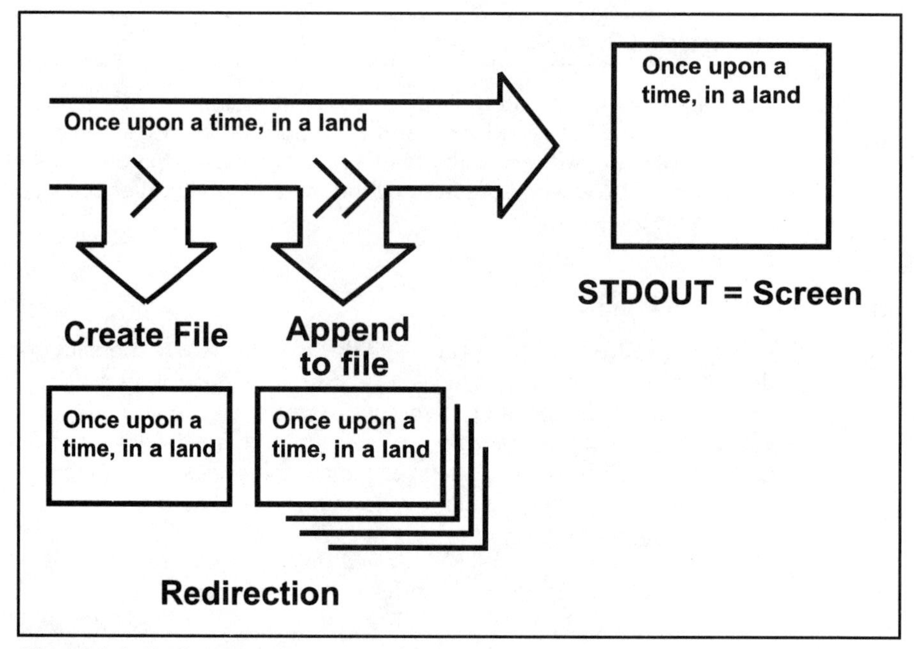


**Figure 1-4:** Redirection with > and >>.

**Exercise 1-2**

The following list contains a few suggestions that you can use to expand your practice sessions (and to add variety to them at the same time):

A. Run the program a few more times to make `hello.txt` grow.

B. Change the contents of the string once in a while to put literary variety into `hello.txt`.

C. Use redirection to capture the output from the Perl version option, such as `C:\dev> perl -v > option.txt`.

## Reading and writing

The following items may seem like a random-looking grocery list of Perl oddities, but they actually lead to a well-stuffed shopping cart the first time down the aisle for reading and writing with Perl:

- Perl likes to read files and will take a filename and try to read anything you put on the command line after the program instruction.
- The `-n` option tells Perl to cycle through a whole file, one line at a time, instead of reading only the first line and then quitting.

- If you don't give `print` a string to work with, Perl prints whatever it has (which usually is the last line it read).

You can pack all these elements together into a one-line program like the following to read a file and print out each line:

```
C:\dev>perl -ne "print" citymile.dat
```

This command line means "Run Perl, read through the entire file one line at a time, print each line as it comes in, and use `citymile.dat` as the file to read and print."

To set up this command, copy the `citymile.dat` file from the \DATA directory on the CD-ROM to your working directory (or copy any short text file you have laying around) and feed it to Perl as shown in the following example. Put the `n` option in front of the `e` option to make `-ne`, as follows:

```
C:\dev>perl -ne "print" citymile.dat
Atlanta, GA, Boston, MA, 1037
Boston, MA, Chicago, IL, 963
Chicago, IL, Cairo, IL, 375
Cairo, IL, St. Louis, MO, 153
St. Louis, MO, Cincinnati, OH, 340
Cincinnati, OH, Cleveland, OH, 244
Cleveland, OH, Dallas, TX, 1159
```

This command works just like the DOS `type` command. So why bother with the duplicate effort, you ask? To get ready for something that `type` can't do: grep a file.

### Exercise 1-3

The following exercises will help you get a handle on reading and writing with Perl:

A. Add redirection to the end of the print program to copy `citymile.dat` into a new file called `citymile.txt`.

B. Append the output from `perl -v` to the new file `citymile.txt` with the redirection symbol (>>).

C. Print the new file to the screen with a `perl -ne "print"` command. Then try it again, using `-en` instead of `-ne`. Does it work? (Remember that `-e` means "Evaluate and execute what comes *next*," and the option `n`, by itself, does not qualify as an executable Perl statement.) Also try separating the options: `perl -n -e "print" citymile.dat`.

D. For viewing a long file, add the DOS `| more` option to the end of your Perl print program line to show the file one screenful at a time.

# Pattern preview: poor man's grep

*Grep* is a program on UNIX systems that scans files for patterns of characters and reports on what it finds. The word `grep` is a semi-acronym which means *global regular expression print,* in reference to the regular-expression, pattern-matching engine that makes `grep` work. Perl uses the same pattern-matching machinery for its search functions.

## Pattern matching with /exp/

The basic pattern for regular expressions is a pair of slashes that set off the string that you want to find. You can look for occurrences of "Mom" with the pattern `/Mom/`. Note that the pattern `/mom/` is different from `/Mom/` or `/MOM/`, however, because patterns are case sensitive. This is only the *basic* form of a regular expression — a bewildering number of variations, operators, and options are available to Perl programmers. I sift through the various possibilities throughout the rest of this book.

For a taste of the power of patterns, consider the following grep-like Perl program that scans a text file for a pattern and prints any line containing that pattern. In this example, I want to find the lines in `citymile.dat` that mention Chicago. The program that does the task is

```
C:\dev>perl -ne "print if /Chicago/" citymile.dat
```

The `if` flow-control construction and the pattern work together to tell Perl "Print the current line if it contains this pattern." The model for this style of flow control is "Perform the action *if* a condition is true." Patterns return True when they match the condition and False when they fail (don't match). When `if` receives a response of True, the `print` function is enabled to run. When `if` receives a False signal, it jumps the program flow out of the instruction and moves on to the next instruction.

The -n option here makes the one-line program repeat in a loop to read the whole file (until no unread data is left). The program reads citymile.dat, checks each line for the pattern /Chicago/, and prints only those lines that match the pattern. It returns this result:

```
Boston, MA, Chicago, IL, 963
Chicago, IL, Cairo, IL, 375
```

This pattern finds matches that appear anywhere in the line — one match was in the middle, and one match was at the beginning of a line. I even can look for something shorter (say, just /Chi/) and get useful results:

```
C:\dev>perl -ne "print if /Chi/" citymile.dat

Boston, MA, Chicago, IL, 963
Chicago, IL, Cairo, IL, 375
```

**Exercise 1-4**

Time to test your Perl knowledge! Answer the following questions:

A. What do you get if you're overconfident in your brevity and try the pattern /C/ ?

B. How do you find lines that mention Ohio?

C. What pattern will find cities that are 1,159 miles apart?

## Pattern matching with wildcards up your sleeve

Perl offers some wildcard characters for more creative matches. For instance, the dot (.) represents a single character of almost any kind, except a line-end character (carriage return or linefeed). The comments in the following lines explain the matches:

```
/K./      # Kelly, but not keg
/.ocket/  # locket, pocket, rocket
/lo..er/  # loafer, loader, logger
/C.....o/ # Chicago, Carl does, but not Cicero
/.../     # any string that has at least three characters in it
```

## Comments in Perl

The hash mark (# — some call it the pound sign) designates a comment in Perl code. Anything after the hash mark on a line of code is a comment, not executable code. Comments do nothing for the operation of a program, but they can be critical to explain what the program is doing.

## Multipliers: + * ?

The symbols +, ?, and * (called plus, hook, and star, respectively — though you may have heard other names for them) have special meaning in regular expressions (Figure 1-5). These symbols are called *multipliers* because they specify how many of a specific character or expression are needed for a match, as follows:

+ = one or more of the preceding character

? = zero or one of the preceding character

* = zero or more of the preceding character

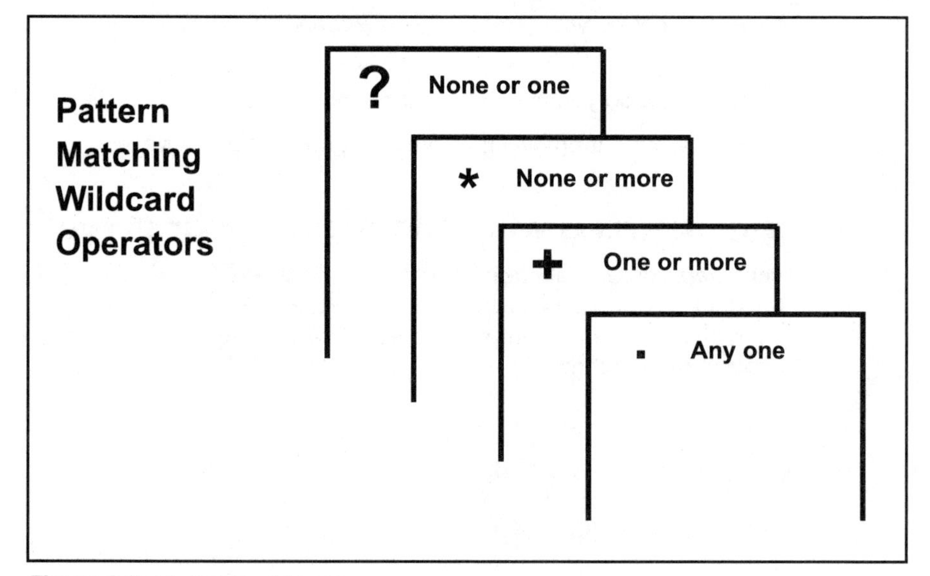


**Figure 1-5:** Multiplier wildcards.

Multipliers work like this:

```
/b+/     # one or more 'b': Abbot, cabbage, rabid, aaaabbbbcccc
/lef?t   # Has to be letter 'l', followed by 'e', followed by 'f' or
         #   nothing (only one 'f', if any), followed by 't':
         #   left, let, letter, leftenant, but not lent (only 'f'
         #   or nothing is allowed between the 'e' and 't')
         #   and not laffter (too many f's in a row).
/g*on/   # zero or more g's followed by 'on':
         #   gone, wagon, won, Rangoon, platoon
         #   Klingon, Raggggonark
```

You can use the dot symbol with the hook, star, and plus multipliers to create wildcard matches:

```
/part.*e/  # part-time, parties, part of the, apartment
/a.....g/  # abcdefg, abiding, bad doggy, not arbitrage
/a.?g/     # age, auger, but not affecting (zero or only one char
           #   following after the letter a)
/ka+.*n/   # Afrikaans, packaging, but not knot (at least one a)
```

**Exercise 1-5**

Try out these patterns on citymile.dat (the basic command to find "Chi" is `C:\dev>perl -ne "print if /Chi/" citymile.dat` ):

A. `/C.*o/`

B. `/Ci*/`

C. `/C.*i/`

D. `/3/`

E. `/3.*5/`

F. `/5.*3/`

## Anchoring a pattern

If you want to match something only when it appears at the beginning or end of a line (Figure 1-6), you can *anchor* the pattern to that position by using the anchor characters (`^`) for the beginning of the line and (`$`) for the end of the line:

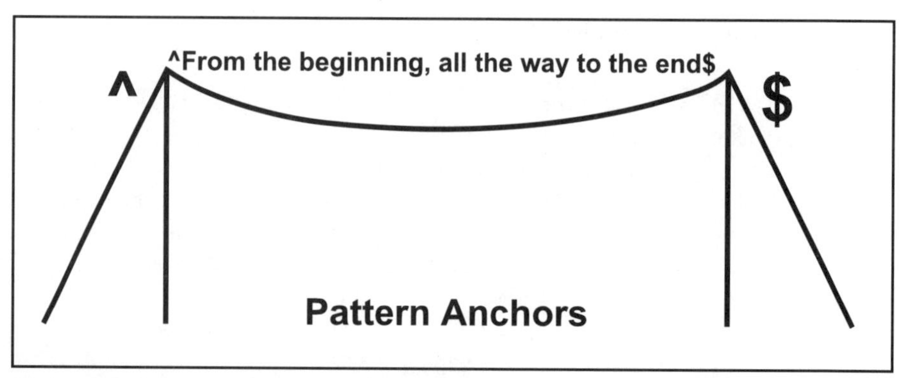


**Figure 1-6:** Pattern anchors ^ and $.

```
/Chicago/   # match Chicago anywhere on the line
/^Chicago/  # match Chicago only if it is exactly at the
            #   beginning of the line
/Chicago$/  # match Chicago only if it is right at the
            #   end of the line, just before the carriage return
```

**Exercise 1-6**

Try these patterns on `citymile.dat`:

A. `/B/     # match B anywhere on the line`

B. `/^B/    # match B only at the beginning of the line`

C. `/^C/    # match C only at the beginning of the line`

D. `/3/     # match 3 anywhere on the line`

E. `/3$/    # match 3 only at the end of the line`

## Matching special characters

Sigmund Freud said "Sometimes, a cigar is just a cigar." How do you make a star (`*`) just a star in Perl? If you want to find the `*` symbol that is acting just as a `*` symbol in a pattern rather than the "zero or more of the preceding character[,]" multiplier, you have to make a special effort. To find the regular `*` symbol in a pattern, precede the star with a backslash (`\*`). For example, to match the string `*TXT` in a file that talks about computer filenames, use the following pattern:

```
/\*TXT/   # match *TXT, not zero or more '\' followed by TXT
```

The backslash, when used to liberate a character from special meaning in a pattern (so that it is just a character), is called an *escape.* The act of making a special character "unspecial" is called *escaping* the character. The dot character in a pattern means "any one character in this position." Use `\.` to make a dot represent just a dot in a pattern search. If you want to find `*.TXT`, you have to escape both the `*` and the `.` symbols to make the pattern work, as follows:

```
/\*\.TXT/  # match *.TXT, not zero of more \
           #   followed by a \ followed by any character
           #   followed by TXT, like you would think
```

The escape character (the backslash) in patterns has the power to force any character that immediately follows it to represent the actual character itself rather than indicate any special Perl meaning that the character usually has in patterns. In other words, the backslash in `\*` changes `*` from meaning "zero or more of the preceding characters" to meaning "just a plain old asterisk." For example

```
/^Address/  # match Address at beginning of line
/\^Address/ # match ^Address, complete with caret, anywhere
/the very last $/  # match phrase 'the very last ' at end of line
/the very last \$/ # match phrase 'the very last $' anywhere
/1+2/  # match one or more number 1 followed by number 2
/1\+2/ # match phrase '1+2', including the plus sign
```

**Exercise 1-7**

Write patterns to match these phrases:

**A.** `Price: $12.56` (at the end of a line)

**B.** `myfile.*` (anywhere in the line)

**C.** `Me, crazy?` (at beginning of the line)

**D.** `mc^2/3`

## Pattern summary

Before moving on to the PerlFacts section, here's a quick review of various patterns that you have learned so far:

| Expression | What It Represents |
|---|---|
| `/abc/` | literal text: “abc” |
| `.` | (dot) any one character except newline |
| `?` | zero or one of preceding character: `/d?/` is zero or one “d” |
| `*` | zero or more of preceding character: `/d*/` is zero or more “d” |
| `+` | at least one or more of preceding character: `/d+/` is one or more “d” |
| `^` | only at start of line: `/^Chi/` |
| `$` | only at end of line: `/Chicago$/` |
| `\` | escape, following character is literal, not wildcard or special meaning: `/good\*/` is good plus asterisk |

# PerlFacts: First Steps

The PerlFacts section of each chapter in this book is a hard-boiled, eyeball-to-eyeball, gloves-off, programming tutorial. No more Mr. Nice Guy! Fire up your two-window, Perl-programming environment, crack your knuckles to loosen up however many fingers you type with, and jump right in.

## Working with scripts

With the exception of `-e`, `-n`, and sometimes `-i` (which I introduce you to much later), Perl's command-line options are special-purpose features that have little application for the ultimate purpose of this book — writing Perl programs to make cool Web pages. For that purpose, your Perl programs have to run on the Web server, the (most likely) UNIX machine in your ISP's remote location. Command-line programs won't help you much there. I only use command-line Perl programs to perform quick, grep-like operations, to peek inside files for something I hope to find, or (occasionally) to show off for people who wonder why so much excitement surrounds Perl these days.

The real power of Perl is in using it with scripts, which is where we are headed now.

## Using multiple windows for edit/test cycles

For Perl scripting, I use two windows: one for editing scripts, and one for testing what I've written (Figure 1-7). Both windows point to the same directory, C:\DEV. The procedure for using these windows to do some Perl scripting is as follows:

1. Write some Perl script.
2. Save it to a file.
3. Leave the Edit window open (like Arnold, you'll be back).
4. Go to the Test window.
5. Run Perl with the script.
6. Examine the results.
7. Go back to Step 1.

This cycle runs continuously until either the program behaves the way you want it or a non-programmer calls you to supper . . . or breakfast.

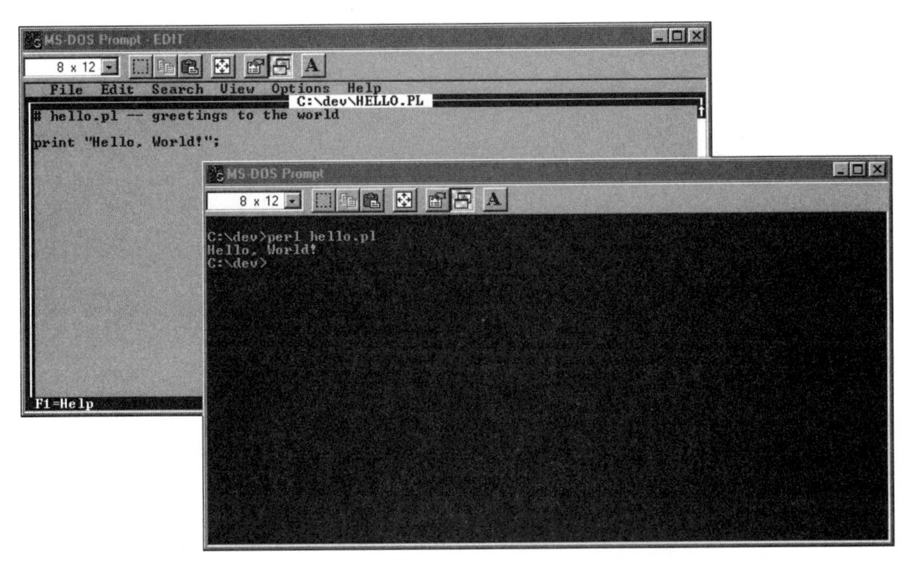


**Figure 1-7:** Setup for editing and testing.

## Edit or Notepad?

For an editor, I use the MS-DOS editor called Edit. It's simple, fast, comfortable, and has sticky indents so that each new line starts at the same indent as the line above it. Edit also accepts the Ctrl+Y (yank) command for deleting a line without selecting the whole thing (having the cursor in that line is enough) and moving it to the paste buffer. These simple enhancements make running Edit in a DOS window much more agile and productive (for me at least) than running Notepad on the desktop.

Other editors with more features are available, such as Write in Windows 3.11 and WordPad in Windows 95. I have included a couple editors on the CD-ROM for you to take a look at, too. Try out some of them when you feel you have outgrown Edit. If you already have a favorite editor, then by all means, continue using it!

## WinPerl: all in one

WinPerl (which comes on the CD-ROM) is a do-it-all Perl environment for Windows. It has a built-in script editor and creates a separate output window as needed (Figure 1-8). WinPerl takes some getting used to, but you may feel more comfortable using this editor if the DOS command line gives you goose bumps.

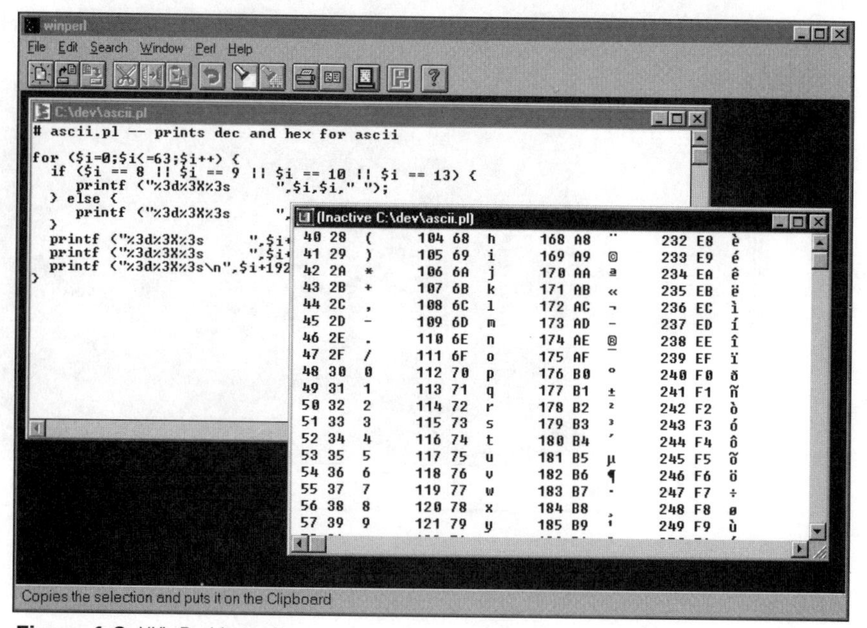


**Figure 1-8:** WinPerl in action.

# print

The `print` function is Perl's portal to the world. You'll quickly learn the ins and outs of `print` because you need it in almost every program you write. The information I've already given you about `print` was just a gentle introduction to this function's power.

To sample the `print` function, open Edit (you can use a different editor, but I'll be using Edit throughout this book), choose File⇨New, and type this familiar line, including the semicolon, which is the statement terminator for Perl:

```
print "Hello, World!";
```

Now choose File⇨Save As, name the file `hello.pl`, and save it. Throughout the known Universe, the two-letter extension `pl` is the accepted identifier for Perl script files. A similar convention applies to Perl modules (library files to be included in other Perl scripts), which are identified with the extension `pm`.

Go to the Test window and check for your new file by using the following command:

```
C:\dev> dir hello.pl
```

If the file is there, you are ready to continue. A `File not found` error message, however, means that your programming setup is not configured properly. To fix this, open both the Edit window and the Test window in the same directory. Enter the command **`C:`** to get to drive C; enter the command **`cd \dev`** to get to the DEV directory (or whatever directory you are using); and then start over.

When you are ready to continue, run the new program in Perl from the Test window by using this command:

```
C:\dev> perl hello.pl
```

Press Enter. Perl runs and announces

```
Hello, World!
```

Congratulations! Your program was successful (see Figure 1-9).

MS-DOS Prompt
8 x 12
C:\dev>perl hello.pl
Hello, World!
C:\dev>

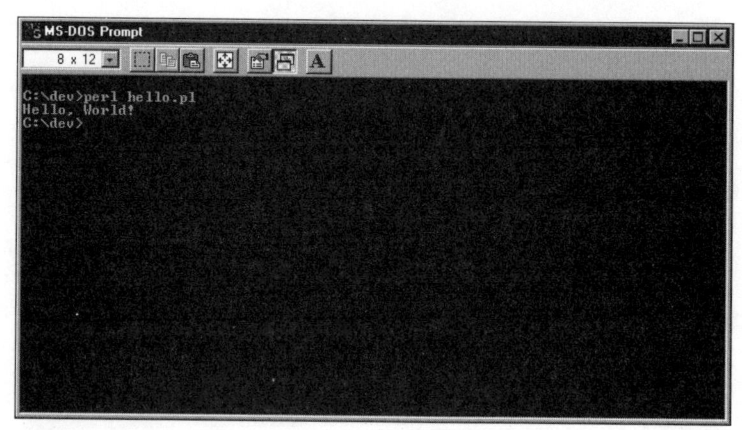

**Figure 1-9:** The birth of a programmer — Hello, World!

# Commenting with #

Comments in program code remind the programmer of what the program does and how it works. Comments do not do anything functional — in fact, they are invisible to the Perl interpreter. To write these handy hidden comments, put a hashmark (# — some call it the pound sign) in front of the comment (Figure 1-10). Anything that appears after a # on a line in a Perl script is treated as a comment. The # may be anywhere on the line — it does not have to be at the beginning. For example, take a look at the following code listing:

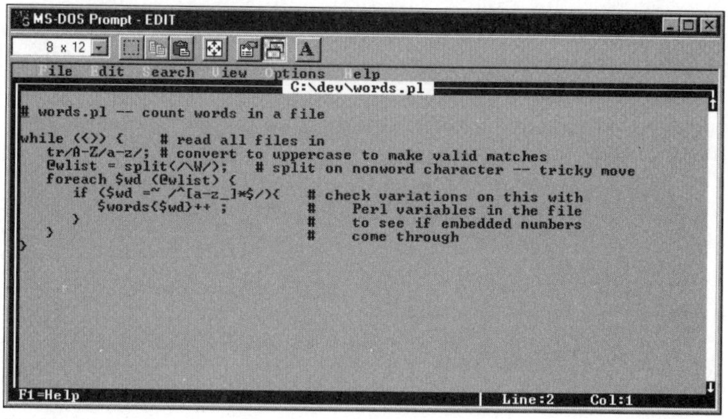

MS-DOS Prompt - EDIT
8 x 12
File Edit Search View Options Help
C:\dev\words.pl
# words.pl -- count words in a file
while (<>) {     # read all files in
tr/A-Z/a-z/; # convert to uppercase to make valid matches
@wlist = split(/\W/);   # split on nonword character -- tricky move
foreach $wd (@wlist) {
if ($wd =~ /^[a-z_]*$/){   # check variations on this with
$words{$wd}++ ;   #    Perl variables in the file
}   #    to see if embedded numbers
}   #    come through
}
F1=Help
Line:2   Col:1

**Figure 1-10:** Perl code with commented reminders to the programmer.

```
while (<>) {     # lunch with Kerrie today
   tr/A-Z/a-z/; # bring lots of money
   @wlist = split(/\W/);
   foreach $wd (@wlist) {
      if ($wd =~ /^[a-z_]*$/){
         $words{$wd}++ ;
      }            # because last time, she
   }               # ate half the Brummer Bldg.
}
```

For now, use a comment on the first line of a program to identify the program's name and purpose. Make room at the top of the program script and add this comment:

```
# hello.pl -- obligatory traditional first program
```

Perl ignores white space (tabs, spaces, blank lines) in a script. Use white space anywhere you think it would help make the program more readable. For example, you can put a blank line between the comment and the code in `hello.pl` to separate your personal note from the working code. I added a caption to the program listing to help you find it later (Listing 1-1).

**Listing 1-1** **hello.pl**

```
# hello.pl -- obligatory traditional first program

print "Hello, World!";
```

Save the script and run it again to confirm that the comment stays out of the way.

# Variables

A *variable* is like a named bucket for carrying data. You can stir up the contents any way you want or dump everything out and put something new into the bucket, but its name doesn't change. In Perl, variable names begin with identifying symbols.

## Scalar variables marked with $

Any name starting with `$` is a *scalar* variable, which means it can hold just one object, though the object can be complex (Figure 1-11). For instance, `$a` can hold something as simple as a single letter `s` or a more complex object made up of many simple objects, like the word "surprise" with all its letters.

Variables are good for describing operations on a type of object when you don't know any specifics about the object itself. It's like telling people how to pass a bucket down a line without telling them whether the bucket contains water or potatoes. In Perl, you can write the instruction

```
print $a;
```

without worrying about what the `$a` bucket contains at the moment — whatever it holds will print.

Variable names can be made up of lowercase and uppercase letters, digits, and the underscore character. The name must have a letter following the identifying symbol. Case matters in Perl, so `$bucket` and `$Bucket` are treated as two different variables. `$My_bucket` is a legal variable name, but for long names I prefer using internal capitalization over the underscore, so I would use `$MyBucket`. For a batch of similar variables, numbers also work well — `$Good1`, `$Good2`, `$Good3`.

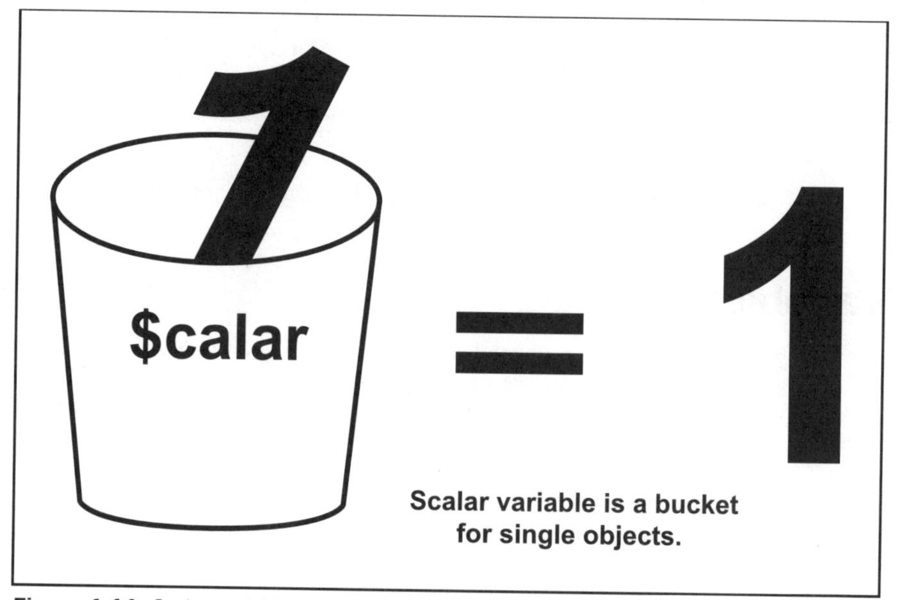


**Figure 1-11:** Scalar variables.

Later I tell you about Perl's useful family of special variables, which includes the `$/` and `$*` objects and punctuation-shorthand names.

## Assigning values with =

To load a variable (fill the bucket), assign a value to it. The equal sign (=) is Perl's assignment operator. Don't say "equals" when you read the = symbol aloud — say "is assigned to" or "takes the value of." This will help you understand more difficult Perl constructions down the line. Try it with these assignments:

```
$a = "apples";
$fruit = "orange";
$address2 = "123 Main Street";
$BIGnum = 24566;
$littleNUM = 4;
```

Sound awkward? Then say "is," as in "dollar littlenum *is* 4."

The assignment operator can transfer the value of one variable to another, similar to dumping new wine into an old bottle:

```
$new = "cranberry";
$old = "burgundy";
$old = $new;   # old bottle now holds cranberry wine
```

Notice the helpful comment explaining the change in contents. Both variables, `$new` and `$old`, now have cranberry contents. The burgundy in `$old` disappeared when Perl poured (transferred) cranberry into `$old` from `$new`. The reason is that assigning a new value to a variable overwrites whatever value the variable currently holds.

Perl uses the same variable type to hold characters, strings, and numbers. For example, the following are all valid assignment statements:

```
$bucket = "g";
$bucket = "Gee, Dad!";
$bucket = "four";   # the word, not the number
$bucket = 4;        # the number, not the word
$pail = "strawberries";
$pail = $bucket;    # now $pail holds the number 4
```

Although the flexibility of this feature is powerful and useful, the potential ambiguity can be troublesome. For example, if `$a` is the number 4 and `$b` is the word "five," how do you get Perl to determine which is larger? Not to worry — I explain how later, right before I threaten you with such comparisons.

### Printing variables

To print by using variables, first assign a value to the variable and then use it in a `print` statement, as in Listing 1-2:

**Listing 1-2** **hello2.pl**

```
# hello2.pl -- use variable to print message

$a = "Hello, World!";
print $a;
```

Running the program yields the expected results:

```
C:\dev>perl hello2.pl
Hello, World!
```

### Creating variables

You create variables simply by using them. That is, the first time you mention `$new` in a line of Perl code, `$new` springs into existence, ready to go to work.

This ease of creation, however, can be the source of puzzling bugs in your code. If you create `$MyAddrs` early in a program and then refer to it as `$MyAddr` (missing an "s") later in the program, your attempted reference actually creates a new variable that does not know about the existence of the original variable or what it holds. As a result, you now have two different variables that look similar but are not the same. Because Perl is case-sensitive, the same situation can arise if you accidentally use a different case when referring to a variable. Thus, starting out with `$BigNum` and ending up with `$BIGNum` is a recipe for frustration.

**Exercise 1-8**

Experiment with different variable names in hello2.pl (Listing 1-2). Keep in mind that variable names must start with the $ symbol immediately followed by a letter, which can be either upper- or lowercase.

## Current line special variable $_

If you tell Perl to print without specifying what it should print, Perl prints the current line (usually the last line that it read from a file). References to the current line are so common that Perl frequently assumes that you meant to use the current line wherever it makes sense to do so unless you specifically tell Perl otherwise. For instance, the Perl statement

```
print;
```

sends the current line out into the world, whereas the statement

```
print "Hello";
```

sends a cheery greeting instead.

Perl uses a special variable — a reserved name — for the current line, which is `$_`. (I pronounce it as *dollar-under.*) This variable behaves like any other variable — you can print it or assign its value to another variable, as you see here:

```
print $_;     # prints the current line
$mine = $_;   # assigns current line to $mine
print $mine;
```

You can go the other way with $_ and assign some arbitrary value to it, overwriting whatever $_ thinks is the current line:

```
$_ = "Hello";
print $_;     # prints Hello
print;        # prints Hello again
```

Why would Perl print `Hello` in the last line of the above example? Because, given a `print` command without a specific object to use, Perl carries out the instruction with whatever is in the magic current-line variable `$_`. Because `$_` was assigned the value of "Hello," Perl prints `Hello`.

This shorthand method of referencing may look confusing at first, but you will quickly get used to it. I show you many more examples of shorthand and special variables when the time is right.

## Array variables marked with @

Array variables hold *arrays,* or lists, of values. Array variables have the @ symbol as the first character in their names to help you tell them apart from scalar variables, which only hold one value at a time (Figure 1-12). After the first character, array variable names follow the same rules as scalar variable names — they consist of a letter first and then any combination of letters and numbers you want.

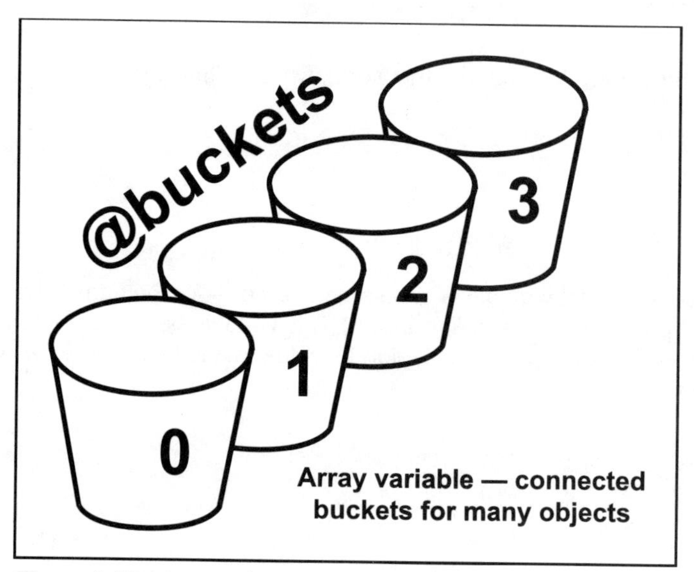


**Figure 1-12:** *Array variables.*

Arrays enable you to handle groups of objects by naming the group rather than by naming all the individual objects. Instead of saying, "Buy bananas, apples, and oranges," you simply say "Buy fruit," and your shopping assistant knows what to do.

### Assigning values to an array

The assignment operator (=) works with arrays but carries a heavier load than it does with scalar variables. Values are assigned to arrays in several different ways. The simplest method is to list the intended contents of the array for the assignment:

```
@fruit = ("banana", "apple", "orange");
```

This single statement creates the array @fruit (if it does not already exist) and simultaneously assigns the three strings "banana", "apple", and "orange" to the array variable. The list is enclosed in parentheses, and each element is separated from the others with a comma. Perl does not require a space after each comma — I added them for readability.

Unlike most other computer languages, Perl accepts a variety of objects in its arrays. The list of values for a particular array can include strings, numbers, variables, and even other arrays. For example

```
@trailmix = ("almond", "raisin", @fruit, 5, "123 Main Street", $a);
```

Notice that the strings are enclosed in quotes, but numbers and variables are not quoted.

## Retrieving values from an array: subscripts

Arrays with names that begin with the @ symbol (another kind of array that you'll meet later is marked with the % symbol) keep their contents in strict, sequential order. If you put an element in the third slot in an array, you'll find it in the third slot when you come back looking for it, provided that you haven't done something to push the array parts around in the meantime. To retrieve the value in a particular slot, ask for it by position number, called the *subscript*. A couple of special tricks occur in this process, however.

The first trick you need to know about is that Perl starts numbering its array slots with 0 rather than 1. Hence, to retrieve the first element, ask for subscript 0; to retrieve the second element, ask for subscript 1; to retrieve the third element, ask for subscript 2; and so on.

The second trick is that the array changes its name when referring to single elements. When working with a single object rather than a whole array, I use a scalar variable that starts with $. When I want just one object from an array, it also is a single object, so I use $ again and @fruit becomes $fruit[]. To use a subscript, put the number in square brackets on the end of the array name in its single-object form: $fruit[2] is the single element at subscript 2 of the array @fruit.

The following listing shows some examples of working with arrays and the individual elements within them. The result is shown in Figure 1-13.

**Figure 1-13:** Array variable subscripts.

```
@fruit = ("banana", "apple", "orange");   # 3-element array
$what = $fruit[0];        # put first element into variable $what
                          #   notice @fruit is now $fruit[]
print $what;              # result: prints banana to STDOUT
$what = $fruit[2];        # put third element into $what
print $what;              # result: prints orange to STDOUT
```

## Adding array elements

You can add an element to an array in at least three different ways. To illustrate these methods, start with the following array:

```
@fruit = ("banana", "apple", "orange");
```

Now assign the whole list of elements again, adding the new element, kiwi, in the normal manner:

```
@fruit = ("banana", "apple", "orange", "kiwi");
```

You also can assign a new variable to an array by using a subscript in a new, higher position:

```
$fruit[3] = "kiwi";    # creates 4th slot for "kiwi"
```

Alternatively, you can use the push function to add an element to the end of an array:

```
push(@fruit, "kiwi");  # pushes "kiwi" onto the array,
                       #   increasing the number of elements by 1
```

## More Print Power

The next program example uses three new features for the print function: printing a whole array, printing a list of objects, and forcing a new line.

To print a whole array, use the array variable name as a print object, such as `print @myArray;`. All the values in the array print out one after another, with no extra spaces or new lines separating them unless you add them yourself.

To print a list of objects with one print statement, write the list after the print function with a comma between each item in the list: `print "one", "two", 3, $m * yVar;`. The elements in the list print one after another, just like printing a whole array.

The Perl print function does not automatically return to the start of a new line after printing an object, unless that object is a "newline" character or contains a newline character. The newline character is a special string represented by `\n`. To force a new line, add `\n` to the list of objects to be printed, such as `print $name, "\n", $address, "\n";` (Listing 1-3):

**Listing 1-3** **addarray.pl**

```
# addarray.pl -- add elements to an array

@my = ("one", 2, "three", 4);  # start small
print @my, "\n";    # show the array so far
$my[4] = "five";    # put "five" at a new subscript
print @my, "\n";    # show the expanded array
push(@my, 6);       # push a value onto the end of array
print @my, "\n";    # show the expanded array
```

Run the program to demonstrate additions to an array:

```
C:\dev>perl addarray.pl
one2three4
one2three4five
one2three4five6
```

One way to insert a space between array elements as-printed is by using the brute-force approach — adding a space to the end of each element in the original assignment statement:

```
@my = ("one ", "2 ", "three", "4 ");
```

As usual with brute-force methods, side-effects occur. In this case, you have to add quotes around the numbers in the list, which converts the numbers into strings.

Another way to print an array with its elements separated by spaces is to wrap the array name in quotes when printing. Try the quote-enhanced version in Listing 1-4 — note the treatment of the array in the last line:

**Listing 1-4 Printing an Array with Auto-Spaces**

```
# addarry2.pl -- add elements to an array

@my = ("one", 2, "three", 4);  # start small
print @my, "\n";    # show the array so far
$my[4] = "five";    # put "five" at a new subscript
print @my, "\n";    # show the expanded array
push(@my, 6);       # push a value onto the end of array
print @my, "\n";    # show the expanded array
print "@my\n";      # show the expanded array
# end of addarry2.pl
```

The program produces this output:

```
one2three4
one2three4five
one2three4five6
one 2 three 4 five 6
```

# Input and output

Perl needs to know where its information is coming from and where to send it. These channels to the outside world are called *filehandles,* a UNIX term for anything that sends or receives data. When the Perl interpreter runs, its first order of business is to set up filehandles (communication channels) for input, output, and error reporting. These three filehandles are created automatically and have reserved names: STDIN, STDOUT, and STDERR (Figure 1-14). The STD part means *standard,* as in *standard equipment.* A Perl reserved name such as these cannot be used for anything but its reserved, built-in meaning.

## Standard output: STDOUT

The three STDs are used so frequently that Perl often assumes that they exist and thus Perl does not require you to mention them explicitly; instead, Perl creates them and automatically assigns channels to them. For example, the rigorous form of the `print` function needs a filehandle to answer the question, “Print where?” Here, the filehandle goes between `print` and the outgoing message. STDOUT usually represents the monitor, or the computer screen. So, to wake up your computer, the Perl command is

```
print STDOUT "Wake up!";
```

If you omit the filehandle in a `print` statement, Perl assumes that you really meant to print to STDOUT and fills in the blank for you. Consequently, the statement

```
print "Wake up!";
```

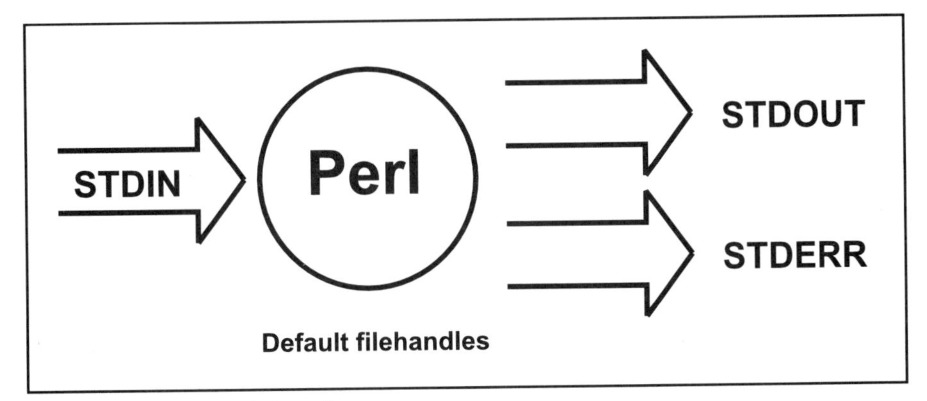


**Figure 1-14:** Default filehandles.

has exactly the same result as

```
print STDOUT "Wake up!";
```

Either statement sends the message `Wake up!` to your screen.

If you want to send the `print` output to another location, however, you need to specify that filehandle. For example, to send a wakeup call to a place called `FHANDLE` (Perl filehandles are conventionally written in all caps), the statement is

```
print FHANDLE "Wake up!";
```

## Standard error: STDERR

Messages sent to `STDERR` go right to your screen, even if you redirected the program's output to a file. Perl wants you to get the message immediately when something goes wrong. To test this feature, create an error in `hello2.pl` by deleting the closing quote mark after World!, save the file as `hello3.pl`, and then run it (Listing 1-5):

**Listing 1-5 hello3.pl Program Containing an Error**

```
# hello.pl -- program with an error

print "Hello, World!;
```

Note how Perl reports the error when you run the program:

```
C:\dev>perl hello3.pl
Can't find string terminator '"' anywhere before EOF at hello2.pl
line 3.
```

Now try to capture the error message by redirecting the program's output into a file, as follows:

```
C:\dev>perl hello3.pl > err.txt
Can't find string terminator '"' anywhere before EOF at hello2.pl
line 3.
```

The error message still appears directly on the screen. Is it also in the new file? No. Although the err.txt file was created by the redirection, the file remains empty. When it reached the error, Perl sent a message to STDERR (the screen) and quit before writing anything to the new file.

## Standard input: STDIN

Perl takes whatever you hand it through STDIN. The source of STDIN may be a file, a stream of data from another program, or simply data entered from your keyboard. You have already seen STDIN working automatically for command-line Perl programs. The DOS redirection symbol (<) feeds a file directly into Perl's STDIN.

## Reading a file with <STDIN>

A pair of angle brackets (<>) is Perl's input, or *read,* operator. If a filehandle such as STDIN appears inside these brackets, the read operator causes Perl to fetch one line at a time from that filehandle. Use a variable (such as $Name) to store the entire line:

```
$Name = <STDIN>;  # read a line from STDIN and
                  #   put it into $Name
```

This program takes several lines, in sequence, from STDIN and then prints them in reverse order (Listing 1-6).

**Listing 1-6** **revline.pl**

```
# revline.pl -- read three lines from keyboard, print in reverse
order

$one = <STDIN>;
$two = <STDIN>;
$three = <STDIN>;

print $three;
print $two;
print $one;
```

Then run the program and start typing lines to fill the sudden silence. My try went like this:

```
C:\dev>perl revline.pl
I really need to know
What crooked row to hoe
No matter where I go
No matter where I go
What crooked row to hoe
I really need to know
```

After I press Enter in the third line Perl prints all three lines in reverse order (Figure 1-15). For an interesting variation on this theme put the input strings into an array (Listing 1-7).

**Listing 1-7** **revline2.pl**

```
# revline2.pl -- read three lines into array, print in reverse order

$one = <STDIN>;
$two = <STDIN>;
$three = <STDIN>;
@lines = ($one, $two, $three);
print $lines[2];
print $lines[1];
print $lines[0];  # that's all
```

STDIN reads
one line at a time
each time
it is invoked

| | |
|---|---|
| $a = <STDIN>; | $a = "STDIN reads" |
| $b = <STDIN>; | $b = "one line at a time" |
| $c = <STDIN>; | $c = "each time" |
| $d = <STDIN>; | $d = "it is invoked" |

**Each <STDIN> reads one line**

**Figure 1-15:** Reading with <STDIN>.

**Exercise 1-9**

Here are a few more exercises to try:

A. Rewrite `revline2.pl` to print the lines in forward sequential order. Save the new program as `revline3.pl`.

B. Rewrite `revline3.pl` and give it four lines of input. Save as `revline4.pl`.

Next up: a looping device for reading a file of unknown length.

## Flow control with `while()`

The `while` operator is one of Perl's flow control, or *conditional,* operators. `while` tells the program to keep repeating a procedure while a certain condition is true and then to stop when it encounters a change that makes the condition false. In Listing 1-8, the flow consists of a loop that reads from `STDIN` while there is anything left to be read. Figure 1-16 shows the results.

**Listing 1-8** **prtfile.pl**

```
 # prtfile.pl -- print from STDIN until the file is done

while (<STDIN>) {
  print;
}
```

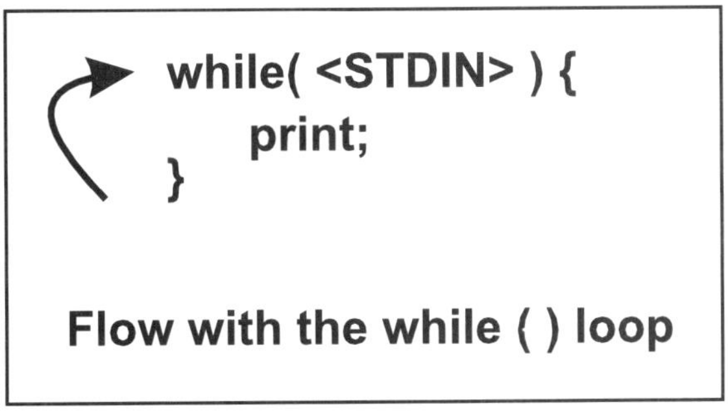

```
while( <STDIN> ) {
    print;
}
```

Flow with the while ( ) loop

**Figure 1-16:** Looping with while( ).

## Reading data with while (<STDIN>)

The while operator is handy for reading all the data from the file specified for STDIN. For example, first run the prtfile.pl program, using citymile.dat as the file-to-read argument:

```
C:\dev>perl prtfile.pl citymile.dat
Atlanta, GA, Boston, MA, 1037
Boston, MA, Chicago, IL, 963
Chicago, IL, Cairo, IL, 375
Cairo, IL, St. Louis, MO, 153
St. Louis, MO, Cincinnati, OH, 340
Cincinnati, OH, Cleveland, OH, 244
Cleveland, OH, Dallas, TX, 1159
```

As you can see, every line in the file gets printed. The while(<STDIN>) statement reads the file one line at a time, as long as there are lines to be read. This program reads the entire file instead of reading a limited number of lines assigned to specific variables, as I did before with

```
$one = <STDIN>;
$two = <STDIN>;
$three = <STDIN>;
```

while operates over a block of code, which can contain several lines of instructions. The curly braces {} mark the beginning and end of the block of code that belongs to this particular while loop. In Listing 1-8, the loop has only one statement, print;, which kicks in every time while runs the loop and prints the current line. Loops typically have many statements in the block of code:

```
while (<STDIN>) {
  print;
  $a = "-----";
  print $a;
  $b = ":::::";
  print $b;
  # plus as many more lines as you need
}
```

The condition that controls the loop (and determines whether the next pass is a go or a no-go) appears in the parentheses following the `while` function. Each time through the loop, `while` checks whether the expression in the parentheses is True or False. This particular expression (`<STDIN>`) means "read a line from `STDIN`." Every time the input operator (<>) fetches a line from `STDIN`, it sends the value for True to `while` and tucks the new line into the Perl *current line* holder. Because the conditional expression is True, `while` runs the loop, and the line gets printed.

When it reaches the end of the file, the input operator <> notifies `while` that nothing is left for it to fetch by sending a "nothing left" signal (a null, but you can think of it as a false signal) to `while`. At this point, `while` terminates the loop by jumping to the instruction after the closing curly brace. Because no more statements appear after the curly brace in `prtline.pl`, the program closes the input and output files and stops.

## Reading keyboard input with `while(<STDIN>)`

To Perl, the keyboard is the source for `STDIN`. If I run `prtfile.pl` without giving it a file to read, the program waits for something to come in through `STDIN`. As long as I keep typing lines, `prtfile.pl` prints every line it reads until it reaches the end of my keyboard "file," which is indicated with the Ctrl+Z, "file-end" character on DOS machines (it's Ctrl+Z on UNIX machines, too). Ctrl+Z must be entered from the keyboard for Perl to break out of the loop:

```
C:\dev>perl prtfile.pl
To Perl,
To Perl,
even the keyboard
even the keyboard
can be a file.
can be a file.
^Z
```

## Opening a specific file to read

`STDIN` is a filehandle used for reading data with the `<STDIN>` construct. The name of the file assigned to the `STDIN` filehandle comes from outside the program (Figure 1-17). If you know in advance the name of the file to be read, you can put that information inside the program by using the `open` function to assign the file to a filehandle, as follows:

```
open (FILEHANDLE, "myfile.dat");
```

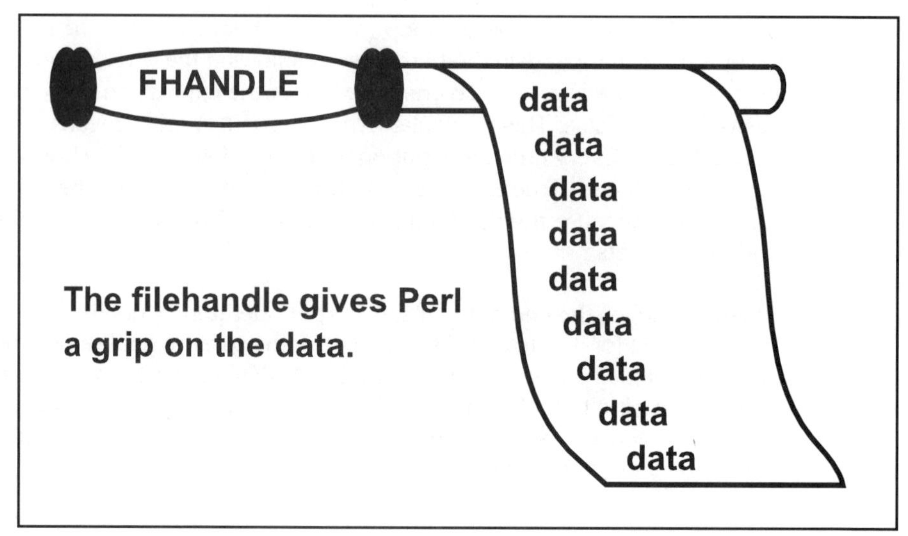


**Figure 1-17:** Filehandles.

You can use any name you want in place of `FILEHANDLE`, but using all caps for filehandle names is customary. `FHANDLE`, `INFILE`, `DATFILE`, and `GREG` all are legal filehandle names. The name of the file does not have to be in a string — it can be a variable:

```
$newfile = "myfile.dat";
open (MYHANDLE, $newfile);
```

In a program script, open the file before trying to read it, such as in Listing 1-9:

**Listing 1-9** `prtafile.pl`

```
# prtafile.pl -- print from FHANDLE until the file is done

open (FHANDLE, "citymile.dat");
while (<FHANDLE>) {
  print;
}
```

This program knows which file to read, so you do not need to enter the filename on the command line after the program name:

```
C:\dev>perl prtafile.pl
Atlanta, GA, Boston, MA, 1037
Boston, MA, Chicago, IL, 963
Chicago, IL, Cairo, IL, 375
Cairo, IL, St. Louis, MO, 153
St. Louis, MO, Cincinnati, OH, 340
Cincinnati, OH, Cleveland, OH, 244
Cleveland, OH, Dallas, TX, 1159
```

**Exercise 1-10**

Here are a few more exercises to help you increase your Perl-programming skills:

A. Change the filename in `prtafile.pl` to make the program read a different file.

B. Make up your own filehandles for the `open` and <> functions.

# Arguments

Programmers love arguments, but to a programmer, *argument* has a special meaning. An argument is a chunk of information passed to a program or a function. For example, in this statement

```
print STDOUT $myWord;
```

both `STDOUT` and `$myWord` are arguments for the `print` function.

## Command-line arguments

Arguments come into programs from the command line, too. By typing

```
C:\dev>edit prtchigo.pl
```

I invoke (start) `edit.com` and pass the argument `prtchigo.pl` to Edit as the file it should fetch for the current work session.

Perl looks for arguments on the command line to determine what you want it to read and do. For example, in the following command

```
C:\dev>perl -ne "print if /Chicago/" citymile.dat
```

everything after perl is part of a series of arguments. The argument -ne is a command-line option passed to perl, whereas "print if /Chicago/" is a one-line program passed to perl and citymile.dat is a filename passed to perl.

By using citymile.dat as an argument for prtfile.pl, I'm telling the program which file it should read:

```
C:\dev>perl prtfile.pl citymile.dat
```

Using arguments in this fashion is typical command-line behavior for running Perl scripts. The typical command-line arguments are the script you want to use and then the name of a file for the script to process, in that order. You can have additional arguments, however, such as a pattern for the program to find in the target file. For example, the command that tells Perl to use the program findtext.pl to look for "Chicago" in citymile.dat is

```
C:\dev>perl findtext.pl "Chicago" citymile.dat
```

## Using command-line arguments in a program: @ARGV

Perl reads command-line arguments and passes them into the script by using a special array variable called @ARGV. By that, I mean that @ARGV tells the program what was on the command line. I can call up @ARGV, examine the command-line arguments one-by-one, and work with them inside a program (Figure 1-18). The next program shows you how, but you'll have to read the paragraphs that follow to see how it works because a batch of new tricks appears in argecho.pl (Listing 1-10).

**Listing 1-10 argecho.pl**

```
# argecho.pl -- show any command-line arguments

$argNum = @ARGV;
$i = 0;
while ($i < $argNum) {
  print $i, " -- ", $ARGV[$i], "\n";
  $i++;
}
```

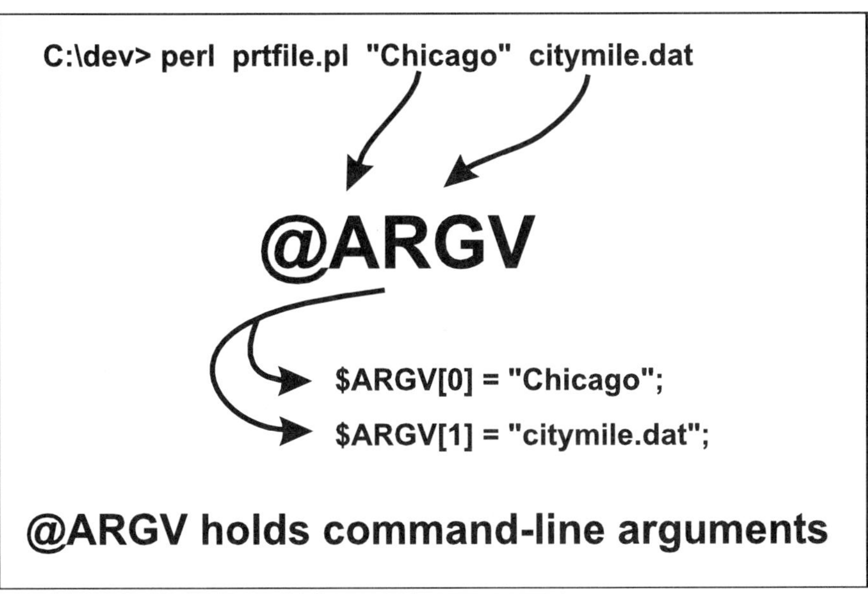


**Figure 1-18:** Command-line arguments in @ARGV.

## The line-by-line secrets of `argecho.pl`

As promised, I've broken down `argecho.pl` line-by-line to show you how it works:

1. **`$argNum = @ARGV`**

   Assigning a whole array to a scalar variable puts the size of the array (the number of elements) into the variable. `@ARGV` holds the arguments from the command line, so now `$argNum` represents the total number of arguments that Perl found.

2. **`$i = 0;`**

   Creates a scalar variable `$i` (for Index) and gives it the value 0.

3. **`while ($i < $argNum) {`**

   Starts a conditional loop. Continues the loop as long as `$i` is less than `$argNum`, the number of arguments. `$i` gets bigger as the program runs. As soon as `$i` equals `$argNum` (is no longer less than `$argNum`), this operator jumps Perl out of the loop.

4. **print $i, " -- ", $ARGV[$i], "\n";**

   A single `print` command prints a list of objects one after the other when the list is presented with each object separated by commas (`print $a, $b, $c;`). Here, the `print` statement prints whatever value is in `$i`, followed by a space, two hyphens, and another space, the array element in the `$i`-th subscript of `@ARGV`, and then the newline `\n` to force a carriage return. In other words, print a sequence number, a dash, the argument for that sequence number, and start a new line. I *told* you the print function had a lot of power!

5. **$i++;**

   The double-plus is an auto-increment operator that does the same task as `$i=$i=1`. It means, "Take the numerical value of this variable, add 1 to that value, and put the new total back into the variable." So if `$i` is 2, after looping through `$i++`, the new value for `$i` is 3. Do another `$i++`, and the value of `$i` is 4.

6. }

   The curly brace sends the program back to the `while` function with a new value in `$i`. The `while` conditional test checks the `$i` value to see if it is still less than the total number of arguments. If everything is still okay, the program numbers and prints the next argument in line and goes back for more, until all the arguments have been picked out of `@ARGV`.

Run `argecho.pl` with a few arguments on the command line after the program name, and the arguments print out in sequence:

```
C:\dev>perl argecho.pl once upon a time
0 -- once
1 -- upon
2 -- a
3 -- time
```

**Exercise 1-11**

Try out these variations on argecho.pl for more practice with arguments:

A. Run `argecho.pl` with different numbers of arguments.

B. Experiment with arguments that look like matching patterns. To use spaces or special characters in an argument, enclose the argument in quotes.

## Patterns and comparison operators

You met the pattern-matching operator, a pair of slashes that include an expression (`/expr/`), in the command-line statement that looks for "Chicago" in `citymile.dat`:

```
C:\dev>perl -ne "print if /Chicago/" citymile.dat
```

Can you use that technique in a program? Yes! For example, take a look at `prtfile.pl` with the `print if` statement written in to turn it into `prtchigo.pl` (Listing 1-11):

**Listing 1-11** **prtchigo.pl**

```
# prtchigo.pl -- print if line has Chicago

while (<STDIN>) {
  print if /Chicago/;
}
```

You run it in the same way as the command-line version, using `citymile.dat` as the file-to-use argument:

```
C:\dev>perl prtchigo.pl citymile.dat
Boston, MA, Chicago, IL, 963
Chicago, IL, Cincinnati, OH, 287
```

### Exercise 1-12

Try out these exercises to add a little variation to the preceding programs:

**A.** Run `prtchigo.pl` by itself, without a filename argument:

```
C:\dev>perl prtchigo.pl
```

**B.** What does the program do? (Hint: Type whatever you want, but be sure to try something with "Chicago" in it. Remember, Ctrl+Z ends `STDIN` from the keyboard.)

## Using variables in patterns

Like the `print` function, the regular expression engine in Perl is smart enough to recognize variables — the $ marker character is the clue. Perl evaluates any variables in a pattern and substitutes values for variables before testing the pattern for a match. For example

```
$findme = "Chicago";    # assign Chicago to the variable $findme
print if /$findme/;     # print the line if it contains Chicago
$findme = "C\.*go";     # assign C\.*go to $findme
print if /$findme/;     # same as: print if /C\.*go/
$findme = "\^Chi";      # assign ^Chi to $findme
print if /$findme/;     # print if /^Chi/; match Chi at start of
                          line
```

# PerlProject: Finding Text Patterns

The PerlProject section found in each chapter of this book is where you build the software tools that help you create cool Web pages with Perl. The programs that you encounter before this section typically are for illustrative purposes only — they simply are intended to demonstrate specific concepts in Perl programming. The programs that you find here (and in other PerlProject sections throughout the book) are the real keepers; these programs are useful in their own right.

The first PerlProject, `findtext.pl`, wraps together the core concepts in Chapter 1. This program uses command-line argument-handling with the `@ARGV` array, variables in a pattern statement, flow control with the `while` loop, the `<FHANDLE>` construct to read a file, decision-making with the `if` conditional, and the elemental form of the `print` function with an assumed filehandle and current-line `$_` variable. This program reads the command line to obtain a regular expression pattern and a filename, searches the file for the pattern, and prints any lines containing the pattern.

Take a brief pause here and go back and reread the preceding sentence. The fact that you understand the programmer tech-talk in that sentence is a clear indication of how much you've learned already. Remarkable, isn't it? Now, on to the main course — see Listing 1-12.

**Listing 1-12** **findtext.pl**

```
# findtext.pl -- use command-line argument for pattern search
    # usage: perl findtext.pl "pattern" filename

$pattern = $ARGV[0];          #1. ARGV[0] holds the pattern string
open (FINDFILE, $ARGV[1]);    #2. open() names a filehandle
while (<FINDFILE>) {          #3. while() to read lines from file
    print if /$pattern/;      #4. print if pattern matches
}
# end of findtext.pl
```

The following steps illustrate how this program works:

1. `ARGV[0]` is the first slot in the command-line list. It holds the pattern string, with the quotes stripped off.
2. The `open` function creates the filehandle `FINDFILE` and assigns the filehandle to the file named in `ARGV[1]`, the second item in the command-line list.
3. The construct `<FINDFILE>` means "read a line from this filehandle," just like `<STDIN>` means "read a line from the standard input filehandle."
4. Perl recognizes the unescaped `$` on `$pattern` as the start of a variable, evaluates the variable to find what it contains, and replaces the variable with its contents as the regular expression for the pattern. If `$pattern` contains "Chicago" ( because it appears on the command line), then the match will be for `/Chicago/`.

The following are some examples of the `findtext.pl` program:

```
C:\dev>perl findtext.pl "Chicago" citymile.dat
C:\dev>perl findtext.pl "C.*ro" citymile.dat
C:\dev>perl findtext.pl "7$" citymile.dat
```

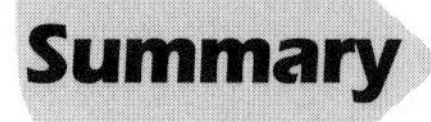


Let's review some of the topics introduced in this chapter:

- Regular expressions are patterns enclosed in a pair of forward slashes.
- Perl runs from the command line. The command invokes the Perl interpreter and gives it instructions.
- Scalar variables are marked with an initial $ in their names and can hold one object. Values are assigned to variables with the assignment operator `=` : `$myVar = "apples"`. Values can be made up of characters or numbers.
- Array variables are marked with an initial @ in their names and hold a list of objects. Values assigned by describing the list: `@fruit = ("apples", "oranges", "pears")`. Values may be strings, numbers, or variables.
- Arrays are accessed by subscripts, starting with 0 as the first element. The @ marker changes to $ when the meaning is a single element: `@fruit = ("apples", "oranges", "pears")`, and `$fruit[2]` is the third element "pears."
- Perl communicates by reading and writing to files identified by special variables called *filehandles*. `STDIN`, `STDOUT`, and `STDERR` are automatic filehandles that are created every time Perl runs. Filehandles are used in print commands and the "read file" construct <>.
- The conditional operator `if` has an inline form — "do something if something is true." For example, `print if /Chicago/`.
- The loop operator `while` repeats statements in a block marked by curly braces, as long as the test condition is true. The read file construct is true until the end of the file. To loop through the standard input and print each line:

```
while (<STDIN>) {
    print if /Chicago/;
}
```

- `@ARGV` is a special array that holds command-line parameters.

# Preparing Pages for Perl

**Skill Targets**

- What CGI is and where it fits into Web site operation
- What kinds of applications CGI makes possible for Web pages
- How HTML forms use CGI
- How to use `while` and `if` operators for flow control in Perl
- Using more regular expressions for pattern-matching

This chapter lays the bedrock for Web tasks that can be addressed with Perl scripts. Then in the PerlProject section at the end of the chapter, I discuss a program called `grepfil.pl`, which finds a pattern in multiple files.

## CGI and Perl

The *Common Gateway Interface* (CGI) is the doorway between a Web page and the Internet server where the page resides. Perl plays an important role in CGI programming, as you'll see in a moment.

### Common Gateway Interface in a nutshell

The browser does a good share of the work involved in presenting a Web page. Text formatting, page layout, graphics display, tables, frames, keystrokes and mouse-clicks, even music and video are handled by the browser and its helper applications. All the server does is handle file-fetching requests. The browser sends requests to the server and the server sends replies. This exchange is a simple matter when the request is to show another Web page. The server fetches the requested HTML file, adds a message to the front of the file (an informational file header), and sends the package off to whomever made the request (Figure 2-1).

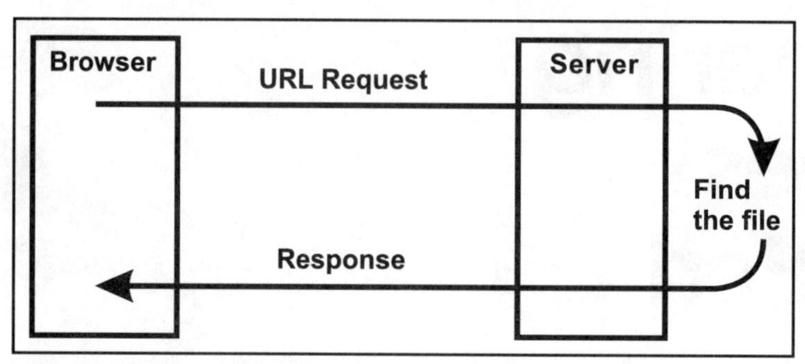


**Figure 2-1:** Browser/server communication.

When a browser wants more than just another Web page or graphic from the server, the request goes to the CGI for processing (Figure 2-2). For example, requests for text searches, data processing, status reports, hit counts, and other data-interactive processes need special handling. CGI programs do the processing, file building, and database access for these special requests.

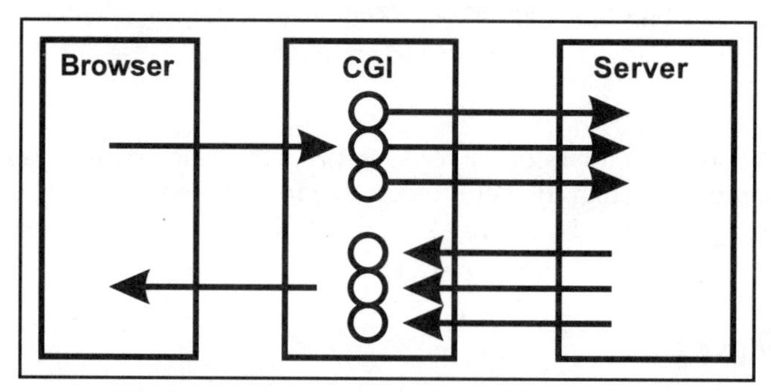


**Figure 2-2:** Communicating through the CGI.

Many of the special-handling CGI programs are written in Perl. And you will write some of the most interesting ones throughout this book.

## The secret life of Perl

Perl (*P*ractical *E*xtraction and *R*eport *L*anguage) started out as a UNIX system administration tool, an enhancement of some of the text processing and formatting tools available on UNIX installations. Larry Wall recognized the need to expand the capabilities of those programs commonly used for managing file systems, passwords, usage reporting, data extraction and summarizing, and other mysterious projects that make UNIX system administrators so valuable. By the time he had a solid set of enhancements, Larry had created a whole new language. Perl was born.

Then Larry Wall turned Perl loose on the world — quite literally. He gave away Perl as freeware, stipulating that everyone could use Perl for free — provided that they maintained free access to Perl interpreters and enhancements for everyone and did not try to exploit the use of Perl for their personal gain. (See `license.txt` in the installed Perl directory for the related official statement.)

The price was right, the software was incredibly powerful, and Larry Wall continued to support, develop, and enhance his creation — and as a result, Perl spread quickly through the computer world. Perl has been ported to every important (and some not-so-important) computer operating system. Thus, if you know how to use Perl, you can produce powerful programs and applications for use on computers you may have heard of because your scripts can play on any computer that has a Perl interpreter.

# HTML and Perl

HTML and Perl cross paths through the CGI. Processing requests flow from the HTML documents through the CGI, where Perl programs receive the requests and massage the information (Figure 2-3). The usual response provided by a Perl CGI program takes the form of another HTML page, which is frequently constructed on-the-fly to meet the specific needs of the requester.

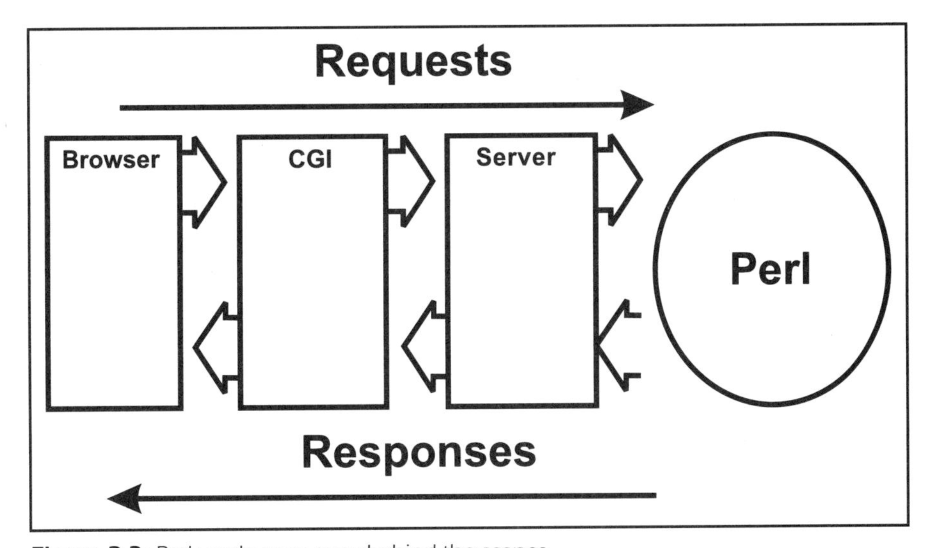


**Figure 2-3:** Perl works way, way behind the scenes.

## Using HTML: A Review of Basic Operations

A Web page is a document designed for viewing on a computer screen. The document is written in *HyperText Markup Language* (HTML). Because the HTML code for a Web page is funny-looking and very different from the document as it appears onscreen, some people think of HTML as a programming language. It's not. Perl is a programming language. HTML is a set of tags written into the document text to provide formatting instructions.

The hypertext part of HTML comes from special tags that set up links that enable the viewer to jump to another part of the Web site. Click on the link, and the browser calls the server with a request to fetch whatever it finds at the other end of the link. If the other end contains a document, the viewing continues. If the link is to a CGI program, the server does some data processing and computing before the viewing continues.

The HTML documents and the CGI programs for a Web site usually are located on the same server. One computer may have a number of Web site accounts, each with its own set of directories. CGI programs in Perl or other languages also reside in separate directories on the server (Figure 2-4). Because CGI programs sometimes must access server files and other resources, security measures with rules and procedures for uploading and using CGI programs is a high priority for Web site system administrators.

```
/cgi  /abc-corp                /abc-corp /cgi
      /big-jim                           /www
      /cococorp                          /logs

/www  /abc-corp                /big-jim /cgi
      /big-jim                          /www
      /cococorp                         /logs

/logs /abc-corp                /cococorp /cgi
      /big-jim                           /www
      /cococorp                          /logs
```

What the directory really is. . . .    And what it looks like to the users

**Figure 2-4:** Possible directory structure on the server.

See Appendix B for a short-course review on HTML coding.

## Tables, frames, forms, and all that jazz

True to the way of the computing world, HTML started out simple and then got complicated. Web pages now use tables for arranging information (Figure 2-5), frames for showing multiple pages simultaneously, graphics to enhance understanding or provide entertainment, and even sound, video, and animation for those presentations where words alone cannot do the job.

HyBrowser: Table Demo

File Reload Home Back Forward View CGI Bookmarks Options Help

**Table done with <PRE>**

```
ITEM #    Description       Cost
--------- ----------------- -----
X3940     Hammer, claw      22.45
X4256     Pliers            12.50
X6435     Saw, crosscut     26.75
```

**Table done with <TABLE>**

| ITEM # | Description | Cost |
|---|---|---|
| X3948 | Hammer, claw | 22.45 |
| X4256 | Pliers | 12.50 |
| X6435 | Saw, crosscut | 26.75 |

**Figure 2-5:** Tables in HTML — old style and new.

The current problem with these more dazzling enhancements is that not all browsers support them.

It isn't enough for users to just receive information; they want to talk back to the Web page. You can add *forms,* however, containing input fields, check boxes, and drop-down selection lists to extract information from viewers (Figure 2-6). After the viewer clicks on the Submit button, the form data goes off to the server for processing. All browsers, even the the text-only ones, support forms and display them in varying degrees of elegance.

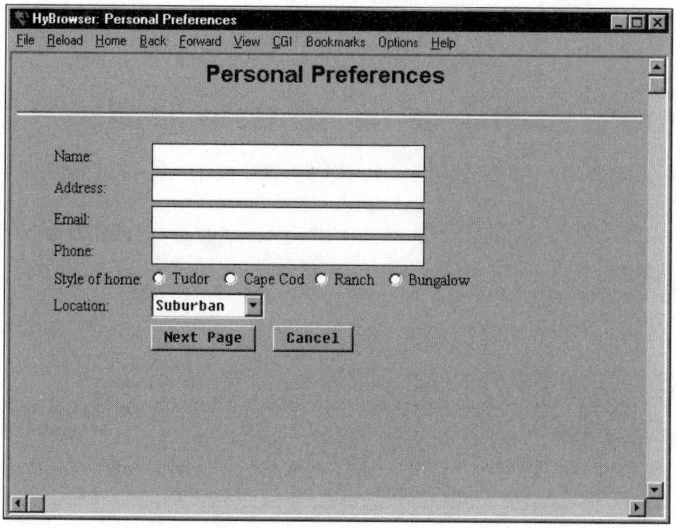

**Figure 2-6:** Personal preferences form.

# Forms and Perl

The basic idea behind a form is simple: Ask the visitor for information, get the information, then do something with the information. The tricky part of dealing with forms is handled behind the scenes by your Perl code.

## Form elements overview

A form can be as simple as a one-word prompt accompanied by a text box for input (Figure 2-7).

Alternatively, a form can be as complex as an IRS 1040C form. How complicated your forms get depends on your needs and the strength of your vistors' motivation for responding to all questions.

After a visitor fills in a form, the browser sends off the data for processing or storage. Typically, the form's data stream feeds into a program that changes the data into a more readable format. The processing program can be a URL anywhere on the Internet. The processing program usually is a Perl script, a UNIX shell script, or a compiled program residing on the server that handles your Web pages.

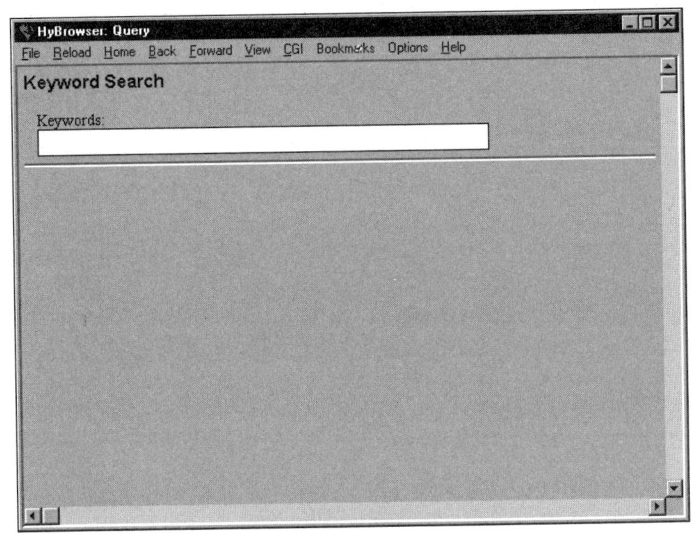


**Figure 2-7:** A simple form that uses a text box for input.

The data from a form flows out in a stream that uses special formatting called *URL encoding*. The term comes from the fact that the data has to be translated into a format that can pass through the Internet, which originally meant pure and simple ASCII text that looked like the typical Web page address — letters and numbers, no spaces, no fancy punctuation, and no funny business with fonts. The process changes "I want to join Kombat Karate because I need the exercise" into the following string for transmission:

```
Comment=I+want+to+join+Kombat+Karate+because+I+need+%0D%0Athe+
exercise.%0D%0A
```

Of course, encoding data is only half the battle — translating the URL-encoded data back into readable text on the other end of the transmission is the other half, and a very good job for Perl. I explain what the data looks like, where it goes, and how it gets handled in Chapter 3.

## Input options

HTML provides a basic set of form elements that accept input from the visitor. You already may know these elements from your experience with software in the modern GUI environment. The following list is a preview of the input options that you will be using shortly. Figure 2-8 shows some of these input options in action.

| Input Elements | Element Types |
|---|---|
| Textbox | Multiline<br>Single line<br>Password |
| Checkbox | |
| Radio button | |
| Select (picklist) | Single selection<br>Multiple selection |
| Command buttons | Reset<br>Submit |

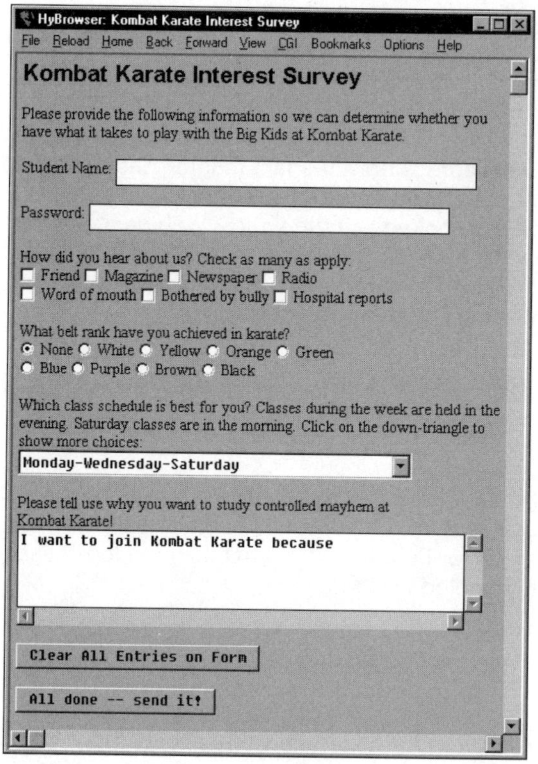

**Figure 2-8:** *A kitchen-sink collection of form elements.*

You've seen these guys or their close relatives before, so you shouldn't find any mysteries in this list.

You can use any or all of these elements in a single form if you like. In fact, that's exactly what I intend to do here in order to show you how to create them and what they all look like. If you just can't wait, take a peek at Chapter 3. But be sure to return to this chapter so that you don't miss the excitement of the rest of this chapter.

## HTML form design

Building a form is easy. Some of the more feature-laden HTML editors do most of the work for you. Designing a form for maximum utility and viewing pleasure, however, is an entirely different matter. The task of designing a form calls on artistic sensibilities that vary widely between designers. For example, you may not care for my designs, but I might view yours with admiration and delight.

Aside from the input fields themselves, the design tools for forms are limited but adequate:

| Design Consideration | Description |
|---|---|
| Prompts | Use a helpful prompt (label) for each field to tell the viewer what to do or how to do it. Put the prompts where the viewer expects to see them: directly above long fields, to the left of short fields, or to the right of checkboxes and radio buttons. |
| Alignment | Forms with several fields need help to keep from looking chaotic. Use the `<PRE>` tag to set up a basic alignment that works with all browsers. If you are confident that your viewers all use browsers that support tables, you can put frame elements into table cells for impressive alignment control. |
| Spacing | Do some thinking about whether a group of checkboxes or radio buttons should be allowed to run across the page or instead be stacked like a list. Remember that the viewer controls the width of the display, so be sure to consider how your prompts and buttons will work with line breaks that differ from what you intended. |
| Equivalents | Use the appropriate input field for your particular form. Resist the temptation to use a select list just to show off if the equivalent group of radio buttons will be easier for the viewer to use. On the other hand, don't avoid select lists just because they look tricky to code when a select list is what you really need. |

Knowing how to use the tools and looking at the form from the viewer's standpoint will help your design effort succeed. Successful designs are what makes cool Web pages work.

## Sending data: GET and POST

The browser sends form data to the server by using one of two methods: GET or POST. I get into the details of these two methods in Chapter 3, but here's a quick overview.

With the GET method, the browser packages the form data into something called an *encoded string* (URL-encoded, to be exact) and tacks it onto the end of an otherwise normal-looking request for a URL. For instance, suppose that my form has a field called Favorite series, and I type the value **Cool Pages** into the input field. When I click on Submit to send the form data to the CGI program at www.some.site/cgi-bin/bookform.pl, the request actually goes out as

```
www.some.site/cgi-bin/bookform.pl?Favorite+
series=Cool+Pages
```

The server handling this request wakes up bookform.pl and hands over the encoded string Favorite+series=Cool+Pages for the program to process. The encoded string then goes through an environmental variable (see the next section) called QUERY_STRING.

The GET method is workable but limited. Servers have length limits for URLs and environmental variables, and a form containing long field names and longer values may reach the limit before all the data goes out.

The POST method, however, can handle much longer coded strings of data (Figure 2-9). POST encodes data the same way, but it sends the data directly to the CGI program through STDIN. The POST method uses the CONTENT_LENGTH environmental variable to tell the server how many bytes to read from STDIN. The data stream coming in can be as long as you require.

Because of the data length limit, almost all forms use the POST method.

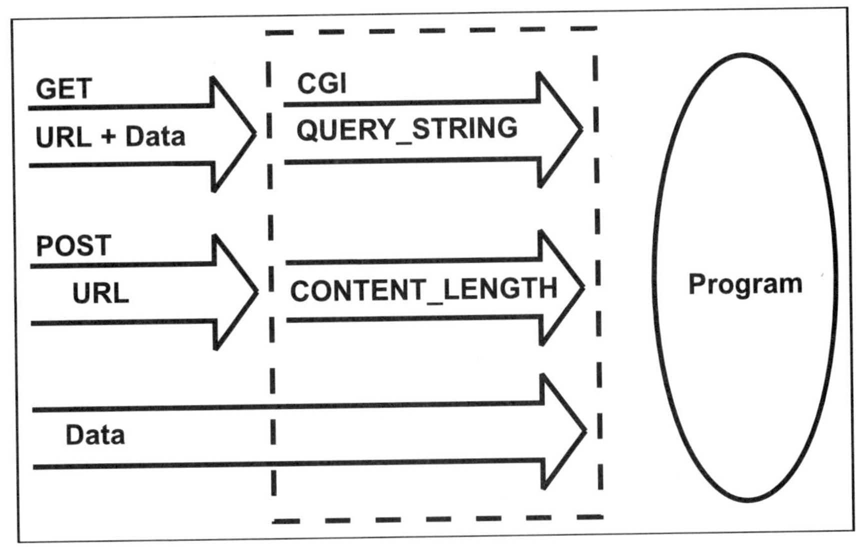


**Figure 2-9:** GET versus POST.

## Environmental (CGI) variables

Functions and processes on a server pass data to each other through environmental variables — named locations in the computer memory for storing handy information. These variables act much like a row of mailboxes. Processes and functions slide information into these variables and then go about their business elsewhere. Other processes and functions stop by to pick up the information they need and drop off data for the next guy to use.

When I talk about CGI programming, I refer to these environmental variables as CGI variables. You met two of the CGI variables a moment ago: `QUERY_STRING` and `CONTENT_LENGTH`. Listing 2-1 shows a sample listing of CGI variables returned by a program I present in Chapter 9, `env2html.pl`:

**Listing 2-1 CGI Variables Returned by `env2html.pl`**

```
DOCUMENT_ROOT=/usr/local/web/mysite
GATEWAY_INTERFACE=CGI/1.1
HTTP_ACCEPT=image/gif, image/x-xbitmap, image/jpeg, image/pjpeg,
*/*
HTTP_CONNECTION=Keep-Alive
HTTP_HOST=www.some.site
HTTP_USER_AGENT=Mozilla/2.0 (Win95; I)
```

*(continued)*

**Listing 2-1** ***(continued)***

```
PATH=/usr/sbin:/usr/bin
QUERY_STRING=
REMOTE_ADDR=127.0.0.0
REMOTE_HOST=some.site
REQUEST_METHOD=GET
SCRIPT_FILENAME=/usr/local/cgi/mysite/env2html.pl
SCRIPT_NAME=/mysite/env2html.pl
SERVER_ADMIN=boss@some.site
SERVER_NAME=some.site
SERVER_PORT=80
SERVER_PROTOCOL=HTTP/1.0
SERVER_SOFTWARE=Apache/1.0.3
TZ=US/Central
```

The CGI variables of most importance for understanding the browser/server communication process are described in the following table:

| Variable | Description |
|---|---|
| `QUERY_STRING` | Incoming data appended to the URL for a `GET` method |
| `REQUEST_METHOD` | Whether the URL request is a `GET` (the default any request that isn't otherwise specified) or `POST` |
| `CONTENT_LENGTH` | How many bytes of the data stream to read for a request with a `POST` method. This variable is only defined for a `POST` method and does not appear in a CGI variable listing (like the preceding one) generated with a `GET` method |

More environmental variables are available. I show you what they are and how to look at them with Perl programs later in this book.

# Perl for forms

Why do you need Perl to process forms if the server is so cooperative about passing data around? You need Perl because HTML can't do the work — it can only help show the results.

The form data goes out as URL-encoded. A Perl program decodes it into a readable format. Then Perl processes the decoded information, perhaps by using it to query a database or check a price list, which produces more information. After completing the processing, Perl formats all new data into a report and adds all the HTML tags needed to turn the report into a Web page. Finally, Perl hands the page over to the server, which in turn can pass the page back to the requesting browser for displaying to the viewer.

# PerlFacts: More Patterns and Flow Control

This chapter's PerlFacts section takes regular expression pattern-matching to a higher level by introducing variables within expressions, classes, and alternatives. It also digs deeper into controlling data flow with variations of `if` and `while`.

## Power tools for patterns

Just when you think you've got your arms around a topic, Perl expands it by making refinements and adding more power. Comparing the regular expression patterns found in Perl to the street-variety search-and-replace functions is like comparing ballet to a baby's first toddling steps.

In this section, I show you some of Perl's methods for handling alternatives in patterns. These grindstone pattern-pieces — such as one out of a group, several but no more than that, anything but numbers, either this word or that word, and whole words only — will sharpen the blades in your pattern toolbox.

### Setting number of repetitions

Suppose that you want to find multiple occurrences of some character set in your file. How would you go about it? Character wildcards look helpful at first. To find one or none of a character, the hook (`?`) multiplier is manageable. But the star (`*`) and plus (`+`) are too loose on the top end for this purpose. Neither the star (none or more) nor the plus (one or more) puts a limit on the maximum number of repetitions of the designated character. For example, if I want to find six of something in my pattern, both star * and plus + will return a match with 7, 8, or 100 occurrences of that something, a far more generous interpretation than I require.

Curly braces to the rescue! To specify an exact number of repetitions (Figure 2-10), you can designate the minimum and maximum number range, separated by a comma, in curly braces as follows:

- {0,3} means from zero to three repetitions
- {2,7} means from two to seven repetitions
- {10,} with nothing after the comma shows no upper range and means ten or more repetitions
- {8} with no comma means exactly eight repetitions

**Repetitions**

**{Min, Max}**

**Figure 2-10:** Repetitions with curly-braced Min and Max.

The general multiplier works well with the dot symbol:

```
/p.{4,9}t/;  # parachute, but not pitiful: must have at least
             #    4 chars but not more than 9 between p and t
/a.{5}g/;    # same as /a.....g/ : exactly 5 chars between a
             #    and g
/xyz{8,}$/;  # xy, then 8 or more z's up the end of the line
/(xyz){8,}/; # 8 or more xyz's
```

**Exercise 2-1**

Write patterns to find the following:

A. Text filenames starting with three numbers.

B. Six-letter words with a space on either side.

C. At the start of a line, eight-letter words ending in "ing."

## Class patterns [aeiou]

To look for a particular set of characters in your match, you can use *class patterns*. You define a set of characters as a character class by enclosing them in square brackets. For example, [aeiou] represents the class of lowercase vowels without the sometimes *y*. You get a true match if any one of the characters in the class appears in that position in the target string:

```
/[AEIOU].*/;  # Olaf, Ellen, myOwnFile, do-re-mi-sO
/ab[aeiou]t/; # abate, abutt, sabotage; not 'about' because
              #    only one char from the class is allowed
```

Instead of entering every member of a class, such as [abcdefghijklmn], use *ranges* to describe the group (Figure 2-11). You designate a range by using single characters for the start and end of a sequential series and connecting them with a hyphen, all in square backets:

```
/[0-9]/;       # much easier than [0123456789]
/[a-z]/;       # much easier than... well, you know
/[A-Z][a-z]/;  # first character uppercase, second one lowercase
/[a-zA-Z]/;    # any one alpha character, lowercase or uppercase:
               #   there is no space between the two sets.
/[A-PR-YO-9];  # phone number, no Q on the keypad
/[a-km-z]/;    # a to k, and m to z, Christmas synonym: no ell
```

**Class Patterns**

**[a-g] # any of these**

**[^a-g] # any *BUT* these**

**Figure 2-11:** "Any one" and "none of these" class patterns.

A caret (^) just inside the first bracket negates a class. In other words, using a caret as the first character of the class signals that the rest of the characters in the class are to be avoided. The match fails if any of the illegal characters turns up in that position in the target string:

```
/.*[^XYZ]$/;     # no match if there's an X, Y, or Z at the end of
                 #   the line
/G[^0-9] size/; # only G followed by 'not a number'
/only the [^a-zA-Z] character/; # anything but a lowercase
                 #   or uppercase letter
```

**Exercise 2-2**

Write patterns to match the following:

A. Telephone number with area codes that start with the number 4.

B. Any mention of a file with a .PL extension and at least three letters before the extension, all with a preceding space.

C. An uppercase letter followed by three to nine numbers and then none or one x.

## Alternative ( / either | or / )

To create a search on alternative choices at a particular position in the target, use the alternative operator, the vertical bar. Unless *scoped* (controlled) with parentheses, the alternatives choices include everything that appears from the opening slash to the vertical bar and everything that appears from the vertical bar to the closing slash:

```
/No smok|Spit/; # matches "No smoking", "Spitting Allowed"
/girls|boys/; # matches 'what are little boys made of'
               #    and  'what are little girls make of'
```

You can use parentheses to specify a more restricted scope for the alternatives. One alternative includes everything between the opening parenthesis and the vertical bar, and the other alternative consists of everything from the vertical bar to the closing parenthesis, as follows:

```
/No (smok|spit).?ing/; # matches "No smoking", "No spitting"
/to the ([0-9]|teeth)/; # dressed to the 9s, dressed to the teeth
```

Without the parentheses in `(/the [0-9]|teeth/)`, the bar operates from slash to slash, and the alternatives would be `to the [0-9]` or `teeth` instead of `[0-9]` or `teeth`.

**Exercise 2-3**

Write patterns to match the following:

A. Lines with “either/or” or “and/or”

B. 800 numbers with either letters or numbers after the 800 part

C. Telephone listings for men’s names with either “jr.”, “Jr.”, or “JR.”

## Special characters (^ $ \r \n \t \f \d \D \w \W \s \S \b \B)

Perl likes economy. Some patterns are used often enough to deserve their own economical shorthand. You already know the caret and dollar symbols:

^ Pattern starts at beginning of string

$ Pattern ends at end of string

Perl uses every character on the keyboard for one special purpose or another. The backslash is the most flexible character and usually acts like a toggle or reversing switch. Used with a special character in a pattern, such as the star (*) or hook (?), the backslash takes away any special meaning ("escapes" the character) and makes the character just a character. The backslash works the other way, too — when used with ordinary characters in patterns and strings, the backslash adds special meaning so that the characters are no longer regular characters.

Table 2-1 shows some familiar faces with the new jobs assigned by the backslash:

**Table 2-1 Special Characters in Patterns**

| Character | What It Represents |
|---|---|
| \r | Carriage return, ASCII 13 decimal |
| \n | Line feed; ASCII 10 decimal in UNIX Perl, ASCII 13 decimal in Macintosh Perl, ASCII 13 + ASCII 10 (two characters) in DOS Perl |
| \t | Tab, ASCII 9 decimal |
| \f | Formfeed, ASCII 12 decimal |
| \d | Digits, same as [0-9] |
| \D | Nondigits, negation of \d same as [^0-9] |
| \w | Same as [a-zA-Z0-9_], matches anything alphanumeric, including the underscore |
| \W | Same as [^a-zA-Z0-9_], negation of \w, matches anything that's not alphanumeric |
| \s | Space — actually whitespace, which includes space, tab, carriage return, line feed, and form feed (ASCII characters 32, 9, 13, 10, and 12), same as [ \r\t\n\f] |
| \S | Not space, negation of \s, same as [^ \r\t\n\f] |

**Table 2-1 *(continued)***

| Character | What It Represents |
|---|---|
| \b | Word boundary; matches punctuation, whitespace, or a nonalphanumeric character at the beginning or end of a string |
| \B | Anything that is not a word boundary, negation of \b |

The following examples show special characters as they appear in Perl scripts:

```
/^\d+\t/;     # beginning of string, one or more digits, and a tab
/\D$/;        # any string ending in a non-digit
/\btrust\b/; # trust as a word bounded by punctuation or space:
              # 'trust' "trust! :trust?, but not mistrust or trusted
/\strust\s/; # trust bounded by whitespace, but not trust? or trusts
```

**Exercise 2-4**

Write patterns to match the following:

**A.** Telephone number, with area code, using special character \d

**B.** URL bounded by whitespace

**C.** A line ending with a five-digit or nine-digit ZIP code

# Operators, conditionals, loops, and subroutines

The flow of events through a program follows a looping, twitching, jumping path, no matter what computer language you use. Chapter 1 touches lightly on the `while` and `if` functions. Now I will drag them into the light for closer examination and add the topic of subroutines for good measure. First, take a quick look at the operators that massage the values in your variables.

## Smooth operators for math

Scalar variables can hold strings or numeric values. The variable doesn't care which kind of value it holds. Sometimes Perl doesn't care, either. If I have the number 4 in `$myVar` and I want to use `$myVar` by adding `$invite`, which holds "Come to my house at," Perl can change the number 4 to the string "4" automatically and tell my friends to "Come to my house at 4."

To make sure that your numbers remain as numeric operators, use math operators (string operators are discussed in the next section). The simple math operators are as follows:

| Symbol | Arithmetic It Performs |
|---|---|
| + | Addition: 3 + 4 = 7 |
| – | Subtraction: 11 – 5 = 6 |
| * | Multiplication: 3 * 5 = 15 |
| ** | Exponentiation: 2**3 = 8 |
| / | Division: 21 / 7 = 3 |
| % | Modulo division (remainder only): 25 / 7 = 4 |

These math operators work with literal numbers, with numberic variables, or any mixture of the two:

```
$one = 1;
$two = 2;
$ans = $one + $two;  # $ans = 3
$ans = $two * 4;     # $ans = 8
$half = $ans / 2;    # $half = 4
$remain = $half % 3; # $remain = 1
$ans = $ans + 4;     # $ans = 12
```

Perl has a special trick for the last expression, a variable that changes its own value. To take a numeric variable, add something to it, and then store the new total in the old variable, use addition and assignment operators together as one operator. For example, `$ans += 4` means "add 4 to `$ans`, so `$ans` is now 4 bigger than it was." You can blend any of the arithmetic operators with the assignment operator, as follows:

| Arithmetic Assignment | Result |
|---|---|
| += | Addition: `$var += 4` means `$var = $var + 4` |
| –= | Subtraction: `$var -= 4` means `$var = $var - 4` |
| *= | Multiplication: `$var *= 4` means `$var = $var * 4` |
| **= | Exponentiation: `$var **= 4` means `$var = $var ** 4` |
| /= | Division: `$var /= 4` means `$var = $var / 4` |
| %= | Modulo division (remainder only): `$var %= 4` means `$var = $var % 4` |

At this point, programming-book authors are supposed to hand out a list of arithmetic examples and exercises. With math topics, that always makes me feel like a third-grader. I want to talk about strings instead.

## Smooth operators for strings

With strings, adding "two" and "three" totals "twothree," not "five." When the strings are hidden in variables that don't care whether they hold words or numbers, using the right string instead of the wrong math operator is critical. Look at what Perl can do with strings and scalar variables holding strings.

`.` (dot) concatenates strings:

```
$dot = "beg" . "end" # $dot now "begend"
```

`.=` (dot assign) concatenates into original variable:

```
$new = "beg";
$new .= "end";        # $new now "begend"
```

`x` (x) makes into multiple copies:

```
$old = "beg" x 3;    # "begbegbeg"
```

`x=` (x assign) makes multiple copies into original variable:

```
$bigger = "big";
$bigger x= 3;        # "bigbigbigbig"
```

That doesn't seem like much for string operations, does it? There's more to come — wait until I start talking about substitution, translation, and, much later, `sprintf`.

## Nothing but the truth

Every branch in a program's flow requires a decision. Left or right? Up or down? Get another line or quit now? Perl makes decisions by testing conditions. The basic condition to test is whether an expression is true or false. Other values that work with decision-making are 0 (False) or not-zero (True); null (nothing — think of it as zero) or anything that's not null; and tests that show whether an object does not exist or does exist.

## Comparing numbers

Numeric comparisons use the following notions:

| Operator | Meaning |
|---|---|
| > | Greater than |
| < | Less than |
| == | Equals |
| >= | Greater than or equal to |
| <= | Less than or equal to |
| != | Does not equal |
| <=> | Compare and return result as –1, 0, or 1 to show how the left side compares with the right side: –1 = left less than right, 0 = left equals right, and 1 = left greater than right. |

The comparisons are easy to evaluate, as the following listing shows:

```
$big = 100;                           # assignment, not evaluation
$small = 10;                          # assignment, not evaluation
$true = "True";
print $true if ($big > $small);       # True
print $true if ($big >= $small);      # True
print $true if ($big == $small);      # doesn't print anything
print $true if ($big != $small);      # True
print $true if ($small < $big);       # True
$result = $big <=> $small;            # $result is -1 (left bigger)
$result = $small <=> $big;            # $result is 1 (left smaller)
$result = ($small * 10) <=> $big;     # $result is now 0 (equal)
print $true if (($small * 10) == $big);  # True!
print $true if (($big / 12) < $small);   # Also True
```

Look at all the parentheses in the last two statements. They set the order, or priority, of evaluation. Without the internal parentheses, Perl would interpret the last statement as

```
print $true if ($big / 12 < $small);
```

Perl knows that this statement was not intended to mean `$big` divided by the evaluation of "Is 12 < `$small` ?," but long collections of objects and operators can be confusing to a human reader. That leaves you, the programmer, in the lurch three weeks later when you are trying to remember what your code was really supposed to do.

Precedence rules exist in Perl to instruct it to divide this first, multiply that, and only then check for the comparison. I put the standard table of precedence rules in the Perl summary appendix for you. But I can never remember what takes precedence over which operator, so I don't expect you to. Just use parentheses to clarify how you want things to work — do the most inside parentheses first, then the next level, and so on. The parentheses won't hurt anything, and they help you think out the process now and be able to understand it later.

## Comparing strings

Can you say whether one string is greater or less than another string? Yes! A string is greater than another string if the first string sorts farther down on an alphabetical list — thus, *backside* is greater than *aspire* in an alphabetical list.

Because variables can hold either numbers or strings, you must tell Perl to compare values as strings by using the string comparision operators, which are character-based to remind you that the comparison deals with strings, not numbers. The string comparison operators are as follows:

| Operator | What It Means |
|---|---|
| `gt` | Greater than |
| `lt` | Less than |
| `eq` | Equals |
| `ge` | Greater than or equal to |
| `le` | Less than or equal to |
| `ne` | Does not equal |
| `cmp` | Compare and return result as –1, 0, or 1 to show how the left side compares with the right side: –1 = left less than right, 0 = left equals right, and 1 = left greater than right. |

String comparisons take some thinking, but you'll get used to doing them. Check out the following examples:

```
$irked = "irritable";              # assignment, not evaluation
$hot = "mad";                      # assignment, not evaluation
$true = "True";
print $true if ($hot gt $irked);   # True, mad comes after irri
                                       table
print $true if ($hot ge $irked);   # True
print $true if ($hot eq $irked);   # False: doesn't print anything
print $true if ($hot ne $irked);   # True
print $true if ($irked le $hot);   # True
$result = $irked cmp $hot;         # $result is now 1,
                                   # pointing to $hot as the
                                       larger
$result = $hot cmp $irked;         # $result is now -1, again
                                   # pointing to $hot as the
                                       larger
```

**Exercise 2-5**

Using this example

```
$n9 = 9; $n10 = 10;
```

perform the following string comparisons:

**A.** What is `$res` in: `$res = $n9 <=> $n10;`

**B.** What is `$res` in: `$res = $n9 cmp $n10;`

## Jumping: `if-elsif-else`

The one-line (or inline) form of `if` works well when both the action and the decision are simple:

```
print if ($a > 4);
print $true if ($tiny lt $huge);
```

The action takes place if the condition is true. Otherwise, nothing happens — the program simply skips to the next statement. To process a whole series of statements instead of just one, Perl offers the block form of `if`:

```
if ($tiny lt $huge) {
    $fixed = $tiny . " aforementioned ";  # concatenate
    print $fixed;
    $tiny = $fixed . $huge
}
```

The condition appears in parentheses after the `if`, and the block-opening curly brace follows right after the condition. When the condition is true, the program processes all statements in the block, from the opening curly brace to the closing curly brace. When the condition is false, the program skips the entire block and picks up the flow with the statement right after the closing curly brace.

So far, I only have one choice — do something or don't. To expand the possibilities, I want to instruct Perl that "If true, do Plan A, otherwise do Plan B." Such a flow-control structure is called if-else. If-else has two blocks — one for the true path and one for the false path, as in the following example:

```
if ($i <= 10) {
    print "Still working \n";    # linefeed \n at end of string
    $i++;                        # increment $i by one
} else {
    print "Greater than 10 \n";
}
```

The `else` branch does not need a condition to evaluate because it feeds from the `if` condition:

- When the condition is true, the program goes through the `if` block and then skips the `else` block.
- When the condition is false, the program skips the `if` block and goes through the `else` block instead.

To check for a secondary condition (if the number is less than 5, do this; but if it is 6, do that), use `elsif`, which uses a condition the same way as `if` :

```
if ($i <= 5) {
    print "Still working \n";
    $i++;
} elsif ($i == 6) {
    print "We've got a 6!\n";
}
```

When $i equals 6, the program flow skips the if clause and goes through the block for the elsif. Any number greater than 6 will skip both blocks. You can chain together as many of the elsif blocks as you need. For example

```
if ($i <= 5) {
    print "Still working \n";
    $i++;
} elsif ($i == 6) {
    print "We've got a 6!\n";
} elsif ($i == 50) {
    print "We've got a 50!\n";
} elsif ($i == 227) {
    print "We've got a 227!\n";
} elsif ($i == 8) {
    print "We've got an 8!\n";
}
```

Whenever $i holds a number not listed in the chain of elsif blocks, the program skips the whole group without a pause. A finishing else block to catch this fall-through is a useful touch (as in the following example):

```
if ($i <= 5) {
    print "Still working \n";
    $i++;
} elsif ($i == 6) {
    print "We've got a 6!\n";
} elsif ($i == 50) {
    print "We've got a 50!\n";
} elsif ($i == 227) {
    print "We've got a 227!\n";
} elsif ($i == 8) {
    print "We've got an 8!\n";
} else {
    print "Nothing we wanted this time.\n";
}
```

The else block catches the in-between and too-big numbers.

## Old Dog, New Trick

Notice that `elsif` only has one "e." I didn't notice that at first, and my oversight cost me a week of frustration early in my Perl career, trying to get my misspelled "`elseif`" clauses to work. I resorted to a long chain of simple `if` blocks instead. That solution worked, but not as well as `elsif`, which Perl optimizes for speed while preparing your script to run. Carryover habits from other computer languages or reckless assumptions can create bugs that you may not see in your own code. When that happens, show your code to someone who knows how to proofread. Perl expertise, though it helps, is not required for proofing your typing, if the proofer has good examples for comparison.

**Exercise 2-6**

Try writing some Perl statements to handle the following scenarios:

A. Greg's salary is secret, but everybody knows that he gets a 10 percent raise if unit sales exceed 25,000 and a 10 percent cut if sales are less than 5,000. Write an `if` block that gives Greg his due. Note: For Perl, don't use commas in numbers. Write them as 25000 and 5000.

B. Write a program that prints a person's last name first if the first name is alphabetically higher and first name first if the last name is higher.

# Looping: `while()` with `last`, `next`, and `(<>)`

The `while` function loops repeatedly through a block of statements, as long as the specified condition is true. One already familiar example is the loop that reads and prints lines coming in through `<STDIN>` :

```
while (<STDIN>) {
    print;
}
```

As long as data is entering through `<STDIN>`, the loop and the printing action continue.

## Nested blocks

To print only those lines that match a pattern, you can use the inline `if`. For example, take a look at the `gold1.pl` program that follows in Listing 2-2.

**Listing 2-2 Using `gold1.pl` to Find "Treasure" in Files**

```
# gold1.pl -- find treasure

while (<STDIN>) {
    print if (/treasure/);
}
print "Done.\n";
```

This program reads the file, prints any line that contains the word *treasure*, and prints `Done.` when it reaches the end of the file. I can rewrite the inline `if` to make an `if` block that does the same job, as with `gold2.pl` (Listing 2-3):

**Listing 2-3 Finding Treasure with `gold2.pl` and `if`-block**

```
# gold2.pl -- find treasure with if-block

while (<STDIN>) {
    if (/treasure/) {
        print;
    }
}
print "Done.\n";
```

You are now looking at nested blocks of conditional statements. The if-block is nested inside the while-block. A large processing loop with smaller decision blocks nested inside appears commonly in programming. You also can add another nested condition to make sure that you found something worthwhile, as in Listing 2-4:

**Listing 2-4 Finding Gold with `gold3.pl`**

```
# gold3.pl -- find gold in the treasure
while (<STDIN>) {
    if (/treasure/) {
        print "Maybe\n";          # line has "treasure" in it
        if (/gold/) {
            print "Dig here!\n";  # "treasure" line also has "gold"
        }
    }
}
print "Done.\n";
# end of gold3.pl
```

A potential problem with nested block structures is that the nesting can become quite intricate. To keep from getting lost, I lined up each block's closing curly brace under the first letter of the statement that opened the block and then indented each block four spaces more to the right. I can easily match the closing braces with the opening statements by using the Up-arrow key to bump up the text cursor from the closing brace to the last statement aligned with that brace, enabling me to see which program actions belong to which block.

**Exercise 2-7**

The following exercise helps you to understand how loops work with Perl:

A. Rewrite the program `findtext.pl` (see Listing 1-1 in the preceding chapter) to change the inline `if` to a block `if`.

B. In the new, revised `findtext.pl`, add an `else` block to the new `if` block so that it prints "Nope" if the line doesn't match the pattern.

C. Delete one of the closing curly braces in the revised `findtext.pl`. Run the program to see what kind of error message Perl sends.

### The `last` statement

In the interest of full disclosure, let's tell the potential gold prospector how many lines have been panned by modifying the script, as in Listing 2-5:

**Listing 2-5 `gold4.pl` Counts the Number of Lines Processed**

```
# gold4.pl -- find gold in the treasure, count lines
while (<STDIN>) {
    $i++;                      # increment $i once each loop
    if (/treasure/) {          # look for treasure
        print "Maybe ";        # say "Maybe" if there's
                                   treasure
        if (/gold/) {          # then look for gold
            print "Dig here! ";    # found it!
        }
    }
    print "Line $i\n";         # print the current value of
                                   $i
}                              # loop back up for another
                                   line
print "Done.\n";               # announce when the loop is
                                   done
```

Listing 2-6 is a test file with a list of geological features on a miner's claim. I'll run this file through the mining program to find likely places to dig:

**Listing 2-6** `goldmine.dat` **Data File**

```
loose shale
gravel moraine
bedrock stream
treasure island
sandy shore
gold treasure chest
rich iron lode
presidential library files
```

You can create `goldmine.dat` by typing it in from the listing or by copying the file from the Examples directory on the CD-ROM. Now, to go digging, enter this command at the prompt:

```
C:\dev>perl gold4.pl goldmine.dat
```

Perl runs the command and returns the following:

```
Line 1
Line 2
Line 3
Maybe Line 4
Line 5
Maybe Dig here! Line 6
Line 7
Line 8
Done.
```

What happened at Line 4? Perl hit treasure and printed `Maybe`, but the search didn't pan out — no gold. As a result, the program skipped down to the closing brace for `if (/gold/)`, went to the closing brace for if `(/treasure/)`, and printed `Line 4` right after `Maybe`.

Line 6 had both treasure and gold, and all the code blocks were processed: `Maybe Dig Here! Line 6`. The program found the spot to dig, but then continued reading the file right through to the bitter end.

Once I find gold, I want to quit reading the file. The `last` statement terminates a loop and jumps out with no further processing. Perl takes a `last` statement to mean, "This is the last statement to process in this loop. Get out, now!"

A `last` statement right after finding gold jumps me out of the file-reading loop and prints `Done`. Listing 2-7shows where to insert the `last` statement.

**Listing 2-7** **gold5.pl**

```
# gold5.pl -- find gold in the treasure, count lines
while (<STDIN>) {
    $i++;
    if (/treasure/) {
        print "Maybe ";
        if (/gold/) {              # found treasure, look for gold
            print "Dig here! ";    # found gold, make announcement
            last;                  # jump out of loop to Done.
        }
    }
    print "Line $i\n";
}                                  # closing brace for 'while'
print "Done.\n";                   # jump lands here
```

Now the resulting report is shorter:

```
Line 1
Line 2
Line 3
Maybe Line 4
Line 5
Maybe Dig here!
```

The program jumps out of the loop, but it still doesn't tell me where to dig. The `while` loop ends just after `print "Line $i\n";` which is inside the `while` loop. The `last` statement comes earlier in the loop and jumps the program flow past `"Line $i\n";` — the line number printing statement. Fixing this little awkwardness looks to me like a good "leave it to the reader" programming exercise!

### Exercise 2-8

Where would you add another print statement to show the line number where gold was found?

## Loop again with `next`

If I'm looking for gold and I find iron instead, I may as well search someplace else. The `next` statement shortcircuits a loop and jumps the program back to the top of the loop for another try. In the gold-digging program, another try means "read the next line" as shown in Listing 2-8:

**Listing 2-8 `gold6.pl` and `next` to Dig Faster**

```
# gold6.pl -- find gold in the treasure, count lines
while (<STDIN>) {
    $i++;
    if (/iron/) {
        next;          # go back up to 'while' for another line
    } elsif (/treasure/) {
        print "Maybe ";
        if (/gold/) {
            print "Dig here! ";
            last;      # jump out of the 'while' loop this point
        }
    }
    print "Line $i\n";
}
print "Done.\n";
```

Any time the program hits a line containing *iron,* the `next` statement skips the remainder of the loop and kicks the flow back up to `while`, so that it can read another line.

## Multi-file input with `while(<>)`

Looking back on the programs and snippets provided so far, I have shown these methods for reading files:

1. Read from `<STDIN>` until end of file (EOF):

```
while (<STDIN>) {
    print;
}
```

2. Read from named file until EOF:

```
open (MYHANDLE, "myfile.dat");
while (<MYHANDLE>) {
    print;
}
```

3. Read file listed on the command line after a pattern:

```
$pattern = $ARGV[0];          #1. ARGV[0] holds the pattern
                                   string
open (FINDFILE, $ARGV[1]);   #2. open() names a filehandle
while (<FINDFILE>) {          #3. while() to read lines
                                   from file
    print if /$pattern/;      #4. print if pattern matches
}
```

Those methods all use a filehandle inside the read-file function (<>), which, in turn, is inside a `while` loop. What if you want to read a bunch of files through a program, or even an entire directory of files? How do you manage all the filehandles?

The solution is to use the `@ARGV` array. The `@ARGV` special array holds all command-line parameters. Start with this command:

```
C:\dev> perl listem.pl first.txt second.text third.txt fourth.txt
```

The program has access to the filenames listed on the command line by looking at `@ARGV`:

```
print $ARGV[0];    # first.txt
print $ARGV[1];    # second.txt
print $ARGV[2];    # third.txt
print $ARGV[3];    # fourth.txt
```

At least two ways are available to read all files in the list. The hard way is to create an index variable and use that variable to cycle through the names in `@ARGV` one at a time, as in Listing 2-9:

**Listing 2-9** **readf01.pl**

```
# readf01.pl -- read files listed on command line
# usage: perl readf01.pl file1 file2 file3 ...

$i = 0;                          # set index to 0
$parnum = @ARGV;                 # set $parnum to number of files
while ($i < $parnum) {           # while index < number of files
    open (FHANDLE, $ARGV[$i]);   # open the file at "index"
                                       element
    while (<FHANDLE>) {          # read the opened file
        print;                   # print the current line
    }                            # go for another line
    close (FHANDLE);             # close the file to tidy up
    $i++;                        # increment the index to next
                                       number
}                                # go back for next file
```

The easy way to read files is to use a special property of the read-file function. The operator <> with nothing in it cycles through the elements in `@ARGV` automatically. An implied `@ARGV` is associated with <>, just as an implied `STDOUT` is associated with print. The `while <>` statement means "read every line in each file in `@ARGV`, one file at a time." The next program, `readf02.pl`, does the same job as `readf01.pl` (Listing 2-10).

**Listing 2-10** **readf02.pl**

```
# readf02.pl -- use while(<>) to read files listed on command
      line
# usage: perl readf02.pl file1 file2 file3 ...

while (<>) {
      print;
}
```

If reading a list of files is so simple, then why do it the hard way? Because you'll run into times when you have no other choice. Using `while (<>)` doesn't work when the command line contains something other than a filename — a search pattern, for instance. In that case, you have to pick `@ARGV` apart to handle filenames and other parameters separately.

**Exercise 2-9**

Special bonus — try wildcards with readf02.pl, like this:

```
C:\dev>perl readf02.pl *.pl *.dat
```

# PerlProject: Multi-file searching

This PerlProject, `grepfil.pl`, draws on the new concepts in this chapter to build a tool for multi-file searching. The programming techniques in `grepfil.pl` are command-line argument handling with `@ARGV`, variables in a pattern statement, `while` loop, `<FHANDLE>` construct to read a file, `if` conditional, `print` function, and regular expression pattern-matching. This program reads the command line to get a regular expression pattern and a file list or mask, searches the files for the pattern, and prints any lines containing the pattern.

Just in case you're wondering, I have to point out that more elegant, Perl-ish ways of performing this task are available than the methods used in Listing 2-11. But first we crawl — then we walk. You'll be delighted at how fast and how far the baby steps in these opening chapters have taken you!

**Listing 2-11** **grepfil.pl**

```
# grepfil.pl -- read files listed on command line to find pattern
# usage: perl readf01.pl "pattern" file1 file2 file3 ...

$i = 1;                           #1 set index to 1 for first
                                         filename
$parnum = @ARGV;                  #2 set $parnum to number of
                                         parameters
$pattern = $ARGV[0]               #3 set $pattern to first
                                         parameter
while ($i < $parnum) {            #4 while index < number of files
    open (FHANDLE, $ARGV[$i]);    #5 open the file at "index"
                                         element
    while (<FHANDLE>) {           #6 read the opened file
        print if /$pattern/;      #7 print the current line if
                                         match
    }                             #8 go for another line
```

```
    close (FHANDLE);                    #9 close the file to tidy up
    $i++;                               #10 increment the index
}                                       #11 go back for next file
# end of grepfil.pl
```

The comments in Listing 2-11 are only terse reminders of what the code is doing. Let me explain in more detail:

1. `$ARGV[0]` holds the pattern, the first parameter on the command line after the name of the Perl program. The pattern comes into **`$pattern`** with the quotes automatically stripped off by DOS. The first filename is in **`$ARGV[1]`**, so the index for filenames has to start at 1.
2. Assigning an array variable to a scalar variable puts the number of elements into the scalar variable.
3. The first element in `@ARGV` is element 0, the pattern.
4. This starts the main loop of the program. `while` checks the size of the number in `$i` with the total number of parameters and terminates when `$i` gets bigger than needed.
5. `$i` is 1, so the open statement assigns `$ARVG[1]` — the second element, which is the first filename — to the filehandle `FHANDLE`.
6. The read-file operator <> reads one line with every pass through the `while` loop.
7. The regular expression operator `/ /` recognizes the string variable, evaluates it, and uses its value as the pattern to find.
8. The closing brace for the while loop sends the program up to read another line from the current file.
9. Once it has no more lines to read, the program drops out of the `while(<FHANDLE>)` loop and executes this line to close the file.
10. To get set for the next file, this line increments `$i` to the next number.
11. The closing brace for the main loop sends the program back up with an incremented `$i` to open the next file. If $i is bigger than the number of parameters in $parnum, the while operator kicks the program back down past this closing brace, and the program ends.

### Exercise 2-10

Note that on each loop through while(<>), ARGV[$i] holds the name of the file being read. Add a variable to hold the filename and then place that variable in the print statement so that the output shows which file contained the found line.

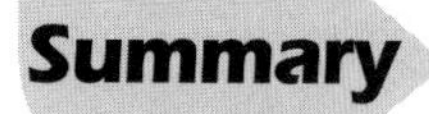


The following is a brief recap of the topics covered in this chapter. Keep the following items in mind for regular expressions:

- Set number of repetitions with number range in braces: {min,max}
- Declare classes (groups) of characters in square brackets: [aeiou], [A-Z]
- Vertical bar separates alternatives: /and|or/
- Special characters: ^ $ \r \n \t \f \d \D \w \W \s \S \b \B

The following points deal with Perl's operators:

- You can combine these math operators with = to perform self-operations: + - * ** / %
- These string operators also can be combined with = to get self operations: .= +=
- The math comparison operators found in Perl are as follows: > < == >= <= != <=>
- You can perform string comparisons in Perl by using these operators: gt lt eq ge le ne cmp

We also discussed flow control in this chapter:

- You can use block statements such as while( ) and if-elsif-else to control flow in Perl.

# Working with Forms: The Basics

**Skill Targets**

Directing a flow of data from the visitor, to the form, to the server, and back to you

HTML form elements, actions, and methods

HTML code to place form elements on a Web page

The format of data generated by forms

Using regular expressions to parse coded strings

Interaction is what the World Wide Web is all about. Enabling active participation with others around the world is the most compelling reason for connecting to the Web. This chapter starts you on the road to getting your Web visitor involved with your portion of the Internet. Let's take a look at how to put a form into a Web page and then receive and process the data you get back from it.

*HyperText Markup Language* (HTML) is the data format of the Web. Every Web page begins life as a script of HTML tags and attributes. I am assuming that you know a little something about HTML but may not have much experience with the tags used to build forms into Web pages. We need forms to accept input on a Web page so that the Perl scripts will have data to process. For that reason, I explore the form tags in some detail in this chapter and the next, but leave all the other fascinating issues of HTML intricacies to your own discovery in the many HTML resources available on the Web and in bookstores across the globe.

## Overview of Forms in HTML

A *form* on a Web page is a collection of input fields that communicates its contents back to the server. Order forms, questionnaires, surveys, guest books, database queries, and "What do you think of my Web page?" comments all carry data back to the owner of a Web page for further processing.

The processing starts with routines to break out the information from its coded format, making the data readable and useful. In this chapter, I show you how to begin this process by starting the construction of a Web site for Kombat Karate, a martial arts training school with students of all ages, sexes, and levels of ability.

# HTML form input types

HTML form elements offer a variety of ways to accept input from the visitor: text line input, multi-line text fields, checkboxes, radio buttons, and picklists of several flavors. I have organized the HTML tags and their related syntaxes in the following list for your reference. If you already are familiar with form elements, the explanations in this chapter may seem to cover old ground for you. If that's the case, travel quickly — but carefully — through this chapter, and watch for new bumps in the path.

The following provides a quick overview of what you should know about form-relevant HTML tags:

## <FORM>...</FORM>

Forms act as a container for holding `INPUT`, `SELECT`, and `TEXTAREA` elements. You need start and end tags to define the form. The start tag uses the following optional attributes:

- `ACTION="URL"`. The name of the script file or program that will handle the data from this form.
- `METHOD="GET"` or `"POST"`. How the data moves from the form to the data handling script.

Example: `<FORM ACTION="/cgi-bin/formecho.pl/" METHOD="POST">`

## <INPUT>

Defines the behavior and placement of a field for accepting visitor data on a form. The TYPE attribute reflects the input options for gathering data. Use only one of the following for each field:

- `TYPE="TEXT"`. A single line of text.
- `TYPE="PASSWORD"`. Hides user input by replacing it with asterisks on-screen.

- TYPE="CHECKBOX". When clicked, puts an X or checkmark to show which choices are selected.
- TYPE="RADIO". When clicked, puts a dot in a circle to show the selected choice; choices are mutually exclusive.
- TYPE="SUBMIT". When clicked, sends the data on its way.
- TYPE="RESET". When clicked, clears all entered data from the form.
- TYPE="HIDDEN". A field that does not appear in the Web page's display. Use it to communicate information that the visitor cannot change easily.
- NAME="myFieldName". The variable name that identifies this field.
- VALUE="myFieldValue". With checkboxes and radio buttons, this specifies which choice the visitor made. Assigning VALUE in a Submit field customizes the button label.
- SIZE=?. The number of characters for the field input box for TEXT and PASSWORD types.
- MAXLENGTH=?. Maximum number of characters allowed in the field for TEXT and PASSWORD types only.

## <SELECT>...</SELECT>

This selection list container defines the contents and placement of a picklist. Its attributes are as follows:

- NAME="myFieldName". The variable name that identifies this field.
- SIZE=?. Specifies the display characteristics for the list: 1 (or SIZE omitted) = a pop-up box; 2 = scrollable box; greater than the number of actual options = scrollable box with a "Nothing" entry tacked onto the end of the list.
- MULTIPLE. Visitor can select more than one choice at a time.
- <OPTION>. Tag to identify the text for a picklist item.
- <OPTION SELECTED>. Tag to identify a picklist item that will be highlighted in the list as the default choice.

## <TEXTAREA>...</TEXTAREA>

This tag is a multi-line textbox container, defines the placement of the textbox on the form. Its attributes are as follows:

- NAME="myFieldName". The variable name that identifies this field.
- ROWS=?. Number of lines deep; how many rows will show in the textbox.
- COLS=?. Number of characters wide; how many characters will show on a row.

## HTML form data — name/value pairs

Form data goes to the CGI (Common Gateway Interface) and then to your Perl program in a coded string that reports on each field in the form. Each field has a `NAME` attribute (so that you know where the data came from) and a `VALUE` attribute (the contents of the field). The coded string sent by the browser pairs each `NAME` in the form with its `VALUE` and connects them with an equal sign: `NAME=VALUE`. If your page contains a field named City, and the visitor enters *Oconomowoc* (the metropolitan pivot of the Lake Country) as the field's value, the resulting coded string contains `City=Oconomowoc` nestled among all the other pieces of data.

The `name/value` pair is the basic data construct for forms and form-processing programs. The simplest CGI reports are made up of lists of `name/value` pairs, such as the following:

```
Name=Jerry Muelver
City=Oconomowoc
Hobby=Karate
```

When naming fields, carefully consider how helpful those names are for describing the function and desired contents of the fields. Taking time to choose the most descriptive names provides solid payback in terms of the clarity and usefulness of your CGI programs and the kinds of replies they generate.

# Building the Form

Kombat Karate wants to use the Web to sign up students, publish tournament announcements, and take orders for clothing and equipment. The Karate Master believes in incremental progress and always starts new students with tiny, basic steps. The same sort of philosophy can be applied to creating a Web page — start with the bare minimum, see how it works, and then gradually add enhancements. I decided to build a demonstration form, adding form input options one at a time, so that the Master can appreciate the tools of the Web.

My plan is to start with a blank HTML page and end up with a multi-modal work of Web art. Then, under your watchful eye, I'll develop the CGI program that reports back the data collected by the form.

## Bare bones beginning

To start small, first open a new blank page in your favorite HTML editor and add the minimum HTML code for setting up a new Web page:

```
<HTML>
<HEAD>
<TITLE>Kombat Karate Interest Survey</TITLE>
</HEAD>
<BODY>
<H1>Kombat Karate Interest Survey</H1>
</BODY>
</HTML>
```

As you can see, the page is not very elegant yet. A quick peek with the browser (see Figure 3-1) shows that the only Web page elements displayed are a title in the window's title bar and a very commanding heading for the form.

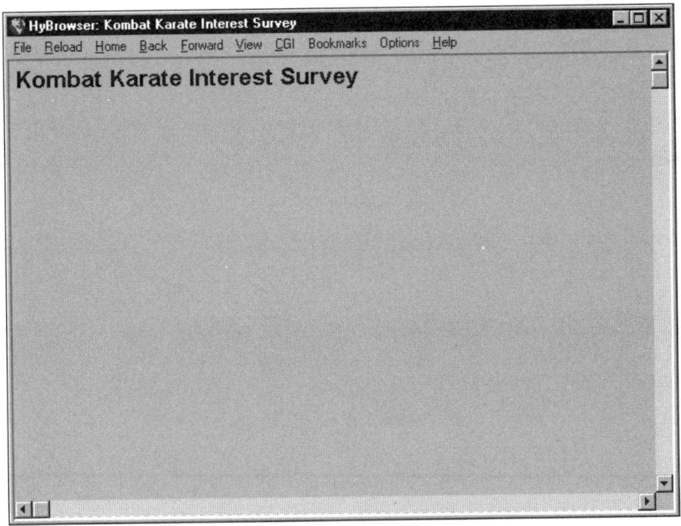


**Figure 3-1:** The bare-bones Kombat Karate page.

## Viewing Web Pages

Figure 3-1 shows the sample Kombat Karate Web page in HyBrowser, the HTML page viewer included on the CD-ROM in the `\hybrowse` directory. You can find installation instructions for this viewer in the `readme.txt` file, in `\hybrowse`. You also can find usage tips and explanations in `hybrowse.htm`, which can be viewed with any browser (including HyBrowser).

You can use any browser you like for viewing the pages developed in this book. HyBrowser, which I wrote specifically for Windows users, has a major advantage over other browsers for CGI development though — HyBrowser handles basic CGI operations without needing to be hooked up to a Web server. That means you can test CGI Perl scripts with HyBrowse right on your computer.

Below the heading, you need to add text that tells the visitor what this form is all about. In the following script snippets, the boldfaced text represents the new material to fix this problem, and the non-boldfaced text shows your location within the script:

```
<H1>Kombat Karate Interest Survey</H1>
<P>Please provide the following information so we can determine
 whether you have what it takes to play with the Big Kids at
 Kombat Karate.
```

Your browser should now display the code as shown in Figure 3-2.

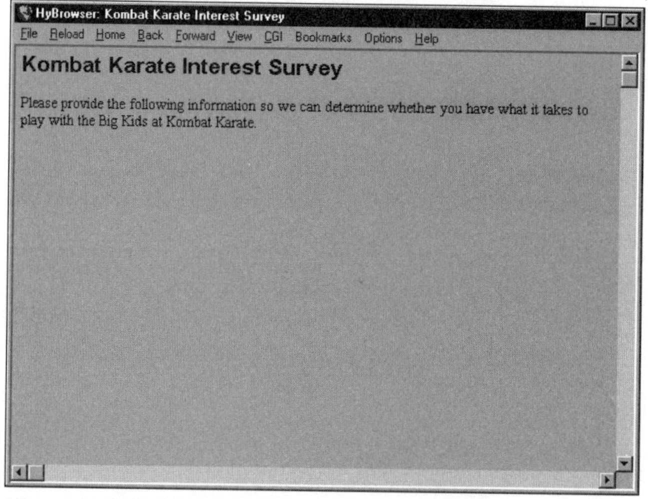


**Figure 3-2:** Building up the Kombat Karate page.

Now add the <FORM>...</FORM> tags to hold the form. Your HTML will look like this:

```
<HTML>
<HEAD>
<TITLE>Kombat Karate Interest Survey</TITLE>
</HEAD>
<BODY>
<H1>Kombat Karate Interest Survey</H1>
<P>Please provide the following information so we can determine
 whether you have what it takes to play with the Big Kids at
 Kombat Karate.
<FORM>
</FORM>
</BODY>
</HTML>
```

The FORM container requires two attributes that I discuss later: ACTION and METHOD. The ACTION value typically consists of the name of a script or program that receives the output of the form. The METHOD attribute is either GET or POST.

The METHOD, ACTION, GET, and POST attributes all are explained in the section "Handling Form Data," which appears later in this chapter.

## Adding text fields

The first order of business for building the form is to ask the visitor for a name. Kombat Karate can use this information to find out who wants to know about the school. The input will be in the form of text, so you want to add a TEXT input field to the form for entering this data. Remember, the data comes back with the NAME of the field matched with a VALUE, so you need to label the field. Give this field the name *Student Name*. The code for assigning the TYPE and NAME attributes is placed in an INPUT tag in the FORM container like this:

```
<FORM>
<INPUT TYPE="text" NAME="Student Name">
</FORM>
```

If you now look at the code in your browser, all you see is the bare textbox without adornment (Figure 3-3).

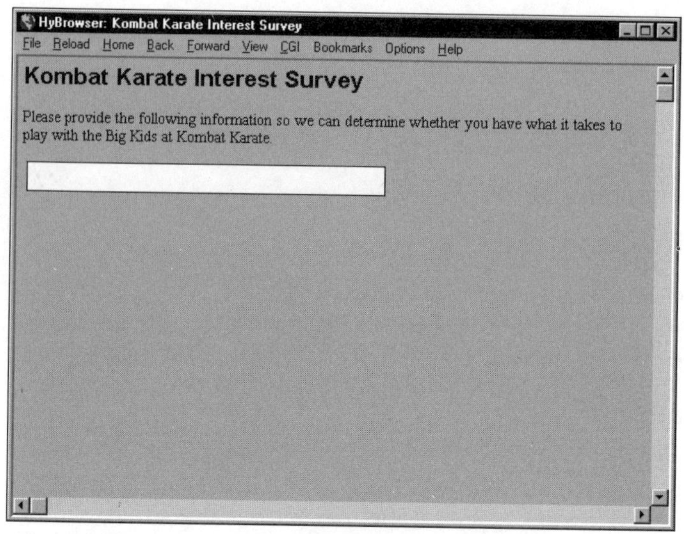


**Figure 3-3:** A form with an input field.

Now add a field prompt (the phrase *Student Name:*) in front of the textbox so that visitors know what information is being requested of them:

```
<FORM>
Student Name: <INPUT TYPE="text" NAME="Student Name">
</FORM>
```

Something that you need to consider now is the size of the entered value. To make the textbox 40 characters wide to accommodate a name such as *His Most Noble Baronship Ron Wodaski*, add a `SIZE` attribute with the value 40:

```
Student Name: <INPUT TYPE="text" NAME="Student Name" SIZE="40">
```

In case someone has a really long name, use the `MAXLENGTH` attribute to set the upper limit for the number of characters that the textbox can accept, which may be more than the number of characters shown. For this form, set the maximum length for the data to 80. With `MAXLENGTH` set to 80, you can type 80 characters into a 40-character textbox, because the box allows the text to scroll beyond its visual limitations. With `MAXLENGTH` added, the textbox definition is as follows:

```
Student Name: <INPUT TYPE="text" NAME="Student Name" SIZE="40"
MAXLENGTH="80">
```

In your browser, you should now see something like Figure 3-4.

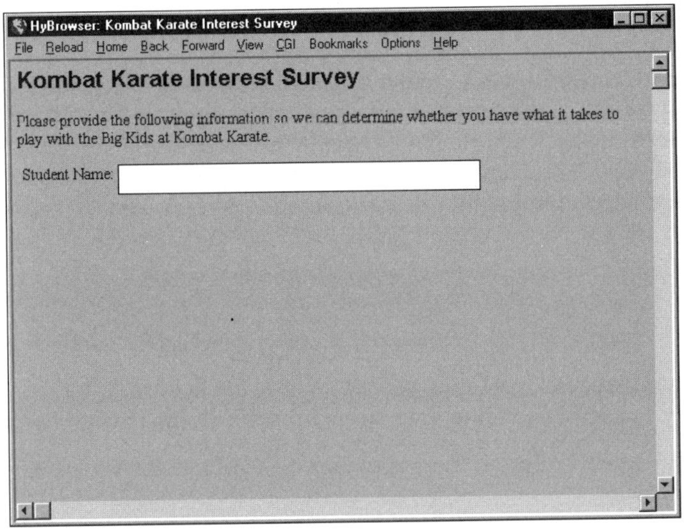

**Figure 3-4:** Form with dressed-up input field.

With the form in the browser, enter some text into the box to see how it works. When your text runs into the end of the box, it will scroll to accept new characters. Use the Left- and Right-arrow keys (and Home and End) to move around in the text.

As you can see, nothing appears on the screen to show where the form begins and ends. The textbox simply floats into place like any other HTML text or graphic object. If you like, you can set off the form from the rest of the screen by using horizontal rules (the <HR> tag) or embedded graphics.

## Caps and Quotes in HTML Code

HTML tags are not case-sensitive. <FORM> is just as good as <form> or <Form> from the browser's point of view. I use uppercase letters for HTML tags to make them easier to see in code examples and text references. Use whatever looks best to you: uppercase, lowercase, or even mixed case.

The quotes in HTML tag attributes ( NAME="Student Name " ) also have some flexibility. For single words, you can get by without quotes: NAME=Student, SIZE=40 . For values made up of several wo**rds or groups of symbols separated by punctuation, quotes are necessary to hold things together: NAME="Student Name". I always use quotes for all attribute values, even short little numbers. Then I know exactly what to look for when I have to do any searching and rerplacing. I can search for 40 and know that I won't get 140 by mistake. And "Name" is certainly going to be different from NAME= , should I have to find "Name" and change it to "FullName" or "Last Name".

## Adding a password field

The Karate Master wants to make sure that a potential student's inquiry won't be "adjusted" by someone else, so you need to obtain a password from prospective students. A `PASSWORD` field description is just like a `TEXT` field, only with a different `TYPE` attribute. As a result, you can just copy the text field description and change the `TYPE` attribute to `password`:

```
Student Name: <INPUT TYPE="password" NAME="Student Name"
SIZE="40" MAXLENGTH="80">
```

This field still needs work. You need to identify the field with the name *Password* so that you know where the data came from. To do this task, change the `NAME` from `Student Name` to `Password`, as follows:

```
Password: <INPUT TYPE="password" NAME="Password" SIZE="40"
MAXLENGTH="80">
```

This code now displays the Password input box shown in Figure 3-5:

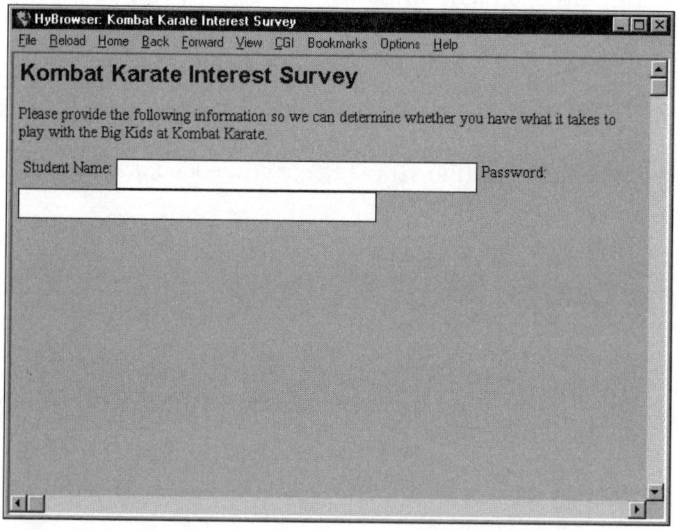

**Figure 3-5:** The form with a password field.

The textbox still doesn't look quite as it should. The label for the Password textbox appears on the same line as the Name field, which is on a separate line from the Password textbox. The <P> tag forces a new paragraph beginning and often finds gainful employment as a form layout tool. You can bump the Password prompt down by using a <P> tag and add <P> tag to the Student Name: prompt, too:

```
<FORM >
<P>Student Name: <INPUT TYPE="text" NAME="Student Name" SIZE="40"
MAXLENGTH="80">
<P>Password: <INPUT TYPE="password" NAME="Password" SIZE="40"
MAXLENGTH="80">
```

When you redisplay the form, the browser shows it with the improved appearance (Figure 3-6).

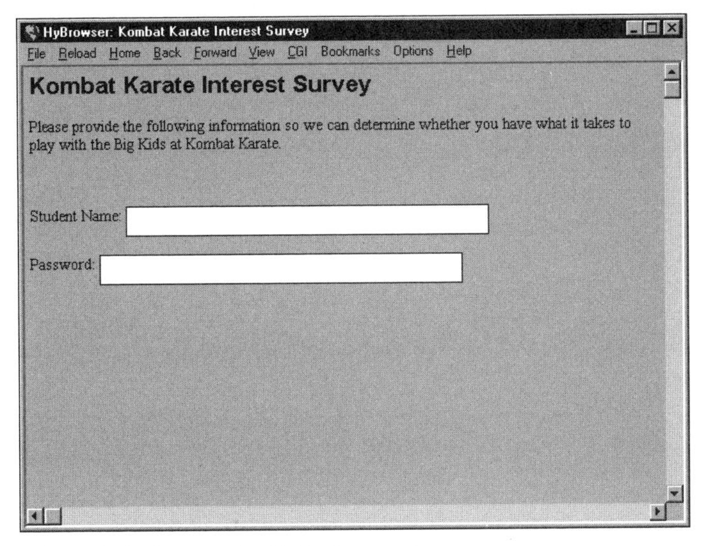


**Figure 3-6:** A form with field alignment.

The form's appearance still is not completely wonderful, but it looks better than it did. The lesson here is that adjusting the position of form elements requires more than just writing the HTML tags for each input type. You sometimes have to coax elements into place.

## Arranging Form Elements

In addition to pushing form elements around with <P> (paragraph) and <BR> (line break), you can use the list containers <UL>...</UL> (unordered list), <OL>...</OL> (ordered list), and <DL>...</DL> (definition list) to position input fields. (See Appendix A for descriptions of HTML tags.) Be aware, however, that different browsers each show variations in interpretations of HTML tags, so the displayed results may vary from one visitor to the next. Visitors with different browsers will see slightly (or drastically!) different views of the same HTML code.

Tables offer another formatting tool for designing forms. Take note that not all browsers can handle tables. If you decide to use tables, you should advise vistiors that their browsers may not show your page properly. Those visitors using text-only or early version browsers (compliant only with HTML 1.0) will appreciate having an alternative page layout available for their viewing.

You see more elegant form design techniques in later chapters of this book. You also can download and examine the code from pages on your favorite Web sites for additional ideas on formatting.

## Adding checkboxes

To evaluate the effectiveness of advertising methods, the Karate Master needs to know how the prospective student learned about Kombat Karate. A list of possible reference sources presented as checkboxes is a good questionnaire technique.

To build such a list, start by inserting a field prompt for the whole set of checkboxes:

```
<P>How did you hear about us? Check as many as apply:
```

Each checkbox needs its own `<INPUT>` tag. Also, each checkbox needs its own name to identify which field is returning data. The `VALUE` attribute provides the data that will be returned when a checkbox is checked. With that in mind, the following code creates the first checkbox:

```
<INPUT TYPE="checkbox" NAME="Friend" VALUE="Yes">
```

When this checkbox is selected, the outgoing data stream contains "`Friend=Yes`." If it is not selected, the data stream won't mention this field at all.

For checkboxes, people expect the field prompt, or description, to follow on the same line as the box, just to the right. Put a space after the angle-bracket that closes the tag and add this field prompt:

```
<INPUT TYPE="checkbox" NAME="Friend" VALUE="Yes"> Friend
```

Now add more checkboxes for reference sources such as magazines, newspapers, radio ads, and so on. Start the set of checkboxes on its own line by using a <P> tag for the field prompt and a <BR> tag to force a newline without introducing too much space after the field prompt, as follows:

```
<P>How did you hear about us? Check as many as apply:
<BR><INPUT TYPE="checkbox" NAME="Friend" VALUE="Yes"> Friend
<INPUT TYPE="checkbox" NAME="Magazine" VALUE="Yes"> Magazine
<INPUT TYPE="checkbox" NAME="Paper" VALUE="Yes"> Newspaper
<INPUT TYPE="checkbox" NAME="Radio" VALUE="Yes"> Radio
<BR>
<INPUT TYPE="checkbox" NAME="Word" VALUE="Yes"> Word of mouth
<INPUT TYPE="checkbox" NAME="Bully" VALUE="Yes"> Bothered by bully
<INPUT TYPE="checkbox" NAME="Hospital" VALUE="Yes"> Hospital
reports
```

Notice the addition of the <BR> tag after the Radio prompt, which makes a reasonable break in the format so that each checkbox stays with its prompt. No set rule exists for determining where to place line breaks for formatting checkbox lists, so trial-and-error is an accepted method. The point of forcing breaks is to avoid a browser-inflicted line wrap that might separate a checkbox from its field prompt. Take a look at how the checkbox code displays in your browser (see Figure 3-7):

You can stack the checkboxes in a column by adding a <BR> tag after each prompt phrase, but for the Kombat Karate form, a horizontal layout fills the screen with more information and less blank space.

The browser sends `name/value` pairs only for those checkboxes that have been checked. Thus, no checkmark, no data. The possible `name/value` pairs for this set of checkboxes could be something like the following:

```
Magazine=Yes
Radio=Yes
Word=Yes
```

The `=Yes` format for checkbox values works well for processing forms.

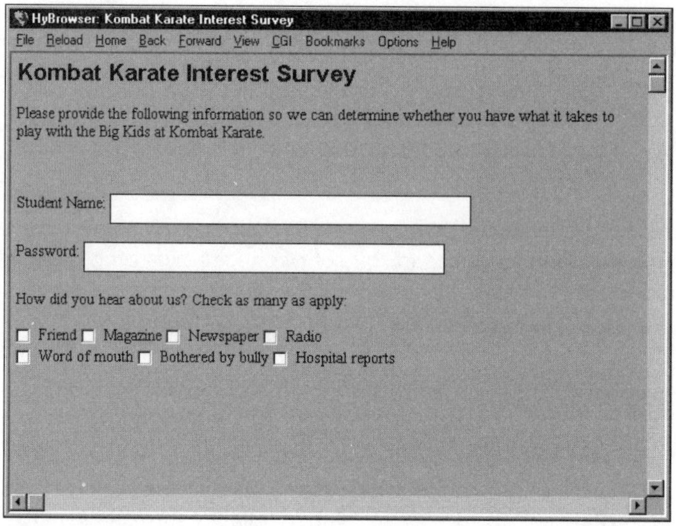

**Figure 3-7:** A form with checkboxes added.

# Adding hidden fields

The TYPE=HIDDEN field has an unusual property for input fields — it doesn't accept any input. In fact, a hidden field doesn't even show up in the browser display for the form. But I'll bet you already guessed that just from the name.

The power of the hidden field lies in its VALUE. Simply give a hidden field a name and a value, and any reports generated from the form automatically have that data — the name/value pair for the hidden field. Using hidden fields has two major advantages:

- The form always has something useful to produce. Even if all fields in the form are left blank, a form with a hidden field has at least one field name/value pair to process.
- Hidden fields are perfect for form identification markers. If you have several forms on a site, or several sites containing forms for you to contend with, knowing which form generated what data is critical to your data processing operation.

Let's add a hidden field to the Kombat Karate form right after the opening <FORM> tag. I use a standard field name for form identification fields: AAFormID. All my processing programs look for this one field name and value to determine which form it is handling. The funny name also rises to the top of any sorted list, so I know just where to look for it:

```
<FORM>
<INPUT TYPE="hidden" NAME="AAFormID" VALUE="Kom01">
Student Name: <INPUT TYPE="text" NAME="Student Name">
```

## Adding a Reset button

People change their minds. The `RESET` type of `INPUT` makes mind-changing possible in your forms. `RESET` is a button on your form that is preprogrammed to clear all data entries in the form back to their original conditions. The basic HTML description for the `Reset` button is

```
<INPUT TYPE="reset">
```

By default, this code creates a button that reads "Reset." For more helpful labels, use the `VALUE` attribute to explain what happens when the visitor clicks on the button, such as the following:

```
<INPUT TYPE="checkbox" NAME="Hospital" VALUE="Yes"> Hospital
 reports
<P><INPUT TYPE="reset" VALUE="Clear All Entries on Form">
```

In the browser, the button now looks like Figure 3-8:

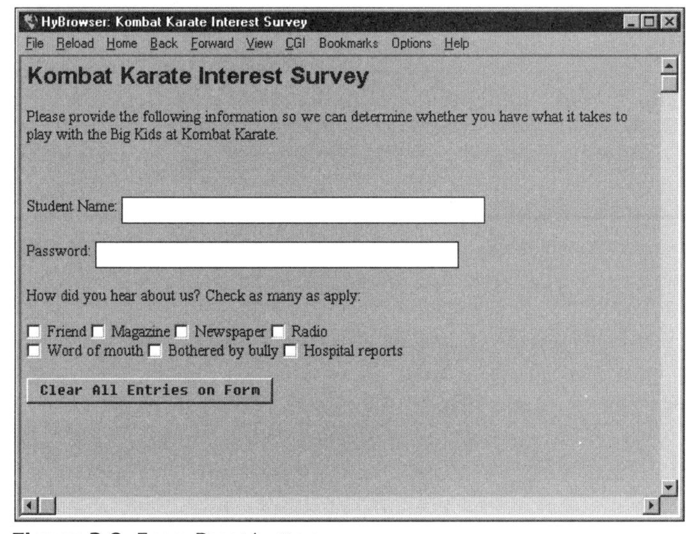


**Figure 3-8:** Form Reset button.

## Adding a Submit button

At last! Wrap it up and send it off by using the SUBMIT type. The format for the Submit button is just like that for the Reset button. You can use the VALUE attribute to clarify the function of the button by changing the label to "All done -- send it!", because the default (without a VALUE setting) is "Submit Query", which is too formal for our puposes:

```
<P><INPUT TYPE="submit" VALUE="All done -- send it!">
```

But wait! You didn't say where to send the data! That job is reserved for the METHOD and ACTION attibutes of the opening <FORM> statement, so you don't need to worry about that here.

## Sending data with ACTION and METHOD

As I hinted at earlier, ACTION and METHOD are the traffic cops for the form. You can use these attributes to send the data from the form to any one of a number of destinations, including the following:

- Your own Perl script, where you can massage the data as you see fit
- An off-the-shelf CGI program produced by someone else
- An e-mail address
- A form-processing program at a URL completely remote from your own

For sound instructional reasons, I want you to use an e-mail address for this form. Add ACTION and METHOD attributes to the opening <FORM> tag now to see how the finished form's code looks. I explain ACTION and METHOD in just a moment, and placing them in a form helps the explanation. In place of me@some.site in the following code, use your own e-mail address. (If you don't have an e-mail address yet, use hybrowser for now instead of mailto:me@some.site — HyBrowser knows how to handle this particular fictitious address.) Your code should look as follows:

```
<FORM ACTION="mailto:me@some.site" METHOD="post">
```

# HTML Code for the Bare Bones Example Form

Listing 3-1 contains the complete source code for the current state of the example form. On the CD-ROM, this file is \code\ch02\KOMSUR01.HTM.

If you have been manually typing in this form, compare your work now before moving on. I inserted a few line spaces to make the code easier to read. The line beginning with <!-- is a comment, closed with the symbol --!>. Figure 3-9 shows how the final form (well, the semi-final Phase 1 form — there's more work ahead) should look in your browser. The next section, "Handling Form Data," shows how the data flows from the form to the server and back to you.

**Listing 3-1 Kombat Karate Interest Survey Phase 1 HTML Code**

```
<HTML>
<HEAD>
<TITLE>Kombat Karate Interest Survey</TITLE>
<!-- Phase 1, still work to be done. -->
</HEAD>
<BODY>
<H1>Kombat Karate Interest Survey</H1>
<P>Please provide the following information so we can determine
 whether you have what it takes to play with the Big Kids at
 Kombat Karate.
<FORM  ACTION="mailto:me@some.site" METHOD="post">
<INPUT TYPE="hidden" NAME="AAFormID" VALUE="Kom01">
<P>Student Name: <INPUT TYPE="text" NAME="Student Name" SIZE="40"
MAXLENGTH="80">
<P>Password: <INPUT TYPE="password" NAME="Password" SIZE="40"
 MAXLENGTH="80">
<P>How did you hear about us? Check as many as apply:
<BR><INPUT TYPE="checkbox" NAME="Friend" VALUE="Yes"> Friend
<INPUT TYPE="checkbox" NAME="Magazine" VALUE="Yes"> Magazine
<INPUT TYPE="checkbox" NAME="Paper" VALUE="Yes"> Newspaper
<INPUT TYPE="checkbox" NAME="Radio" VALUE="Yes"> Radio
<BR>
<INPUT TYPE="checkbox" NAME="Word" VALUE="Yes"> Word of mouth
<INPUT TYPE="checkbox" NAME="Bully" VALUE="Yes"> Bothered by
 bully
<INPUT TYPE="checkbox" NAME="Hospital" VALUE="Yes"> Hospital
 reports
<P><INPUT TYPE="reset" VALUE="Clear All Entries on Form">
<P><INPUT TYPE="submit" VALUE="All done -- send it!">
</FORM>
</BODY>
</HTML>
```

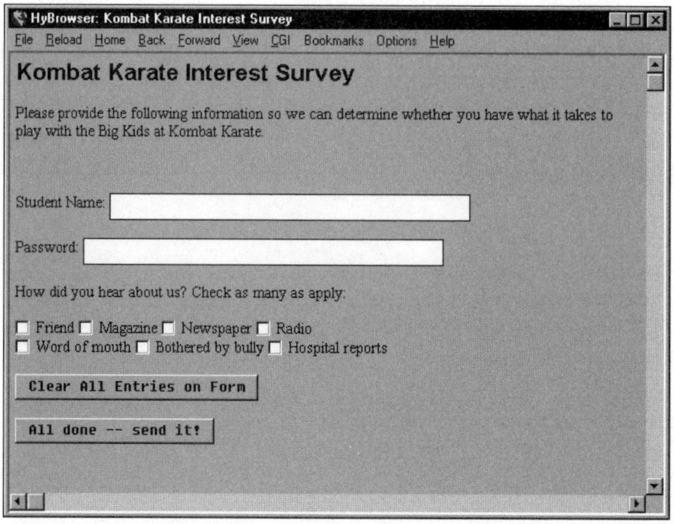

**Figure 3-9:** Kombat Karate Interest Survey Form — Phase 1.

# Handling Form Data

Forms spit out their data in standard URL format. The main rules for encoding form data into this format are as follows:

- For each field in the form, print the field's `NAME`, then an equal sign, and then the field's `VALUE`. A field named *Name,* containing my name, looks almost like this:

```
Name=Jerry Muelver
```

- Replace all spaces with a plus-sign, exactly like this:

```
Name=Jerry+Muelver
```

- Replace any remaining nontext characters with the ASCII value for that character, written in hexadecimal numbers (shown in base 16 instead of base 10) with a percent sign in front of it. A line break in an entry on a DOS system is represented by a carriage return followed by a line feed. This combination of characters, usually referred to by the acronym CRLF (Carriage Return/Line Feed), is represented by ASCII characters 13 (for carriage return) and 10 (for line feed), which are hexadecimal 0D and 0A. As a result, a comment field with a couple of carriage returns in it comes out as follows:

```
Comment=I+want+to+join+Kombat+Karate+because+I%0D%0A
    need+the+exercise.%0D%0A
```

- Hook sequential pairs of NAME=VALUE together by using ampersands as delimiters (separator characters), such as in the following example:

```
Name=Jerry+Muelver&Password=BigJer&Friend=Yes
```

Following these rules, the data from the Phase-2 Kombat Karate survey form (with the enhancements that I add in Chapter 4) becomes a URL-coded string that looks something like this:

```
AAFormID=Kom02&Name=Jerry+Muelver&Password=BigJer&Friend=
Yes&Word=Yes&Radio=Yes&Belt=Brown&Classes=MWS&Comment=I+want+to+join+
Kombat+Karate+because+I%0D%0Aneed+the+exercise.%0D%0A
```

I'd much rather have it formatted in NAME=VALUE pairs, each on a separate line (such as the following), so that I can do data processing more easily:

```
AAFormID=Kom02
Name=Jerry Muelver
Password=BigJer
Radio=Yes
Word=Yes
Belt=Brown
Classes=MWS
Comment=I want to join Kombat Karate because I need the exercise.
```

Formatting the data this way is a job for Perl and regular expressions. But first, we need a closer look at the METHOD and ACTION attributes of the FORM tag because these attributes specify where the data stream goes when it leaves the browser.

## Using the ACTION attribute

The value for the ACTION attribute in the <FORM> tag is a URL — a pointer to something that acts on the data from the form. The URL target typically is a program or a program script (usually written in Perl) that can pick apart the data and reformat it. If you have a script in the cgi-bin directory of your Web server that you want to point your data to, the <FORM> tag ACTION attribute may look like this:

```
<FORM ACTION="http://www.some.site/cgi-bin/myscript.pl">
```

If you omit the ACTION attribute, the browser tries to send the data to the current URL — which is your document with the form on it. Nothing useful happens in that case because the document can't perform any processing.

The kind of processing you need starts with regular expressions. The following mailto: ACTION attribute used by the Kombat Karate survey form skips the CGI processing and diverts the URL-encoded form data directly into a mail message:

```
<FORM ACTION="mailto:me@some.site" METHOD="post">
```

The "PerlProject" section for this chapter describes a translator program that decodes the data found in such a mail message.

## Using the METHOD attribute

The METHOD attribute tells the browser how to send data from the form. The two values for a form's METHOD attribute are as follows:

| | |
|---|---|
| POST | Send the data as a string for input to a program |
| GET | Splice the data string onto a URL |

The syntax for defining METHOD is as follows:

```
<FORM METHOD="get">
```

or

```
<FORM METHOD="post">
```

It doesn't matter whether GET or POST are uppercase or lowercase. If you omit the METHOD attribute entirely, Perl uses the GET value by default.

### GET

The GET method appends the data stream to the end of the URL — not to the end of the document at the URL, but to the actual URL itself, pasting it right onto the address with a question-mark identifier. Using the Kombat Karate example, the following URL

```
<FORM ACTION="http://www.some.site/cgi-bin/myscript.pl">
```

now becomes

```
http://www.some.site/cgi-bin/myscript.pl?AAFormID=Kom02
&Name=Jerry+Muelver&Password=BigJer&Friend=Yes&Word=Yes&Radio=Yes
&Belt=Brown&Classes=MWS&Comment=I+want+to+join+Kombat+Karate+
because+I+need%0D%0Athe+exercise.%0D%0A
```

This data stream starts with `?AAFormID=Kom02` and goes on for some length. Everything that appears in the URL after the question mark goes into an environmental CGI variable called `QUERY_STRING`. Next, CGI wakes up the program at the URL destination and tells it to look in the `QUERY_STRING` environmental variable for the data. `GET` has its uses, but tacking the form output onto the URL has one severe limitation — `GET` can't handle much data. The server's CGI treats a `GET` URL as one long address, and servers are limited in how much space they allot for CGI variables and how many characters they can handle in a URL address.

### POST

You almost always will prefer to use the `POST` method rather than the `GET` method. The `POST` method also sends the data stream as a tack-on to a URL, but the server's CGI knows that this add-on is a `POST` and uses a different handling technique from the one it uses with `GET`.

The CGI senses the `POST`, finds the question mark in the URL and splits the basic URL from the data string. The URL goes into a CGI variable and the data channeled into the STDIN for whatever program the CGI finds at that URL. Now all you need is a Perl program to handle the data flowing in through `STDIN`. For that, you are going to need more Perl power.

## PerlFacts: More on Regular Expressions

Until now, I have only shown you how to use regular expressions to find patterns. But finding the pattern is only the first step in a find-and-replace operation. Using patterns for substitutions, translations, and substring extractions opens up some potent possibilities. Tables 3-1 and 3-2 list the regular expressions and special pattern operators that you can use to perform these operations. I'll get into these expressions in more dramatic detail in the following sections. Fold the corner of this page over, so that you can find and use these pattern secrets without having to memorize the whole list.

<table>
<tr><th>Table 3-1</th><th>Regular Expressions</th></tr>
<tr><th>Element</th><th>Matching Function</th></tr>
<tr><td>.</td><td>Match any character except newline</td></tr>
<tr><td>(...)</td><td>Group elements together</td></tr>
<tr><td>$1..$9</td><td>Backreference grouped elements</td></tr>
<tr><td>+</td><td>One or more of preceding element</td></tr>
<tr><td>?</td><td>Zero or one of preceding element</td></tr>
<tr><td>*</td><td>Zero or more of preceding element</td></tr>
<tr><td>{x,y}</td><td>x, y are min and max number of preceding element to match</td></tr>
<tr><td>{x}</td><td>Match preceding element exactly x times</td></tr>
<tr><td>{x,}</td><td>Match preceding element x or more times</td></tr>
<tr><td>[...]</td><td>Match any element in this class</td></tr>
<tr><td>(...|...|...)</td><td>Match alternatives</td></tr>
<tr><td>\</td><td>Escape meanings for special-function characters + ? . * ( ) { } [ ] | \ /</td></tr>
<tr><td>^</td><td>Beginning of string, used right after the first front-slash</td></tr>
<tr><td>$</td><td>End of string</td></tr>
<tr><td>\r</td><td>Carriage return, ASCII 13 decimal</td></tr>
<tr><td>\n</td><td>Line feed, ASCII 10 decimal</td></tr>
<tr><td>\t</td><td>Tab, ASCII 9 decimal</td></tr>
<tr><td>\f</td><td>Form feed, ASCII 12 decimal</td></tr>
<tr><td>\d</td><td>Digits, same as [0-9]</td></tr>
<tr><td>\D</td><td>Nondigits, negation of \d, same as [^0-9]</td></tr>
<tr><td>\w</td><td>Same as [a-zA-Z0-9_], matches alphanumeric, including the underscore</td></tr>
<tr><td>\W</td><td>Same as [^a-zA-Z0-9_], negation of \w, anything not alphanumeric</td></tr>
</table>

| | |
|---|---|
| `\s` | Space, actually whitespace: space, tab, carriage return, line feed, and form feed (ASCII characters 32, 9, 13, 10, and 12), same as `[ \r\t\n\f]` |
| `\S` | Not space, negation of `\s`, same as `[^ \r\t\n\f]` |
| `\b` | Word boundary; matches punctuation, whitespace; also matches a nonalphanumeric character at the beginning or end of a string |
| `\B` | Anything that's not a word boundary, negation of \b |
| `/ /i` | Ignore case |

**Table 3-2 Special Pattern Operators and Variables**

| Pattern Operator/ Variable | Function |
|---|---|
| `=~` | Reassign target for pattern matching from default `$_` (current line) to a named variable |
| `s/ / /` | Substitution, swap match in first expression for string in second expression |
| `s/ / /i` | Ignore case in finding match for substitution |
| `s/ / /g` | Global, substitute every such match found in the target |
| `s/ / /e` | Evaluate the swap portion as a Perl expression, then perform the replacement |
| `s/( )/$1/` | Subexpression substitution or grouped elements by numbered reference — `s/a(..)a/b$1b/` replaces two characters between a's with the same two characters between b's |
| `tr/ / /` | Transliteration operator, swap letters from first expression for letters in second expression in target |
| `$&` | Contents of last previous pattern match |
| `` $` `` | Portion of target string to the left of last previous pattern match |
| `$'` | Portion of target string to the right of last previous pattern match |
| `$1..$9` | Reference to subexpressions in last previous pattern match |

## Switching targets with =~

There are times when you'd rather not use $_ (the default current line) for the target string of a matching pattern — for example, if you have another string (or array of strings) that needs urgent processing. Perl's =~ operator enables you to play another target (a variable or input) against the pattern:

```
$_ = "Once upon a time";
$newTarget = "there lived a fair Princess";
$nextTarget = "in a castle in the woods.";
/upon/;                        # matches current line $_
/Princess/;                    # not a match for current line
$newTarget =~ /Princess/;  # this is a match
$newTarget =~ /castle/;     # not a match
$nextTarget =~ /castle/;    # this is a match
```

The ability to switch targets for a pattern match means anything can be tested. Pattern-matching is not restricted to just the current line.

## Ignoring case with i

Unadorned patterns are case-sensitive. For example, `/menu/` will not match `"Menu."` The ignore operator (`i` placed to the right of the closing slash) makes the pattern case-insensitive. Thus, you get the following matches with this operator:

```
/menu/i;       # matches menu, not Menu, MENU, menU
/menu/i;       # matches menu and Menu, MENU, menU
/ y/i;         # yes, Ypsilanti, TODAY
/[aeiou]m+/i; # amend, Amanda, iMMEDiate
```

## Substituting with s/ / /

The substitute operator `s///` takes a matched pattern between the first two slashes and swaps in a designated replacement string from the second two slashes. The form is `s/find/replace/` and it works as shown in this series of changes:

```
$_ = "They sold the house.";
s/old/new/;           # replace old: They snew the house.
s/s.+w/bought/;       # replace snew: They bought the house.
s/the house/a farm/; # replace the house: They bought a farm.
```

Each step in the series rewrites the value of $_. On its own, the substitute operator replaces only the first occurrence of a match in the target:

```
$_ = "Children are little men and little women.";
s/little/big/;  # Children are big men and little women
```

The global operator g, tacked onto the search pattern, forces substitutions on every instance of the match in the target, as follows:

```
$_ = "The only thing we have to fear is fear itself.";
$ slogan = $_;
s/fear/love/;  # Changes current line $_, one substitution only -
-
               # The only thing we have to love is fear itself.
               # Starting over with the original quote tucked
               #   into $slogan, using =~ to switch targets --
$slogan =~ s/fear/love/g;
               # g forces all possible substitions --
               # The only thing we have to love is love itself.
```

Use the ignore operator i with or without the global operator g to remove case-sensitivity for the match half of the substitution pattern — the swap half maintains its specified case, as follows:

```
$_ = "Men here, women there.";
s/men/boys/ig; # boys here, woboys there.
```

In the preceding example, the match found both *Men* and *men* and replaced both with lowercase *boy*. Without the global operator g, only *Men* would have been replaced.

Let's take a look at another example. The substitution operator renames *Chicago* in the following program (Listing 3-2):

**Listing 3-2 Changing Chicago to Windy City with chiwindy.pl.**

```
# chiwindy.pl -- change Chicago to Windy City
# usage: perl chiwindy.pl citymile.dat
while (<>) {
  s/Chicago/Windy City/;
  print;
}
```

**Exercise 3-1**

Try these variations on Listing 3-2 to see how substitution works:

A. Rewrite `chiwindy.pl` to change IL to Illinois.

B. What pattern changes IL to Illinois for the Chicago to Cairo route?

C. What pattern changes `<form>` to `<FORM>`? `</form>` to `</FORM>`? Can you change both with one pattern?

## Using variables in a substitution pattern

With variables, you can build patterns while the program is running instead of coding exactly what the pattern must be. Perl picks out variables from a pattern and interpolates them, using their values when applying them to the pattern:

```
$gender = "man";                #1
$_ = "a remarkable woman";      #2
/remarkable ..$gender/;         #3 true: ..man matches woman
$_ = "Woman mans firetruck";    #4
s/$gender/mbat/g;  #5 Wombat    mbats firetruck
s/mbat/$gender/g;  #6 fixed     again: Woman mans firetruck
```

The point of this example is that you can use a variable in a pattern, and the pattern operator will evaluate the variable and use its contents to perform the match test. Let's run through the demo again, line by line:

1. Assign the word *man* to the variable `$gender`.
2. Assign *a remarkable woman* to the current-line variable `$_`.
3. Check the current line for the pattern *remarkable,* space, two unknown characters, and the word *man* stored in `$gender`. The current line holds *a remakable woman* so the pattern match with *remarkable ..man* succeeds. The regular expression evaluates `$gender`, so the pattern runs as `/remarkable ..man/`.
4. Assign a new string to the current line variable `$_`.
5. Perform a substitution on the current line, replacing *man* with *mbat.* The *man* to find is in the variable `$gender`. The substitution pattern evaluates `$gender` and performs the substitution as `s/man/mbat/`.
6. Perform a substitution on the current line, replacing *mbat* with the *man* in the variable `$gender`. Again, the variable is evaluated, so the pattern runs as `s/mbat/man/`.

Command-line parameters can find their way into substitution patterns through variables. Listing 3-3 shows the start of a search-and-replace program:

**Listing 3-3 `sandr.pl` for searching and replacing patterns in files**

```
# sandr.pl -- search and replace pattern in files
# usage: perl sandr.pl "old" "new" filename
$old = $ARGV[0];                    #1
$new = $ARGV[1];                    #2
$nrFiles = @ARGV;                   #3
$i = 2;                             #4
while ($i <= $nrFiles) {            #5
    open (FHANDLE, $ARGV[$i]);      #6
    while (<FHANDLE>){              #7
        s/$old/$new/g;              #8
        print;                      #9
    }
    close (FHANDLE);
    $i++;                          #10
}
```

SearchANDReplace, `sandr.pl`, works like this:

1. Put first command line argument into `$old`. This is the *find* pattern.
2. Put the second argument into `$new`. This is the *replace* pattern.
3. Set `$nrFiles` equal to the total number of command-line arguments. Assigning an array to a scalar variable returns the total number of elements in the array.
4. Start with `$i` at 2. You'll see why in a moment.
5. The `while` loop runs as long as `$i` is less than the total number of arguments on the command line. Arrays start at `[0]`, so the final array element is `[size-1]`.
6. Open the file named by the $i-th argument. Because `$i` starts at 2, the first file to be opened will be whatever was named in the third command-line argument, `$ARGV[2]`. If the command line was

```
perl sandr.pl "Utah" "Idaho" salt.txt potato.txt corn.txt
```

   the `$ARGV[2]` is `salt.txt`.

7. Loop through each line in the opened file.

8. Perform the substitution globally on the current line (for instance, replace all Utah with Idaho).
9. Print the (possibly modified) current line. This statement prints every line in the file, whether it was modified or not.
10. Increment the value of $i, to open the next file in the command line list.

To save the output of `sandr.pl`, use the save-to redirection symbol (>) as in the following command to replace misspelled *hte* with the more socially acceptable *the* in the file `mynote.txt` and save the results in `goodnote.txt`:

```
C:\dev> perl sandr.pl " hte " " the " mynote.txt > goodnote.txt
```

## Transliterating with `tr/ / /`

The transliteration operator, `tr///`, is basically a substitution with a character mission. It examines the target for any characters in the find pattern and then swaps that character with a corresponding one in the replace pattern. For example, `tr/abc/xyz/` changes any *a* to *x*, any *b* to *y*, and any *c* to *z*. Take a look at the following examples to get a better grasp of how this operator works:

```
$_ = "Once upon a midnight dreary.";
tr/aeiou/AEIOU/; # OncE UpOn A mIdnIght drEAry.
$_ = "All things come to him who waits.";
tr/[a-i]/[1-9]/; # All t89ngs 3om5 to 89m w80 w19ts.
$newVal = "yes no up down true ";
$newVal =~ tr/ /\+/; # plus into space: yes+no+up+down+true
```

### Exercise 3-2

Write a `tr///` pattern for URL-encoded strings that will change pluses `(+)` into spaces, and ampersands `(&)` into newlines. Hint: don't forget to escape the plus!

## Subexpressions with `(..)` and `$1 )`

Suppose, to cut down on gasoline usage, that Congress prohibits interstate travel. Now you have to convert your mileage charts so that they show distance only between cities within a state. The data file runs on this layout:

```
Chicago, IL, Peoria, IL, 170
Peoria, IL, Hannibal, MO, 143
```

You could go state by state to find intrastate distances with patterns such as the following:

```
print if /IL.*IL/;
print if /MO.*MO/;
```

Or, you could use something to find the first state mentioned in a record and see if that same state is repeated later in that record. In other words, find something inside an expression and remember what you found so you can use it again. This neat trick is called a memory pattern or subexpression.

Before I explain what these items are, take a look at this example. Subexpressions look like the following:

```
/(back)up $1wards/;
```

The subexpression of this example is `(back)`. Here, the memory of the subexpression is `$1`. The subexpression is repeated wherever `$1` appears in the pattern. Thus, the whole pattern is looking for "backup backwards" as the match. This minor variation

```
/(b..k)up $1wards/;
```

remembers exactly what was found in the parentheses and uses that part of the pattern again. This version will match `bookup bookwards`, `backup backwards`, and `buckup buckwards`, but not `backup bookwards`.

To remember the match for a subexpression, enclose it in parentheses. To recall and re-use the matched subexpression, refer to it with a backslash-digit pair that tells which subexpression should be used, counting from left to right. If there is only one subexpression in the statement, its number is `$1`. If two subexpressions are in the statement, the leftmost one is `$1` and the other subexpression is `$2`. For example, this pattern

```
/([A-Z][A-Z]).*$1/; # find two uppercase letters together,
                    # then any number of characters, then the
                    # same two letters we found earlier
```

will match

```
Chicago, IL, Peoria, IL, 170        # one IL, then another one
Oconomowoc, WI, Delafield, WI, 4    # one WI, then another one
```

but not

```
Peoria, IL, Hannibal, MO, 143       # one IL, but no repeat
```

You can also use subexpressions for more literary applications, such as the following:

```
/\b(..).*$1\b/; # word that begins and ends with the same two
                    chars
                # in the same order: educated, revere, not
                    serves,
/\b(.)(.).*$2$1\b/; # any word whose first two letters are
                    reversed
                    # at the end: deed, serves, severes, detained
/best (of times), worst $1/; # best of times, worst of times
/(my) (time) (is) (your) $2, $4 $2 $3 $1 $2/;
                    # my time is your time, your time is my time
```

To work through those examples, figure out what subexpression could be in the parentheses, then find a matching backslash-digit to insert the remembered subexpression. Subexpressions also work in a substitution pattern, even across the find/replace slash, as follows:

```
$_ = "yes no up down true ";
s/([a-z]+)\s/$1_val,/g;
       # any lowercase character followed by a space in the
         target
       # has "_val," added to it in place of the space
print; # prints: yes_val,no_val,up_val,down_val,true_val,
```

What's going on? The search pattern is constructed like this:

| | |
|---|---|
| `[a-z]` | Any lowercase letter |
| `[a-z]+` | Any one or more lowercase letters |

| [a-z]+\s | Any one or more lowercase letters followed by a whitespace character (space or tab) |
|---|---|
| ([a-z]+)\s | Remember any group of lowercase letters followed by whitespace. Because the whitespace is not included in the group, it won't be remembered. |
| $1_val, | Remember that lowercase word you just remembered? Well, take that word, whatever it was, and replace it with that very same word plus "_val," (notice the comma) so that "yes" is replaced with "yes_val," and "no" is replaced with "no_val," all by the very same substitution pattern! |

## Remembering matches: Special variables

$_ is a special variable that refers to the current line of the input stream. Perl has many special variables and special arrays — remember @ARGV? Some special variables refer to pattern matches and are perfect for processing matched text, pieces of matched text, and even pieces of text that are only close to a pattern match. The following list describes the special variables available:

| Variable | What It Represents |
|---|---|
| $& | Most recent pattern match |
| $` | The part of the string that comes before the pattern match (mnemonic — the apostrophe tilts toward the left) |
| $' | The part of the string that comes after the pattern match (mnemonic — the apostrophe tilts toward the right) |
| $1...$9 | Contents of corresponding subexpressions in the most recent pattern match; carries the memory of the match outside the regular expression pattern, whereas \1...\9 works only while still within the pattern itself |

These variables help you perform parsing operations by making it easy to refer to the elements surrounding a match within a string. Take a look at the following listing for example:

```
$_ = "When in the course of human events";
/ course /;
print $&;  # prints: course
print $';  # prints: When in the
print $';  # prints; of human events
print "$`$&$'\n";    #prints: When in the course of human events
                        $data = "Company Name = XYZ Development";
                        $data =~ s/XYZ/ABC/; # name-change here
print $&;              # prints: XYZ
print $';              # prints: Company Name =
print $';              # prints: Development
print "\n$`$&$'\n";  # prints: Company Name = XYZ Development
print "$data\n";      # prints: Company Name = ABC Development
                        $data =~ /(.*y)(.*e )(. )/;
print "\n", $&;       # prints: Company Name =
print "\n$3$2$1\n";  # prints:  = Name Company
```

Notice that `$&` and `$1...$9` report on the match, not the swap, for substitution patterns.

## Associative arrays: Name that bucket

I only gave you part of Perl's array story — just the evening news sound byte, really — when I introduced normal, numerically indexed arrays earlier in this book. The real story, or the special event and star performer in Perl, is the *associative array*. The associative array is indexed by strings instead of numbers for the element subscript. Table 3-3 shows some of the Perl functions that work on arrays. Take a quick look just to see what I am going to throw at you in the following sections. As usual, detailed explanations are coming right up.

**Table 3-3 Array Functions**

| Array | Function |
|---|---|
| `@var = (list of values)` | Create normal array |
| `$nmbr = @var` | Set `$nmbr` to the number of elements in the array `@var` |
| `$nmlast = $#var` | Set `$nmlast` to the highest numbered subscript in the array `@var`. Because arrays are numbered from 0, `$nmbr = $nmlast + 1`. |

| | |
|---|---|
| `%var = (list of key/value pairs)` | Create associative array |
| `$var($i)` | Reference normal array element by numerical index — use parentheses |
| `$var{$i}` | Reference associative array element by string index — use curly braces |
| `print @var` | Print each element in the array, without adding spaces or newlines |
| `print "@var"` | Print each element in the array, adding a space between each element |
| `@var = split/expr/$string/` | Break `$string` into list of substrings using `expr` pattern as the separator |
| `foreach (@var)` | Cycle through `@var` array one element at a time |
| `foreach $tmp (@var)` | Cycle through `@var` array one element at a time, loading the element into `$tmp` each time |
| `%avar = keys(%var)` | Return list of associative array `%var` index keys into normal array `@avar` |
| `foreach $tmp (keys(%var))` | Cycle through `%var` associative array one key at a time, loading the key into `$tmp` each time |
| `while (($keyvar,$valvar) = each(%var))` | Cycle through associative array `%var` one key/value pair at a time, placing the key in `$keyvar` and the value in `$valval` |

## Review of numerically-indexed arrays

A quick review of arrays is in order. You already know that normal arrays are simple lists of objects. `@fruit`, for instance, may have five elements numbered 0 through 4. Create `@fruit` by declaring it with a list of objects:

```
@fruit = ("apple", "banana", "mango", "orange", "pear");
```

To refer to an element in an array, change the variable mark from `@` to `$` to show that the reference is to a scalar variable (one object only) and place the subscript number of the referenced element in square brackets, like this:

$fruit[1] is "banana" and $fruit[4] is "pear". To add "kiwi" to the list, use a new index number for the assignment:

```
$fruit[5] = "kiwi"; # creates 6th slot, fills it with kiwi
```

The numerical index for normal arrays is handy for retrieving values from an array. Listing 3-3, sandr.pl, uses $i++ (an auto-incrementing index) to step through the command-line parameters in @ARGV. The auto-increment operator (++) adds 1 to the value of the variable ($i++ is $i + 1), and is very commonly used to cycle through normal arrays.

Now I want you to meet a powerful structure called the associative array.

## String-indexed associative arrays

Suppose that I have a list of favorites: color, burgandy; pie, apple; ice cream, chocolate almond; fruit, banana; pasta, linguini. If you ask me for my favorite pie, I look up "pie" in the list and find that "pie" is paired with "apple". Perl's associative arrays work exactly the same way. I can look for the "pie" subscript in the favorite array and find its associated element "apple".

Associative arrays use the percent sign % as the symbol for indicating the variable type. Create an associative array by assigning a list of value pairs to a variable whose name begins with %. The array interprets the odd-numbered values in the list as *keys* and the even-numbered values as *elements,* such as in the following example:

```
%favorite = ("color","burgandy","pie","apple","ice cream",
"chocolate almond","fruit","banana","pasta","linguini");
```

The keys in %favorite are the strings "color", "pie", "ice cream", "fruit", and "pasta". To retrieve the elements (more properly called *values*) of an associative array, first change the variable marker from % to the familiar $ symbol, which identifies the variable as a one-object scalar variable: so %favorite becomes $favorite. Numerical arrays use square brackets to hold the key, but associative arrays are fancier and use strings as keys, so you also want to use fancier brackets — curly braces:

```
$dessert = $favorite{"pie"};
```

The key "pie" points to the eslement "apple". In the preceding example, if I don't care for apple pie, I can ask for

```
$dessert = $favorite{"ice cream"};
```

and enjoy a dish of chocolate almond (the element for ice cream) while you savor the concept of associative arrays.

## Why use curly braces for associative arrays?

Scalar variables can act as keys for arrays, such as in this example:

```
$fuitNr = @fruit;  # load $fruitNr with number of elements
$i = 0;
while ($i <= $#fruit) {
    print $fruit[$i];
    $i++;
}
```

The variable `$i` holds a number that acts as the subscript for the array elements, starting at 0 and running up via the auto-increment operator one step at a time until it reaches the last element number in the array. That last number is returned by the special array variable `$#fruit`. Scalar variables take either numeric or string values and even convert from one to the other when it makes sense to do so. Perl determines whether to consider a variable's value as a number or a string by the operators working on the variable. For example, `$a >= $b` is a numerical expression, whereas `$a ge $b` is a statement dealing with strings.

In the same way, the square brackets tell Perl that `$fruit[$i]` is a normal array, so `$i` must be a numerical value. The curly braces tell Perl that `$favorite{$i}` is an associative array and that `$i` must now hold a string value.

This automatic conversion can cause problems with arrays. If `$i` contains `"pie"` and `$i` turns up as the index in `$favorite[$i]`, Perl sees the square brackets and converts `"pie"` to a no-value number — 0. As a result, you end up looking at the first element in the normal `@favorite` array, rather than the `"pie-th"` element in the associative `%favorite` array. Therefore, remember to use fancy curly braces when indexing associative arrays.

## Adding elements to associative arrays

To add an element to an associative array, assign a value to a new key, as in the following example:

```
%favorite = ("color","burgandy","pie","apple","ice cream",
"chocolate almond","fruit","banana","pasta","linguini");
$favorite{"language"} = "Perl";
```

Assigning a value to an existing key changes the contents of that key.

## Dumping @ array into % array

Assigning a normal array to an associative array causes Perl to load the normal array elements into the associative array in key/value order, similar to declaring the elements in a list:

```
@parts = ("hammer",4,"pliers",1,"saw",3,"nail",1562);
%inventory = @parts;
print $inventory{"nail"};    #prints: 1562
```

The normal array `@parts` looks like this:

| Key | Element (value) |
|---|---|
| 0 | hammer |
| 1 | 4 |
| 2 | pliers |
| 3 | 1 |
| 4 | saw |
| 5 | 3 |
| 6 | nail |
| 7 | 1562 |

The associative array `%inventory` looks like this:

| Key | Element (value) |
|---|---|
| hammer | 4 |
| pliers | 1 |
| saw | 3 |
| nail | 1562 |

Going back the other way (assigning an associative array to a normal array) also works. However, the sequence of values coming from the associative array is not guaranteed, so not much use exists for a direct, associative-to-normal array assignment. Perl does not sort or otherwise impose a sequence ordering on the key/value pairs in associative arrays, so without performing extra processing, the pairs come out in an unpredictable order.

## Looping through arrays

I just showed you one way to loop through an array to peek at the contents of each element — use an *auto-incrementing index,* such as `$i++` in the following:

```
$fruitNr = $#fruit;
$i = 0;
while ($i <= $fruitNr) {
    print $fruit[$i];
    $i++;
}
```

This method works well for normal arrays, but how can I auto-increment an index for an associative array? That is, how do I get from “soup” to “nuts” when I want a full meal?

### Using `foreach( )` with normal arrays

Perl has a list-reading function for looping through arrays: `foreach`. The `foreach` function is a block statement that acts like a `while` block for arrays. The statement `foreach (@fruit)` means “step through the `@fruit` array, one element at a time”:

```
@fruit = ("apple", "banana", "mango", "orange", "pear");
foreach (@fruit) {
    print;
}          # prints: applebananamangoorangepear
```

This example relies on the implied current line variable $_ as the object for printing. Fortunately, foreach enables you to create a local variable, a feature useful for treating each element as something more than just the current line. You create the variable by inserting its name between foreach and the parentheses. This local variable refers to each element in turn and lives only for the duration of the foreach block:

```
@fruit = ("apple", "banana", "mango", "orange", "pear");
foreach $choice (@fruit) {
    print $choice, " ";
}                           # prints: apple banana mango orange pear
print $choice, "done";      # prints: done
                            # $choice is empty outside the block
```

Somewhat disappointing is the discovery that foreach *almost* works for associative arrays, as you can see in the following example:

```
%favorite = ("color","burgandy","pie","apple","ice cream",
"chocolate almond","fruit","banana","pasta","linguini");
foreach $my (%favorite) {
    print $my, " ";
}                           # prints: pasta linguini ice cream
                               chocolate
                            # almond fruit banana pie apple color
                               burgandy
```

The problem is that the keys and values are intermingled. Each key is still paired with its value, but the order of the pairs is not predicatable.

## Retrieving associative array index with keys( )

The keys function returns a list of the keys in an associative array:

```
%favorite = ("color","burgandy","pie","apple","ice cream",
"chocolate almond","fruit","banana","pasta","linguini");
@mykeys = keys(%favorite);
```

The normal array @mykeys now holds "pasta", "ice cream", "fruit", "pie", and "color".

### Exercise 3-3

Extend the example code to use foreach for printing the keys of the associative array %favorite.

## Using `foreach (keys( ))` with associative arrays

A special case of `foreach` breaks associative array keys out of the list. You can call for these keys by using this construct:

```
foreach $my (keys(%favorite))
```

Each loop delivers another key from the array. Because these keys are not sorted or ordered in storage, you cannot (without extra effort) predict what sequence of keys will be used. Take a look at the following example:

```
%favorite = ("color","burgandy","pie","apple","ice cream",
"chocolate almond","fruit","banana","pasta","linguini");
foreach $my (keys(%favorite)) {
    print $my, " ";
}                     # prints: pasta ice cream fruit pie color
```

With access to the keys, I can find the values:

```
%favorite = ("color","burgandy","pie","apple","ice cream",
"chocolate almond","fruit","banana","pasta","linguini");
foreach $my (keys(%favorite)) {
    print $favorite{$my}, " ";
}        # prints: apple linquini burgandy banana chocolate
almond
```

Now I have the values, in strange order, with no keys. Add a little more code to perform a lookup with each key by using the key to retrieve its value from the associative array `%favorite`:

```
%favorite = ("color","burgandy","pie","apple","ice cream",
"chocolate almond","fruit","banana","pasta","linguini");
foreach $my (keys(%favorite)) {
    print $my, "=", $favorite{$my}, " \n";
}
```

Finally, I get a list of keys paired with values:

```
pie=apple
pasta=linguini
color=burgandy
fruit=banana
ice cream=chocolate almond
```

A better method of obtaining the values for keys is available: the each function.

### Using while (each( )) with associative arrays

The each function retrieves associative array keys and elements, one pair at a time. When placed within a while loop, each steps through the entire array, returning an empty list when all the keys have been used. The empty list terminates the while loop. Instead of having one local variable, as in foreach, each has two — one for the key and one for the element, such as in the following example:

```
%favorite = ("color","burgandy","pie","apple","ice cream",
"chocolate almond","fruit","banana","pasta","linguini");
while (($mykey, $myval) = each(%favorite)) {
    print $mykey, "=", $myval, " \n";
}
```

The output is the same as the foreach with lookup version in the previous example. The advantage to using each for associative array looping is efficiency and clarity.

## Converting strings into lists with split( / expr /, $string )

The split operator extracts substring pieces from a string and stuffs all the pieces into an array as a list. The syntax for split is as follows:

```
@var = split(/expr/,"string to split")
```

In this statement, `@var` is the array variable that holds the list and `/expr/` is the pattern Perl matches to determine where to split the string. Typically, the splitting expression is a single character, such as a comma or a colon, but it also can be a group of characters such as comma-space.

## `split` into a normal array

Suppose that you have a string of indecisions connected by hyphens, such as the following:

```
$valString = "yes-no-up-down-true-false";
```

To break `$valString` into a list of words, set up the pattern expression in `split` to find the hyphens as follows:

```
@newVals = split(/-/,$valString); # @newVals now holds the list:
                                  #"yes","no","up","down","true","false"
print $newVals[2];                # prints: up
```

The default pattern for `split` is whitespace: a space, a tab, or the like. The default string is whatever you have set for `$_`. This can produce elegant shorthand for splitting text into words and numbers and stand-alone symbols — the text units programmers call *tokens* when they want to keep secrets. The next example splits a string into tokens:

```
$_ = "It was a dark and stormy night.";
@tale = split;
# @tale now holds "It","was","a","dark","and","stormy","night."
print $tale[3];    # prints: dark
```

## `split` into an associative array

Associative arrays accept the list returned by the from `split` function, taking the even-numbered elements as keys and pairing each key with its following substring as the value:

```
$toolbox = "hammer:4:pliers:1:saw:3:nail:1562";
%inventory = split(/:/,$toolbox);
print $inventory{"saw"}, "\n";   # prints: 3
while (($mykey, $myval) = each(%inventory)) {
    print $mykey, "=", $myval, " \n";
}
```

The first `print` statement puts 3 (the value for the key *saw*) on a line by itself. The `while(each)` loop then delivers key/value pairs:

```
3
hammer=4
saw=3
pliers=1
nail=1562
```

## `split` into list of variables

The `split` function works on the right side of the assignment operator = and doesn't care what receives the list on the left side of =. The receiver can be a normal array, an associative array, or a list of variables acting as the equivalent of an array, such as follows:

```
$supplies = "paper+carton";
@onhand = split(/+/,$supplies);
                        # @onhand[0] = paper, onhand[1] = carton
%buylist = split(/+/,$supplies);
                        # $buylist{"paper"} = "carton"
($item,$quantity) = split(/+/,$supplies);
                        # $item = "paper", $quantity = "carton"
```

### Exercise 3-4

You can practice your splits by trying this sample exercise:

1. Write a `split` statement to break a URL string into a list of name/value substrings. Start with this string:

   ```
   name=Mary+Jones&address=123+Main+Street&city=Rome&state=WI
   ```

   and retrieve a list of strings such as `"name=Mary+Jones"` and `"city=Rome"`.
2. Add statements to split each substring into a name string and a value string. Place the name and value in separate variables.
3. Add statements to accumulate the name/value pairs into an associative array.

# Character conversion with hex and pack

Computer data is not always formatted as nice, readable ASCII text files. More often than not, binary data gets mixed in with it. For instance, tabs and carriage returns and formfeed characters are sprinkled into text files all the time. A quick peek at any word-processing or spreadsheet file will tell you that there is much more to computer files than the safe, kindly ASCII characters seen on the screen. To solve this non-ASCII character-handling problem, Perl translates between binary data and textual data by using the `pack` and `hex` functions (Figure 3-10). Converting data types is an advanced topic, but you need to know about it to parse form data. The conversion process also relates to patterns and substitutions, so let's look at this process now.

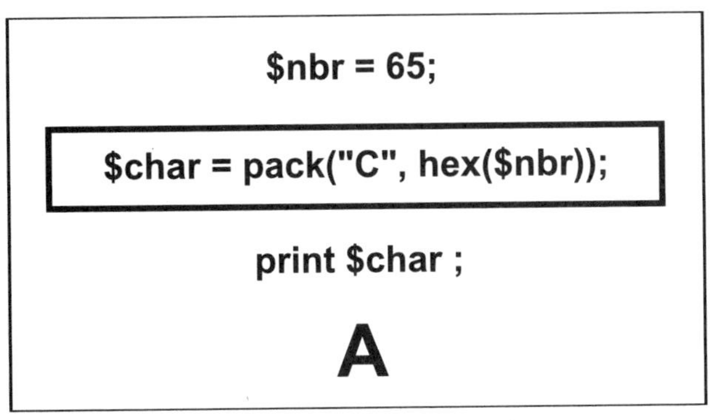


**Figure 3-10:** `Pack` and `hex`, hard at work.

## URL encoding

Form data passes from the browser to the server as URL-encoded strings. The encoding is necessary to make all non-printing characters in the data visible to the server. The server understands that character triplets beginning with a percent sign are special. Carriage returns and tabs entered into an input field by the visitor are coded as `%0D%0A` and `%09`, for instance.

This coding also prevents the server from confusing the meaning of certain characters. In the coded string, the ampersand signals the division between `NAME/VALUE` pairs. If the visitor types an ampersand (&) into a field, the browser converts the character into `%26` so that the server won't get confused. Without such coding, the & symbol would cause a false separation in the `NAME/VALUE` reading. The equal sign is another example. The equal sign is the separator between a `NAME` and its `VALUE`, so any equal sign entered into an input field is converted to `%3D`, which passes into the server without being confused as a separator =.

Other characters that may be encoded are quotes, apostrophes, exclamation marks, and other punctuation symbols that have special meaning or mysterious powers when transmitted as part of a URL. All encoded items need to be decoded so that the final format for a database form entry or a Web page description has the appropriate cast of characters (Figure 3-11).

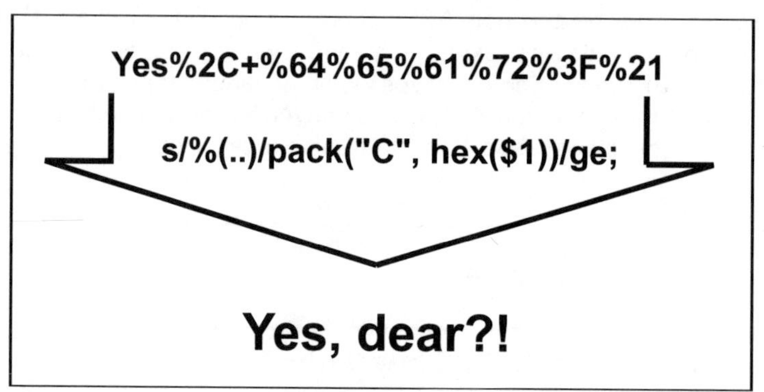


**Figure 3-11:** URL character conversions.

## Hexadecimal to decimal

The `hex` function returns the decimal value for a hexadecimal number. *Hexadecimal* means counting by 16s — 0 through 9, then A for 10, B for 11, and so on through hex F. Why do you care about hex numbers? Because the URL-encoded percent-sign triplets, such as `%3D`, are hex representations. Your Perl CGI programs have to manipulate hex numbers to read the URL strings, so you have to know how to conduct the manipulation. The `hex` and the `pack` functions work together to convert the `%3D` appearing in a URL string to an equal sign on a page.

To convert from hex to decimal numbers, multiply the value of the first character by 16 and add the value of the second character. Thus, Hex F is decimal 15, and hex 10 (read as one-oh) is decimal 16. The following table shows some of these conversions:

| Hex | Calculation | Decimal |
|---|---|---|
| 05 | 0 x 16 + 5 | 5 |
| 1B | 1 x 16 + 11 | 27 |
| 8C | 8 x 16 + 12 | 140 |
| A5 | 10 x 16 + 5 | 165 |
| FF | 15 x 16 + 15 | 255 |

Unless you write computer programs for a living, you will find it easier to look up hex numbers in a hex-to-decimal table than to deal with hex numbers directly. Appendix A has a table showing hex and decimal conversions for embedding special characters in HTML code and translating characters for URL encoding. The Perl program that generates the table is called `hextbl.pl` and is found in the \tools directory on the CD-ROM.

Perl's `hex` function starts the conversion work for you. The `print` function understands strings of ASCII characters expressed in decimal numbers: ASCII 65 is A, ASCII 61 is =, and so on. So, how do you print a hex number like `3D` with a function that wants decimal numbers such as the equivalent 61? If you are working with an operation that needs a decimal number and you only have hexadecimal numbers handy to pass on to it, use `hex` to make the conversion, as in the following example:

```
$myDecimal = hex("3D"); # take hex 3D and convert it to decimal
print $myDecimal;       # prints: 61
$myDecimal = hex("22"); # convert hex 22 into decimal
print $myDecimal;       # prints: 34
```

So far, I can convert hexadecimal to decimal, but the characters are still not printing. Rather, just the decimal numbers for those characters are printing. I need to do one more step and I'll have what I'm after.

## Convert numbers to characters with pack

The `pack` function is a type converter that offers several conversion options. The `pack` function takes two parameters to work wonders: a template, or instruction for what kind of conversion to perform, and a list of decimal numbers to convert. The form of the template for `pack` is a string of characters that varies depending on the type of conversion you want to do and the number of decimal numbers in the list. The letter used for that character represents the type of conversion, and the string contains one of that character for each number in the list.

The types to which you can convert are the various storage types (machine format) used internally by the operating system: integer, long integer, single- or double-precision floating point, and the rest of the bit and byte structures that computers have in their diets. For example, the template "C" converts numbers ranging from 0 to 255 into ASCII character-storage format. The following table lists some useful conversion templates for the purposes of this book (although many more are available):

| Template | Number Type |
|---|---|
| "c" | Signed (plus or minus) character –127 to +127 |
| "C" | Unsigned character from 0 to 255 |
| "i" | Signed integer from –16383 to +16383 |
| "I" | Unsigned integer from 0 to 32767 |

Look up "A" in the ASCII character table in Appendix A — the ASCII decimal is 65. To convert that 65 into the format used by the computer to represent "A" internally, use pack like this:

```
$letter = pack("C",65);   # convert 65 to an unsigned character
print $letter;            # prints: A
```

To convert more decimals, use more templates, as follows in this coded message to Orphan Annie from her dog Sandy:

```
$word = pack("CCCC",65,114,102,33);
print $word;                  # prints: Arf!
```

A 41 in hexadecimal notation means 4 x 16 + 1 or 65 in decimal notation. You can get from hex 41 to A by using a script similar to the following:

```
$dec = hex(41);               # converts hex 41 to decimal 65
$letter = pack("C",$dec);     # converts decimal 65 to letter A
print $letter;                # prints: A
```

A more "Perl way" of doing this task is to put the hex function inside the pack function:

```
$letter = pack("C",hex("41"));
print $letter;                # prints: A
$crlf = pack("CC",hex("0D"),hex("0A"));
print "A", $crlf, "B";        # prints: A on one line and B on the
 next
                              # or A \n B
```

We're getting closer to solving the URL-decoding problem!

## Evaluate functions in s/ / / with e option

The substitution function, `s///`, can accept options to modify its behavior. One such option is `i` (for ignore), which makes the search pattern case-insensitive. Another handy option is `g` (for global), which forces the substitution to take effect on all matches in the target string instead of quitting after the first substitution.

Meet the new option, `e` (for evaluate) — today's star performer. Evaluate means that Perl should interpret the substitution string as a Perl statement, evaluate it as program code to resolve any functions or operations, and then use the results of the evaluation for the substitution. The following listing shows examples of using options and combinations of options with the substitution function, including the `e` option:

```
$_ = "banana"; s/an/1+2 /; print;  # prints: b1+2ana
$_ = "banana"; s/an/1+2/g; print;  # prints: b1+21+2a
$_ = "banana"; s/an/1+2/e; print;  # prints: b3ana
$_ = "banana"; s/an/1+2/eg; print; # prints: b33a
```

With the `e` option, the substitution function evaluates 1+2 and uses the result, 3, for the substitution string.

The `e` option evaluates functions as well as expressions. Take a look at the same example using expressions:

```
$_ = "banana";
s/a/pack("C",65)/; print;    # no e option, prints:
                               bpack("C",65)nana
$_ = "banana";
s/a/pack("C",65)/e; print;   # prints: bAnana
s/a/pack("C",65)/eg; print;  # prints: bAnAnA
```

Hex 41 is ASCII 65. Dare you use the `hex` function inside of the `pack` function inside of the substitution operator? Yes!

```
$_ = "banana";
s/a/pack("C",hex(41))/e; print;   # prints: bAnana
```

The folllowing section describes the payoff of using such a setup.

## Using subexpressions with s/ / /e

A while ago, I showed you how to use subexpressions for substitutions. For a subexpression, you put something in parentheses and refer to the something later by using a number reference, as follows:

```
$_ = "my 44xlm shoe";
s/(..)x/#$1#x/; print;    # prints: my #44#xlm shoe
```

Now try that with a fake URL-encoded string:

```
$myURL = "Use+the+%3CFORM%3E+tag.";
$myURL =~ s/%(..)/pack("C",hex($1))/eg;
print $myURL;  # prints: Use+the+<FORM>+tag.
```

This process is so marvelous, I have to explain it step-by-step just to savor the elegance of Perl:

1. `s/%` finds a percent sign.
2. `s/%(..)` tells the Perl to remember the two characters following the percent sign.
3. `s/%(..)/pack` replaces the percent and two characters following it with a pack-ed decimal number.
4. `pack("C",` converts a decimal number into a character.
5. `pack("C",hex` gets the decimal number by using the `hex` function.
6. `hex($1)` feeds the `hex` function the two characters following the percent sign.
7. `s/%(..)/pack("C",hex($1))/e` evaluates the replacement string as a Perl statement.
8. `s/%(..)/pack("C",hex($1))/eg` performs the substitution on every possible match.

In other words, replace every percent-character-character triplet (URL-encoded hex number) with the ASCII character that the triplet represents.

The first time I saw this construct, I had no idea how it could possibly work. It took me nearly a week to figure it out. When the light bulb finally went on, I was so excited that I had to drive into town and treat myself to a steak and eggs breakfast. I covered two place mats with ballpoint scribblings to show the waitress how it worked. She called the cook out of the kitchen so that he could see, too. He gave me an extra order of hash-browns in appreciation.

# PerlProject: Parsing URL-Encoded Strings

This PerlProject, `mail2htm.pl`, is a parsing program that translates URL-encoded strings and formats the `name/value` data as a simple HTML page. The coded string may be in a file by itself (extracted from a form by HyBrowser, for example) or it may be part of an e-mail message, such as the response from a form containing `ACTION="mailto:me@some.site"`. This version of the parser looks for the magic designator `AAFormID=` to determine whether it has found the URL-encoded string. If your e-mail format allows it, you may be able to look for just the first equal sign in a mail message to pick out the URL string. Figure 3-12 shows what the e-mail message looks like and how `mail2htm.pl` converts the URL-encoded string into a Web page.

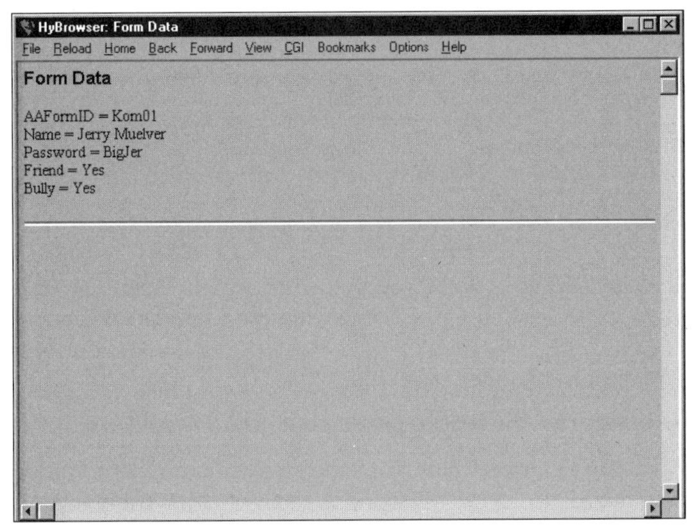


**Figure 3-12:** *An e-mail message returning a URL-encoded string, and the resulting HTML page generated by* `mail2htm.pl`.

The program itself is a great deal simpler than the explanation that follows it, or so I've been told. You can see in Listing 3-4 that `mail2htm.pl` uses just about every Perl trick you've learned up to this point. As you read through the program and its explanation, you really should be congratulating yourself on how far — and how fast! — you've traveled down the Perl path.

**Listing 3-4** **mail2htm.pl**

```
# mail2htm.pl -- parse URL-encoded strings into HTML file
# usage: perl mail2htm.pl msgfile > outputfile
print "<HTML>\n<HEAD><TITLE>Form Data</TITLE></HEAD>\n";  #1
print "<BODY>\n<H2>Form Data</H2>\n<HR>\n";                #2
while (<>) {                                               #3
    if (/AAFormID=/) {                                     #4
        chop();                                            #5
        @url = split(/&/);                                 #6

     foreach (@url) {                                      #7
            tr/+/ /;                                       #8
            s/=/ = /;                                      #9
            s/%(..)/pack("C",hex($1))/ge;                  #10
            print "$_<BR>\n";                              #11
        }
        print "<P><HR>\n";                                 #12
    }
}
print "</BODY>\n</HTML>\n";                                #13
# end of mail2htm.pl;
```

The following list guides you through the parts of the script and the steps `mail2htm.pl` takes in the preceding example to parse URL-encoded strings:

1. Minimum head for HTML file.
2. Heading for the report, plus a page-dividing rule.
3. The `while` statement reads the files listed on the command line. DOS wildcards (`*.msg`) will work. A redirect (>) symbol to save the output into a file does not confuse the input functions. For example, the following command works:

    ```
    perl mail3htm.pl *.msg > newmail.htm
    ```

4. Look for `AAFormID=`, the `NAME` from the form's hidden field. A string with this code in it will most likely be an encoded URL string.
5. Cut off the new line at the end of the string.
6. Cut the string into `name/value` pairs by splitting it at each ampersand and inserting the equal-sign-connected pair into `@url` array.

7. Cycle through the `@url` array one element at a time.
8. Translate plus signs in the current element into spaces.
9. Add a space on either side of the plus sign for readability.
10. Any %-character-character triplets are hex numbers. Replace each triplet with the ASCII character that the triplet represents.
11. Print the element (contained in `$_`) plus `<BR>` and a new line.
12. The URL string has been processed. Print a `<P>` for vertical space followed by a page-dividing rule, just in case you find more URL strings in this file to process.
13. There are no more strings, so you can add the closing tags for the HTML file.

## Exercise 3-5

Use HyBrowser to create a small set of URL-encoded strings. Run mail2htm.pl to process the strings into HTML files. Open the new HTML files in HyBrowser to check your work.

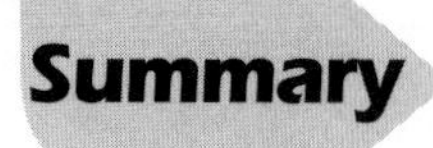


Some of the highlights from this action-packed chapter are

- Basic HTML coding for form elements `HIDDEN`, `TEXT`, `PASSWORD`, `CHECKBOX`, `RESET`, and `SUBMIT`.
- Sending data from a form with `GET` and `POST` methods.
- Pattern options `i` (ignore case), `g` (global), and `e` (evaluate).
- Subsitution `s/ / /`, translation `tr/ / /` and sub-expression operators.
- Associative array manipulation and magic
- String disassembly with the `split` function
- Character conversion with `hex` and `pack`
- Converting cryptic URL-encoded data into readable Web pages

# Working with Forms: Advanced

**Skill Targets**

How to use radio buttons and select lists in HTML forms

How to use Perl to write a form-response page on-the-fly

How to upload and install Perl CGI scripts on the server

What MIME types are and how to use them

The basics of HTTP headers and their uses

Advanced string and array manipulation

In this chapter, we finish constructing the survey form for Kombat Karate by adding radio buttons, select lists, and textarea input to the form. The PerlProject program introduced at the end of the chapter comes in handy once you finish the form — it is a generic forms digester that runs as a CGI program on the HTTP server and sends data from the completed form to the browser.

## Fancier Form Elements

Kombat Karate wants to offer lists of items to its clients from its instruction and merchandise catalogs. Because the form is still in the exploratory stage, the Karate Master desires to see the full range of HTML input and selection options. Having learned long ago that the Karate Master's wishes need serious consideration well in advance of the next sparring class, I hope you understand my urgent desire to demonstrate the remaining HTML form elements by completing the Kombat Karate Interest Survey form.

## Radio buttons

The Karate Master wants to know whether the prospective student has previous experience in other styles of karate. To ask what rank the prospective student has attained, I provided a group of *radio buttons* with belt ranks from which to pick.

A set of radio buttons works much like a batch of checkboxes except that you can select only one button at a time. Clicking one button automatically unclicks any other button in the set. This interdependence derives from using the same `NAME` attribute for all radio button fields in the set. All radio buttons that have the same `NAME` communicate with each another. Give each button a different `VALUE` so that you can tell which one was clicked when the form was submitted. Notice that this is the opposite of how checkbox groups are handled, where all fields must have different names but can have the same value.

To create the set of radio buttons for the Kombat Karate form, first open `komsur01.htm`, rename it to `komsur02.htm`, and start by adding a newline and a field prompt (shown in boldface) between the last checkbox field and the Reset button.

```
<INPUT TYPE="checkbox" NAME="Hospital" VALUE="Yes"> Hospital
reports
<P>What belt rank have you achieved in karate?<BR>

<P><INPUT TYPE="reset" VALUE="Clear All Entries on Form">
```

The first line of code (in boldface) describes the radio button much like the checkbox:

```
<P>What belt rank have you achieved in karate?<BR>
<INPUT TYPE="radio" NAME="Belt" VALUE="None"> None
```

Turn on the button for this field by adding the `CHECKED` attribute. This attribute also returns a useful value if the visitor submits the report without first making a personal choice in the button group. Even if the visitor skips this group of radio buttons, the form at least returns the `Belt=None` name/value pair, such as the following:

```
<INPUT TYPE="radio" NAME="Belt" VALUE="None" CHECKED> None
```

As mentioned earlier, the main difference between radio buttons and checkbox descriptions is that radio buttons from the same group all have the same NAME. For example, the following listing shows the entire group:

```
<INPUT TYPE="radio" NAME="Belt" VALUE="None" CHECKED> None
<INPUT TYPE="radio" NAME="Belt" VALUE="White"> White
<INPUT TYPE="radio" NAME="Belt" VALUE="Yellow"> Yellow
<INPUT TYPE="radio" NAME="Belt" VALUE="Orange"> Orange
<INPUT TYPE="radio" NAME="Belt" VALUE="Green"> Green
<BR>
<INPUT TYPE="radio" NAME="Belt" VALUE="Blue"> Blue
<INPUT TYPE="radio" NAME="Belt" VALUE="Purple"> Purple
<INPUT TYPE="radio" NAME="Belt" VALUE="Brown"> Brown
<INPUT TYPE="radio" NAME="Belt" VALUE="Black"> Black
```

Your browser's view of the radio buttons should be something like Figure 4-1.

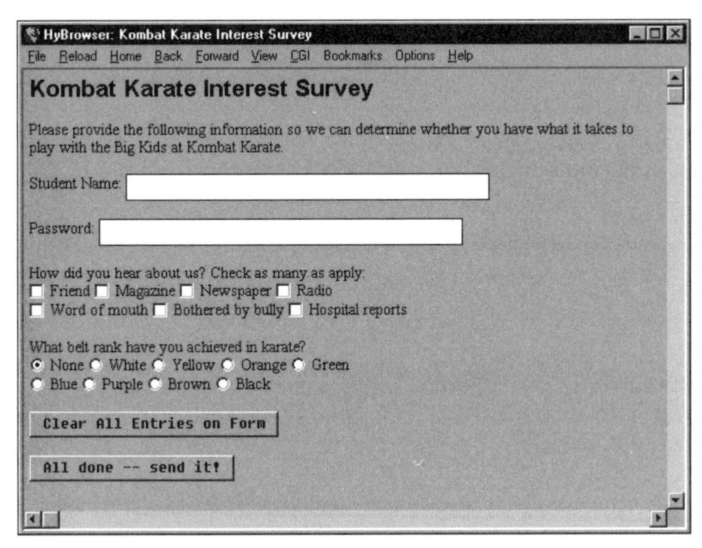


**Figure 4-1:** Group of radio buttons.

This group of buttons actually works — try it!

## Select lists (picklists)

Although this Web page is running out of available real estate, the Karate Master still wants to add more information. To plan his class schedule, he needs to know what classes the prospective student is likely to attend. I like to use </SELECT>. . .</SELECT> tags to create a picklist of such choices.

As usual, to do this task, use an informative field prompt (shown in boldface) to tell the visitor what this part of the form requires from him or her, as follows:

```
<INPUT TYPE="radio" NAME="Belt" VALUE="Black"> Black
<P>Which class schedule is best for you? Classes during the week
are held in the evening. Saturday classes are in the morning.
Click on the down-triangle to show more choices:<BR>
```

Place the list box on your form. The </SELECT>. . .</SELECT> tag pair is a container, so begin by adding the start and end tags right after the field prompt:

```
<SELECT>
</SELECT>
```

Add a NAME attribute inside the <SELECT> start tag:

```
<SELECT NAME="Classes">
</SELECT>
```

Now fill in the container with OPTION tags. Each OPTION tag holds the value that is sent to your Perl code if that option is selected. Write the text (the list of days for classes, shown in boldface) for each picklist entry right after the OPTION tag, as follows:

```
<SELECT NAME="Classes">
<OPTION VALUE="MWS"> Monday-Wednesday-Saturday
<OPTION VALUE="TTS"> Tuesday-Thursday-Saturday
<OPTION VALUE="MWFS"> Monday-Wednesday-Friday-Saturday
<OPTION VALUE="MTTF"> Monday-Tuesday-Thursday-Friday
<OPTION VALUE="MTWTF"> Monday-Tuesday-Wednesday-Thursday-Friday
<OPTION VALUE="S"> Saturday Only
</SELECT>
```

The Karate Master really wants Fridays off, so you encourage sign-ups for Monday-Wednesday-Saturday by preselecting that option with the SELECTED attribute, as follows:

```
<OPTION VALUE="MWS" SELECTED > Monday-Wednesday-Saturday
```

What kind of select list should this be? Your choices are a pop-up list (click in the corner to expand) or an open, scrollable list box. The SIZE attribute defines the style of list box. The following table lists the settings of the SIZE attribute:

| SIZE **Setting** | **List-Box Style** |
|---|---|
| SIZE="1" or SIZE simply omitted | Pop-up list |
| SIZE="2" | Scrollable box, 2 lines showing |
| SIZE="3" | Scrollable box, 3 lines showing |
| SIZE larger than the number of choices | Browser adds a "Nothing" entry to the list and forces a scrollable box |

Try SIZE="1" for the pop-up list. The whole construction now is as follows:

```
<P>Which class schedule is best for you? Classes during the week
are held in the evening. Saturday classes are in the morning.
Click on the down-triangle to show more choices:<BR>
<SELECT Name="Classes" SIZE="1">
<OPTION SELECTED VALUE="selMWS"> Monday-Wednesday-Saturday
<OPTION VALUE="TTS"> Tuesday-Thursday-Saturday
<OPTION VALUE="MWFS"> Monday-Wednesday-Friday-Saturday
<OPTION VALUE="MTTF"> Monday-Tuesday-Thursday-Friday
<OPTION VALUE="MTWTF"> Monday-Tuesday-Wednesday-Thursday-Friday
<OPTION VALUE="S"> Saturday Only
</SELECT>
```

In the browser, the selection list starts out collapsed, with only one (unselected) option as shown in Figure 4-2:

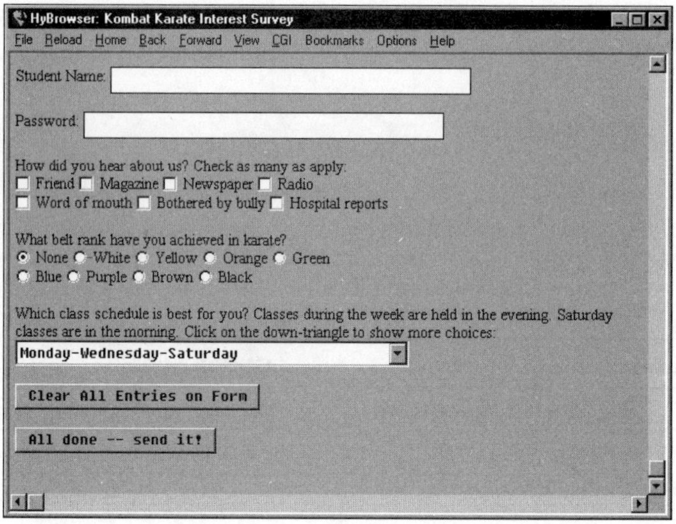

HyBrowser: Kombat Karate Interest Survey

File Reload Home Back Forward View CGI Bookmarks Options Help

Student Name:

Password:

How did you hear about us? Check as many as apply:
Friend Magazine Newspaper Radio
Word of mouth Bothered by bully Hospital reports

What belt rank have you achieved in karate?
None White Yellow Orange Green
Blue Purple Brown Black

Which class schedule is best for you? Classes during the week are held in the evening. Saturday classes are in the morning. Click on the down-triangle to show more choices:

Monday-Wednesday-Saturday

Clear All Entries on Form

All done -- send it!

**Figure 4-2:** Selection list, initial view.

After you click the down-arrow box, the list expands to show all options, as shown in Figure 4-3:

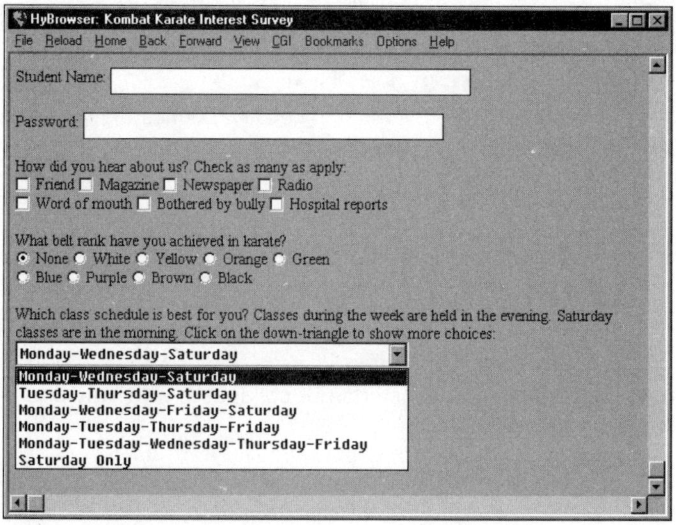

HyBrowser: Kombat Karate Interest Survey

File Reload Home Back Forward View CGI Bookmarks Options Help

Student Name:

Password:

How did you hear about us? Check as many as apply:
Friend Magazine Newspaper Radio
Word of mouth Bothered by bully Hospital reports

What belt rank have you achieved in karate?
None White Yellow Orange Green
Blue Purple Brown Black

Which class schedule is best for you? Classes during the week are held in the evening. Saturday classes are in the morning. Click on the down-triangle to show more choices:

Monday-Wednesday-Saturday

Monday-Wednesday-Saturday
Tuesday-Thursday-Saturday
Monday-Wednesday-Friday-Saturday
Monday-Tuesday-Thursday-Friday
Monday-Tuesday-Wednesday-Thursday-Friday
Saturday Only

**Figure 4-3:** Selection list, open view.

# Textarea (multi-line textbox)

Asking for comments is like asking for pasta — you don't know how much you're going to get or even what kind. You're not even sure if you'll like it once you get it. HTML accommodates such ambiguity in input by using the <TEXTAREA> element: a scrollable, write-as-much-as-you-want textbox. Here you use it to probe into the prospective student's motivation for wanting to take up exchanging of thumps and bumps as a hobby.

The <TEXTAREA>. . .</TEXTAREA> tag pair is a container. The start tag holds the NAME, ROWS, and COLS attributes. The space between the start and end tags is available for you to add anything you would like to show as default text in the textbox.

Use the following HTML code as one way to ask for comments:

```
<P>Please tell us why you want to study controlled mayhem at<BR>
Kombat Karate:<BR>
<TEXTAREA NAME="Comment" ROWS="4" COLS="50">I want to join Kombat
Karate because
</TEXTAREA>
```

These few lines of code added between the select list box and the Reset button produce something like Figure 4-4:

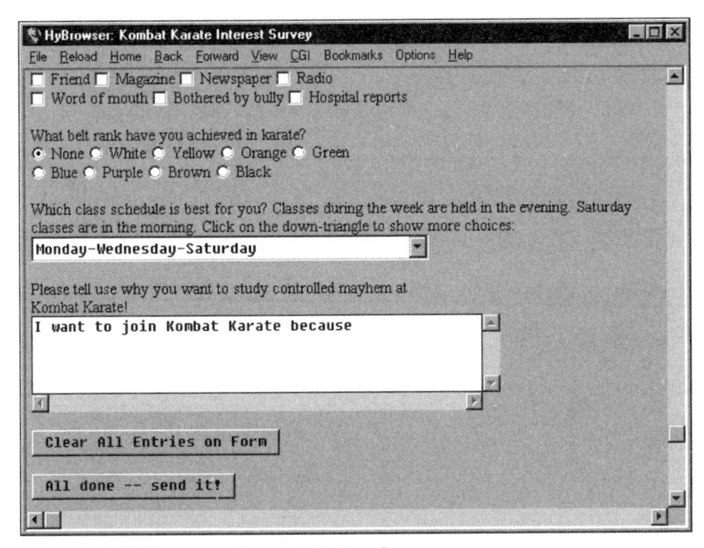


**Figure 4-4:** Textarea box added to form.

You still have room for four lines of 50 characters each. Many browsers don't support automatic word-wrapping for input fields, so the input you receive from textarea boxes often contains visitor-entered line breaks that must be processed. The box enables scrolling both horizontally and vertically to accept longer lines or deeper thoughts.

Some browsers (that is, Netscape 2.0 and above) entertain additional options for `TEXTAREA` to control word-wrapping within the box:

| | |
|---|---|
| `WRAP="OFF"` | Disables word-wrapping. Visitor must actually type any newlines needed. |
| `WRAP="VIRTUAL"` | Word-wrapping occurs automatically to fit text within the text box width, but the new lines do not appear in the data transmitted from the form. |
| `WRAP="PHYSICAL"` | Word-wrapping occurs automatically, and the new lines (line breaks) are included in the data transmitted from the form. |

Browsers that do not recognize the `WRAP` option simply ignore it. When that happens, the visitor will manually insert line breaks in the text, so your CGI programs need to make allowances for the possible newlines.

# HTML for Complete Survey Form

The Kombat Karate demonstration survey is completed. This Phase 2 version (Listing 4-1) is on the CD-ROM as `\code\ch04\komsur02.htm`. Use the program as is for testing in HyBrowser or change the `mailto:` address to your e-mail address to receive the form data via e-mail and parse it separately.

**Listing 4-1 Kombat Karate Interest Survey Phase 2**

```
<HTML>
<HEAD>
<TITLE>Kombat Karate Interest Survey</TITLE>
<!-- Phase 2 -->
</HEAD>
<BODY>
<H1>Kombat Karate Interest Survey</H1>
<P>Please provide the following information so we can determine
whether you have what it takes to play with the Big Kids at
Kombat Karate.
<FORM  ACTION="mailto:hybrowser" METHOD="post">
<INPUT TYPE="hidden" NAME="AAFormID" VALUE="Kom02">
```

```
<P>Student Name: <INPUT TYPE="text" NAME="Name" SIZE="40"
MAXLENGTH="80">
<P>Password: <INPUT TYPE="password" NAME="Password" SIZE="40"
MAXLENGTH="80">
<P>How did you hear about us? Check as many as apply:
<BR><INPUT TYPE="checkbox" NAME="Friend" VALUE="Yes"> Friend
<INPUT TYPE="checkbox" NAME="Magazine" VALUE="Yes"> Magazine
<INPUT TYPE="checkbox" NAME="Paper" VALUE="Yes"> Newspaper
<INPUT TYPE="checkbox" NAME="Radio" VALUE="Yes"> Radio
<BR>
<INPUT TYPE="checkbox" NAME="Word" VALUE="Yes"> Word of mouth
<INPUT TYPE="checkbox" NAME="Bully" VALUE="Yes"> Bothered by
bully
<INPUT TYPE="checkbox" NAME="Hospital" VALUE="Yes"> Hospital
reports
<P>What belt rank have you achieved in karate?<BR>
<INPUT TYPE="radio" NAME="Belt" VALUE="None" CHECKED> None
<INPUT TYPE="radio" NAME="Belt" VALUE="White"> White
<INPUT TYPE="radio" NAME="Belt" VALUE="Yellow"> Yellow
<INPUT TYPE="radio" NAME="Belt" VALUE="Orange"> Orange
<INPUT TYPE="radio" NAME="Belt" VALUE="Green"> Green
<BR>
<INPUT TYPE="radio" NAME="Belt" VALUE="Blue"> Blue
<INPUT TYPE="radio" NAME="Belt" VALUE="Purple"> Purple
<INPUT TYPE="radio" NAME="Belt" VALUE="Brown"> Brown
<INPUT TYPE="radio" NAME="Belt" VALUE="Black"> Black
<P>Which class schedule is best for you? Classes during the week
are held in the evening. Saturday classes are in the morning.
Click on the down-triangle to show more choices:<BR>
<SELECT Name="Classes" SIZE="1">
<OPTION VALUE="MWS"> Monday-Wednesday-Saturday
<OPTION VALUE="TTS"> Tuesday-Thursday-Saturday
<OPTION VALUE="MWFS"> Monday-Wednesday-Friday-Saturday
<OPTION VALUE="MTTF"> Monday-Tuesday-Thursday-Friday
<OPTION VALUE="MTWTF"> Monday-Tuesday-Wednesday-Thursday-Friday
<OPTION VALUE="S"> Saturday Only
</SELECT>
<P>Please tell us why you want to study controlled mayhem at<BR>
Kombat Karate:<BR>
<TEXTAREA NAME="Comment" ROWS="4" COLS="50">I want to join Kombat
Karate because
</TEXTAREA>
<P><INPUT TYPE="reset" VALUE="Clear All Entries on Form">
<P><INPUT TYPE="submit" VALUE="All done — send it!">
</FORM>
</BODY>
</HTML>
```

The form looks lean and mean, just like the Karate Master (Figure 4-5).

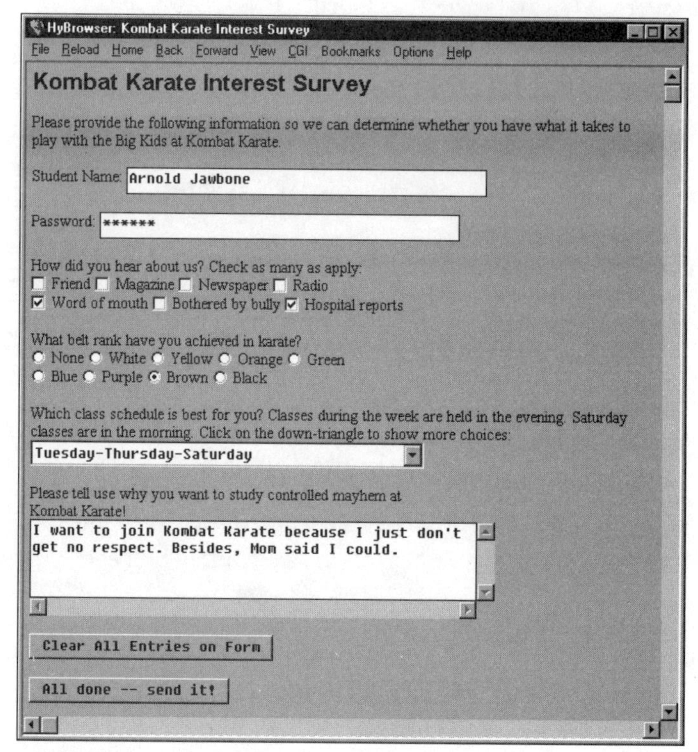


**Figure 4-5:** Kombat Karate Interest Survey.

# Arranging Form Elements

The easiest guide to laying out and formatting forms is common sense. Group related entries together, present questions in a normal flow (not backwards, such as state, city, address, phone, name), and use appropriate input types — radio buttons for obtaining single choices in a group, checkboxes for obtaining multiple choices, and select pop-ups for obtaining lengthy lists of alternatives. Artful use of <P> and <BR> can help you maintain clarity and organization in your forms. Once in a while, you have to resort to some serious pushing-around.

## <PRE>. . .</PRE>

Input fields are text elements, just like words, and can be pushed along a line with spaces. In HTML, however, multiple spaces do not work. The browser collapses groups of spaces down to a single space. Fortunately, workarounds exist.

Originally intended to format tables set up with tabs and text, the <PRE>. . . </PRE> tag now finds service as a form-formatting device. The <PRE> tag prevents the browser from collapsing spaces, but at the expense of typographic elegance. Everything between the starting <PRE> tag and the closing </PRE> tag is displayed exactly as it is laid out but in a monospace (typewriter) font. What is useful about the tag, from my viewpoint, is that <PRE> works for all browsers. For instance, the following HTML code appears on the screen much as you see it here, monospaced font and all:

```
<PRE>
        Be still,               Stand up
        my pounding             and shout
        heart.                  it out!
</PRE>
```

Only the tags are hidden. The indented, lined-up text holds its place.

For large blocks of text, the monospace font looks antiquated. But in forms — where the visitor is interested in data rather than font design — the improvement in layout is more important than the font (such as in the following example):

```
<FORM>
Name: <INPUT TYPE="TEXT" NAME="Name" SIZE="25"><BR>
Shipping address: <INPUT TYPE="TEXT" NAME="Shipping"
SIZE="40"><BR>
City: <INPUT TYPE="TEXT" NAME="Shipping" SIZE="40"> State: <INPUT
TYPE="TEXT" NAME="State" SIZE="2"><BR>
9-digit Zip Code: <INPUT TYPE="TEXT" NAME="Zip" SIZE="10">
<P>
<PRE>
            Name: <INPUT TYPE="TEXT" NAME="Name" SIZE="25">
Shipping address: <INPUT TYPE="TEXT" NAME="Shipping" SIZE="40">
            City: <INPUT TYPE="TEXT" NAME="Shipping" SIZE="40">
           State: <INPUT TYPE="TEXT" NAME="State" SIZE="2">
9-digit Zip Code: <INPUT TYPE="TEXT" NAME="Zip" SIZE="10">
</PRE>
</FORM>
```

Figure 4-6 shows the result.

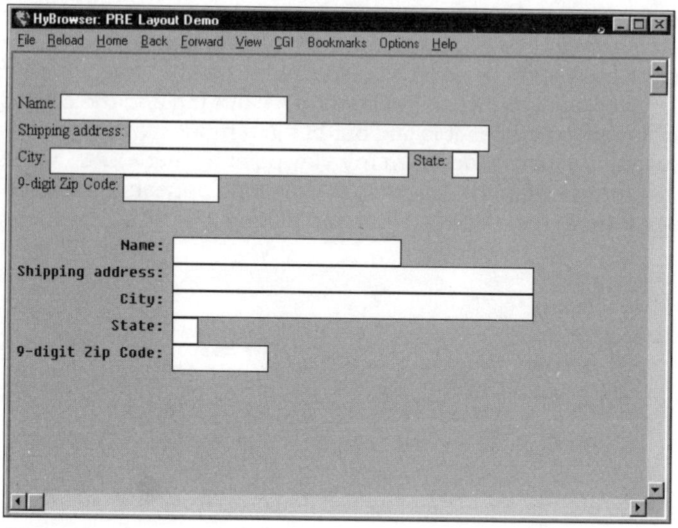

**Figure 4-6:** Layout with <PRE>.

I think visitors can live with the typewriter font, don't you?

## Tables

Tables are trickier to use for form layout than <PRE>, but many people feel the final result is well worth the extra effort. You get to keep the proportional font and have your layout, too, if the visitor is using a browser that understands tables (and almost all of them do these days). The following example shows the code for using tables as the layout element for the address textboxes:

```
<FORM>
<TABLE BORDER="0">
<TR><TD ALIGN="RIGHT">Name:</TD>
    <TD><INPUT TYPE="TEXT" NAME="Shipping" SIZE="40"></TD></TR>
<TR><TD ALIGN="RIGHT">Shipping address:</TD>
    <TD><INPUT TYPE="TEXT" NAME="Shipping" SIZE="40"></TD></TR>
<TR><TD ALIGN="RIGHT">City:</TD>
    <TD><INPUT TYPE="TEXT" NAME="Shipping" SIZE="40"></TD></TR>
<TR><TD ALIGN="RIGHT">State:</TD>
    <TD><INPUT TYPE="TEXT" NAME="State" SIZE="2"></TD></TR>
<TR><TD ALIGN="RIGHT">9-digit Zip Code:</TD>
    <TD><INPUT TYPE="TEXT" NAME="Zip" SIZE="10"></TD></TR>
</TABLE>
</FORM>
```

And how does it look? Just fine for browsers that understand tables (Figure 4-7).

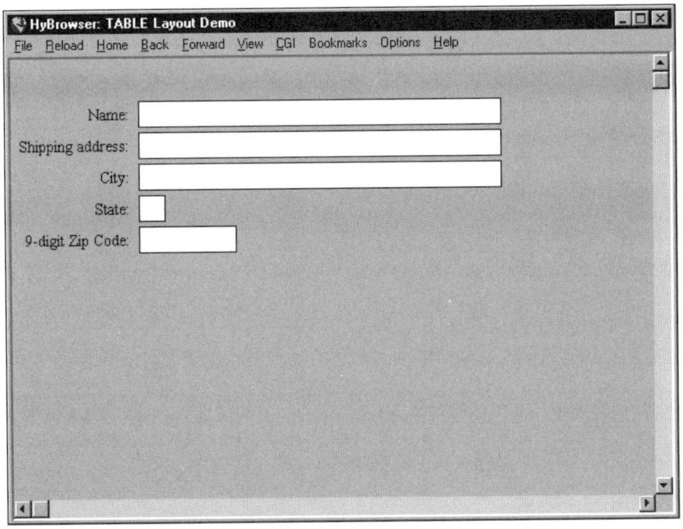

**Figure 4-7:** Layout with <TABLE>.

But the appearance is not so nice if the browser cannot deal with tables (Figure 4-8).

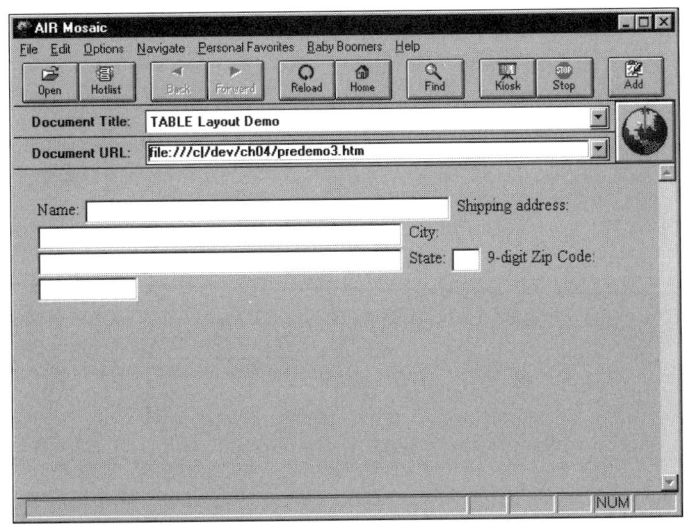


**Figure 4-8:** Layout with <TABLE> in a browser that does not understand tables.

**Exercise 4-1**

Adjust the Kombat Karate survey form by changing the checkbox and radio button fields into two vertical columns each.

# MIME Meets Perl

Multipurpose Internet Mail Extensions (MIME) are specifications for types of files that move through the Internet. The purpose of MIME is to enable computers on different platforms and configurations to pass information to one another and to understand how to process the information with the least amount of fuss and bother. Different MIME types are available for text, images, video, audio, messages, applications, and others. Within the MIME types are subtypes for particular uses. HTML is text, and its MIME type is `text/html`. You usually can find a listing of the MIME types supported by your browser in the browser's Preferences or Options menus.

## MIME types

No browser processes all MIME types and subtypes. Sometimes special MIME types (such as audio and video) require *helper* applications on the receiving end, separate programs that the browser calls in to assist with trickier forms of data. The CD-ROM contains lists of the available MIME types and subtypes, along with the file extensions that go with each type.

After it receives a request to send a file, the server checks the file's extension to determine the file's MIME type. You already know about .HTM, .HTML, and .GIF extensions, I'm sure. You also should know that you can't use arbitrary extensions such as .HHH for HTML files or .JIF for GIF files. The reason you have such constraints with file extensions is that servers rely on the expected use of extensions to determine a file's type.

## HTTP headers

Files must be "well-dressed" in order to shuffle around the Internet. Every request from a browser to a server and, conversely, every file or file-like response from the server to the browser, has a chunk of identifying data called a *header* pasted onto the front (head) of the file.

### Request headers

The first piece of information that the browser sends as part of a request to the server is a `Method` request header. This header consists of just one line of text containing three items in a special format, with each item separated by a space:

```
Method URL Version
```

`Method` is the same method used in the HTML `<FORM>` tag: `POST` or `GET`. URL specifies the location of the requested document. Version indicates the highest level of HTTP protocol that the browser understands. (HTTP protocol refers to the tags and language used for conversation between browser and server.) Thus, the request header may look like this:

```
GET http://www.some.site/index.html HTTP/1.0
```

Once you provide the server with the appropriate header information, the server knows what to do.

After sending the `Method` request header, the browser may follow up with additional headers to provide more information to the server or to request special handling. When the server answers, it tacks on these headers to the front of the files being sent. After the browser receives the server's response, it is the browser's turn to convert the header data into handling instructions. These request and response headers are listed on the CD-ROM.

CGI programs do not deal directly with the request headers coming from the browser. The server tucks header information into CGI variables like stuffing letters into a mailbox, and the CGI program checks the contents of the relevant variable to find the data. You don't have to understand much about the format and content of request headers; you just need to know where to look for the data brought in by the header. You are welcome to explore the information on headers found on the CD-ROM, but I promise to reveal what you have to know about request headers in time to use the revelations in your Perl scripts.

## Response headers

Response headers (those that come back from the server to the browser) will be of more interest to you. The server uses response headers to tell the browser the particulars about the incoming file: its type, length, date last modified, and so on. CGI programs are files, but you don't send these out — you run them. So where does the header come in?

CGI programs typically return information to the browser by sending a file or by producing a series of `print` commands — which looks like a file to the browser — to `STDOUT`. In order to flow it through the Internet to the browser, the file needs a header. Because of the way CGI works, your program has to create its own response header to get a message back to the browser.

Often I use a very simple response header. For a response in HTML page format, the browser only needs to know whether the incoming file is text, and if so, whether it should be treated and displayed as HTML. The header for this lightweight communication task is

```
Content-type: text/html
```

This header looks like a name/value pair, doesn't it? If the output to the browser is a dirt-simple text message, the header is

```
Content-type: text/plain
```

A quick look at the list on the CD-ROM reveals that the value for `Content-type:` is always a MIME type.

## Headers end with a blank line

When the server adds a header to a file being sent to a browser, a blank line — a newline with no other characters — separates the header from the file. Your CGI program must do the same. Without the blank line, you have no way to tell where the header ends and the file begins. To provide a blank line separator, the Perl code for the header must end with two newlines before the next line of the file is printed:

```
print "Content-type: text/html\n\n";
print "<HTML><TITLE>Test Page</TITLE></HEAD>\n";
print "<BODY>Rest of page text.</BODY></HTML>\n";
```

### Important: Number One CGI Beginner Mistake

Every CGI and Perl forum and newsgroup is familiar with this desperate plea for help:

"My CGI program won't work! Nothing comes back from the server. What's wrong with my code?!"

Then follows a dozen lines of Perl or UNIX shell code. At the top of the code you find the CGI Beginner's Number One Mistake — the programmer forgot to separate the header from the file with a blank line. In Perl, that means *two* newlines (`\n\n`): one to end the string, and one to make the blank line.

The browser sees the header separated by a blank line and gives these results:

```
Content-type: text/html
<HTML><TITLE>Test Page</TITLE></HEAD>
<BODY>Rest of page text.</BODY></HTML>
```

The blank line is easy to forget, especially with multi-line headers.

# PerlFacts: Manipulating Strings and Arrays

This edition of PerlFacts further unravels the tangled world of strings and arrays. In this section, I lead off with some file-reading tricks, look at string analysis and extraction functions, and finish up with further explorations in arrays and lists.

## Reading a whole file into a string or array

The file-reading operation that I've introduced you to so far has been based on treating the file (or `STDIN`) as a stream — take a trickle in, process it, and get another trickle, one line at a time. Another way to process files is to read the entire file in a one giant gulp. As long as your computer has enough memory, or if the file is small enough, pulling the entire file into your program at once offers the advantages of speed, direct access to all parts of the file, speed, simplified programming, and speed. (Did I mention speed?)

### File input with <>

To help illustrate the difference between the two methods of reading files, let's do a quick review. To read a file one line at a time, open the file, give it a filehandle, and then use the read-from operator (<>) in a loop, as follows:

```
open (FHANDLE, "myfile.txt");
while (<FHANDLE>) {
    print;       # prints current line
}
```

To read each line into a specific variable, assign the read-from operator to the variable, as shown here:

```
open (FHANDLE, "myfile.txt");
while ($line = <FHANDLE>) {
    print $line;
}
```

To read the *entire* file into an array, assign the read-from operator <> to the array in a single statement:

```
open (FHANDLE, "myfile.txt");
@myLines = <FHANDLE>;
$i = 1;
foreach $line (@myLines) {
    print "$i++: $line";    # prints a number for each line
}
```

With the file held entirely in memory, jumping from line to line around the array for comparisons, manipulations, and sorting operations is a snap.

## File input with `read( )`

The `read()` function accesses files that may not already be arranged in nice, neat lines. Database files, binary files, and data flowing through CGI fall into this category. The syntax for `read()` is

```
read (FHANDLE, $var, $length);
```

where `FHANDLE` is the familiar filehandle, `$var` is the string that will hold the incoming data, and `$length` is the number of characters to read. For example, the following shows how the `read()` function works to grab the first 30 characters of `citymile.dat`:

```
open (FHANDLE, "citymile.dat");
$chars = 30;
read (FHANDLE, $chunk, $chars);
print "$chunk\n";   # prints first 30 characters of citymile.dat
```

Why would I want to restrict the number of characters? In database applications, the data spreads though the file in specific chunks of known length. Thus, the procedure for data retrieval is

1. Find out where to start reading in the file.
2. Find out how many characters to read.
3. Read just that number of characters to make sure that the data from only one record is being pulled into the program.

For CGI programs, the request header on a data stream tells the server how many characters belong to the data by stuffing that information into the `CONTENT_LENGTH` CGI variable. When a Perl program fetches the data stream, the program has to know exactly how many characters to fetch in order to keep its fingers out of someone else's pie.

## String functions

In addition to its pattern-based string operations, Perl provides the same string manipulations found in some other computer languages. Perl also performs some string-related tasks that no other languages do, so Perl programmers tend to develop high confidence levels in the face of text-manipulation projects.

### chop

Strings coming into a Perl program through `STDIN` make their appearance as a complete line. By "complete," I mean that the line can stand by itself because it has a newline character at the end. There are times when I like having newlines on my strings and there are times when I don't. When you have to shuffle pieces of strings around to build an elegant report, for instance, creating embedded newlines is as cumbersome as knitting with piano wire. On the other hand, newlines at the end of each string in a normal array make it a snap to print out the array in a nice, neat column of text.

Let's look at an example. Listing 4-2 shows a program that concatenates strings on input.

**Listing 4-2** **catstr.pl**

```
# catstr.pl - concatenate strings on input
while (<STDIN>) {
    $a .= $_;
}
print $a;
```

## Cross-Platform Trap

If you produce data files on a DOS platform, the newlines will be two characters — CR (carriage return) and LF (linefeed). These DOS data files retain the CRLF newlines when you transfer them to a UNIX platform unless you take special pains to convert the files to UNIX format. If you use `chop` in UNIX on files that came from DOS with CRLF intact, the chop will remove only the LF character. The surviving CR character produces mystery line breaks when the data shuffles back to DOS in a generated HTML page.

The moral of the story is: Use UNIX format for files that will be processed on a UNIX platform.

A trial run of `catstr.pl` results in this printout:

```
C:\dev> perl catstr.pl
String concatenations
include newlines
if there are any to be found.
^Z
String concatenations
include newlines
if there are any to be found.
```

To get all those strings to concatenate on one line, I use the `chop` function, which cuts the last character off a string. The syntax is

```
chop($var);
```

where `$var` is the string to be chopped. If no `$var` is mentioned, `chop` assumes that `$_` is the target.

In Listing 4-3, because the last character on a string coming through `STDIN` is the newline, `chop` cuts off the newline, and the strings behave as expected. They print with no unruly line breaks because the embedded newlines have been removed. Notice in Listing 4-3 that I added a space after each `$_` to make the line more readable. Notice also that I added a newline `\n` to the concatenated string to print it properly.

**Listing 4-3 catstr2.pl**

```
# catstr2.pl — concatenate chopped strings on input
while (<STDIN>) {
    chop($_);
    $a .= "$_ ";
}
print "$a\n";
```

A trial run of `catstr2.pl`, with three lines of explanatory text for input, produces this:

```
C:\dev> perl catstr2.pl
String concatenations
include newlines
if there are any to be found.
So, chop them off.
^Z
String concatenations include newlines if there are any to be
found. So, chop them off.
```

Perl adjusts the `chop` function for each platform. On UNIX, the newline is ASCII 10 (Perl's `\n`); on Mac, it is ASCII 13 (`\r`); and on DOS (and Windows), it is ASCII 13 plus ASCII 10. Whether it consists of one or two characters, in each case, `chop` removes the newline.The default target string for `chop` is `$_`, so the working code from `catstr2.pl` can be written as

```
while (<STDIN>) {
    chop;
    $a .= "$_ ";
}
```

## index

The `index` function finds the location of a designated substring within the target string. The syntax is

```
$pos = index(target, substring [,offset]);
```

where the various parts of the function represent the following:

| | |
|---|---|
| `$pos` | The variable that holds the result (character position of the found substring, or –1 if it not found) |
| `target` | The string to be searched |
| `substring` | The string to be found |
| `offset` | Optionally, the character position (number of characters to skip) to start the search |

The character position returned by `index` is a bit tricky — it actually represents the number of characters skipped. A match with the first character of the string returns `0`, because no characters were skipped. A match with the fourth character of the string returns `3`.

A common use for `index` is to convert objects into numbers, as follows:

```
$months = "JanFebMarAprMayJunJulAugSepOctNovDec";
$myMonth = "Apr";
$moNum = index($months, $myMonth);  # $moNum = 9
```

This snippet of code needs work before the conversion from April to 4 will succeed (currently, it shows the month number as 9). Prepare for mass confusion — my explanation is much more involved than the corresponding Perl code. I should have divided by 3, which allows for having three letters in each month's abbreviation. Because a hit on the first character of the string is 0, `"Jan"` would give me a 0 to divide by 3. And `"Apr"` divided by 3 is 3, not the 4 that I really want. So I add 3 to the number returned by `index` and then divide by 3 to get the traditional April=4 result, as follows:

```
$myMonth = "Apr";
$moNum = (index($months, $myMonth) + 3) / 3; #moNum = 4
```

A matching pattern tells you whether or not a substring is in a target string. But `index` can tell you how many times the substring can be found. Use the optional `offset` parameter to march through the string by incrementing the `offset` after each found match:

```
$target = "His theory is more theatrical than useful.";
print "$` \|" if ($target =~ /the/);
                  # prints: His (everything before the match).
$thePos = 0;
```

```
while (1) {                          # always true, so loop forever.
    $found = index($target, "the", $thePos);  # starts at zero.
    if ($found >= 0) {               # made a hit.
        $nrHits++;                   # increment the hit counter.
        $thePos = $found + 1;        # increment the offset.
    } else {                         # no "the" in remainder of string,
        last;                        # so quit.
    }
}
print "Found \"the\" $nrHits times.\n";
```

**Exercise 4-2**

How would you use `s///g` to count hits? Show the technique by rewriting the preceding "theatrical" example. Hint: set `$_ = $target`. Another hint: `s///g` returns the number of substitutions made. Be careful in your value assignments and be mindful of the difference between `=`, `=~`, and `==`.

## rindex

To search for a substring backward, starting from the end of a target string, use `rindex`, which works the same way as `index` except that the starting position is the end of the target string. The syntax is as follows:

```
$pos = rindex(target, substring [,offset]);
```

where the parts of the function represent the following:

| | |
|---|---|
| `$pos` | The variable that holds the result (number of characters skipped before finding a match, or –1 if no match was found) |
| `target` | The string to be searched |
| `substring` | The string to be found |
| `offset` | (Optional) The character position to start the search — number of characters from the start of the target string to skip before scanning for the substring |

The value returned by `rindex` is the number of characters skipped from the front of the string to the hit position.

Because the optional offset is measured from the left end of the target, and the position of the hit also is measured from the left end of the target, stepping through a string with `rindex` takes more arithmetic and logic than it is worth. The most typical use for `rindex` is to find the last occurrence of a substring in a target string and be happy with that:

```
$target = "His theory is more theatrical than useful.";
$rpos = rindex($target, "the");
print $rpos;    # prints: 19
                #    chars skipped to 'theatrical'
```

## length

Knowing the length of a string often is the first step in comparisons, reports, page formatting, and parsing operations. The Perl `length` function is direct and clear, as follows:

```
$myString = "abcdefghi";
$len = length($myString);    # $len is 9
```

### Exercise 4-3

Try these steps to enhance your understanding of how the `length` function works:

1. Write a program that prints each word in a string followed by the length of the word. Use a `word=length` format, with one entry on each line.
2. Expand the `word=length` program to read an entire file.
3. Enhance the `word=length` program to print each word only once, skipping duplicates.

## substr

String disassembly is a common need in text manipulation programs. Given a position within a string, you can access a piece of the string with the `substring` function. The syntax is:

```
$myStr = substr(source, start[, length]);
```

where

| | |
|---|---|
| `$myStr` | = the variable that holds the resulting substring |
| `source` | = the string to be disassembled |
| `start` | = number of characters to skip before slicing the substring |
| `length` | = optional, number of characters to take for the substring |

If you don't specify a `length` parameter, the substring will begin with the character at `start` and continue through the end of the string. The source string is not modified by `substr`.

```
$myStr = "Unusual circumstances require";
$theSub = substr($myStr, 8);
print $theSub, "\n";     # prints: circumstances require
print substr($myStr, 14, 6), "\n";  # prints: stance
```

`substr` not only returns a piece of a string, it also accepts a substring for injecting into a target. When you assign a string into a `substr` function, the assignment has the same effect as using the Copy/Paste commands in an editor:

```
$shortStr = "Once upon a time, in a land far away,";
$newStr = "midnight dreary";
substr($shortStr, 12, 4) = $newStr;  # selecting 'time'
print $shortStr;
# prints: Once upon a midnight dreary, in a land far away,
```

If the pasted string is longer than the selected substring, the target string enlarges itself to accommodate the new size. If the pasted string is shorter than the selected substring, the target string is shortened appropriately, as follows:

```
$shortStr = "Once upon a time, in a land far away,";
$newStr = "long ago";
substr($shortStr, 5, 11) = $newStr;  # selecting 'upon a time'
print $shortStr;
# prints: Once long ago, in a land far away,
```

# Array and list juggling

So far, you have learned how to do the following with arrays:

- Create normal and associative arrays
- Assign values to array elements
- Use array elements for assignments and quoted strings
- Convert from an associative array to a normal array and back again
- Cycle through normal arrays one element at a time with `foreach`
- Retrieve a list of keys from an associative array with `keys` and use the list of keys to go through the associative array one element at a time

But sitting up and rolling over isn't enough for the array puppy — you can teach him to jump through hoops, too, with a little more effort.

## chop

This `chop` is the same one that works on strings. When `chop` is applied to an array, it removes the last character of every element in the array, as in the following:

```
@myList = ("a01 ","b02 ","c03 ","d04 ");
print @myList, "\n";  # prints: a01 b02 c03 d04
chop(@myList);        # cuts the space off each element
print @myList;        # prints: a01b02c03d04
```

**Exercise 4-4**

Rewrite the `chop` example to build the list with newlines instead of spaces.

## split

In Chapter 3, I showed how to use `split` to break a string into an array or break a string into a list of variables. The basic `split` function is straightforward, as the following example shows:

```
$collection = "necklace:watch:car:bankroll:home videos";
@valuables = split(/:/,$collection);
foreach $item (@valuables) {
   print "$item\n";
}
```

The result of this script is as follows:

```
necklace
watch
car
bankroll
home videos
```

Splitting into variables is just as reasonable:

```
$pair = "price=15.50";
($name,$value) = split(/=/,$pair);
                        # $name = "price", $value = "12.50"
```

The `split` function pays attention to the receivers of the split pieces. If only two receivers exist for five available pieces, `split` puts the first piece in the first receiver, the second piece in the second receiver, and throws the rest away. For example

```
$basket = "fruit:apple:banana:pear:kiwi";
($type,$item) = split(/:/,$basket);
print "$type\n$item\n";
```

results in

```
fruit
apple
```

Maybe if I gave `split` an array for the items in the preceding example, it could make room for the remaining pieces:

```
$basket = "fruit:apple:banana:pear:kiwi";
($type,@item) = split(/:/,$basket);
print "$type\n@item\n";
```

The preceding script results in

```
fruit
apple banana pear kiwi
```

That's interesting! I can put the first element into a scalar variable and the rest into an array and still get rid of the delimiter. Notice that printing the array `@item` as part of a quoted string inserts single spaces between elements.

One more option is available for `split` — restricting the number of pieces retrieved. The syntax for this option is `split(/expr/,source,num)`, where `num` is the maximum number of pieces:

```
$basket = "fruit:apple:banana:pear:kiwi";
(@item) = split(/:/,$basket,3);
foreach $element (@item) {
   print $element, "\n";
}
```

This result can be really useful:

```
fruit
apple
banana:pear:kiwi
```

For the last piece in a limited list, `split` tosses in the remainder of the string. This time, the delimiter (:) comes along with the string. Thus, `split(/:/, $basket,2)` produces two pieces in a head-and-tail fashion:

```
fruit
apple:banana:pear:kiwi
```

With its various options, the `split` function can be a flexible tool for working with database applications.

## join

If a `split` exists, it is only fair that a `join` should be available, too. The `join` function places all elements of an array into a string together and connects the elements with a specified delimiter. The syntax is

```
join("str",@array)
```

where `"str"` is a string expression that describes the delimiter (the glue for the operation), and `@array` is the normal array or specific list that provides the elements for the new string. For example

```
@shorts = ("if","of","an","or","be","is","it");      #1
$ignore = join("|",@shorts);                         #2
print $ignore, "\n";  #3 prints: if|of|an|or|be|is|it
$special = join("::",("check",@shorts));  #4
print $special, "\n";
          # prints - check::if::of::an::or::be::is::it
```

Some discussion is in order. The previous code snippet performs the following operations:

1. Assembles a list of short words into the array `@short`.
2. Uses `join` to splice the array elements with the vertical bar character and assign the resulting string to `$ignore`.
3. Prints the newly assembled string to prove that join worked as expected.
4. Uses `join` again to splice *check* and each of the elements in `@shorts` into one long string, this time with a double colon as a two-character delimiter.

## push

The `push` function adds another element, or list of elements, to the end of an array. The syntax is

```
push(@array,list)
```

where `@array` is the target array to be expanded and `list` is the element or list of elements to be added. The following example shows the `push` function in action:

```
@ordinals = ("first","second","third","fourth");
$numElements = @ordinals;
print $numElements, "\n";          # prints: 4
push(@ordinals,"fifth");
$numElements = @ordinals;
print $numElements, "\n";          # prints: 5
print $ordinals[4], "\n";          # prints: fifth
```

Remember, assigning an array to a scalar variable puts the total number of elements into the variable, so `$numElements` shows that `push` extends the array.

## pop

The pop function is the opposite of push — it returns the last element of an array and shortens the length of the array by one element:

```
@ordinals = ("first","second","third","fourth");
$numElements = @ordinals;
print $numElements, "\n";   # prints: 4
$final = pop(@ordinals);
print $final, "\n";         # prints: fourth
$numElements = @ordinals;
print $numElements;         # prints: 3
```

Not only did pop retrieve the last element in the array (fourth), pop also deleted that element and shortened the array.

## shift

The shift function performs the same action to the front of an array that pop performs to the back of an array — shift retrieves an element, deletes it from the array, and shifts all remaining elements up a notch to fill in the gap. The syntax is

```
$var = shift(@array)
```

where $var is the variable that receives the retrieved element, and @array is the array that surrenders its first element for the retrieval. The following shows how it works:

```
@ordinals = ("first","second","third","fourth");
$numElements = @ordinals;
print $numElements, "\n";          # prints: 4
$initial = shift(@ordinals);
print $initial, "\n";              # prints: first
$numElements = @ordinals;
print $numElements, "\n";          # prints: 3
print $ordinals[0], "\n";          # prints: second
```

The first element has been stripped off and all other elements moved up one slot in the index.

## unshift

The unshift function adds an element or list to the front of an array and moves the other elements of the array down one slot in the index. These functions might be easier to remember if `shift` was the adder and `unshift` was the subtracter, but they aren't. The syntax for `unshift` is

```
unshift(@array,list);
```

where `@array` is the array that receives the new front end and `list` is the element or list to be added. For example

```
@ordinals = ("first","second","third","fourth");
$numElements = @ordinals;
print $numElements, "\n";          # prints: 4
unshift(@ordinals,"zero");
$numElements = @ordinals;
print $numElements, "\n";          # prints: 5
print $ordinals[0], "\n";          # prints: zero
```

The array was extended by one element, and the new element `"zero"` was inserted at the front of the array.

## sort

You saw the `keys` function in Chapter 3, so you can consider the next couple of paragraphs to be a review before I get into `sort`. I'm building up to some major moves with associative arrays.

Associative arrays are not organized alphabetically or even by sequence of construction — the first element inserted into the array may not be the first element returned. Associative arrays are designed for instant retrieval of values when you know what the key is. Because no method exists for imposing order directly on an associative array, you have to deal with organized access outside the array. To create a list of the keys (subscripts) from an associative array, use `keys` to assign the list to a normal array:

```
@keylist = keys(%myArray);
```

Remember, `@keylist` holds the keys from `%myArray`, but you have no guarantee about their order. Printing `@keylist` directly provides an unpredictable sequence of keys.

## Auto-sorted Associative Arrays

Some implementations of Perl (WinPerl, for example) may have autosorted associative arrays. In these helpful versions, associative arrays are stored and retrieved with their keys arranged in sorted order. This case is not likely to be true for the version of Perl running on your ISP server, so don't skip the following explanation of the `sort` function. This is must-know Perl stuff.

Perl provides a really easy way out of this dilemma. The `sort` function arranges the elements of a normal array in alphabetic (ASCII) order. The syntax is

```
@ordered = sort(@mixedup);
```

where `@mixedup` is a normal array being sorted into `@ordered`. Using this function to dip into my favorite fruit basket results in the following:

```
@fruit = ("Banana","Apple","Pear","Kiwi");
print @fruit, "\n";  # prints: BananaApplePearKiwi
@basket = sort(@fruit);
print @basket, "\n"; # prints: AppleBananaKiwiPear
     # just to check, reprint @fruit
print @fruit, "\n";  # prints: BananaApplePearKiwi
```

The `sort` takes place during the assignment and does not affect the source array.

To get a fruit basket inventory using an associative array `%fruit`, I capture the keys into a normal array and sort them. Then I use the keys to print the inventory from the associative array in an orderly fashion, as follows:

```
%fruit = ("Banana",5,"Apple",2,"Pear",4,"Kiwi",8);
print %fruit, "\n"; # prints: Pear4Banana5Apple2Kiwi8
@basket = sort(keys(%fruit));  # sort and assign
print @basket, "\n"; # prints: AppleBananaKiwiPear
foreach $item (@basket){
   print "$item $fruit{$item}\n";
}
```

The foreach loop uses the sorted keys in @basket to print the fruit list:

```
Apple 2
Banana 5
Kiwi 8
Pear 4
```

### Exercise 4-5

Rewrite the fruit basket example without the step marked # sort and assign. Hint: Move the sort and assign operation right into the foreach statement.

## reverse

The reverse function turns an array upside down, reversing the order of the elements. The syntax is

```
@revlist = reverse(@myarray);
```

Like the sort function, reverse must be assigned to an array variable to hold the output of the function, like this:

```
@fruit = ("Banana","Apple","Pear","Kiwi");
print "@fruit\n";  # prints: Banana Apple Pear Kiwi
@basket = sort(@fruit);
print "@basket\n"; # prints: Apple Banana Kiwi Pear
@unbasket = reverse(@basket);
print "@unbasket\n"; # prints: Pear Kiwi Banana Apple
```

## values

Where you find keys, you will also find values. The values function generates a list of all values in an associative array. The syntax is

```
@valList = values( %array);
```

The @valList array contains the values from %array, but they will not be arranged in a predictable order. I haven't come up with a really good application for this function yet, but maybe you will.

## each

The each function is another review item from Chapter 3 that I'm mentioning here for the sake of completeness. The each function returns a different key/value pair from an associative array every time Perl calls it. The syntax is

```
@pair = each (%array);
```

The @pair normal array retrieves two elements from %array — a key and its value. Exactly which pair of elements is returned is unpredictable. The each function is useful, however, for processing an associative array when the sequence of keys is not important — for example, when the output will be dumped into a database that has its own sorting requirements and tools.

## delete

In an associative array, no front or back end exists, so the push, pop, unshift, and shift functions have no application for associative arrays. Adding elements to associative arrays is easy — just declare a new key in curly braces and assign a value, as follows:

```
$myArray{"new key"} = "Brand new value";
```

What about deleting elements from an associative array? Use delete. The syntax is

```
delete $array{"key"};
```

You can assign the deletion to a variable. The delete function returns the value of the deleted element and deletes both the key and the value from the array, as follows:

```
%fruit = ("Banana",5,"Apple",2,"Pear",4,"Kiwi",8);
print %fruit, "\n";   # prints: Pear4Banana5Apple2Kiwi8
$gone = delete $fruit{"Apple"};
print %fruit, "\n";   # prints: Pear4Banana5Kiwi8
print $gone, "\n";    # prints: 2
```

In most applications, you won't care about the value of the deleted element, so a simple delete statement without an assignment suffices:

```
delete $fruit{"Apple"};
```

# PerlProject: Returning Form Data to the Visitor

The point of writing programs is to produce code that works. To be sure it works, you have to test your programs.

## Local testing

For security reasons, most ISPs require CGI programs to be analyzed before they can be run. Such an analysis can take several days if the ISP is busy or understaffed; hence, program development grinds to a halt without a local testing setup. HyBrowser is designed to test CGI programs locally on your computer without having to hook up to the Internet and transfer files.

### Plugging CGI Security Leaks

Potential security problems resulting from design flaws in CGI programs are the things that go "bump" in the night and disturb the sleep of your ISP's Webmaster. Unlike the intelligent, gentle people who read this book, some Web surfers log on with less than good intentions. Mischief-makers abound on the Web, and they probe for weaknesses in Web site installations. Before approving the installation of your CGI programs, your ISP will check the code for potential programming trouble spots like these:

1. *File creating and writing procedures* — temporary, visitor data, password, log files and like, could be subject to tampering, tinkering, and redirection.
2. *System commands* — any program commands that set or change permissions (`chmod`, `chown`, `chgrp`) need careful scrutiny.
3. *System access* — program calls like `exec` and `system`, or calls to the operating system shell, are immediately under suspicion.
4. *Password visibility* — some Web site designers just don't think (or worse, don't know!) that the visitor has one-click access to the HTML code for the page, including the URLs (and data strings appended to URLs) for CGI programs.

Your ISP will make additional checks, but those listed here are the usual starting points. Be prepared to do some rewriting to make your code acceptable. It's all for your own good!

The procedure for testing with HyBrowser (see Figure 4-9) is as follows:

1. Write the CGI program.
2. Write the HTML page that calls the CGI program.
3. Load the HTML page into HyBrowser.
4. Activate the link to the CGI program (click on the link or use the Submit button to submit a form).
5. Trap the URL call to the CGI program and dump the data to an intermediate file.
6. Run the CGI program to access the file.
7. Load the CGI program's output into HyBrowser.

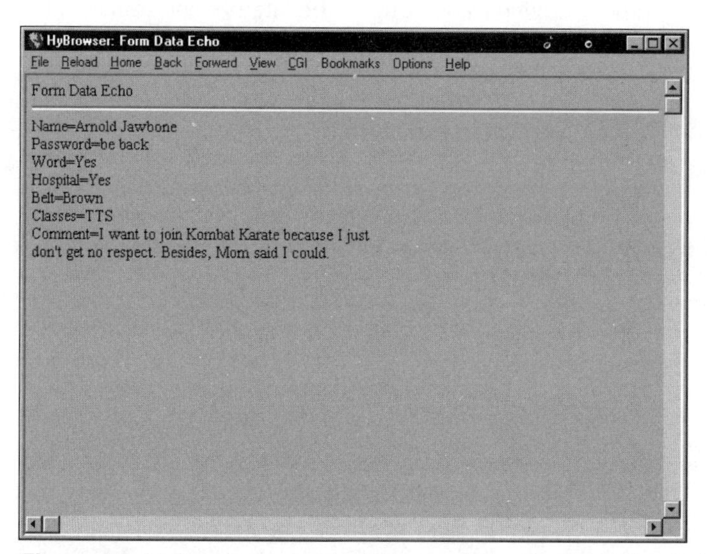


**Figure 4-9:** HyBrowser generates URL-encoded string for testing Perl programs.

Differences exist between the Perl program as-tested and the Perl program as-CGI, but you at least can verify the internal workings and logic of your program in a timely and orderly fashion. I explain how to adjust the Perl script for the testing and runtime variations in the comments within each program that follows.

# Turning your Perl script into a UNIX CGI program

On DOS, you run a Perl script by invoking the Perl interpreter from the command line, as follows:

```
C:\dev> perl listall.pl *.pl
```

You could run Perl the same way in UNIX on your ISP's Web server — if you were sitting at the UNIX workstation, that is. Because you're not sitting there, you must run Perl by remote control. That means you have to teach Perl scripts to run themselves!

In UNIX, certain kinds of program scripts, such as Perl scripts, can be converted from just plain scripts into runnable programs. Performing this magic requires five critical steps:

1. Insert a message inside the script to tell UNIX where to find the interpreter that runs the script.
2. Convert the Perl script to UNIX text. In UNIX, lines terminate with the linefeed character (ASCII 10, called LF). In DOS, the terminating symbol is carriage-return (CR) + linefeed (LF) to make ASCII 13 + ASCII 10 (called CRLF for short).
3. Upload the script to the directory designated by your ISP for your CGI programs.
4. Change the operating mode property of the script so that UNIX knows that the script is almost directly runnable.
5. Change the access rights to the script to enable your Web site visitors to run the script as a CGI program.

Your ISP should provide you with step-by-step instructions and tools for accomplishing these CGI program installation procedures. The following paragraphs tell you what to look for in these instructions.

## Locating and designating Perl's home

The Perl script uses a special comment inserted as the first line in the script to tell the server where to find the Perl interpreter. Your ISP will tell you what directory holds Perl. On my server, Perl resides in the following directory:

```
/usr/local/bin
```

Notice that the directory levels use forward slashes on UNIX platforms and backslashes on MSDOS platforms.

I use this information in my programs to activate the Perl interpreter. The first line in my Perl programs is a comment that references the directory and tells the server to find Perl in that location:

```
#!/usr/local/bin/perl
```

Notice that the comment uses a special format with a `!` bang (exclamation point) after the # comment symbol. UNIX has a magic data file that is used to recognize files. `#!/usr/local/pin/perl` is magic. When UNIX has instructions to run a file, it looks for this hash-bang combination in the first line of the file. This special comment is an instruction to UNIX to find and run the program named in the instruction — and then pass the file along to the target program as a script. In other words, give the job to the guy who knows how to do it. Without this special-format line, UNIX won't find Perl or know that my script is supposed to be runnable, and my CGI programming won't work. A minimal CGI program looks something like Listing 4-4:

**Listing 4-4** **minimum.pl**

```
#!/usr/local/bin/perl
# minimum.pl — HTML test page generator
print "Content-type: text/html\n\n";
print "<HTML><TITLE>Test Page</TITLE></HEAD>\n";
print "<BODY>Rest of page text.</BODY></HTML>\n";
# end of minimum.pl
```

To verify Perl's location, connect to the server via TELNET, and use the `where` command on the UNIX command line (the colon is the TELNET command-line prompt):

```
: where perl
/usr/local/bin/perl
```

## DOS to UNIX

Depending on the services offered by your ISP, you can upload your program and convert it on the server, or you may have to convert it yourself before uploading it.

Many servers have a conversion utility, typically called `dos2unix`, that you can run on the UNIX command line to convert your script line-endings to the UNIX format. With such a converter available, if you have just uploaded `minimum.pl` to your CGI directory, connect via TELNET to the server, navigate to the CGI directory, and call the conversion program (as follows):

```
: dos2unix minimum.pl
```

If you must do the conversion yourself before uploading the program to your ISP, this Perl program can accomplish the task (Listing 4-5).

**Listing 4-5 crlf2lf.pl**

```
# crlf2lf.pl — convert DOS crlf to UNIX lf line-ending
binmode(STDOUT);
while (<STDIN>) {
   chop;
   print "$_\n";
}
# end of crlf2lf.pl
```

The `binmode` function sets `STDOUT` to binary mode rather than standard text mode. In DOS text mode (the default), the newline symbol `\n` is treated as two characters: CR and LF. In binary mode, the newline symbol is treated as just one character: LF. This little program leaves the input (`STDIN`) in text mode, so that `chop` cuts off two characters, but changes the output (`STDOUT`) to binary mode, so that using `\n` only adds one character — the LF needed for UNIX. Try it out with any old DOS text file named any.dos to create any.unx (such as the following):

```
C:\dev> perl crlf2lf.pl < any.dos > any.unx
```

## Uploading via FTP

The FTP route for uploading your Web pages to your ISP is the same one used for uploading CGI programs. The destination directories may be different, however. Typically, the CGI directory is specific for your account and is something like this:

```
www.some.site.com/yourlogin-cgi
```

The specifics may vary for your ISP. After you upload `minimum.pl` to your CGI directory, any calls from HTML links to your CGI program use that directory for the URL, as follows:

```
<A HREF="http://www.yourcompany.com/yourlogin-cgi/
name_of_program">
```

For example, in a Web page on my site, the reference would be

```
<A HREF="http://www.some.site/some-cgi/minimum.pl">
Make my page.</A>
```

### Modifying attributes with chmod and chgroup

Once uploaded and converted for line-endings, your CGI program is almost ready to run. The final step is to set the permissions for your program so that your visitors can enjoy the fruit of your labors. Permissions (access rights) are set from the command line during a TELNET connection. The requirements for your site may be different, but to set the ownership group and permissions and the access mode for `minimum.pl`, I use these commands in a TELNET connection:

```
: chgrp web minimum.pl; chmod 750 minimum.pl;
```

The `chgrp` command sets the group for `minimum.pl`. In this case, `web` is the name of a very large group, all members of which have "read and execute" rights to files assigned to their group. The `chmod` command sets the file's mode from plain old script to fully executable (so UNIX will look for and act on the hash-bang instruction), and fine-tunes the permissions. Both the group and permissions have to be set exactly as your ISP specifies, or your programs won't work and your files won't open when you need them.

### Uploading to ISP for approval

CGI programs can be a doorway to disaster. If they misbehave or allow access to files and programs outside the scope of your account, CGI programs can be source of misery for an ISP. Because of the security issues, ISPs usually require that CGI programs be submitted for analysis and evaluation before they allow you to use them. As I warned before, be prepared for this approval step — it's for your own protection, too.

## Returning form data

The Kombat Karate Interest Survey is useful only if the Karate Master can get his callused hands on the data. You already have the tools to retrieve data with a `mailto:` action. Some browsers don't understand how to handle the `mailto:` action, so you now must enter the world of CGI.

The next program, echo2htm.pl, fixes this problem by parsing the URL-encoded data from a form, minimally formatting the name/value pairs, and writing a simple report in HTML format. The instant the HTML page goes through STDOUT from echo2htm.pl to the server, the server hands over the page to the requesting browser as it would a real file.

To use echo2htm.pl, type it in from Listing 4-6 (or copy it from the CD-ROM), upload the program to the CGI directory on your server after converting the line-ends to UNIX format. Then set the permissions for the program, name the echo2htm.pl as the URL in the komsur2.htm ACTION attribute, and try it out. Here it is, with full explanation following the listing:

**Listing 4-6** **echo2htm.pl**

```
#!/usr/local/bin/perl
# echo2htm.pl -- echo decoded URL string back to requester
print "Content-type: text/html\n\n";                #1
read(STDIN, $formdat, $ENV{'CONTENT_LENGTH'});    #2
print "<HTML><HEAD>\n";                             #3
print "<TITLE>Form Data Echo</TITLE>\n";
print "</HEAD><BODY>\n";
print "Form Data Echo\n";
print "<HR>\n";
@namevals = split(/&/,$formdat);                    #4
foreach (@namevals) {                               #5
   tr/+/ /;
   s/=/ = /;
   s/%(..)/pack("C",hex($1))/ge;
   print "$_<BR>\n";                                #6
}
print "<P><HR>\n";
print "</BODY>\n</HTML>\n";                         #7
```

Notice that the first line of the program is a UNIX-specific comment that designates the path to the server's Perl interpreter. This line may be different for your ISP's server. Here's how echo2htm.pl works (see the corresponding numbers in Listing 4-6):

1. This response header is required when sending a file back to the browser, to alert the browser that this file is an HTML file. Notice the two newlines (\n\n) used to create a blank line between the header and the file itself.

2. echo2htm.pl retrieves the length of the data stream from the CONTENT_LENGTH element in the special %ENV array of CGI variables and then uses that length for the read() function to put the data string into $formdat.
3. echo2htm.pl prints the heading information for the HTML page.
4. echo2htm.pl breaks the name/value pairs out of the $formdat string and inserts them into the @namevals array.
5. This set of statements, from Chapter 3's mail2html.pl, parses the name/value pair to make it readable.
6. Here, echo2htm.pl sends the current string, with its name/value pair neatly formatted, to STDOUT.
7. echo2htm.pl closes out the HTML page.

### Exercise 4-6

Use <PRE> to add more formatting to the name/value pair printout.

In this chapter, you learned the following:

- *Request headers* are information lines sent from the browser to the server.
- *Response headers* are information lines attached by the server to files being returned to the browser. Headers must be separated from the attached file by at least one blank line.
- You can identify MIME (Multipurpose Internet Mail Extension) files moving through the Internet by their specific MIME types and format in a Content-type: notation in the file header.

These functions were introduced for string handling:

- `chop($var)` removes the last character (or two characters if they are CRLF) from a specific string or from every string in an array.
- `index($target, $substring [,offset])` returns the number of characters skipped to find `$substring` in `$target` or –1 if `$substring` was not found.
- `rindex($target, $substring [,offset])` is the same as `index()`, but it works from end of string and returns position of last `$substring` in `$target`.
- `length($var)` returns the length of the string.
- `substr($source, start [, length])` returns substring from `$source`, starting at character number `start` and continuing for `length` characters. With no length designation, returns balance of `$source` from `start` to end of string.

These array functions also appeared in this chapter:

- `chop(@array)` removes the last character (or two characters if they are `CRLF`) from every string in an array.
- `split(/expr/, $var)` returns a list of substrings from `$var`, using the expression in `/expr/` as the substring delimiter.
- `join("str", @array)` returns a string composed of all elements of `@array` joined together with the delimiter `str`.

- `push(@array, list)` adds `list` (a list or single variable) to the end of `@array`.
- `pop(@array)` returns the last element in `@array` and then deletes the element from `@array`.
- `unshift(@array, list)` adds `list` (a list or single variable) to the front of `@array`.
- `shift(@array)` returns the first element of `@array`, and deletes that element from `@array`.
- `sort(@array)` returns sorted copy of `@array`, typically assigned to a new array. Some implementations of Perl have autosorted associative arrays.
- `values(%array)` returns list of values from associative array.
- `keys(%array)` returns list of keys from associative array.
- `each(%array)` returns key/value pair from associative array. In a loop, returns a different pair each time it is called until the array is exhausted.
- `delete $array{$key}` returns value for `$key` from associative array and removes `$key` and `value` from the array.

# Making Web Pages Dynamic

**Skill Targets**

Server-side includes

Subroutines

Libraries

Sending form data through e-mail

"Terminate with message" — the `|| die( )` construct

One of the most exciting ways of using Perl scripts is to make Web pages respond to the visitor. Perl's powerful text-manipulation capability automates many of the production steps and page-generation techniques used for converting bits and pieces of information into dynamic Web pages. In this chapter, I touch lightly on the subject of dynamic pages and then go into more detail than I intended on a non-Perl topic (Server-Side Includes). The PerlFacts section explores subroutines and libraries. The PerlProject brings the mail home — I plug the Kombat Karate Interest Survey into the Internet mail system.

## Types of Dynamic Pages

A dynamic page is one with lively parts (as Figure 5-1 suggests). A page that looks different every time you view it suspends the dulling effect of familiarity. Everyone is geared toward paying attention to things that change, a trait probably derived from a couple million years of experience in sorting out the dynamic, edible parts of the environment from static rocks. Web designers capitalize on viewers' sensitivity to change by including dynamic appetizers (such as Server-Side Includes) or an entire moveable feast (such as custom-tailored forms) in their pages.

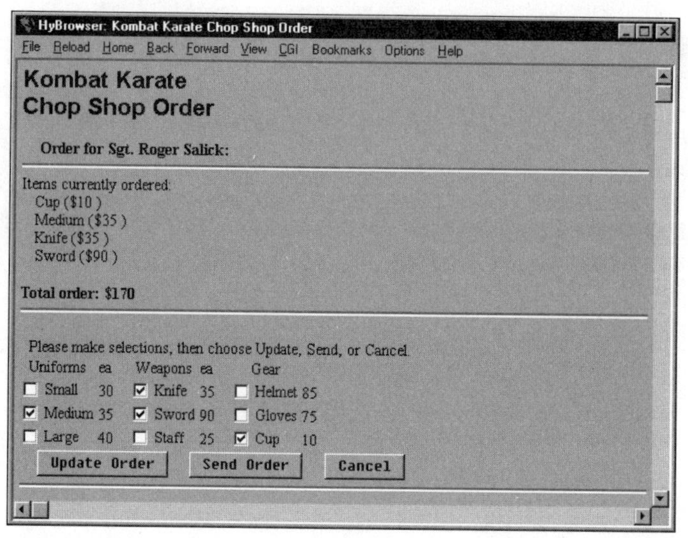


**Figure 5-1:** This order verification page shows additions to the viewer's shopping cart.

## Query responses

Once upon a time, the only way to communicate with a Web site (aside from clicking on anchor links) was with a query. A special tag called `<ISINDEX>`, located in the `<HEAD>...</HEAD>` section of the HTML document, triggered the browser to activate a one-line text input field, which usually appeared somewhere in the browser's window border. The visitor typed a couple of keywords in the field and pressed Enter, which then prompted the browser to URL-encode the keywords, append them to the URL, and send them off to the server for processing (Figure 5-2).

This process was similiar to the task that a one-line form performs with `METHOD=GET`. These days, a one-line form can do the same job by using the `METHOD=POST` procedure that we already understand. Because a form has much greater flexibility and enjoys a look and behavior that visitors can fully comprehend, I don't use `<ISINDEX>`. In fact, I don't know anyone who still uses `<ISINDEX>`.

If you just can't live without creating an `<ISINDEX>` query page, you'll have to chase down the information in some other source. I would like to help you, but I'm a forms guy.

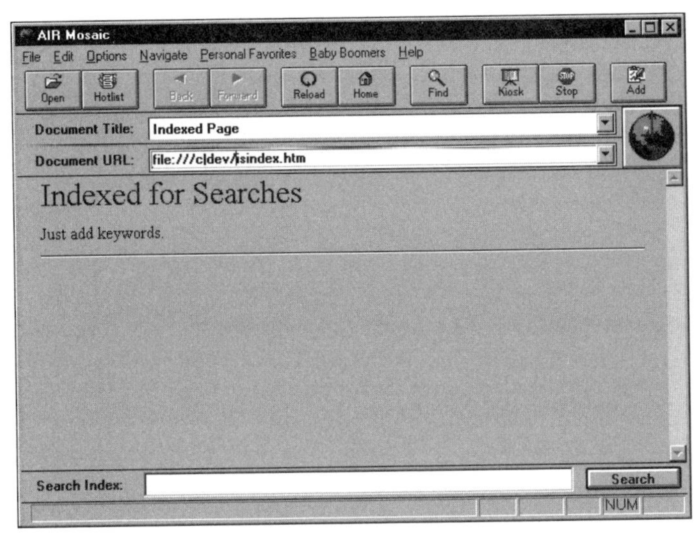


**Figure 5-2:** Some browsers ask for query input with a subtle question line in the lower border of the window.

# Form submit response

Chapter 4's PerlProject, `echo2htm.pl`, was the first baby-step toward using CGI programs for processing HTML form submit requests. I agree, however, that the visitor feedback for a submit request needs to be more elegant than a simple listing of the name/value pairs (see Figure 5-3). You'll find some response enhancements in the PerlFacts section of this chapter.

The design of the response for a form submission depends on the nature of the form, the purpose of the interaction, and the expectations of the visitor. At minimum, the response tells the visitor that the submission was successful. A good response design provides the visitor with options for continuing the interaction (see Figure 5-4), usually by following a link to a main or menu page. Some designs present additional forms that are custom-tailored for the visitor according to the specifics of the data submitted by the visitor from the first form.

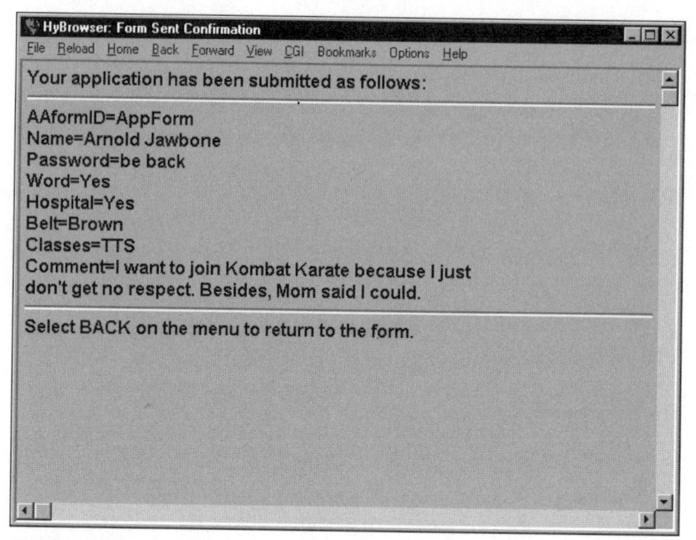


**Figure 5-3:** The brute-force "here's what you sent" feedback technique is easy to program, but it lacks charm.

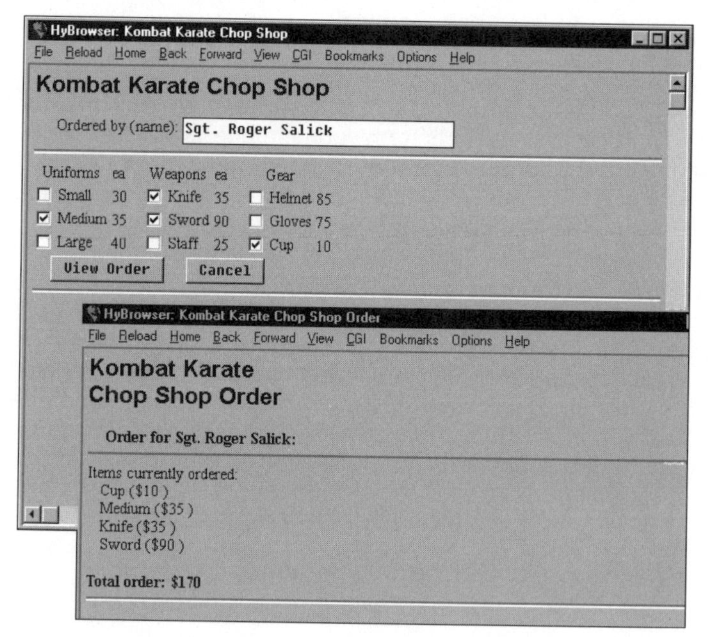


**Figure 5-4:** CGI program generating a second form based on data submitted in the first form in an extended interaction with the visitor.

# Server-Side Includes

*Server-side includes* (SSIs) are HTML commands that work like macros. These commands are specially formatted HTML comments that the server picks up and uses as instructions for inserting information into the HTML script in place of comments.

Usually, HTML comments are in a tag container opened with <!-- and closed with -->, like this:

```
<HTML><HEAD>
<!-- This is a comment -->
<TITLE>My document</TITLE>
```

The special format for SSI instructions adds a hash # to the tag opener. For example, the comment in this line of HTML

```
<P>The current local time is: <!--#ECHO VAR="DATE_LOCAL" -->
```

is replaced with a formatted date-time stamp (as shown in Figure 5-5). When the page reaches the browser's display, the date-time stamp shows up on the screen as if you had manually typed it into the code and uploaded it just a minute ago.

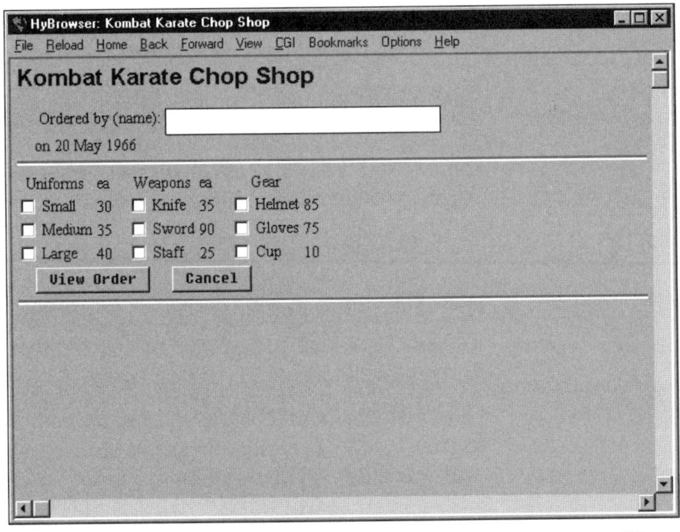


**Figure 5-5:** Date and time data automatically inserted by an SSI command.

## Parsing SSI documents

The use of server-side includes is an option on servers running the NCSA HTTP server software. The server needs a special configuration to enable the SSI option, and SSI documents need special names to let the server know that the document contains SSI codes. The most common naming convention is to use `shtml` for the document type-extension instead of the usual `html`.

When the server fetches a document with the `shtml` extension, it gives the document special handling. To find and operate on server-side includes, the server parses the HTML code, looking for SSI comment tags that begin with `<!--#` . The parsing process slows down file transfers because the file is being read and rewritten rather than just passed along. Even if you have just one SSI command in a large file, the entire file must be parsed. Degraded performance due to parsing accumulates its effect if you have many SSI files. A directory full of files with `shtml` extensions can keep your server busier than a giraffe in a double-rope-jumping contest.

## SSI commands

Table 5-1 shows a roundup of server-side-include commands. An example and explanation follow the summary table. In keeping with the conventions I use in this book, the syntax examples show the code for commands in uppercase. You can use lowercase for command words, however. The spacing of elements in the special comments is critical — no spaces are allowed until after the first command word.

**Table 5-1 Server-Side Include Commands**

| Command | Syntax/Meaning |
|---|---|
| `include` | `<!--#INCLUDE FILE="mynext.html" -->` Inserts the named file in the relative path (current directory, or subdirectory of current directory). |
| `include` | `<!--#INCLUDE VIRTUAL="/incs/myfile.html" -->` Inserts the named file in the path beginning at the root of server directories. |
| `config` | `<!--#CONFIG SIZEFMT="BYTES" -->` Sets the format for file size insertion to bytes, such as `4028`. |
| `config` | `<!--#CONFIG SIZEFMT="ABBREV" -->` Sets the format for file size insertion to kilobytes, abbreviated and rounded off, such as `4K`. |

| Command | Syntax/Meaning |
| --- | --- |
| config | `<!--#CONFIG TIMEFMT="%A" -->` Sets the format for time and date insertions. The quoted element is onc of the templates described in Table 5-2. |
| echo | `<!--#ECHO VAR="DATE_GMT" -->` Greenwich Mean Time |
| echo | `<!--#ECHO VAR="DATE_LOCAL" -->` Local date and time, in local format |
| echo | `<!--#ECHO VAR="LAST_MODIFIED" -->` Main file modification date and timestamp |
| echo | `<!--#ECHO VAR="DOCUMENT_URI" -->` The local path and filename of main file (URI stands for Uniform Document Identifier. |
| echo | `<!--#ECHO VAR="DOCUMENT_NAME" -->` Main filename |
| flastmod | `<!--#FLASTMOD FILE="mynext.html" -->` Inserts the last modification date of the named file in relative path (current directory or subdirectory of current directory). |
| flastmod | `<!--#FLASTMOD VIRTUAL="/incs/myfile.html" -->` Inserts the last modification date of the named file in the path beginning at root of server directories. |
| fsize | `<!--#FSIZE FILE="mynext.html" -->` Inserts the size of the named file in relative path (current directory or subdirectory of current directory). |
| fsize | `<!--#FSIZE VIRTUAL="/incs/myfile.html" -->` Inserts the size of the named file in path beginning at the root of server directories. |
| exec | `<!--#EXEC CMD="pwd ../graphics" -->` Executes the UNIX command in quotes as if it were typed on the command line. |
| exec | `<!--#EXEC CGI="/usr/local/bin/counter.pl" -->` Executes the CGI program in quotes as if it were called from an anchor link (`<A HREF="/usr/local/bin/counter.pl">`). |

Something else that you need to know regarding the echo command is that LAST_MODIFIED, DOCUMENT_URI, and DOCUMENT_NAME are set by the first SSI file that the server parses and do not reflect the status of any files included in that main file.

Table 5-2 shows the various time and date templates that you use with the config command.

**Table 5-2 Time and Date Templates Used with the config Command**

| Template | Format |
|---|---|
| %c | Thu Sep 5 14:30 1996 |
| %a | Thu |
| %b | Sep |
| %X | 14:30:25 |
| %H | 14 (hour in 24-hour format) |
| %M | 30 (minute) |
| %S | 25 (second) |
| %A | Thursday |
| %B | September |
| %Y | 1996 |
| %x | 09/05/96 |
| %m | 9 (number of month in year) |
| %d | 5 (number of day in month) |
| %y | 96 (leaves off the century) |
| %I | 2 (hour in 12-hour format) |
| %p | a.m. (or p.m.) |
| %Z | EST (time zone, Eastern Standard Time) |

Some SSI-enabled sites may have exec disabled for security reasons. Webmasters are uncomfortable with functions that enable UNIX commands to be directly passed down to the command line from a Web connection.

## SSI demo page

Figure 5-6 shows the browser view of a demo SSI page. The code for the page is shown in Listing 5-1. The included page, `sigline.html`, uses the HTML code shown in Listing 5-2. Notice the use of a template string `"%X on %A, %B %Y"` in the `CONFIG` command just before the line that shows `GMT`. The template tokens act like Perl variables in a quoted string.

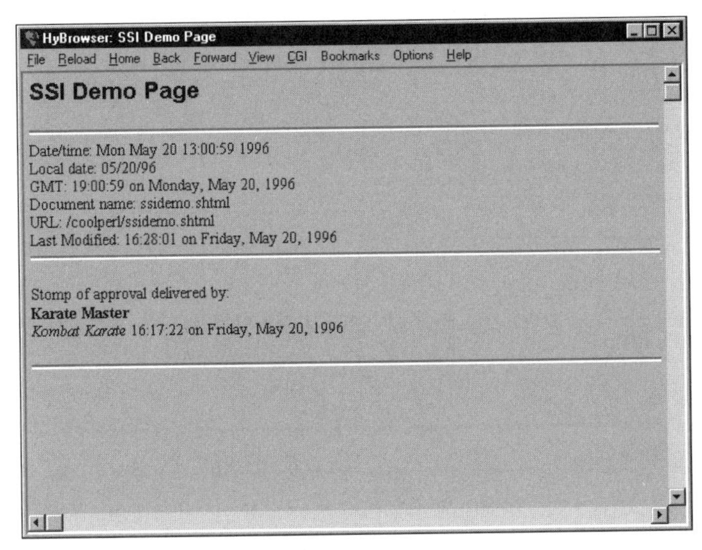


**Figure 5-6:** SSI demo page in browser.

**Listing 5-1** **ssdemo.shtml**

```
<HTML><HEAD><TITLE>SSI Demo Page
</TITLE></HEAD><BODY>
<H1>SSI Demo Page</H1><HR>
<!--#CONFIG TIMEFMT="%c" -->
Date/time: <!--#ECHO VAR="DATE_LOCAL" --><BR>
<!--#CONFIG TIMEFMT="%x" -->
Local date: <!--#ECHO VAR="DATE_LOCAL"--><BR>
<!--#CONFIG TIMEFMT="%X on %A, %B, %d %Y" -->
GMT: <!--#ECHO VAR="DATE_GMT" --><BR>
Document name: <!--#ECHO VAR="DOCUMENT_NAME" -->
URL: <!--#ECHO VAR="DOCUMENT_URI" --><BR>
Last Modified: <!--#ECHO VAR="LAST_MODIFIED" --><BR>
```

*(continued)*

**Listing 5-1 *(continued)***

```
<!--#INCLUDE FILE="sigline.html" -->
<!--#FLASTMOD FILE="sigline.html" --><P>
<HR>
</BODY></HTML>
```

**Listing 5-2 Included File `sigline.html`**

```
<HR>
<P>Stomp of approval delivered by:<BR>
<B>Karate Master</B><BR>
<I>Kombat Karate</I><BR>
```

To run the example, upload Listing 5-1 as `ssidemo.shtml` and Listing 5-2 as `sigline.html` to your ISP account and then point your browser at `ssidemo.shtml`.

**Exercise 5-1**

Write `<!--#CONFIG TIMEFMT=` statements that will produce the following time/date formats:

**A.** Monday, July 1, at 10:00 a.m. sharp

**B.** 1996/Aug/29

# Page Production Methods

Page production is automating, or at least simplifying, the process of generating Web pages. A little polished Perl works wonders for text file automation, but don't discount the power of trusty old cut-and-paste for page production.

## Using templates

Page production based on Perl starts by using templates for the core text of the HTML code. A template is a framework, an overlay structure that gives shape and form to a new production. Using templates gives you a running start on page-building. Listing 5-3 shows a basic template for HTML pages.

**Listing 5-3 Basic HTML Template**

```
<HTML><HEAD><TITLE>
Page title here.
</TITLE></HEAD><BODY>
<H1>Head 1 here.</H1>
Text here.<P>
<HR>
<ADDRESS>
Signature lines here.</ADDRESS>
</BODY></HTML>
```

To use this template, I open a blank page in my HTML editor, copy the template from a file, and paste it into the new page. Then I replace the "something here" text notations with real information and I get an instant Web page (see Figure 5-7).

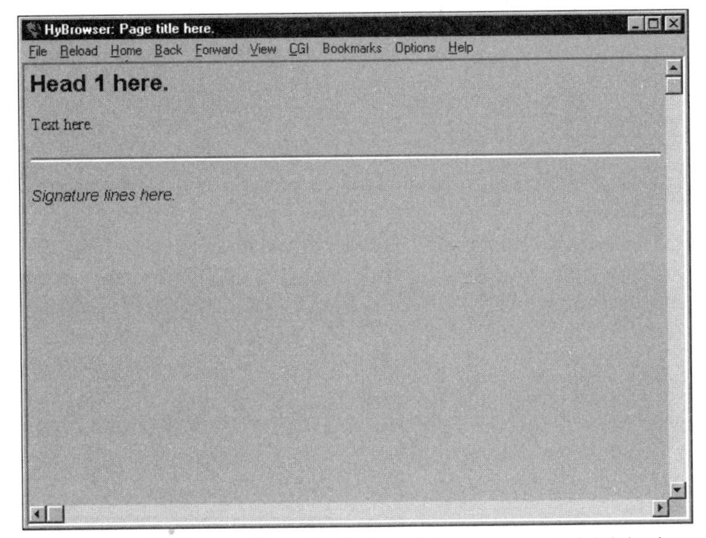


**Figure 5-7:** Web page from basic template — you wouldn't look very pretty in just your bones, either.

After creating several pages with the basic template, I noticed that the copy I use for the signature lines in the `<ADDRESS> . . . </ADDRESS>` block is always the same — same name, same e-mail address for contact, same copyright notice. I wrote those items right into the template (Figure 5-8) in place of `Signature lines here`. Whenever you discover something that crops up repeatedly in your pages, that something is a good candidate for inclusion in your template.

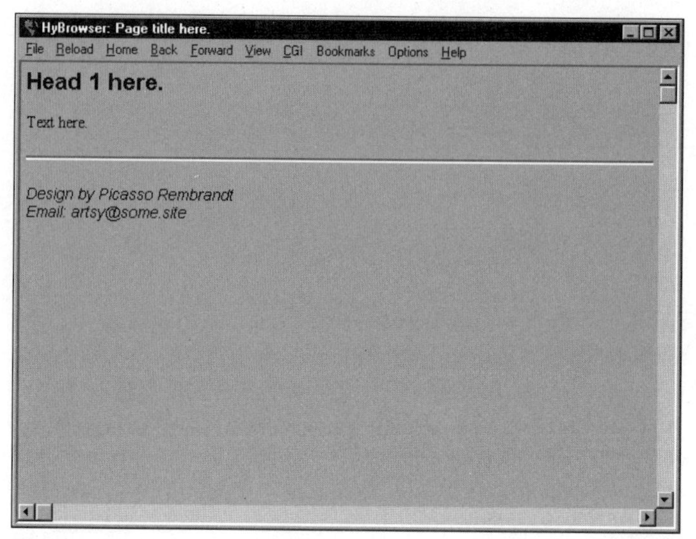


**Figure 5-8:** Enhanced template saves retyping address info for each new page.

## Embedding text

If a template is a quick start, then embedded text is a high-octane fuel additive.

Embedded text (also called *boilerplate*) consists of paragraphs, phrases, instructional snippets, and the like that are so useful, you can't resist copying and pasting them into appropriate spots on your pages. For instance, I use a standard menu bar for the top of long text pages to help the visitor navigate them.

In the boilerplate for the menu bar, every line that appears after the first line begins with a vertical bar and a space and then ends with a space. The last line ends with a space and a vertical bar (Listing 5-4):

**Listing 5-4 Menu Bar for Top of Text Page**

```
<A NAME="top"></A>
| <A HREF="main.html">Home</A>
| <A HREF="contents.html">Contents</A>
| <A HREF="#bottom">Bottom</A>
| <A HREF="p.html">Previous</A>
| <A HREF="n.html">Next</A>
| <A HREF="pindex.html">Index</A>
| <A HREF="phelp.html">Help</A> |
```

To add the menu bar to my page, I paste this boilerplate into the HTML script for the page so that the menu line appears at the top of the page. Then I change `p.html` to the URL of the previous page and `n.html` to the address of the next page, and the menu bar is done. A similar menu bar at the bottom of the page (Listing 5-5) refers to the "top" anchor.

**Listing 5-5 Menu Bar for Bottom of Text Page**

```
<A NAME="bottom"></A>
 | <A HREF="main.html">Home</A>
 | <A HREF="contents.html">Contents</A>
 | <A HREF="#top">Top</A>
 | <A HREF="p.html">Previous</A>
 | <A HREF="n.html">Next</A>
 | <A HREF="pindex.html">Index</A>
 | <A HREF="phelp.html">Help</A> |
```

This time, updating `p.html` and `n.html` consists of a simple cut-and-paste operation, using the corresponding top-menu items as the source for the embedded text. With very little effort (once the embedded text is created and saved), I have a page that looks like Figure 5-9.

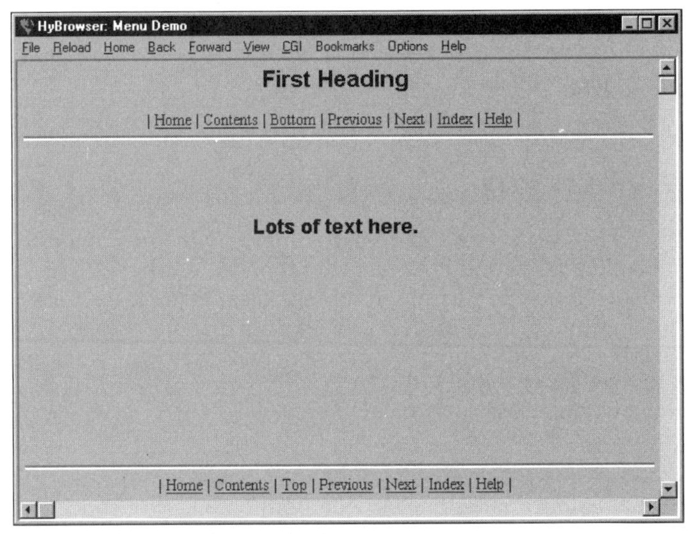


**Figure 5-9:** Boilerplate navigation menus.

Other likely candidates for embedded text are described in the following table.

| Element | Description |
|---|---|
| Prompts for forms | Checkbox and radio button groups sometimes need help, and pop-up selection lists usually need some standard explanation or directions. |
| Submit and Reset | A standard arrangement and button-labeling style is worth preserving and re-using. |
| Table formats | Tables can be tricky to work out — once you have one right, save it as boilerplate text. |
| Inline graphics | Bullets, buttons, and new flags beg for automation. |
| List formats | Lists take work to make them look simple, especially formatted `<DL>` lists that use `<DT><B>Term</B> <DD>Definition` sequences. Preserve the code that makes your lists lovely. |
| Disclaimers | If you've paid good money to have your text legally scrutinized, you don't want to negate the legal impact with an accidental, ad-lib typo. |
| Anything used more than three times | Typing something once is interesting; the second time, it is familiar; by the third time, however, you'll get the idea that you should be using embedded text. |

I accumulate embedded text gems in a reference file and keep that file open in a separate window while I am doing Web work.

## Batch page creation

In the olden days, when I had to do my computing by the glow of a kerosene lamp, database reports and text file generation were done with batch processing. I would get everything set up in tidy bundles, index lists, mark-up tags, and linked files; make sure that no one else needed the computer for the next serveral hours; start the batch process; and go home for supper. The next morning, the whole job would be done — more or less. If any errors were encountered, I'd fix them and re-run the batch.

In today's age of instant gratification, batch processing lost favor. Then along came the Web and its voracious appetite for content, and suddenly batches were cool again.

Suppose that you have a collection of articles or stories or a book, like this one, that you want to publish on a Web site. Are you going to plow though your manuscript and manually type the HTML code for every heading and paragraph of text? No — you're going to automate the operation with word-processing macros and perhaps a Perl program so that it scans the file, inserts tags and embedded text, and creates Web pages by using computer magic. I discuss the details for heavy-duty document conversion methods in a later chapter.

## Real-time page creation

The SSI experiments earlier in this chapter are one example of real-time page enhancement. CGI programs running in Perl raise the ante from the mere embellishment of pages to the generation of forms, pages, and whole sets of linked pages. Database and indexing operations also generate pages in real time with lists of records and URLs for responding to queries. Early experiments in Web page video — using real-time GIF conversions of images from video cameras aimed at bridges, buildings, and campus walkways — have progressed to enable the real-time transmission of rock concerts through the Internet.

Although these tasks are not as ambitious as, say, the real-time presentation of heart surgery instruction, you can accomplish some modest goals by using templates, embedded text, and Perl. These goals include enabling the following:

- Help-file-like answers to queries and Frequently Asked Questions (FAQ)
- Listed URLs for special topic selections
- Hypertext computer-based instruction
- Catalog sheets with items selected specifically for the current visitor, based on size, color preferences, or matching with existing equipment, and so on.
- Anything that be constructed from a "pick one from column A and two from column B"-type of option selections

## <PRE> text versus formatting

For brute-force conversions of text into Web pages, the `<PRE> . . . </PRE>` container is hard to beat. Unless you want fonts and automatic word-wrap, that is.

Simplicity in implementation has a great deal of charm. Because <PRE> preserves the spacing and line-endings of the original ASCII text, all you need for instant Web pages is a formatted ASCII file, an embedded text snippet containing an HTML page header and a <PRE> tag, and another text snippet containing a </PRE> tag and an HTML page close tag.

In some applications, that format provides all that the visitor wants (as in Figure 5-10). In fact, looking for specific information in a word-wrapped, proportional-font formatted table of numbers can be agonizing. A simple typewriter-font arrangement of rows and columns — the format of a <PRE>...</PRE> table — is preferable for financial and other dense numerical data.

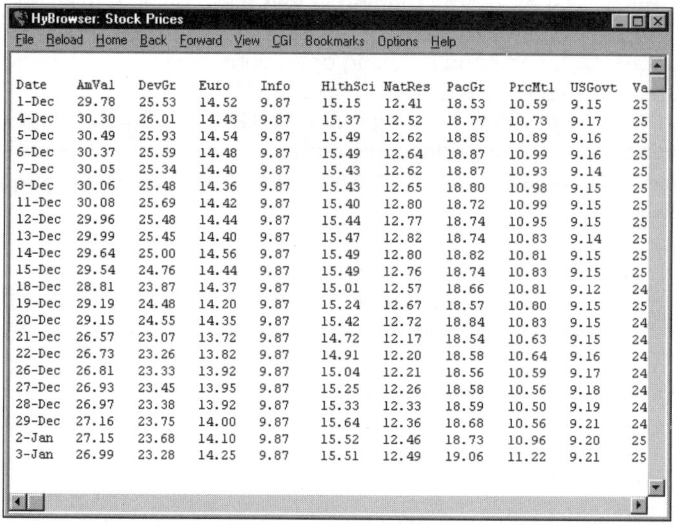

HyBrowser: Stock Prices

File Reload Home Back Forward View CGI Bookmarks Options Help

| Date | AmVal | DevGr | Euro | Info | HlthSci | NatRes | PacGr | PrcMtl | USGovt | Va |
|---|---|---|---|---|---|---|---|---|---|---|
| 1-Dec | 29.78 | 25.53 | 14.52 | 9.87 | 15.15 | 12.41 | 18.53 | 10.59 | 9.15 | 25 |
| 4-Dec | 30.30 | 26.01 | 14.43 | 9.87 | 15.37 | 12.52 | 18.77 | 10.73 | 9.17 | 25 |
| 5-Dec | 30.49 | 25.93 | 14.54 | 9.87 | 15.49 | 12.62 | 18.85 | 10.89 | 9.16 | 25 |
| 6-Dec | 30.37 | 25.59 | 14.48 | 9.87 | 15.49 | 12.64 | 18.87 | 10.99 | 9.16 | 25 |
| 7-Dec | 30.05 | 25.34 | 14.40 | 9.87 | 15.43 | 12.62 | 18.87 | 10.93 | 9.14 | 25 |
| 8-Dec | 30.06 | 25.48 | 14.36 | 9.87 | 15.43 | 12.65 | 18.80 | 10.98 | 9.15 | 25 |
| 11-Dec | 30.08 | 25.69 | 14.42 | 9.87 | 15.40 | 12.80 | 18.72 | 10.99 | 9.15 | 25 |
| 12-Dec | 29.96 | 25.48 | 14.44 | 9.87 | 15.44 | 12.77 | 18.74 | 10.95 | 9.15 | 25 |
| 13-Dec | 29.99 | 25.45 | 14.40 | 9.87 | 15.47 | 12.82 | 18.74 | 10.83 | 9.14 | 25 |
| 14-Dec | 29.64 | 25.00 | 14.56 | 9.87 | 15.49 | 12.80 | 18.82 | 10.81 | 9.15 | 25 |
| 15-Dec | 29.54 | 24.76 | 14.44 | 9.87 | 15.49 | 12.76 | 18.74 | 10.83 | 9.15 | 25 |
| 18-Dec | 28.81 | 23.87 | 14.37 | 9.87 | 15.01 | 12.57 | 18.66 | 10.81 | 9.12 | 24 |
| 19-Dec | 29.19 | 24.48 | 14.20 | 9.87 | 15.24 | 12.67 | 18.57 | 10.80 | 9.15 | 25 |
| 20-Dec | 29.15 | 24.55 | 14.35 | 9.87 | 15.42 | 12.72 | 18.84 | 10.83 | 9.15 | 24 |
| 21-Dec | 26.57 | 23.07 | 13.72 | 9.87 | 14.72 | 12.17 | 18.54 | 10.63 | 9.15 | 24 |
| 22-Dec | 26.73 | 23.26 | 13.82 | 9.87 | 14.91 | 12.20 | 18.58 | 10.64 | 9.16 | 24 |
| 26-Dec | 26.81 | 23.33 | 13.92 | 9.87 | 15.04 | 12.21 | 18.56 | 10.59 | 9.17 | 24 |
| 27-Dec | 26.93 | 23.45 | 13.95 | 9.87 | 15.25 | 12.26 | 18.58 | 10.56 | 9.18 | 24 |
| 28-Dec | 26.97 | 23.38 | 13.92 | 9.87 | 15.33 | 12.33 | 18.59 | 10.50 | 9.19 | 24 |
| 29-Dec | 27.16 | 23.75 | 14.00 | 9.87 | 15.64 | 12.36 | 18.68 | 10.56 | 9.21 | 24 |
| 2-Jan | 27.15 | 23.68 | 14.10 | 9.87 | 15.52 | 12.46 | 18.73 | 10.96 | 9.20 | 25 |
| 3-Jan | 26.99 | 23.28 | 14.25 | 9.87 | 15.51 | 12.49 | 19.06 | 11.22 | 9.21 | 25 |

**Figure 5-10:** <PRE> formatting for tables — sometimes the simple solutions are the best.

# PerlFacts: Subroutines and Libraries

Functions such as `print` and `index` are convenient to use. Each has a job to do: `print` performs an output action on an amazing variety of objects and collections, and `index` does some minor pattern matching and reports where it found the pattern. To combine these tasks into a new job, you must write a series of statements that go through one step after another. To repeat the new job later in the program, use the same steps by copying and pasting them into the right place.

After several repetitions, you have chunks of identical code scattered throughout your program, as in the code snippet shown in Listing 5-6:

**Listing 5-6 Code Snippet with Repeated Procedures — *not recommended!***

```
print "\n";
$i++;
print "$fname[$i] $lname[$i]\n";
print "$addr[$i]\n";
print "$city[$i], $state[$i] $zip[$i]\n";
print "\n";
$i++;
print "$fname[$i] $lname[$i]\n";
print "$addr[$i]\n";
print "$city[$i], $state[$i] $zip[$i]\n";
print "\n";
$i++;
print "$fname[$i] $lname[$i]\n";
print "$addr[$i]\n";
print "$city[$i], $state[$i] $zip[$i]\n";
print "\n";
$i++;
```

Perl doesn't care and runs repetitious code just fine. But suppose that you come up with an improvement for that procedure and want to update the program? Now you have search through the program to find and repair every instance of repeated code. If you miss even one, you end up with a very hard-to-find bug.

For that reason, subroutines and libraries are better ways to repeat code usage.

## User-defined functions: subroutines for all seasons

The functions in Perl are pre-defined: `index` is already there for you to use. A *subroutine* is a user-defined function. You write the code that makes the function work and then give the new code a name that identifies it as a subroutine. Subroutine names are marked with the ampersand (`&`) so Perl can determine which functions are Perl-defined and which are user-defined. You can use the subroutine just like a regular Perl function: Call it by name, feed it something to work on, and watch it to produce useful results.

The following example is a familiar snippet that uses `index` to perform a conversion task:

```
$myMonth = "Apr";
$months = "JanFebMarAprMayJunJulAugSepOctNovDec";
$monthNum = (index($months, $myMonth) + 3) / 3; #moNum = 4
```

I have a program that uses this code in several places to return the number of a month from its abbreviation. To use it, I copy the code, change `$myMonth` to the current need, and retrieve the mystery number from `$moNum`. That constitutes a great deal of work, however. I'd rather do the job once and be done with it. I need a function that works like this:

```
$month = moNum($myMonth);
```

No `moNum` function exists in Perl, so I'll write my own and call it `&moNum`.

## Formatting a subroutine

Although you can use a subroutine several times in a program, the actual code only appears once. The reserved word `sub`, followed by the name of the new user-defined function, defines the subroutine declaration as follows:

```
sub moNum
```

Notice that no ampersand appears in the function name yet. The ampersand marker calls the function from somewhere else in the program. The subroutine definition uses the unadorned name for the function.

The code for `moNum` follows in a block defined by curly braces:

```
sub moNum {
   $months = "JanFebMarAprMayJunJulAugSepOctNovDec";
   $monthNum = (index($months, $myMonth) + 3) / 3;
}
```

Now the subroutine defined by `sub moNum` is ready to work. To use it, call the subroutine by its working name, `&moNum`, anywhere in the program.

Subroutine code is isolated from the program flow. Perl reads the subroutine and interprets the code but doesn't actually execute the statements just yet. Because of the protected isolation, program flow automatically skips over subroutine blocks wherever they appear in the code. You can scatter subroutines throughout the program or collect them all at the front of the program and it wouldn't make any difference to Perl. Perl finds each subroutine, interprets it, and has it ready to fire when called, no matter where it is located.

I like to bunch all subroutines at the end of program. If I have a large number of subroutines, I organize the bunching in alphabetic order so that I can easily keep track of them.

So far, so good. The new subroutine looks official, but it needs a way to accept data so that I can tell `&moNum` which month to look up and calculate.

## Using global values in a subroutine

Variables in Perl are global variables. By global, I mean "everywhere," of course. If you use `$myMonth` in line 3 and again in line 147 of your program, the variable is the same `$myMonth`. If you change `$myMonth` in line 3, the `$myMonth` in line 147 will reflect that same change.

This "globalness" feature applies to subroutines, too. Global variable changes pass right through the picket fence of curly braces surrounding a subroutine declaration. Thus, if you change `$myMonth` in line 3, Perl applies the same change to `$myMonth` in the subroutine `&moNum`. Therefore, one way to easily pass information in and out of a subroutine is to set the value of a variable outside the subroutine and use that same variable inside the subroutine. Then pick a variable that receives a value inside the subroutine and use that variable on the outside to find out what happened, as in Listing 5-7.

**Listing 5-7 Subroutine &moNum Demonstration**

```
# monum.pl -- sub returns month number
$monthNum = 1;         # testing... set value to 1
$myMonth = "May";      # assign value to $myMonth
&moNum;                # uses $myMonth to calculate $monthNum
print $monthNum;       # new value: 5, was changed in sub
sub moNum {
   $months = "JanFebMarAprMayJunJulAugSepOctNovDec";
   $monthNum = (index($months, $myMonth) + 3) / 3;
}
# end monum.pl
```

The steps for using global variables with subroutines in `monum.pl` are clear:

1. Assign a value to `$monthNum` as a test.
2. Assign a value to `$myMonth` outside of the subroutine.
3. Call up `&moNum` to start the subroutine code. The subroutine calculates a new value for `$monthNum` by using the value in `$myMonth`.
4. Check for the results by printing `$monthNum`.

Relying on global variables to communicate with a subroutine works and is great for particular applications, but it also produces some side-effects. First, you are restricted to using the exact variable names used within the subroutine. That fact sends you searching through your code to make sure that you have everything exactly right. Second, you are prohibited from using the subroutine's variables anywhere that could accidentally affect the results of subroutine calls from somewhere else. That restriction sends you searching through your code again.

## Receiving function values through `return`

The data hand-off mechanism for subroutines is the reserved word `return`. The `return` function takes a value and passes it back as an assignable value to the statement that called the subroutine. The syntax is

```
return val;
```

where `val` is either a variable such as `$monthNum` or a literal value such as "1" or "All done."

To use `return` in `&moNum`, hand over the month number stored in `$monthNum`, using the line shown in boldface:

```
sub moNum {
   $months = "JanFebMarAprMayJunJulAugSepOctNovDec";
   $monthNum = (index($months, $myMonth) + 3) / 3;
   return $monthNum;
}
```

Now that `&moNum` returns a value, you are free to use any variable you want to receive the results of the month-to-number conversion. For example

```
$myMonth = "May";            # assign value to $myMonth
$a = &moNum;                 # uses $myMonth to calculate $monthNum
print "$a\n";                # prints: 5
print "$monthNum\n";         # prints: 5 (global in &moNum)
$myMonth = "Sep";
$b = &moNum;
print "$b $a $monthNum\n" # prints: 9 5 9
$myMonth = "Dec";
print &moNum, "\n";          # prints: 12
print "$b $monthNum\n";      # prints: 9 12
```

The `return` function also can report on errors. The trick here is to use `return` more than once and give it a different value each time, as follows:

```
sub moNum {
   $months = "JanFebMarAprMayJunJulAugSepOctNovDec";
   $monthNum = (index($months, $myMonth) + 3) / 3;
   if ($monthNum < 1) { # index failed, $monthNum = 2/3
      return 0;
   } else {
      return $monthNum;
   }
}
```

The `return` function is a shortcut out of the subroutine. No matter how convoluted the subroutine is, when Perl runs into a `return`, it grabs the `return` value and leaves immediately. The rest of the subroutine is not executed.

To use the error-reporting version of `&moNum`, assign the function to a variable and test the result, such as follows:

```
$myMonth = "July";
$vacation = &moNum;
if ($vacation > 0){
   print "SmyMonth = $test\n";
} else {
   print "$myMonth is no good -- try again.\n"
}
```

Notice that this version still requires you to preload $myMonth with some value for &moNum because the input value for the user-defined function depends on the global variable $myMonth.

## Implied return

User-defined functions return a value even if no specific return statement exists. The return function is implicit. If you leave it out of a subroutine, Perl fills in the blank for return with the value of the last statement evaluated in the subroutine. The last evaluated statement does not necessarily mean the last statement in the subroutine — more specifically, it means the last statement touched by Perl before falling out or jumping out of the subroutine. For instance

```
sub moNum {
    $months = "JanFebMarAprMayJunJulAugSepOctNovDec";
    $monthNum = (index($months, $myMonth) + 3) / 3;
    if ($monthNum < 1) { # index failed, $monthNum = 2/3
        $noGood = 0;
    } else {
        $goodCall = $monthNum;
    }
}
```

The if-else block provides the way out of the subroutine. If $monthNum is less than 1, Perl evaluates $noGood = 0; and leaves the subroutine. The last statement evaluated is $noGood = 0; and the value for an assignment statement is whatever passes over the equal sign. In this case, that value is 0. The variable doesn't matter — it just holds the value, and the value is what Perl takes. On the other end, the calling statement receives a 0 from the subroutine.

If the variable doesn't matter, can I just use the assignment value by itself? Yes. I also can use a variable that already has a value, such as $monthNum in this modified example:

```
$monthNum = (index($months, $myMonth) + 3) / 3;
if ($monthNum < 1) { # index failed, $monthNum = 2/3
        0;
    } else {
        $monthNum;
    }
```

## Should I Use an Implied or a Specific Return?

The preferred Perl idiom is to use the implied rather than the specific `return` because using a specific `return` function is a bit slower than just going home after evaluating the last statement. Although the implied `return` is a slick trick, it also can cause you grief if you misjudge which statement is the last one evaluated in a subroutine. The easy way out is to specify a `return` while you are testing and experimenting and then go back when your code is solid and change each `return` to an evaluated statement. Just make sure that the exit out of the subroutine still returns the value you expect.

## Local variables for subroutine input

The opposite of global is local, at least for computer languages. The *local function* creates a list of variables that only apply to a certain subroutine. The syntax is

```
local(list);
```

where `list` is a single variable or array or a whole series of them. Each variable in the list belongs, heart and soul, to the subroutine. If the same variable name appears outside the subroutine, the outside variable is independent of the local variable. Any changes made outside the subroutine do not affect local variables inside the subroutine.

### Creating local variables

To make the variables in `&moNum` local, list them in a `local` function just after the `sub` name declaration:

```
sub moNum {
   local($months, $myMonth, $monthNum);
```

Now `$months`, `$myMonth`, `$monthNum` are local to `&moNum`. If a `$months` variable is located elsewhere in the program, it has nothing to do with the `$months` in `&moNum`. For instance

```
$monthNum = 5;
$test = "Feb";
$a = &moNum(test);
print $monthNum;  # prints: 5
```

The external, global $monthNum variable kept its value, even though the $monthNum variable inside the subroutine was changed. These variables are two different entities who just happen to have the same name. Perl keeps local variables sorted from any would-be, identical-name twins and, like George Foreman with his four sons named George, always knows which one is which.

## Passing values to local variables with @_

Because local variables are private and protected from outside influences, how do you talk to them? Perl has a special gateway for passing values to subroutines: the @_ array.

The @_ array does for function parameters what @ARGV does for command-line parameters. The @_ array collects the values passed to a subroutine, keeps the values in a list, and dishes them out when you ask for them. For instance, I send May out to &moNum like this:

```
$test = &moNum("May");
```

This one-element list arrives at &moNum as the only element in @_. That means $_[0] holds "May". The following statement

```
$a = $_[0];
```

assigns "May" to $a.

### $_[0] Does Not a $_ Make!

There may be a strong family resemblance, but $_[0] is not the same as $_ .

$_[0] is an element of the @_ array, which holds a list of values passed as parameters to a subroutine.

$_ is still the old, familiar variable that refers to the current line (or most recent line read in from a file).

Perl has a lot of close calls like this. Thus, attention to detail is a high-priority item on the list of programmer attributes.

I can rewrite &moNum to assign an incoming value to $myMonth:

```
sub moNum {
   local($months, $myMonth, $monthNum);
   $myMonth = $_[0];    # the first parameter
   $months = "JanFebMarAprMayJunJulAugSepOctNovDec";
   $monthNum = (index($months, $myMonth) + 3) / 3;
   if ($monthNum < 1) { # index failed, $monthNum = 2/3
      0;
   } else {
      $monthNum;
   }
}
```

Finally, &moNum works like a real Perl function, with parameters passed in parentheses. I can use any variable or string I like to send a parameter and any variable to receive the result:

```
$a = "Jun";
$brideMo = &moNum($a);          # $brideMo holds 6
$coldMo = &moNum("Feb");        # $coldMo holds 2
$hotMo = &moNum("A"."u"."g"); # $hotMo holds 8
```

## Passing multiple values to subroutines

All of the normal (for Perl!) array assignment and manipulation tricks work for passing parameters to variables in a subroutine:

- One element at a time:

  ```
  $a = $_[0];
  $b = $_[1];
  $c = $_[2];
  ```

- Batches of elements (if there are fewer receiving variables in the list than there are parameters in @_, the extra parameters are thrown away):

  ```
  ($a, $b, $c) = @_;
  ```

- Processing loops:

  ```
  foreach $item (@_) {
    $a += $item;
  }
  ```

- Total array assignment:

```
@basket = @_;
```

- String assembly:

```
$fruitCompote = join("+",@_);
```

- Combine local declaration with assignment:

```
local($petTrick) = @_;
```

- Compound variable and array assignment:

```
local($head, @tokens) = @_;
```

**Exercise 5-2**

Write a subroutine that accepts two strings — a first name and a last name, in that order — and returns one concatenated name string in last name, comma, first name sequence.

## Subroutines as building blocks

Because the variables in a subroutine can be isolated with the `local` function, subroutines can be copied from one program and pasted into another. A well-armored subroutine will perform its expected mission regardless of who is at the helm or how seaworthy the craft is. You are free to use any variable names required by the subject of your program without being concerned about possible side-effects running rampant in your subroutines.

Constructing programs with subroutine building-blocks has an important beneficial effect on maintenance cost and effort. If a bug crops up in the logic of the procedures in a subroutine, fixing it in one place instantly fixes the bug everywhere you use the subroutine.

# Libraries

Subroutines are internal program building blocks. User-defined functions usually appear in the program listing toward the end of the program but still in the same script.

*Libraries* are external program building blocks that live outside the program but operate as if they were actually part of the code. A library is a script with a tether, and a good library can be a lifesaver on a rope.

## Attaching libraries with the require function

A library is a separate, standalone piece of Perl code with statements, comments, and subroutines. You can copy the code from the script and paste it into your program, but you don't have to. Libraries are attachable. You hook a library to your program simply by expressing your intentions in a `require` function and then acting as though everything in the library — all the statements, global variables, subroutines, and clever programming you didn't have time to invent — is actually wired right into your program.

The syntax is

```
require ("myLib.pl");
```

where `myLib.pl` is a Perl script separate from your program but available on your computer.

After Perl finds a `require` function, it locates the requested library file. Then, as part of the interpreting process, Perl compiles and executes the library file. The signal for successful execution is a non-zero return value from the library. Like subroutines, libraries in a require function return a value from the last executed statement. If no returned value exists or if the value is zero, the `require` function has failed, and Perl terminates the entire program with an error message.

Often, a library file is a collection of subroutines. If no processing is taking place, how does the library return a non-zero value? The easiest way to return a non-zero value is to have it evaluate as 1. The following framework is `toss.pl`, a fictitious library file of monetary subroutines:

```
sub heads {
  ... # code here
}
sub tails {
  ... # code here
}
1;
```

The return value is the 1 right at the end: `1;` is the last statement evaluated. The `require` statement in a program that uses `&heads` and `&tails` such as:

```
require("snake.pl");
```

receives a non-zero value where the "1" is evaluated and the library installation succeeds. Now the program can flip between `&heads` and `&tails` with impunity and parameters.

## Creating libraries

I suggested earlier that repeated code sequences are good candidates for creating subroutines. Moving to the next higher level, repeated subroutines are good candidates for creating libraries.

Some people favor collections of small libraries that contain just one to a few related subroutines in a file. Other Perl libraries — such as those containing document conversions and formatting routines — are huge, often several times larger than the programs they support. Size is not nearly as important a consideration as useability. Access to a few elegantly crafted and throughly tested libraries can save hundreds of hours of programming.

To create your own libraries, build files of your favorite subroutines with copy-and-paste sweeps through your scripts. I like to use subroutines that are as isolated as possible from side-effects by `local` functions that cover every variable and array in the subroutine. If any overlooked global variables are hiding in the subroutine code, they usually make themselves known during a critical demonstration to an important client. Clients are reluctant to forgive programmers who accidentally modify values in a remote corner of a program by using the name of a global variable in an unprotected subroutine.

Be sure to make the new libraries available to your programs. When working on your own machine, simply put the libraries in the same directories with the programs or in a `/lib` directory that you can call by pathname. On the Internet Service Provider's setup, libraries and CGI programs are stored in different locations. Check with your ISP for any special handling needed to get your programs connected to your libraries. Some things to watch out for are potential naming conflicts. For example, most ISPs already have a file called `cgi-lib.pl` or something close to that. Thus, if you name *your* library file `cgi-lib.pl`, you may run into access problems. Which of the two files with the same name actually gets called depends on the directory-search priorities defined in the system's configuration. Avoid potential naming conflicts by checking your ISP's library resources first.

## Finding libraries

Perl is free, and so are many Perl libraries. The Web sites listed on the CD-ROM file `sources.htm` provide links to libraries to start you on your search. These library sites contain descriptions of what's available for Perl libraries, what platforms and configurations are required to use them, and where you can find more. Libraries are available for CGI applications, database work, text and book formatting, and all kinds of scientific and engineering reports — models are available for virtually anything you may want to do. Figure 5-11 provides an example.

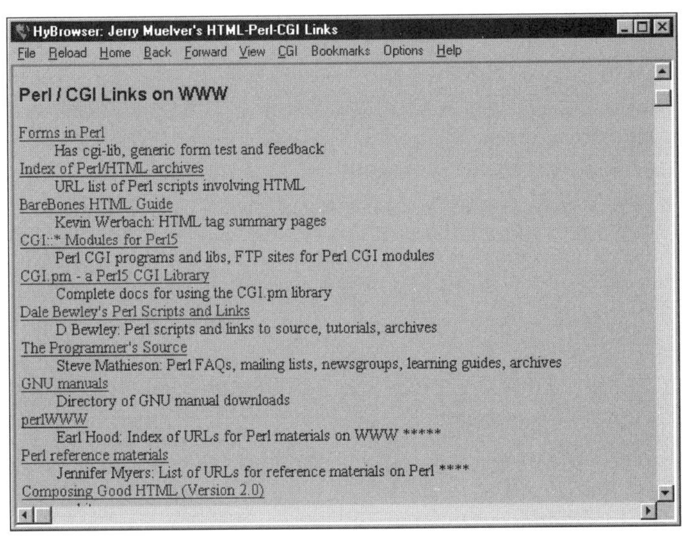


**Figure 5-11:** Partial listing of links to Perl library sources on the Web from the Perl Resource page at `http://www.hytext.com/coolperl`.

A visit to the Web search sites can yield lists with thousands of script titles. Alta Vista requires some refinement in your search request — use the advanced query entries. Yahoo! has specific catagories from which you can start your search. Take a look at `http://www.yahoo.com Computers_and_Internet /Languages/Perl/`.

# PerlProject: Automating Form Data Return

This project refines the data formatting and reporting tools for Kombat Karate's Interest Survey form. The program `frm2mail.pl` parses the data, returns a formatted report to your e-mail address, and reports the successful submission to the visitor.

## Setting up on the server

This project uses the Internet mail program on your ISP's server to send a message directly to your Internet e-mail address. The basic setup procedures are the same as they were for the echo2htm.pl program in Chapter 4. Note that you must copy komsur03.html to a new file, komsur04.html, and edit it to point the ACTION attribute to the new CGI program. To do that, follow these steps:

1. Edit frm2mail.pl to insert your own e-mail address.
2. Upload the program (converted to UNIX text format if needed) to the appropriate directory on your ISP's server.
3. Set the chgrp and chmod attributes for the program file.
4. Verify that the first-line #!/usr/local/bin/perl is correct for your server.
5. Copy komsur03.html to komsur04.html for editing on your computer. Edit komsur04.html and verify that the ACTION attribute for komsur04.html is properly set for the path to frm2mail.pl. on your ISP's equipment.
6. Upload the programs, make chmod adjustments as needed, and test komsur04.html.

## Error logs

Servers have *error logs;* Figure 5-12 shows an example. Every time something goes wrong in a program or file transaction, the operating system makes a note about the problem in an error log. The logs for your Web site may be available to you directly by TELNET — they certainly are available to your ISP's Webmaster. My error log is located in the ~/logs directory. To access it, I connect to it by TELNET, navigate to the ~/logs directory, and issue a cat error.log command (cat is UNIX's type command). All of my programming sins of omission and commission for the past few weeks scroll before my wondering eyes.

Perl communicates with the error logs, too. Messages to STDERR are routed into the logs. A peek in the log reveals messages such as the following:

```
Literal @mysite now requires backslash at /usr/local/cgi/
somesite/frm2mail.pl line 4, within string
syntax error at /usr/local/cgi/somesite/frm2mail.pl line 25, near
"print"
Execution of /usr/local/cgi/somesite/frm2mail.pl aborted due to
compilation errors
```

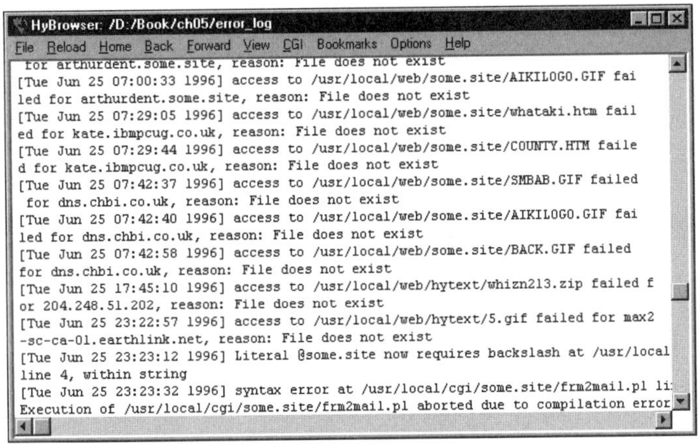

```
HyBrowser: /D:/Book/ch05/error_log
File Reload Home Back Forward View CGI Bookmarks Options Help
 for arthurdent.some.site, reason: File does not exist
[Tue Jun 25 07:00:33 1996] access to /usr/local/web/some.site/AIKILOGO.GIF fai
led for arthurdent.some.site, reason: File does not exist
[Tue Jun 25 07:29:05 1996] access to /usr/local/web/some.site/whataki.htm fail
ed for kate.ibmpcug.co.uk, reason: File does not exist
[Tue Jun 25 07:29:44 1996] access to /usr/local/web/some.site/COUNTY.HTM faile
d for kate.ibmpcug.co.uk, reason: File does not exist
[Tue Jun 25 07:42:37 1996] access to /usr/local/web/some.site/SMBAB.GIF failed
 for dns.chbi.co.uk, reason: File does not exist
[Tue Jun 25 07:42:40 1996] access to /usr/local/web/some.site/AIKILOGO.GIF fai
led for dns.chbi.co.uk, reason: File does not exist
[Tue Jun 25 07:42:58 1996] access to /usr/local/web/some.site/BACK.GIF failed
for dns.chbi.co.uk, reason: File does not exist
[Tue Jun 25 17:45:10 1996] access to /usr/local/web/hytext/whizn213.zip failed f
or 204.248.51.202, reason: File does not exist
[Tue Jun 25 23:22:57 1996] access to /usr/local/web/hytext/5.gif failed for max2
-sc-ca-01.earthlink.net, reason: File does not exist
[Tue Jun 25 23:23:12 1996] Literal @some.site now requires backslash at /usr/local
line 4, within string
[Tue Jun 25 23:23:32 1996] syntax error at /usr/local/cgi/some.site/frm2mail.pl li
Execution of /usr/local/cgi/some.site/frm2mail.pl aborted due to compilation error
```

**Figure 5-12:** TELNET session showing an error log.

These messages tell me that I forgot to escape the `@` with a backslash in the e-mail address in `frm2mail.pl` and that I had a syntax error in line 25 (which turned out to be a missing semicolon), after which Perl gave up in despair and aborted the execution of my flawed program. I fixed what the log said was broken, uploaded the program again, and enjoyed the little rush of success that comes from winning a battle with a finicky computer.

## New function: do or `die`

File access is a chancy exercise, especially in the CGI situation where you are out of touch with the command line and have to rely on error-free code to do the work. If the code is not error-free, a report on what went wrong is critical to the recovery process. Perl tries to tell you why the program quit when something went wrong, but sometimes the messages are cryptic and misleading. For example, if the program quits because of a file-access problem, you have to know more than `Reason: file does not exist.`

The drastic-sounding `die` function, when hooked to a file-access operation, terminates the program immediately and fires a message into `STDERR` if the file operation fails. As the following syntax example shows, you determine what the message is:

```
die ("my error message");
```

You can use `die` in an `if-else` block because `open` returns a non-zero result when it succeeds:

```
if open(FHANDLE, "todays.tmp") {
   ... # do some file-reading...
} else {
   die "Can't open file todays.tmp\n";
}
```

However, the special or-else operator (||) is the more common idiom for Perl. In this snippet, || means "open the file successfully, or else the program terminates with extreme prejudice and a helpful message," such as the following:

```
open(FHANDLE, "todays.tmp") ||
   die "Can't open file todays.tmp\n";
```

For even more detail, leave the newline `\n` off the message string. When `die` sends out a message with no newline on it, Perl adds the program name and the line number, such as in the following example:

```
open(FHANDLE, "todays.tmp") ||
   die "Can't open file todays.tmp";
```

If `todays.tmp` file is missing or being used by someone else, the program quits and the reason appears on the monitor:

```
C:\dev>Can't open file todays.tmp at catorder.pl line 22
```

The message from `die` goes to `STDERR`, which is the screen unless you redirect error output. On the ISP's server, `STDERR` in CGI programs goes to the error log file.

## Returning form data via e-mail

This project's program, `frm2mail.pl`, uses the same URL string-parsing procedures from Chapter 4's `echo2htm.pl`. This time, the name/value pairs print into the body of an e-mail message. Using the server's mail facilities directly has four advantages over returning form data via a `mailto:` action statement:

- frm2mail.pl works for all visitors. The mailto: technique is browser-specific, and not all browsers can send form data through mailto: .
- frm2mail.pl enables your page to provide feedback to the visitor. The mailto: technique, when it works, does its work silently, providing no feedback to the visitor.
- frm2mail.pl program arrives parsed and formatted any way you like it. The mailto: technique sends data that must be parsed and formatted after it is received.
- frm2mail.pl protects the visitor's security. Because the server does the mailing, the only information transmitted from the visitor is what the visitor has put into the form. The mailto: technique users the visitor's mail facilities and transmits the visitor's e-mail address if that information is set up in the browser configuration.

To use frm2mail.pl after you have installed it in the CGI program directory for your Web site, name the program in the ACTION attribute for the <FORM> tag in a page, like this:

```
<FORM  ACTION="http://www.some.site/cgi-bin/frm2mail.pl"
METHOD="post">
```

Listing 5-8 shows the code for frm2mail.pl. This a remarkably simple program, considering that it receives and parses form data, and sends both an e-mail message and HTML page.

**Listing 5-8** **frm2mail.pl**

```
#!/usr/local/bin/perl
# frm2mail.pl -- return form data via e-mail
# your e-mail address goes here -- be sure to
# escape the @ with a backslash -- \@
$e-mail = "me\@some.site";                           #1
read(STDIN, $formdat, $ENV{'CONTENT_LENGTH'});      #2
open(MAILOUT, "| mail $e-mail") ||                  #3
   die "Can't start mail program.";                 #4
@namevals = split(/&/,$formdat);                    #5
foreach (@namevals) {
   tr/+/ /;
   s/=/ = /;
   s/%(..)/pack("C",hex($1))/ge;
   print MAILOUT "$_\n";                            #6
```

*(continued)*

**Listing 5-8 *(continued)***

```
}
close(MAILOUT);                                         #7
print "Content-type: text/html\n\n";                    #8
print "<HTML><HEAD>\n";                                 #9
print "<TITLE>Form Data Sent</TITLE>\n";
print "</HEAD><BODY>\n";
print "<H3>Form Data Sent</H3>\n";
print "<HR>\n";
print "Your completed form was delivered.<BR>\n";
print "Click the browser's BACK button to return.\n";
print "<P><HR>\n";
print "</BODY>\n</HTML>\n";
# end of frm2mail.pl
```

To help you understand how `frm2mail.pl` works, I identified the steps the program goes through in the preceding example and explain them in more detail here:

1. Set the e-mail address for your address in this line.
2. Retrieve the length of the data stream from the `CONTENT_LENGTH` element in the special `%ENV` array of CGI variables and then use that length for the `read()` function to put the data string into `$formdat`.
3. Open a filehandle (`MAILOUT`) to communicate with the server's mail program. The vertical bar (|) in front of `mail` is a UNIX pipe symbol. This statement opens the connection between the filehandle and the mail program so that data sent to the filehandle goes into the mail message. In this form, the message goes out with nothing on the Subject line. To add a subject to the message, use the `-s` with the subject in escaped quotes, like this:

   ```
   open(MAILOUT, "| mail -s \"Hot Form Data\" $email") ||
   ```

4. The `die` function, which is connected to the file `open` operation by the or-else operator (`||`), terminates the program if `mail` won't connect.
5. The URL-encoded string parsing starts here.
6. The `print` function sends the string to the mail message via the filehandle `MAILOUT`.
7. Tidy up and close the filehandle.

8. Print the heading information for the HTML page to report back to the visitor. A really cool technique is to place this MIME heading line at the top of the script, so debugging messages and print commands anywhere in the program script will be sent back to the browser.

9. Format and send the feedback page.

## Summary

This chapter talks about the following:

- The syntax for declaring subroutines is

```
sub mysub {
      ... # statements
   }
```

- The syntax for calling subrountines is

```
&mysub;
   $var = &mysub;
   $var = &mysub($var1, $var2...);
```

- `return()` returns value to calling statement

- In subroutines with no specific `return()`, or an implied `return()`, the value of the last statement evaluated is return to the calling statement.

- `local()` declares variables as local, or private, to the subroutine.

- The `@` denotes a special array that contains a list of parameter values sent to the subroutine by the calling statement.

- The format of libraries is standard Perl script without Perl interpreter location comment.

- Libraries typically contain a collection of subroutines.

- You can include libraries in a main Perl program with a require("filename") function. Successful inclusion is indicated by the require function receiving a non-zero value. The library file should have a final statement that evaluates to non-zero, like 1;.

- `die()` is a new function that terminates program and sends a message to `STDERR`. If the message does not have a newline, die adds the program name and line number to the message.

- Another new function introduced in this chapter is the `||Or-else` operator. Used for file operations. If the file operation fails, the statement after the or-else || operator fires. Mostly used for connecting die functions to file open operations.

- Another new function, the UNIX pipe command | mail, directs program output to mail program.

# Working with Data

**Skill Targets**

- Manipulating sequential files
- Building database information from HTML form data
- Accessing databases to answer queries via HTML
- Generating reports from a data file

An estimated 16 billion pages of information are sloshing around the Internet. Putting up information on a Web page, however, does not necessarily mean that you've done anything useful. Information is worthless if no one can use it.

Perl is a great tool for creating Web front ends to databases. You can start small and simple right on your computer, get the system working, add enhancements one at a time, and finally upload a viable database system to your Web site. In this chapter, I discuss database concepts and techniques and show you ways of implementing data storage and manipulating data in Perl.

Other database topics exist that I don't cover or even look at in this book. Remember, this book is intended for people who want to try their hand at using Perl to create cool Web pages. That means the focus is on do-it-yourself solutions, which may be exciting for the Web hobbyist or adventurist entrepreneur, but not quite the right cup of tea for a Director of Corporate Information Services for North America.

## Databases: The Server Realities

Accessing databases on the Web is not as straightforward as accessing the address book, financial records, or stock listings you may have on your computer. When you are the only one running the program, all the resources of your computer are at your disposal. On a Web server, however, resources are spread among a dozen, a hundred, or even a thousand visitors at a time. I have trouble with resource overload when I'm on the phone and the doorbell rings at the same time. Imagine directing Internet traffic at one of the giant Web search sites such as Yahoo! or Alta Vista, which can have a million hits per day!

## Interfacing and databasing

When two or more users are playing with the same database at the same time, someone has to wait for his or her turn. For example, if Mary is editing the Leeds Card Shop account record, no one else can get into that account until Mary completes her task and sends the record to the file (Figure 6-1). To prevent user collisions from destroying the database or corrupting it with uncoordinated changes, the software puts a lock on the accessed record (or, more likely, on a whole page or block of associated records) so that only one person can access a particular record at a time. This locking-reading-writing-unlocking process may happen very fast (taking only 10 or 20 milliseconds), but it still occurs.

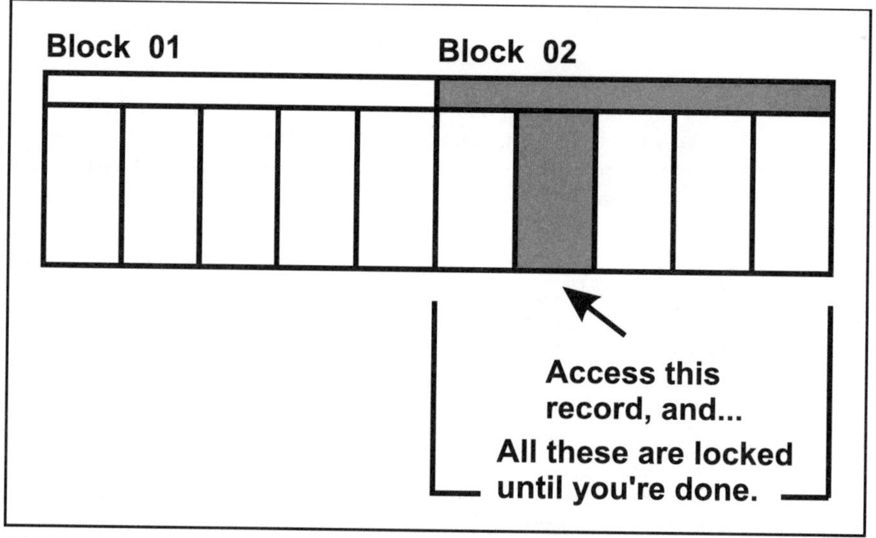


**Figure 6-1:** Database records are locked to prevent multiple simultaneous access.

Web sites present some scary challenges to the database designer. Data on the Web is not passed back and forth through a dedicated, constant-flow channel. Rather, it is tossed through space. Web connections are not continuous. I request a document, and the server sends it. After that, the server thinks it is done with my request and goes off to find a document for some other user.

Meanwhile, the browser puts the connection on "ignore" status while I read the document, find what I want, and click on a link to make another request. To the server, this click represents a whole new transaction. In fact, my browser effectively makes a new connection with the server and starts the relationship all over again (Figure 6-2).

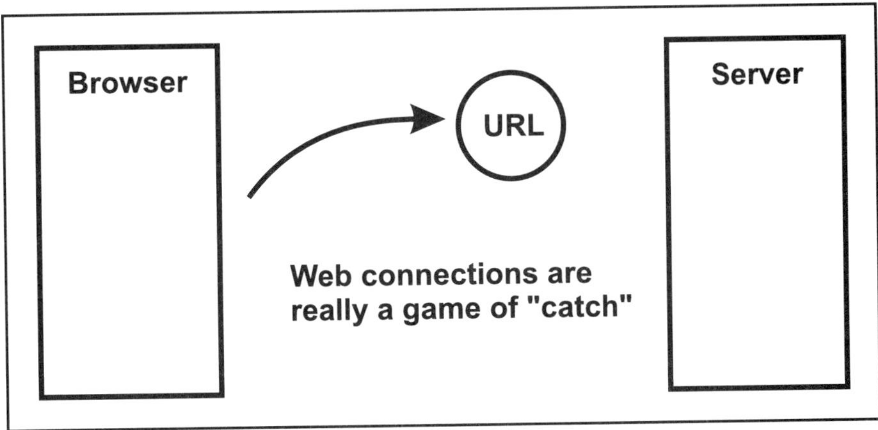


**Figure 6-2:** Web connections are made up of discrete chunks, not continuous conversations.

These intermittent-connection characteristics of the Web make it largely unsuitable for transaction-intensive database applications.

Consider this scenario: What if I make a request to get a record, and the server passes the record to me and locks up a chunk of the file to protect my ownership? Then suppose I get a phone call. The caller tells me the circus is in town and that the parade is just starting. I run out the door. The server keeps my record locked for me. When I come back hours later, the monitor is in screen-save mode, and I just turn off the computer. The server waits a week for me to get back to it. Eighty-five people succumb to malnourishment while waiting for their turns at the database.

There's trouble, folks, right here in River City.

## Oracle, Sybase, and their heavy-metal kin

Only slightly scaled down from their mainframe corporate and enterprise ancestry, database systems by Oracle and Sybase and their ilk are at the top of the data-munching heap. But I'm a realist. I know it's unlikely (all right, unthinkable) that you — as creative, gifted, and motivated as you must be to have gotten this far in the book — would be invited to whip up some Perl scripts that access the corporate database unless you already are part of the crew that builds and maintains the database. If that is the case, however, you already know that Oracle, Sybase, and all others in that class provide tested, proven tools for accessing their databases from the Web or from Web-like Intranet connections (Figure 6-3).

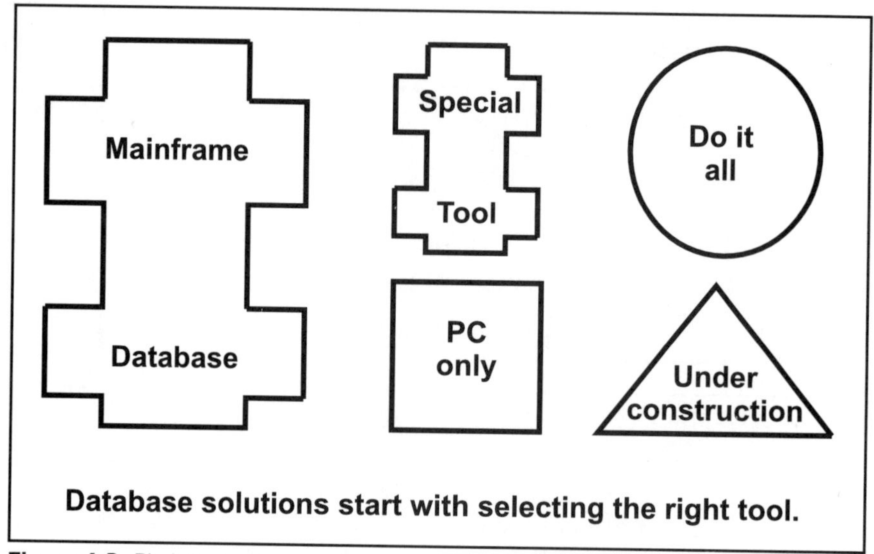


**Figure 6-3:** Big-iron database tools work with specialized scripts.

The Web connection tools for the corporate databases, more often than not, consist of very high-tech Perl libraries with complicated process-management and database security subroutines. I use the very same Perl in this book to start with, but here I'm aiming my sights a little closer — showing how to create homebrewed databases for the up-and-coming, midnight Web adventurer who likes to write the tools personally in order to understand the technology better.

## SQL and Perl

*Structured Query Language* (SQL) is the language database people use to talk to huge, corporate databases. SQL has reserved words and functions like Perl, but these terms are specialized for database applications. The data engines on UNIX and mainframe computers have SQL interpreters built-in. In fact, even desktop database programs such as Access, FoxPro, dBASE, and others understand SQL commands.

Simple SQL statements are easy to understand with a minimum of coaching. The basic SQL operators use boolean logic for juggling file, table, and field names to find and update records by performing searchs with operators like those shown in this partial list:

| Operator | Example | Result |
|---|---|---|
| AND | `Cstate="WI" AND Orders>100` | Select if both conditions are true — select accounts in Wisconsin that have more than 100 orders. |
| OR | `Cstate="WI" OR Cstate="MI"` | Select if either condition is true — select accounts from either Wisconsin or Michigan. |
| NOT | `NOT Cstate="NJ"` | Select if the condition is false — don't select any accounts from New Jersey. |
| =, >, < | `Camount > 500` | Typical comparison operators — select accounts with amounts greater than $500. |

To extract a listing of names and addresses of customers in Wisconsin from a customer database, the SQL statement looks like this:

```
SELECT CName, CAddress, CCity, CState, CZip from Customer WHERE
 CState = "WI"
```

That SQL statement builds a new table of the selected records from the database and presents the table to the query writer in the program's display window (Figure 6-4). Printing a report or labels from the records is another step, which also can be programmed in SQL.

Perl can compose and send SQL commands directly to a program or into a script file for later processing. If you know SQL, you will be able to figure out the Perl to do the job — just use `print` statements to send the commands. If you don't know SQL, the odds are that you don't have a critical need for it at the moment and won't mind my pressing on to other topics.

## Non-UNIX options

Macs, VAX, Wins, and NTs all have Web server software. If your ISP is based on a non-UNIX platform, the database tools come in different flavors, too. You may (and, most likely, will) run into SQL as a database interface option.

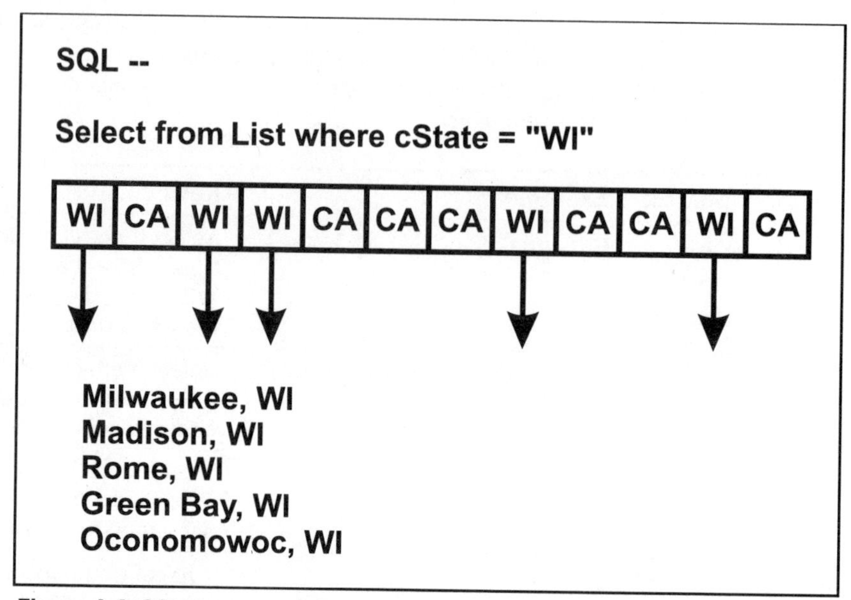


**Figure 6-4:** SQL statement defines which data records are displayed.

All these platforms have Perl available. Contact your ISP to find out about access rights and permissions and the specifics of creating and modifying files for CGI on that platform. Even if you are unable to run database applications on the server, you at least will have the tools to retrieve and transmit queries from your Web pages to your own computer and then process the data there, under your personal control. This "bring home the bacon, then fry it" approach is the one I use in the PerlProject for this chapter.

# Perl's DBM

You may see references in the Perl documentation to `dbmopen` and `dbmclose`, functions that work with the DBM (database management) library implemented on many Perl installations. Because of the intricate installation required to set up and run the DBM library, and because the latest implementations of Perl are pushing to supersede DBM calls with the new `tie()` and `untie()` commands, I consider DBM an advanced topic and won't explore it in this book.

Don't worry — you'll have more than enough to keep you busy with just the sequential and random-access file topics.

# PerlFacts: Handling Data in Sequential Files

Common data process operations apply to any file type — create a file, write to it, close it, open it, read it, and close it again. The reading and writing parts represent most of the challenge. With sequential files, the normal approach is to start at the beginning of the file and read (or write) straight through to the end. Random-access files are designed for hopping and skipping about, with reads and writes occurring anywhere in the file. Each format has advantages and limitations that are best understood by digging in and experimenting with them.

If some of the following material is too basic for you, please skim through it quickly. Many happy computer users are out there who have never worried about data files and records and fields before, and I feel obligated to give them something to worry about.

## Sequential files

Sequential files are typically text files — your basic, human-readable ASCII file. The defining characteristics of text files are (1) that the file is human-readable because it uses normal printable characters only, and (2) that the file formats text in lines by using a newline (CRLF, CR, or LF) at the end of each line (Figure 6-5). Your hard disk is full of text files with extensions such as `.TXT`, `.INI`, `.PL`, and `.HTM`. A text file becomes a sequential data file when you

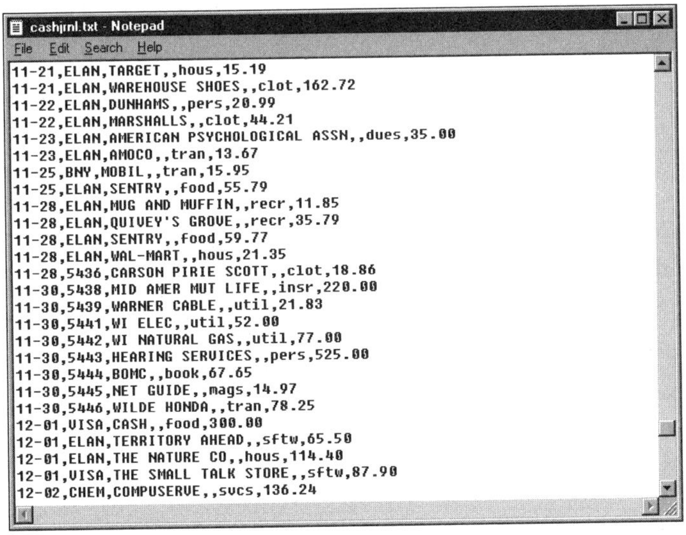

```
cashjrnl.txt - Notepad
File  Edit  Search  Help
11-21,ELAN,TARGET,,hous,15.19
11-21,ELAN,WAREHOUSE SHOES,,clot,162.72
11-22,ELAN,DUNHAMS,,pers,20.99
11-22,ELAN,MARSHALLS,,clot,44.21
11-23,ELAN,AMERICAN PSYCHOLOGICAL ASSN,,dues,35.00
11-23,ELAN,AMOCO,,tran,13.67
11-25,BNY,MOBIL,,tran,15.95
11-25,ELAN,SENTRY,,food,55.79
11-28,ELAN,MUG AND MUFFIN,,recr,11.85
11-28,ELAN,QUIVEY'S GROVE,,recr,35.79
11-28,ELAN,SENTRY,,food,59.77
11-28,ELAN,WAL-MART,,hous,21.35
11-28,5436,CARSON PIRIE SCOTT,,clot,18.86
11-30,5438,MID AMER MUT LIFE,,insr,220.00
11-30,5439,WARNER CABLE,,util,21.83
11-30,5441,WI ELEC,,util,52.00
11-30,5442,WI NATURAL GAS,,util,77.00
11-30,5443,HEARING SERVICES,,pers,525.00
11-30,5444,BOMC,,book,67.65
11-30,5445,NET GUIDE,,mags,14.97
11-30,5446,WILDE HONDA,,tran,78.25
12-01,VISA,CASH,,food,300.00
12-01,ELAN,TERRITORY AHEAD,,sftw,65.50
12-01,ELAN,THE NATURE CO,,hous,114.40
12-01,VISA,THE SMALL TALK STORE,,sftw,87.90
12-02,CHEM,COMPUSERVE,,svcs,136.24
```

**Figure 6-5:** Financial data in a sequential file.

decide to treat it like one by reading it from beginning to end, in sequence. You can open sequential files either for reading or writing (appending counts as writing), but not to do both reading and writing simultaneously.

## Review: file open, read, write

Let's get the cards out on the table before playing the file game. To ante up, Table 6-1 shows a summary of relevant input and output operations. You'll be amazed at how much you already know.

**Table 6-1 File Input and Output Operations Summary**

| Operation | Description |
|---|---|
| <STDIN>; | Read one line from STDIN (keyboard or redirected file). Default line variable $_ holds the line. |
| $a = <STDIN>; | Read one line from STDIN (keyboard or redirected file) into scalar variable. |
| while (<STDIN>) {print;} | Read one line at time from STDIN until reaching the end of the file (or Ctrl-Z if input is from keyboard). The print statement here is only to show some kind of processing. |
| while ($a=<STDIN>) | Read one line at time from STDIN {print $a;} until reaching the end of the file (or Ctrl-Z if input is from keyboard), assigning each line to a scalar variable. |
| while (<>) {print;} | Given a list of list of filenames (or a wildcard token than generates a list of filenames) on the command line and process one file after another, one line at a time. |
| $thisFile = $ARGV; | Assign the name of the current file, when reading files with the while(<>) construct, to the scalar variable $thisFile. |
| while (<"*.txt">) {print;} | Process all files with the extension .txt in the current directory, one line at a time. This substitutes for entering the file descriptor *.txt on the command line. |

**Table 6-1 File Input and Output Operations Summary**

<table>
<tr><th>Operation</th><th>Description</th></tr>
<tr><td>open (MYFILE, "filename.txt");</td><td>Open a file named filename.txt and assign a filehandle called MYFILE. The default mode for a file opened like this is read mode.</td></tr>
<tr><td>open (MYFILE, "<filename.txt");</td><td>Open a file named filename.txt and assign a filehandle called MYFILE. The left-angle bracket sets the file to read mode.</td></tr>
<tr><td>open (MYFILE, ">filename.txt");</td><td>Open a file named filename.txt and assign a filehandle called MYFILE. The right-angle bracket sets the file to write mode. This statement will create filename.txt if it does not exist and will overwrite filename.txt if it exists already.</td></tr>
<tr><td>open (MYFILE, ">>filename.txt");</td><td>Open a file named filename.txt, assign a filehandle called MYFILE. The double-angle bracket sets the file to the append mode. This statement will create filename.txt if it does not exist or append print commands to the file if it already exists.</td></tr>
<tr><td>$a = <MYFILE>;</td><td>Read one line from the file opened and assigned to the filehandle MYFILE. The scalar variable can only hold one object, which limits the read to a single line.</td></tr>
<tr><td>@lines = <MYFILE>;</td><td>Read entire file into the array @lines, one line per array element. The list variable can hold many objects, which allows the reading of multiple lines.</td></tr>
<tr><td>@lines = <>;</td><td>Read all the lines of all the files listed on the command line (or in a command-line wildcard descriptor) into the array @lines.</td></tr>
<tr><td>open(MYFILE,"filename.txt") || die ("Problem opening $filename.txt");</td><td>File error; reports file opening error, terminates program.</td></tr>
</table>

Whew!

## Interface

Perl is a language for manipulating files. The design of the language simply ignores the nicities of screen layouts, buttons, and menus. All user interaction in Perl is boiled down to command-line options, with the occasional possibility of using STDIN for question-and-answer sessions, as in the following example:

```
print "Your name? ";
$myName = <STDIN>;
chop($myName);
print "\nYour age? ";
$myAge = <STDIN>;
chop($myAge);
print "\nYour name is $myName and you are $myAge years old.\n";
```

Bill Gates and the Windows Graphic User Interface design crew have little to fear from Perl.

What can you use as a user interface for sequential files? Whatever you have on hand! Notepad and WordPad on the Windows platform and Edit in a DOS window are free, convenient, and quite adequate to the task of reading and writing text files. I build my data files in Notepad (Figure 6-6), massage them with Perl programs, and reread the results with Notepad (or with WordPad, if the file grows too big for Notepad).

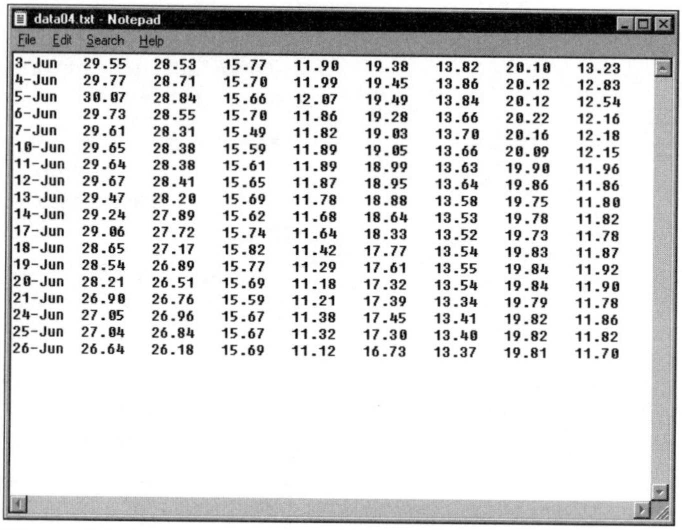

data04.txt - Notepad

File Edit Search Help

| | | | | | | | | |
|---|---|---|---|---|---|---|---|---|
| 3-Jun | 29.55 | 28.53 | 15.77 | 11.90 | 19.38 | 13.82 | 20.10 | 13.23 |
| 4-Jun | 29.77 | 28.71 | 15.70 | 11.99 | 19.45 | 13.86 | 20.12 | 12.83 |
| 5-Jun | 30.07 | 28.84 | 15.66 | 12.07 | 19.49 | 13.84 | 20.12 | 12.54 |
| 6-Jun | 29.73 | 28.55 | 15.70 | 11.86 | 19.28 | 13.66 | 20.22 | 12.16 |
| 7-Jun | 29.61 | 28.31 | 15.49 | 11.82 | 19.03 | 13.70 | 20.16 | 12.18 |
| 10-Jun | 29.65 | 28.38 | 15.59 | 11.89 | 19.05 | 13.66 | 20.09 | 12.15 |
| 11-Jun | 29.64 | 28.38 | 15.61 | 11.89 | 18.99 | 13.63 | 19.90 | 11.96 |
| 12-Jun | 29.67 | 28.41 | 15.65 | 11.87 | 18.95 | 13.64 | 19.86 | 11.86 |
| 13-Jun | 29.47 | 28.20 | 15.69 | 11.78 | 18.88 | 13.58 | 19.75 | 11.80 |
| 14-Jun | 29.24 | 27.89 | 15.62 | 11.68 | 18.64 | 13.53 | 19.78 | 11.82 |
| 17-Jun | 29.06 | 27.72 | 15.74 | 11.64 | 18.33 | 13.52 | 19.73 | 11.78 |
| 18-Jun | 28.65 | 27.17 | 15.82 | 11.42 | 17.77 | 13.54 | 19.83 | 11.87 |
| 19-Jun | 28.54 | 26.89 | 15.77 | 11.29 | 17.61 | 13.55 | 19.84 | 11.92 |
| 20-Jun | 28.21 | 26.51 | 15.69 | 11.18 | 17.32 | 13.54 | 19.84 | 11.90 |
| 21-Jun | 26.90 | 26.76 | 15.59 | 11.21 | 17.39 | 13.34 | 19.79 | 11.78 |
| 24-Jun | 27.05 | 26.96 | 15.67 | 11.38 | 17.45 | 13.41 | 19.82 | 11.86 |
| 25-Jun | 27.04 | 26.84 | 15.67 | 11.32 | 17.30 | 13.40 | 19.82 | 11.82 |
| 26-Jun | 26.64 | 26.18 | 15.69 | 11.12 | 16.73 | 13.37 | 19.81 | 11.70 |

**Figure 6-6:** Notepad — the programmer's database entry tool.

# Record formats

Data files have *records*. Sequential data files have sequential records that run one after the other all the way through the file. The usual *record delimiter* (a character or set of characters that separate one record from another) in sequential files is the newline — ASCII 13+10 in DOS, ASCII 10 in UNIX, ASCII 13 in Macintosh files. In other words, you have one record per line, like those just shown in Figure 6-6.

## Character-delimited

*Fields* are chunks of data that belong to a particular record. A record can have many fields, each separated by some distinguishing character called a *field delimiter*. The ubiquitous comma is a favorite field delimiter for sequential files. For example, the file format I use for my financial records holds data that looks like this:

```
0307,5516,A-1 Mortgage Corp,Mar,mort,350.00
0307,visa,Fred's Cafe,lunch,meal,6.50
0308,5517,Wanda's Foods,party groceries,entr,35.76
```

Each record has the same kind of information in the same position. The fields are set up as:

```
date,number,who,memo,account,amount
```

Dates appear in MMDD format (two digits for month, two digits for day). `number` is a check number or credit card flag. `who` and `memo` are what you usually write on your checks. The `account` field identifies the category for the entry — some of them are mort, util, meal, medi, insr, trvl.

Primitive? I suppose so, if you think colors and boxes and mouse-buttons are essential components for a bookkeeping system. It takes far fewer keystrokes and mouse clicks to enter data in this text-file format, however, than it takes in any of the hi-tech GUI systems I've tried.

When using any delimited format, the delimiters have to be present even if a field is empty. Data programs reading the files use these delimiters to find the fields but also depend on each record to have the right number of fields. Flow-control loops are very finicky about such matters. If a field is empty, the delimiters still have to be there. For example, a car-pooling database may contain people who don't have cars. If you listed the name, vehicle, number of passengers, and availability, the list might look like this:

```
JHenry,Ford,6,open
BHackett,Yugo,4,full
BRubble,,,looking
JBenny,Maxwell,4,no-share
```

Everybody has to have three commas, even if they don't have four wheels.

If any field in a sequential file record could possibly contain a comma, the delimiter should be something else that is not likely to be used in a value. Colons, vertical bars, tabs, and tildes all have appeared as delimiters in files displayed on my screen (Figure 6-7). Tab-delimited fields are popular on the UNIX and VAX platforms. DOS programs like spreadsheet dumps, and text-exports from databases rely more on CSV (Comma-Separated Values), which I explain in the next section.

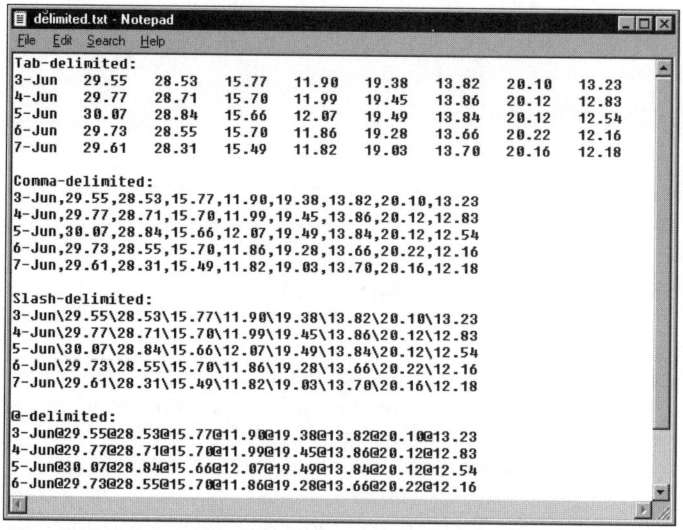

```
delimited.txt - Notepad
File Edit Search Help
Tab-delimited:
3-Jun	29.55	28.53	15.77	11.90	19.38	13.82	20.10	13.23
4-Jun	29.77	28.71	15.70	11.99	19.45	13.86	20.12	12.83
5-Jun	30.07	28.84	15.66	12.07	19.49	13.84	20.12	12.54
6-Jun	29.73	28.55	15.70	11.86	19.28	13.66	20.22	12.16
7-Jun	29.61	28.31	15.49	11.82	19.03	13.70	20.16	12.18

Comma-delimited:
3-Jun,29.55,28.53,15.77,11.90,19.38,13.82,20.10,13.23
4-Jun,29.77,28.71,15.70,11.99,19.45,13.86,20.12,12.83
5-Jun,30.07,28.84,15.66,12.07,19.49,13.84,20.12,12.54
6-Jun,29.73,28.55,15.70,11.86,19.28,13.66,20.22,12.16
7-Jun,29.61,28.31,15.49,11.82,19.03,13.70,20.16,12.18

Slash-delimited:
3-Jun\29.55\28.53\15.77\11.90\19.38\13.82\20.10\13.23
4-Jun\29.77\28.71\15.70\11.99\19.45\13.86\20.12\12.83
5-Jun\30.07\28.84\15.66\12.07\19.49\13.84\20.12\12.54
6-Jun\29.73\28.55\15.70\11.86\19.28\13.66\20.22\12.16
7-Jun\29.61\28.31\15.49\11.82\19.03\13.70\20.16\12.18

@-delimited:
3-Jun@29.55@28.53@15.77@11.90@19.38@13.82@20.10@13.23
4-Jun@29.77@28.71@15.70@11.99@19.45@13.86@20.12@12.83
5-Jun@30.07@28.84@15.66@12.07@19.49@13.84@20.12@12.54
6-Jun@29.73@28.55@15.70@11.86@19.28@13.66@20.22@12.16
```

**Figure 6-7:** Some common field delimiters in action.

## CSV

Spreadsheets and databases offer a text-export format called CSV (Comma-Separated Values). In addition to adding commas between each field, this format adds quote marks around strings, although it leaves numerical values unadorned. The quotes protect any commas or other punctuation embedded in the strings. For example

```
"hammer, ball-peen",12,"Acme"
"pliers, needle-nose",4,"Ace"
```

Programs that import these files have the tools needed to pick out the data from fields. Flavors of Basic (such as Visual, Quick, and Q) thrive on CSV and read and write the format with enthusiasm and verve. I personally don't like CSV because it's a pain to parse. I have to think and experiment to get it right. Give me a clean, comma-delimited data file, and I'll give you a `split(/,/, $myRecord)` without even blinking.

## Line-delimited

A format that allows any and all punctuation in a field is the blank-line delimited file. Each field ends in a newline, and each record ends with a double-newline or a blank line, such as in the following example:

```
Delicious, Red
Red or dark-red skin; bland, crisp white fruit.
Washington

Delicious, Yellow
Yellow or yellow-green skin. More tart than Red Delicious!
Washington

Macintosh
Motorola or PowerPC.
California
```

Blank-line delimited files can run into trouble with empty fields because a blank field is interpreted as a blank line marking the end of a record. Empty fields must have something to hold their place — a space works nicely, although a hyphen is easier to spot on a line than a space when reading the file. Here's a wedding reception dinner list with some guests who haven't decided on their meal:

```
Jones
roast beef
red wine

Johnson
chicken
white wine
```

*(continued)*

*(continued)*

```
Klamath
-
beer

Klein
lobster
champagne
```

Because Klamath has a hyphen for his dinner choice, the database program avoids the awkwardness of hitting a blank line (record delimiter!) where it is expecting to find a field. A blank line here could have ended the record, reset the data scanner to look for a guest's name, and accidentally created a new guest by the name of `"beer"`.

## Tagged-field

Some record formats, like those used in INI files, need more flexibility. The tagged-field format enables a record to hold varying numbers and kinds of fields or even no fields at all. Each field actually is a name/value pair, like the pairs in a URL-encoded string. Each record is marked with a delimiter, which usually is a blank line. The format is perfect for a Perl associative array with the tag in the key and the rest of the field in the value:

```
type:deposit
amnt:1400.00
source:paycheck
type:draft
amnt:1500.00
destination:Rio
type:overdraw penalty
amnt:30.00
```

INI files mark a record by using a left square bracket in the first character position of the line, as in the following `[Extensions]` line. The fields are in a `name=value` format, with one field per line:

```
[Extensions]
crd=cardfile.exe ^.crd
trm=terminal.exe ^.trm
txt=notepad.exe ^.txt
```

The name to the left of the equal sign is the tag for the field. Everything to the right of the equal sign is the value. In this example, the value has two parts — a program name and a template for the filename extension associated with that program.

## Sequential file format summary

The following table summarizes the sequential file formats and their characteristics:

| Type | Rec Delim | Field Delim | Nr Fields | Blank Fields |
|---|---|---|---|---|
| Delimited | Newline | Character | Fixed | Must be delimited |
| CSV | Newline | Comma with quoted strings | Fixed | Must be delimited |
| Blank Delimited | Blank line | Newline | Fixed | Must have character |
| Tagged | Any of the above | Any of the above | Variable | Ignored |

# Extracting and reporting

You've been reading and extracting data from sequential files since Chapter 1, so the process should now be familiar:

1. Open the file.
2. Read one line at a time (or read the entire file into an array with one line in each element).
3. Process the lines (or array elements).
4. Write the line (or processed array) out to a file.

Now roll up your sleeves and dig into some data extraction.

## Extract links from HTML files

Suppose that you have a directory containing a slew of HTML files with HREF tags scattered throughout them, and you now want to generate a manageable list of the links between the files. The process is as follows:

1. Open and read each HTML file.
2. Find each HREF call and copy the URL it contains into a list.
3. Print the filename and the URL-like name/value pairs into a data file.

The first cut at a workable program is a proof of concept. Just open the files, find the URLs, and see what a pattern match looks like. In Listing 6-1, I'm assuming that the URLs listed in an HREF tag are enclosed in quotes, so part of the search pattern looks for the opening and closing quotes.

**Listing 6-1** **listurl1.pl**

```
# listurl1.pl -- print list of URLs from HTML files
while (<>) {
   if (/href=\"(.*)\">/i) {
      print "$ARGV, $1\n";
   }
}
```

I place this program in a directory full of HTML files and run it with the following command:

```
C:\dev> perl listurl1.pl *.htm > listurl1.dat
```

Upon checking the DAT file, I see that it actually works quite well — too well, in fact. First, external sites are included. I only want links between the files within a directory on my computer, not those across the Internet. The pattern `/href=\"(.*)\">/i` picks up every HREF tag, internal and external. Perhaps a non-match with http (`!/http/i`), such as in Listing 6-2, will filter out the external references.

```
bio.html, index.html
cheese.html, http://www.cris.com/%7emsmoo/cheese/
cheese.html, http://www.mei.com/other/mpm/welcome.html
cheese.html, http://www.uwm.educ/~brooklyn/bar.html
cheese.html, http://www.livel.com
cheese.html, http://www.execpc.com/bigscreen
cheese.html, http://www.myp.com
cheese.html, http://nba.starwave.com/bucks
cheese.html, http://www.execpc.com/~jwhouk/admirals.html
chili.html, musthave.html
chili.html, index.html
chili.html, musthave.html
```

**Listing 6-2** **listurl2.pl**

```
# listurl2.pl -- print list of URLs from HTML files
#   excluding HTTP references
while (<>) {
   if (/href=\"(.*)\">/i) {
      if (!/http/i) {
         print "$ARGV, $1\n";
      }
   }
}
```

The results are better — at least the external references are gone. All the external references to cheese are gone, but at least I have my chili:

```
bio.html, index.html
chili.html, musthave.html
chili.html, index.html
chili.html, musthave.html
```

But some of the listings further down the page are odd. For instance, a line with two links in it, like this:

```
<A HREF="#top"> Top </A> | <A HREF="#bottom"> Bottom </A>
```

generates an extended listing, like this:

```
menu.html, #top"> Top </A> | <A HREF="#bottom
```

What I want is:

```
menu.html, #top
menu.html, #bottom
```

I've been snookered by Perl's wildcard over-reach. Instead of stopping at the first quote-angle (`">`) combination in the line, the pattern goes all the way to the last quote-angle it can find. Patterns with wildcard multipliers extend the "anything" match as far as possible toward the end of the string. This over-reach is called the *leftmost longest, or greedy, match*. The star multiplier in the pattern `/href=\"(.*)\">/` means "any number of characters from the equal-sign-quote pair up to the last quote-angle pair in the string," so the pattern reaches past the first quote-angle to look for more quote-angles "> on the same line. What I really need is the *leftmost shortest match.*

## Leftmost longest problem with .* and .+

Patterns with wildcard multipliers find the leftmost longest possible match in a string. For example:

```
$_ = "banana";
/ban/;  print "$&\n";  # ban
/.an/;  print "$&\n";  # ban
/b.n/;  print "$&\n";  # ban
/b.*n/; print "$&\n";  # banan
/.*n/;  print "$&\n";  # banan
/b.*a/; print "$&\n";  # banana
```

How can I get the leftmost shortest — in this case, `ban`— by using a dot-star wildcard?

In Perl 5, use the hook `?` operator as a special stopper, meaning "keep the preceding dot-star as short as possible to make the match." For example:

```
$_ = "banana";
/b.*n/;  print "$&\n";  # banan
/b.*?n/; print "$&\n";  # ban
/b.*a/;  print "$&\n";  # banana
/b.*?a/; print "$&\n";  # ba
```

In Perl 4, however, lines with the `.*?` sequence generate an error message that reads `nested *?/ in line 3` or something similar. The capability to use the hook operator as a leftmost-shortest stopper is a Perl 5 enhancement.

When I need a leftmost shortest match in Perl 4, I set up a loop to test whether I really have the shortest match in the string (Listing 6-3):

**Listing 6-3** **leftmo.pl**

```
# leftmo.pl -- find shortest leftmost match
$a = "banana";
while ($a =~ /b.*a/) {
```

```
    $b = $&;   # store the match, hoping for shortest
    $a = $&;
    print "$a\n";
    chop($a);
}
print "\n$b\n";  # pattern failed, so this is shortest
# end of leftmo.pl
```

The output shows the sequence of reduction:

```
C:\dev> perl leftmo.pl
banana
bana
ba
```

Reformulating the code as a subroutine causes it to evolve into the function in Listing 6-4.

**Listing 6-4** **sub leftmost**

```
sub leftmost {
   local ($a, $pat, $b);
   ($a, $pat) = @_;
   $b = "#"; # return symbol for no-match
   while ($a =~ /$pat/i) {
      $b = $1;   # group within the match
      $a = $&;   # take the longest match
      chop($a);  # cut it down
   }
   $b;
}
# end of leftmost.pl
```

Note that the assignment of `$1` to `$b` in the statement `$b = $1;` means that the subroutine is expecting a parentheses-marked group in the most recently tested pattern. That would be whatever is passed to the subroutine in `$pat`. In the URL search, the pattern `/href=\"(.*)\">/i` provides dot-star in such a group — anything between the quotes following `href=` in a line. To use the new sub in a program, call `&leftmost` with a target string and a pattern string (Listing 6-5).

**Listing 6-5** **testleft.pl**

```
# testleft.pl -- test leftmost sub
$ref = '<A HREF="#top"> Top </A> | <A HREF="#bottom"> Bottom </
A>"';
$urlpat = 'href=\"(.*)\">';  # single quotes to keep literal
while ($url = &leftmost ($ref, $urlpat)) {
   print "found $url\n" if ($url ne "#");
   $ref = substr($ref,index($ref,$url)+length($url));
}
sub leftmost {
   local ($a, $pat, $b);
   ($a, $pat) = @_;
$b = ""Ø;      # return symbol for no-match
while ($a =~ /$pat/i) {
      $b = $1;
      $a = $&;
      chop($a);
   }
   $b;
}
# end of testleft.pl
```

The result follows:

```
C:\dev> perl testleft.pl
found #top
found #bottom
```

Just like downtown.

The next step is to fold this hard-won knowledge into the URL-lisitng program.

## Listing local URLs

All of the fine points have been worked out. The programs in Listing 6-6 and 6-7 build data files showing the HTML filename with each local URL `HREF` tag in the file, in both Perl 5 (with leftmost shortest pattern match) and Perl 4 (with leftmost shortest subroutine).

**Listing 6-6** **listurl5.pl**

```
# listurl5.pl -- print list of URLs from HTML files
#   exclude HTTP references, pick up multiple
#   references on the same line: Perl 5 version
# usage: perl listurl5.pl *.htm > listurl.dat
while (<>) {
   $line = $_;
   while ($line =~ /href=\"(.*?)\">/i) {
      $a = $1;
      if (!($a =~ /http/i)) {
         print "$ARGV, $a\n";
      }
      $line = substr($line,index($line,$a)+length($a));
   }
}
# end of listurl5.pl
```

**Listing 6-7** **listurl4.pl**

```
# listurl4.pl -- print list of URLs from HTML files
#   exclude HTTP references, pick up multiple
#   references on the same line: Perl 4 version
# usage: perl listurl4.pl *.htm > listurl.dat
$urlpat = 'href=\"(.*)\">';  # single quotes to keep literal
while (<>) {
   $line = $_;
   while ($a = &leftmost ($line, $urlpat)) {
      if (!($a =~ /http/i)) {
         print "$ARGV, $a\n";
      }
      $line = substr($line,index($line,$a)+length($a));
   }
}
sub leftmost {
   local ($a, $pat, $b);
   ($a, $pat) = @_;
   $b = 0; # return if no match
   while ($a =~ /$pat/i) {
       $b = $1;
       $a = $&;
       chop($a);
```

*(continued)*

**Listing 6-7** ***(continued)***

```
    }
    $b;
}
# end of listurl4.pl
```

When called with the following command (or `listurl5.pl`)

```
C:\dev> perl listurl4.pl *.htm > listurl.dat
```

the program produces a file with this format:

```
guest.html, #guestform
guest.html, index.html
contract.html, toolbox.html
contract.html, index.html
contract.html, toolbox.html
contract.html, index.html
index.html, bio.html
index.html, musthave.html
index.html, toolbox.html
index.html, octagon.html
index.html, octagon.html
index.html, hops.html
hops.html, index.html
hops.html, #top
hops.html, #top
hops.html, index.html
```

I now have a sequential data file, comma-delimited, with two fields in each record. The data needs at least two clean-up operations: sorting and unduplicating. I don't know if *unduplicating* is a legitimate word yet, but it will be someday.

## Sorting and unduplicating

Computer languages without associative arrays require a file to be sorted before duplicates can be matched and thrown out. The procedure is to sort the elements and then go through and toss out the repeaters — which is easy to do when they are next to each other. Perl can go the other way around and do the dupe removal automatically. If a key assignment to an associative array finds an identical key there already, the old key takes a new value instead of trying to insert a duplicate key. Associative arrays just can't have duplicate keys. Look at what this does for sorting and unduplicating (Listing 6-8):

**Listing 6-8** **srtundup.pl**

```
# srtundup.pl -- sort an input file, remove duplicate records
# usage: perl srtundup.pl <infile >outfile
while (<STDIN>) {
   $dupes{$_} = 1;   # duplicates get overwritten
}
@srtArray = sort(keys(%dupes));
foreach $line (@srtArray) {
   print $line;
}
#end of srtundup.pl
```

Each line from `STDIN` is dropped into the associative array, `%dupes` by the `$dupes{$_} = 1;` statement. If a record already is in the array as a key, the duplicate only serves to reaffirm that the value for that key is 1. All the values for the entire array will be 1. The bogus (actually, place-keeping) values are thrown away when `sort(keys(%dupes))` builds a new, normal array out of the records, sorting them on-the-fly. To do this task, run the program with a redirect in and a redirect out, just like the following DOS `sort` command:

```
C:\dev> perl srtundup.pl < listurl.dat > srtulr.dat
```

Suppose `listurl.dat` starts out like this:

```
guest.html, #guestform
guest.html, index.html
contract.html, toolbox.html
contract.html, index.html
contract.html, toolbox.html
contract.html, index.html
index.html, bio.html
index.html, musthave.html
index.html, toolbox.html
index.html, octagon.html
index.html, octagon.html
index.html, hops.html
```

*(continued)*

*(continued)*

```
hops.html, index.html
hops.html, #top
hops.html, #top
hops.html, index.html
```

After running `listurl.dat` through `srtundup.pl` with the DOS command recommended earlier, the newly created `srtulr.dat` looks much better. The records are sorted, and all the duplicates are removed:

```
contract.html, toolbox.html
contract.html, index.html
guest.html, #guestform
guest.html, index.html
hops.html, #top
hops.html, index.html
index.html, bio.html
index.html, hops.html
index.html, musthave.html
index.html, octagon.html
index.html, toolbox.html
```

My first sort and undupe program, which I wrote 15 years ago on a 64k RAM Apple II, took nearly a half-hour to clean up and sort a list of 50 words. Either I've gotten a lot smarter or computers run a lot faster these days.

## Build a multilevel link table with `grep( )`

Armed with a list of files and links, I now am ready to build a link-list chart to show each file, all of its links, and all links for those links. A *link-list chart* is a tracing tool that helps keep track of the effects of changing links in a file to answer the question, "If I drop this link, what else will be affected?" The chart should look like this:

```
fileA, linkA1
fileA, fileD
    fileD, linkD1
    fileD, linkD2
    fileD, fileC
fileB, linkB1
fileC, linkC1
fileD, linkD1
fileD, linkD2
```

```
fileD, fileC
    fileC, linkC1
```

The procedure for producing the link-list chart is

1. Load the data.
2. For each filename, print the name and a link.
3. If the link is a filename, print the links from the link filename.

The required tools for this process are (1) a normal array containing only the filenames, and (2) a way to find those filenames when they are listed as links. Time for another Perl wonder tool — the `grep` function. Like its UNIX namesake, Perl's `grep` looks for pattern matches, but it searches in an array rather than in a set of files. This marvelous array searcher takes a pattern and an array name and returns a list of matching elements from the array. The syntax is

```
@found = grep(/expr/,list);
```

where `@found` is an array to hold the matches, `/expr/` is a regular expression pattern, and `list` is the array or list to search.

To use `grep` for building a linklist chart, I feed it possible links by splitting the test value from the input line (Listing 6-9). Note that the lines have `chop` applied to them this time because the end part of the string will be used for a comparison, and the appended newline would cause the match to fail.

**Listing 6-9** **linklist.pl**

```
# linklist.pl -- extend the link connections one more level
@links = <STDIN>;
chop(@links);
foreach $lnk (@links) {
   print "$lnk\n";
   ($head,$tail) = split(/, /,$lnk);
   @tolinks = grep(/$tail, /,@links);
   $nrlinks = @tolinks;    # number of links found
   if ($nrlinks > 0) {
      foreach $found (@tolinks) {
         print "    $found\n";
      }
   }
}
```

A fragment from the resulting file follows:

```
toolbox.html, index.html
    index.html, bio.html
    index.html, hops.html
    index.html, musthave.html
    index.html, octagon.html
    index.html, toolbox.html
toolbox.html, #next
toolbox.html, #previous
toolbox.html, process.html
    process.html, index.html
    process.html, toolbox.html
toolbox.html, schedule.html
    schedule.html, index.html
    schedule.html, toolbox.html
```

Internal references (`#next`) stand alone, whereas external references are kicked in a sublist.

### Exercise 6-1

Try these exercises:

A. What pattern will extract external (other site) links only?

B. What pattern will extract image calls?

C. How do you build a reverse listing of images, showing each image file and all pages that use it?

# Updating

Sequential files are contiguous. Because they do not have handy pockets, slots, and subdivisions, you cannot easily dip in and out of sequential files to update a couple of lines here and add a few more in the middle of the file without the danger of overwriting data that you'll wish you hadn't. The traditional approach to updating a sequential file is to rewrite the entire file. Either copy the file one line at a time to a new file with a different name, folding in the changes as you go, or read in the entire file simultaneously and overwrite the old file after the changes have been made.

### FYI — Nice to Know, but Use with Care

The following discussion on editing in-place is more informational than tutorial. For sequential files, I would rather read in one file and write out to a different file than try to do the editing in-place in the same file. In-place editing is a part of Perl that you may see used in your source code explorations, so I want you to know about it. My recommendation is to keep file changes understandable and simple — read from one file and write to another, so that everything remains under your control.

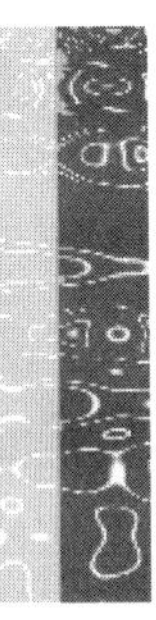

## Editing in-place

The command-line option -i is a step toward automating the sequential file update process. When used with programs processing files with the empty read-file <> operator (empty means <>, not <STDIN>), -i tells Perl to edit the files in-place. Actually, however, the files are not edited in-place — it just looks that way. Perl copies the file to a temporary file, reads in the temporary file, and overwrites the original file during output. You can save the temporary file by using an extension with the -i command. The effect is to create a backup file. The syntax is

```
C:\dev> perl -i .bak myprog.pl file1 file2 file3
```

or

```
C:\dev> perl -i .bak myprog.pl *.ext
```

Assuming that myprog.pl is using the read-file <> operator, the program takes each file in the list or wildcard description in turn, renames the file with a .bak extension, processes the data, and overwrites the old file with new data. The result is an edited file with the old name and a .bak file with the original, unedited data. Using the -i command without the optional extension, as in the following example, does not create any backup files:

```
C:\dev> perl -i myprog.pl file1 file2 file3
```

This version of the command uses temporary files to do the work but creates no backup files. If your program has a bug (it happens, you know), your data may be destroyed, leaving you with no backup for recovery. Therefore, always use the backup option with -i.

## Embedding command-line options in code

Perl scripts running on UNIX need that first comment line to tell the system where to find the Perl interpreter, as in the following example:

```
#!/usr/local/bin/perl
```

The system interprets any additional information in the comment as command-line options. For instance, to use the edit in-place `-i` command, you can embed the command in the code like this:

```
#!/usr/local/bin/perl -i .bak
```

This embedded command-line option has the same effect as this comparable command:

```
C:\dev> perl -i .bak myprog.pl file1 file2 file3
```

Note: The UNIX versions of Perl do not allow a space between the `-i` and the `.bak`, so for embedded instructions intended to run on a UNIX machine, the instruction should be `-i.bak`. On MSDOS, some versions of Perl need a space between `-i` and `.bak`. You'll have to test it to see which way it works for you.

## Invoking in-place editing with `$^I`

Using the in-place option `-i` on the command line actually sets a Perl special variable with the name of `$^I`. When this variable has been set with a value (such as `.bak` or `.000`), Perl activates in-place editing for files coming into the program through the read-file <> operator. The files have the `$^I` value tacked onto their names, and input comes from the renamed files, with output for each file going to a new file with the old file's name. Explicitly defining `$^I` in a program has the same effect. For example, you can change all lowercase <body> tags in a directory's `.HTM` files to uppercase <BODY> tags by using the program in Listing 6-10.

**Listing 6-10** **bodyup.pl**

```
# bodyup.pl -- changes <body to <BODY with in-place editing
# usage: perl bodyup.pl *.htm
$^I = ".bak";
```

```
while (<>) {
   s/<body/<BODY/;
   print;
}
# end of bodyup.pl
```

The command for using the file is shown in the `#usage:` comment.

For instance, I start with a file called `minimum.htm` that looks like this:

```
<html><head>
<title>Title here.</title>
</head><body>
<h1>Heading here.</h1>
<p>Text here.
</body></html>
```

Then I process the file with this command:

```
c:\dev> perl bodyup.pl minimum.htm
```

After the Perl program runs, I check the directory and (in Win95) find two files:

```
minimum.htm.bak
minimum.htm
```

The program created a backup file to preserve the original contents and a new version of `minimum.htm` with these contents:

```
<html><head>
<title>Title here.</title>
</head><BODY>
<h1>Heading here.</h1>
<p>Text here.
</body></html>
```

### Caveat

If you want to experiment with the `-i` command-line option, copy all target files into an experimental directory and have at it. I don't use `-i` for CGI processing for a couple of reasons:

1. Little need exists for in-place file editing in small Web sites.
2. Doing in-place file editing takes too long and gums up the works for multiple users in large, high-volume Web sites.

On my computer, I use in-place editing after thoroughly testing the Perl program. I always — ALWAYS — use the backup option (`-i .bak` or `$^I = ".bak"`) with in-place editing.

# PerlProject: Building a Visitor Database

The Karate Master likes his Web operation so far. Now he wants to take the next step and build a database of prospective students by collecting information from interested Kombat Karate home-page visitors. The design is simple: Ask for the information, feed a Thank You to the visitor, send the information via e-mail, and capture the information from the e-mail messages into a database on Kombat Karate's computer.

## Visitor info form

I pulled the "proof of concept" demo survey into my editor and came up with the form shown in Figure 6-8.

The HTML code in Listing 6-11 shows how the Visitor Info form is put together.

**Listing 6-11 HTML for Kombat Karate Visitor Info Form**

```
<HTML>
<HEAD>
<TITLE>Kombat Karate Visitor Info</TITLE>
<!-- Phase 3 -->
</HEAD>
<BODY>
<H1>Kombat Karate Visitor Info</H1>
<P>If you would like to receive more information about
```

```
Kombat Karate in the mail, please provide your name
and mailing address. If you prefer to call instead,
our phone number is <B>555-1234</B>. Or, visit our
dojo in downtown Osaka.
<FORM  ACTION="http://www.some.sit/some-cgi/frm2mail.pl"
 METHOD="post">
<INPUT TYPE="hidden" NAME="AAFormID" VALUE="Kom6">
<B><PRE>
          First  Mid.Initial   Last
   Name: <INPUT TYPE="text" NAME="Name" SIZE="40" MAXLENGTH="80">
Address: <INPUT TYPE="text" NAME="Address" SIZE="40"
 MAXLENGTH="80">
   City: <INPUT TYPE="text" NAME="City" SIZE="40" MAXLENGTH="80">
  State: <INPUT TYPE="text" NAME="State" SIZE="4" MAXLENGTH="4">
 Zip:<INPUT TYPE="text" NAME="Zip" SIZE="10" MAXLENGTH="10">
  Phone: <INPUT TYPE="text" NAME="Phone" SIZE="13"
 MAXLENGTH="14">
</PRE></B>
How did you hear about us? Check as many as apply:<BR>
<INPUT TYPE="checkbox" NAME="Friend" VALUE="Yes"> Friend  
<INPUT TYPE="checkbox" NAME="Magazine" VALUE="Yes"> Magazine
  
<INPUT TYPE="checkbox" NAME="Paper" VALUE="Yes"> Newspaper  
<INPUT TYPE="checkbox" NAME="Radio" VALUE="Yes"> Radio
<BR>
<INPUT TYPE="checkbox" NAME="Word" VALUE="Yes"> Word of mouth
  
<INPUT TYPE="checkbox" NAME="Dojo" VALUE="Yes"> Saw the dojo
  
<INPUT TYPE="checkbox" NAME="Hospital" VALUE="Yes"> Hospital
reports
<P>What belt rank have you achieved in karate?<BR>
<INPUT TYPE="radio" NAME="Belt" VALUE="None" CHECKED> None  
<INPUT TYPE="radio" NAME="Belt" VALUE="White"> White  
<INPUT TYPE="radio" NAME="Belt" VALUE="Yellow"> Yellow  
<INPUT TYPE="radio" NAME="Belt" VALUE="Orange"> Orange  
<INPUT TYPE="radio" NAME="Belt" VALUE="Green"> Green
<BR>
<INPUT TYPE="radio" NAME="Belt" VALUE="Blue"> Blue  
<INPUT TYPE="radio" NAME="Belt" VALUE="Purple"> Purple  
<INPUT TYPE="radio" NAME="Belt" VALUE="Red"> Red  
<INPUT TYPE="radio" NAME="Belt" VALUE="Brown"> Brown  
```

*(continued)*

**Listing 6-11** ***(continued)***

```
<INPUT TYPE="radio" NAME="Belt" VALUE="Black"> Black
<P><INPUT TYPE="submit" VALUE="Send Info to Kombat Ka
rate">    
<INPUT TYPE="reset" VALUE="Cancel">
</FORM></BODY></HTML>
```

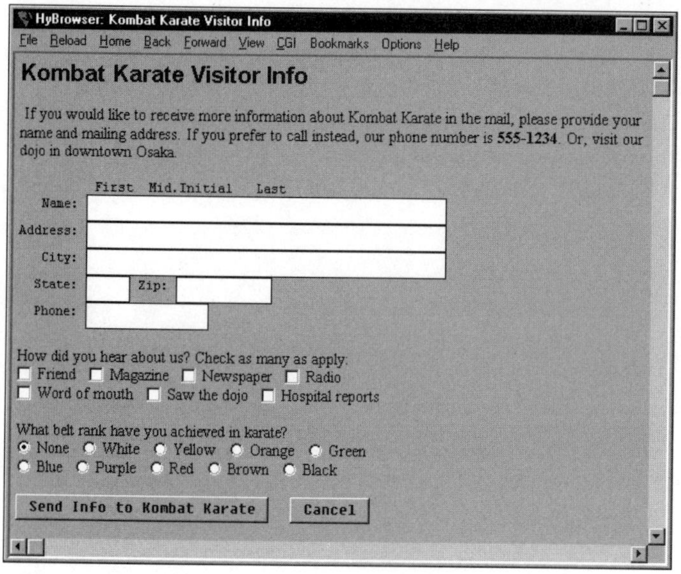

**Figure 6-8:** Kombat Karate Visitor Registration Form.

# CGI processing for visitor info

The first step in CGI processing is to collect the form data and send it on its way via e-mail. The second step is to run a program that builds a database by reading data from the collected e-mail messages.

## Processing the form

The Perl script called by the form in Listing 6-12 is an enhanced verison of `frm2mail.pl` from Chapter 5. This version sorts the name/value pairs. Sorting is probably not needed for short forms containing only a few fields, but for larger forms, sorted lists are a definite plus.

**Listing 6-12** **srt2mail.pl**

```
#!/usr/local/bin/perl
# srt2mail.pl -- return form data via e-mail
# your e-mail address goes here -- be sure to
# escape the @ with a backslash -- \@
$email = "me\@mymail.com";                          #1
read(STDIN, $formdat, $ENV{'CONTENT_LENGTH'});  #2
open(MAILOUT, "| mail $email") ||                   #3
   die "Can't start mail program.";                 #4
@namevals = sort(split(/&/,$formdat));              #5
foreach (@namevals) {
   tr/+/ /;
   s/=/:/;                                          #6
   s/%(..)/pack("C",hex($1))/ge;
   print MAILOUT "$_\n";                            #7
}
print MAILOUT "zzForm\n\n";
close(MAILOUT);                                     #8
print "Content-type: text/html\n\n";                #9
print "<HTML><HEAD>\n";                             #10
print "<TITLE>Form Data Sent</TITLE>\n";
print "</HEAD><BODY>\n";
print "<H3>Form Data Sent</H3>\n";
print "<HR>\n";
print "Your completed form was delivered.<BR>\n";
print "Click the browser's BACK button to return.\n";
print "<P><HR>\n";
print "</BODY>\n</HTML>\n";
# end of frm2mail.pl
```

The following steps correspond to the lines in Listing 6-12 and describe the sorting process in more detail:

1. Set the e-mail address for your address in this line.
2. Retrieve the length of the data stream from the `CONTENT_LENGTH` element in the special `%ENV` array of CGI variables and then use that length with the `read()` function to put the data string into `$formdat`.
3. Open a filehandle (`MAILOUT`) to communicate with the server's mail program. The vertical bar | in front of `mail` is a UNIX pipe symbol. This statement opens the connection between the filehandle and the mail program, so that data sent to the filehandle goes into the mail message.

4. The `die` function, connected to the file `open` operation by the or-else operator `||`, terminates the program if `mail` won't connect.
5. The URL-encoded string parsing starts here. The `split` function generates a list, and the `sort` function operates on a list, so that the output from `split` embedded in `sort` is a sorted list.
6. Set the colon (:) as the delimiter for the name/value pair.
7. The `print` function sends the string to the mail message via the filehandle `MAILOUT`.
8. Tidy up and close the filehandle.
9. Print the heading information for the HTML page to report back to the visitor.
10. Format and send the feedback page.

Figure 6-9 shows the feedback page as it appears to the visitor:

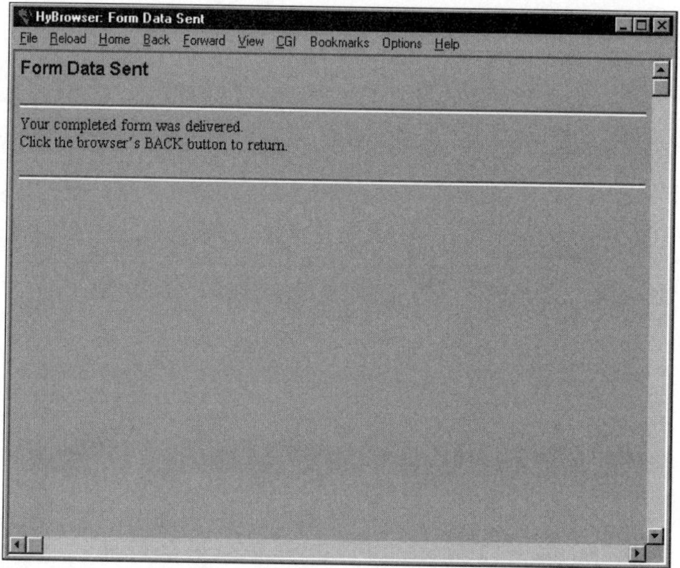


**Figure 6-9:** Visitor Info feedback page.

## Processing e-mail into a database

The e-mail processor, `mail2dat.pl`, extracts name/value pairs from e-mail returned by a form. The format of content section of the e-mail message, generated by `frm2mail.pl`, looks like this

```
AAFormID:Kom6
Address:1222 Byte St.
Belt:None
City:Bitsville
Dojo:Yes

Name:Vern A. Visitor
Phone:414-555-5432
State:WI
Word:Yes
Zip:53202
zzForm
```

Because each block of form data is identified by `AAFormID` at the start and `zzForm` at the end, the e-mail processor can scan for more than one form in a file. Some e-mail programs keep incoming mail concatenated in a single, large file, whereas others keep a batch of separate message files in a directory. Most people will take anything they can get.

The target data file is a tag-delimited sequential file using the same format as the e-mail data. The task for `mail2dat.pl` is to find the `AAFormID` pattern and then copy lines from the e-mail message until the `zzForm` pattern pops up (Listing 6-13).

**Listing 6-13** **`mail2dat.pl`**

```
# mail2dat.pl -- extract form data from e-mail into database
# usage: perl mail2dat.pl infiledesc   (may be *.msg)
open(MDAT, ">>komvis.dat");        #1
while(<>) {                        #2
   if (/AAFormID/) {               #3
      print MDAT $_;               #4
      $a = <ARGV>;                 #5
      while(!$a =~ /zzForm/) {     #6
         print MDAT $a;            #7
         $a = <ARGV>;              #8
      }
      print MDAT $a;               #9
   }
}
close(MDAT);
# end of mail2dat.pl
```

Here's how `mail2dat.pl` works:

1. Open (create, if needed) the data file for appending.
2. Read all lines of all files in the command line file list or descriptor.
3. Look at the pattern that marks the start of the data lines. Because the data name/value pairs were sorted by the CGI program, this pattern marks the start of the data for a form.
4. Print the `AAFormID` line.
5. `ARGV` is the filehandle of the current file coming in through the read-file `<>` operator. Use that name to fetch one line at a time with the read-line `<ARGV>` operator.
6. Watch for `zzForm`, which marks the end of a block of data. Remember, `!~` is the equivalent of "does not match this pattern."
7. Print the current line from the current file out to the data file.
8. Fetch another line from the current data block.
9. The `while` loop terminates when `$a` becomes `zzForm`. Print `$a` as the marker for the end of the current data block.

To use `mail2dat.pl`, place the program in the same directory with the e-mail message files. If the program is located in a file separate from the e-mail messages, use a full or relative pathname in the file descriptor on the command line.

## Generating a phone directory

Data is useless until you use it. Although the Karate Master admired the cleverness of the visitor form and the resulting database, he suggested that the information would be more useful in a phone directory format, perhaps even sorted by last name. I cheerfully agreed, without telling him that the names were coming from the form in first-name-first order and would need to be carved up and reassembled. I figured I could use something like `($first, $last) = split(/ /, $fullname)` to break Vern A. Visitor apart and rebuild him as Vistor Vern A. It turned out to be a little trickier than that, but I had the right idea, as you can see in Listing 6-14.

The directory generator, `dat2phone.pl`, must be able to read the file, find each record, rebuild the Name field, sort the records by last name, and print out a formatted list. Listing 6-14 shows one way to do it.

**Listing 6-14** **dat2phone.pl**

```
# dat2phone.pl -- make phone list from data file
open(DAT, "komvis.dat");                       #1
@alldat = <DAT>;                               #2
close(DAT);
chop(@alldat);                                 #3
open(PHON, ">komphon.txt");                    #4
$pad = "                                   ";  #5
foreach $line (@alldat) {
($head, $tail) = split (/:/,$line);            #6
  if ($head eq "AAFormID") {                   #7
    $alphname = "";                            #8
    $phone = "";
    $addr = "";
    $city = "";
    $state = "";
    $zip = "";
 } elsif ($head eq "zzForm") {                 #9
      $alphname .= $phone . "\n    "          #10
                 . $addr . "\n    "
                 . $city . ", "
                 . $state . "  "
                 . $zip . "\n";
     $rec{$alphname} = 1;                     #11
 } elsif ($head eq "Name") {
      @fullname = split (/ /,$tail);          #12
      $alphname = pop(@fullname) . ", "; #13
      $alphname .= join(" ",@fullname)        #14
                  . $pad;                     #15
      $alphname = substr($alphname, 0, 35);
   } elsif ($head eq "Address") {             #16
      $addr = $tail;
   } elsif ($head eq "City") {
      $city = $tail;
    } elsif ($head eq "State") {
      $state = $tail;
 } elsif ($head eq "Zip") {
      $zip = $tail;
   } elsif ($head eq "Phone") {
      $phone = $tail;
```

*(continued)*

**Listing 6-14** ***(continued)***

```
   }
}
@phones = sort(keys(%rec));                          #17
foreach $visitor (@phones) {                         #18
   print PHON$visitor;
}
# end of datphone.pl
```

The following list describes the parts/ functions of `dat2phone.pl`:

1. Open data file for reading.
2. Load entire data file into array `@alldat`.
3. Cut newlines off every line in the array.
4. Open output file for phone directory, overwriting any existing file with the same name.
5. Create string of spaces for later use.
6. Split the line into `$head` and `$tail`.
7. Start of record.
8. Clear the work variables, so that no leftovers get into the new directory entry by accident.
9. End of record. Build the directory entry.
10. Assemble the directory entry by concatenating work variables and inserting newlines and indent spaces.
11. Load the directory entry into associative array by using the entire assembled entry as the key and the number 1 as the value. This step filters out any duplicates.
12. Split the `Name` field into words by using the space character.
13. Remove the last element of the array and place it in `$alphname` along with a comma and a space.
14. Add the rest of the words from `@fullname` to the end of `$alphname`, separating each word with a space. The name field has now been assembled into `"Last, First Middle"`.
15. Add a string of spaces to the end of the name field and then trim the whole name, with trailing spaces, to 35 characters.
16. Assign each field to an appropriate work variable.

17. All records have been processed and loaded into the associative array `%rec` as keys. Sort the keys from `%rec` into `@phones` to alphabetize the phone listings.

18. March through the phone directory listings, printing each one to the output file.

The directory turns out to be quite usable. It looks like this:

```
Amphibious, Toad A.                     414-555-1234
    100 Slippery Way
    Lily, WI  53201
Crusher, Carl the
    707 Bone Drive
    Smudge, WI  53201
Frilly, Fern                            414-555-2345
    300 Shady Lane
    Frond, WI  53201
```

It seems that Carl doesn't have a phone. I think that's for the better.

## Summary

- Character-delimited fields are fields marked by a separating character, usually punctuation. Character delimited fields use a fixed number of fields — empty fields still must be delimited.

- CSV (Comma-Separated Values) fields are separated by commas, have strings enclosed in quotes, and may have embedded commas. Numbers often are left unquoted. CSV also requires a fixed number of fields, so empty fields must be delimited.

- In line-delimited format, records are separated by a blank line and fields are entered one per line. This format uses a fixed number of fields, so blank fields must have a filling character (usually hyphen).

- Tagged-field is a sequential data-file record format that usually is a variant of line-delimited. Fields are made up of name/value pairs. Records may have varying numbers and types of fields.

- Patterns using the dot-star (.*) or plus-star ( +*) wildcards find the leftmost longest match.

- Perl 5 uses the hook ? operator in conjunction wtih the wildcard (.*?) to find the leftmost shortest match. Special processing is required for Perl 4 to find the leftmost shortest match (see Lisiting 6-3).

- Associative arrays cannot have duplicate keys. Loading an associative array automatically unduplicates the keys in a list.

- The command-line option `-i.bak` (or the program `statement $^I = ".bak"`) invokes editing in-place for programs using the empty read-file < > operator for input.

# Random-Access Files with Perl

**Skill Targets**

- Constructing random-access files
- Retrieving data from random-access files
- Binary file operations with Perl
- Building and maintaining a Web site guestbook with (or without!) CGI

The bulk of the programming done in Perl is aimed at sequential text files. When the topic turns to database projects, Perl is mostly seen as a scripting language: Good for feeding SQL statements into a database and reformatting the data into reports. But Perl has its own database powers — tools for accessing random-access and binary files — that make it a handy tool for working with small databases.

Understanding database operations down at the bit and byte levels provides a basis for understanding the global database represented by the Web.

## Distributing Information on the Web

The Web is a passive source of information. Data on the Web sits and waits until you find it. That passive mode of operation makes Web sites more like books in a library and less like television shows than most people believe. At least, that's how the Web started out.

More recently, the flavor of the Web has changed from library to bookstore. Entrepreneurs and established businesses alike are exploring ways to generate income from Web sites. Information that used to be free for the asking now, more and more often, has a price tag on it, or at least an ad stuck to it (Figure 7-1).

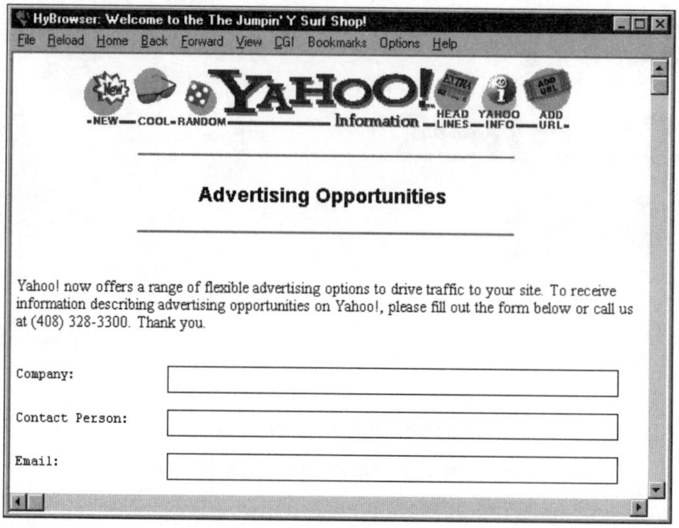

**Figure 7-1:** Billboards on the Information Superhighway — revenue-generating ads now appear on high-count sites.

The inherent value of information keeps the content-rich sites open and thriving (Figure 7-2). Content isn't everything, but without it, there isn't much left. Whether the information on your Web site is free or pay-as-you-go, it should be interesting and useful. Plenty of neglected side-trails and dead-ends already exist on the Information Highway.

## Link lists

On the Web, the basic coin of the realm is the *link*. I cannot recall ever seeing a Web site that did not have links to other sites offering still more links to more sites. A good measure of a Web site's information or entertainment value is the number of links to that site from pages around the world.

A page of links, or a *link list*, is easy to manage if only a few items are on it (Figure 7-3). Updating the list to add or delete a link is a minor HTML editing exercise. Some link lists, like those generated by a search on Yahoo! or Alta Vista, are monsters. The first search I did on Alta Vista came back with a list of 22,000 URLs for my topic. Creating such a list would be a great deal of work if it had to be typed manually. To avoid that route, I later show you how to build a Perl tool to format lists from a file into a Web page when experimenting with sequential data files.

**Figure 7-2:** Home page of the Internal Revenue Service.

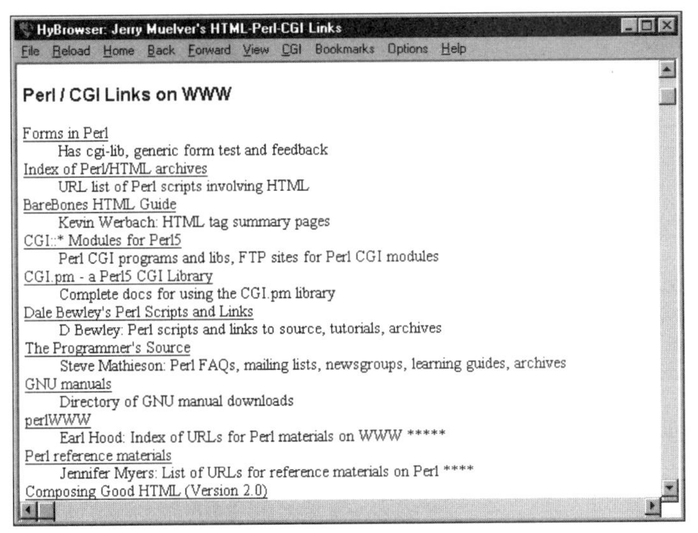


**Figure 7-3:** Page of links to sites with Perl scripts and information.

# Catalogs

A catalog can be a simple list of checkboxes or pages of text flowing around elegant pictorials (Figure 7-4). By their nature, catalogs are not constructed on-the-fly, although the process for ordering from catalogs can be Perl-automated. The most direct way to handle catalog orders is with the `frm2mail.pl` program in Chapter 5, which gets the data in-house. Then process the order into a human-readable format, such as a basic order form, with another Perl program. If you have to process 3,000 orders a day, however, you will require more database power than I can offer in this little book.

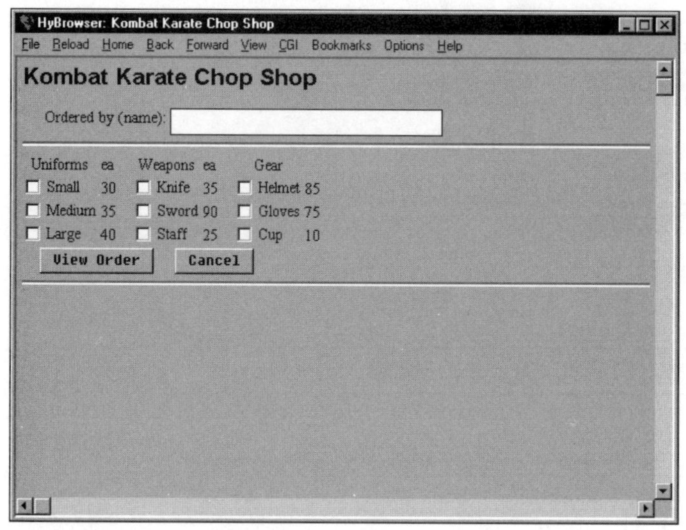


**Figure 7-4:** Online catalogs cater to the digital shopper.

# Spec sheets

Specification sheets and tables are compressed versions of item and catalog lists. Spec sheets usually are static — once the information is set up, it only changes if a new product or version update is introduced, in which case the whole sheet is created anew. You still need the old sheet for the old product, however. Perl's role in spec-sheet generation is a formatting job much like the task of generating link lists (Figure 7-5).

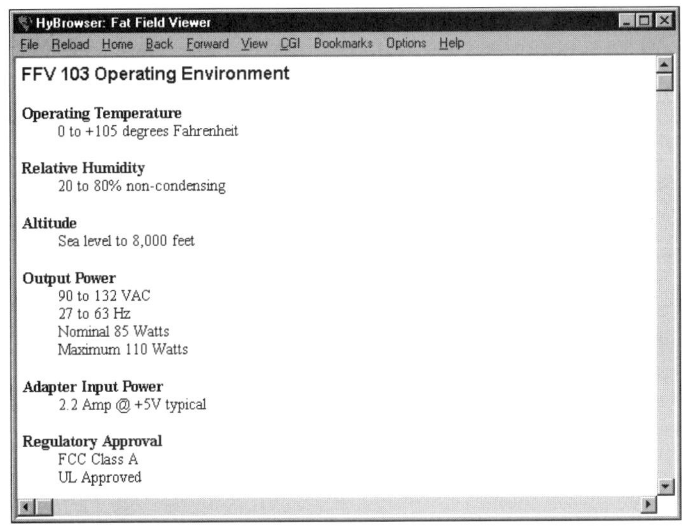


**Figure 7-5:** Product specification sheets are a boon to technical information seekers.

## Libraries

You met Perl libraries in Chapter 5. Although Perl libraries are scattered all across the Web, the libraries I am talking about here are more along the lines of the Library of Congress (Figure 7-6). Every college and university with an Internet connection (which means every college and university) has an access route into their catalog of books and periodicals. Most libraries run long-established, dial-in, text-menu systems. But the trickle toward a Web-page interface is growing into a rushing flood. Behind the interface are the creaky, old, Big Iron mainframe computers that the academic world loves so much. I won't have you do any library cataloguing in Perl here, but you can rest assured that it has been done on mainframe computers — and done well — in Perl.

# Random-Access Basics

*Random-access files* are the backbone of the data industry. Sequential files are great for storing masses of contiguous data but beastly for storing information that needs constant revising and updating. The structured approach of random-access files is the better way for high-access data. By providing an index system and rigid format for data records, random-access file systems deliver information and handle updates with little fuss or bother. The difference in application for random-access and sequential files is much like the difference between using a library's subject/author/title cardfile to find a book and going directly to the stacks to check the title of each book in sequence (Figure 7-7).

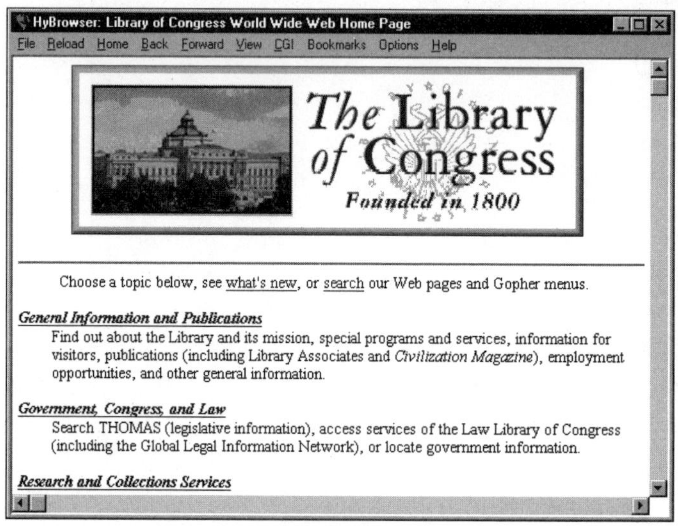


**Figure 7-6:** Library of Congress home page.

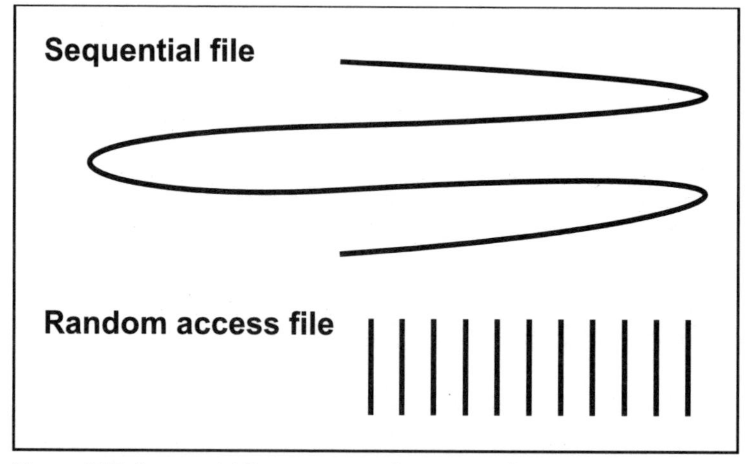


**Figure 7-7:** Sequential files versus random-access files.

## Record formats

Records in a random-access file commonly all have the same length because that is the easiest way to implement random access. If record #3 has 32 characters, then record #10 also has 32 characters. This consistency in record length is the key to random access because the structure leads the way to the data. To find a particular 32-character record, count how many 32s it takes to get there and then use that number to skip right to the record, instead of reading everything from the front of the file to find your data. There is no need to mark the end of a record with a newline, a colon, or anything else. Just start at the beginning of a record and read in the right number of characters to get just the one record, the whole record, and nothing but the record.

## Fixed-length fields

The fixed-length field format keeps the size for a particular field the same for all records. The length of the field's content may vary, but it has to fit into the specified field length. In a phonebook file, for example, suppose that all names have the same space (20 characters) and that all phone numbers are 12 characters long. An 8-character name is padded with spaces to fill the rest of the field. A 26-character name is truncated to fit. Either way, you can count on the phone number to start at byte 20 in every record and use the next 12 characters. The next record starts 32 bytes after the start of the previous record, such as in the following:

```
Wolfman.............414-555-1234Dracula.............414-555-
2345Bride.of.Frankenstei414-555-3456
```

Although the records are laid out end-to-end in the file, thinking of them as stacked rows is easier:

```
Wolfman.............414-555-1234
Dracula.............414-555-2345
Bride.of.Frankenstei414-555-3456
```

You do not need to use delimiters to mark either the records or the fields because everything is set up with fixed lengths. To retrieve data, find the start of a record or field and retrieve the required number of characters for the data element.

## File headers

Some database file formats, such as the ones used by dBase and its progeny, carry additional baggage along with the data. The first section of the file is reserved as a stash for information about the database file: the number of records; the number of fields in each record; the names, lengths, and type of each field; and so on. Database programs read the header first and then use the extracted information to set up arrays and access variables to handle the actual data.

Perl has the tools to read dBase-style database file headers and to manipulate the files, but the exercise is more involved than it is worth. Perl libraries are available on the Web that have all the problems already worked out. If you have an extensive collection of dBase files to integrate with a Web site, your best option is to hook up to one of the available libraries (Figure 7-8). Some wheels are just not fun to reinvent.

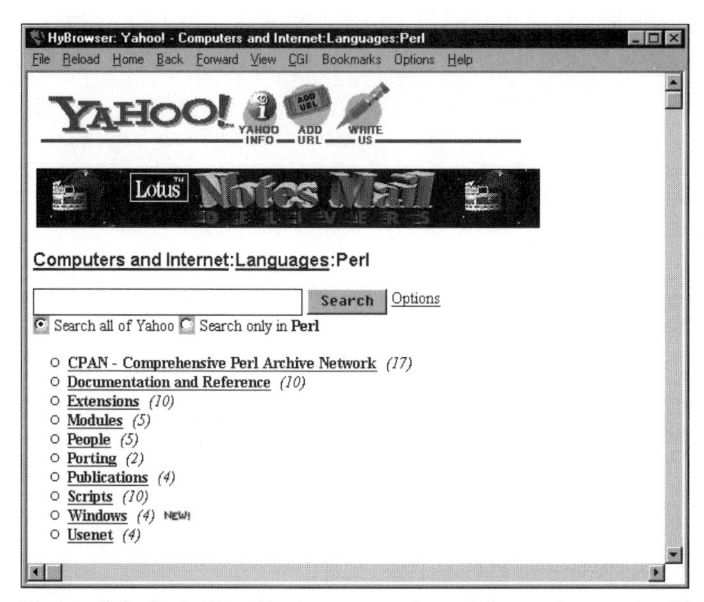


**Figure 7-8:** Partial list of Perl source-code and library sites on the Web.

I discuss file-header construction and behavior after the PerlFacts section, which provides the necessary concepts and vocabulary that you need to understand these topics.

## Binary files

Files with extensions such as .EXE and .DLL and almost everything else on your hard drive are *binary files*. This category includes all program files, compressed files, and the host-mystery things that look like smiley-face garbage when you peek at the file with Notepad, Write, or WordPad. Binary files are not meant to be readable by anything other than another computer program.

So why do we care about binary files? Some database program operations may use binary files. Index files often are binary in format, as are data files, especially the data for number-crunching programs and financial operations.

Perl can read binary files, but it does encounter problems. With a binary file you have to know beforehand exactly what you are getting into in order to make any sense out of it. For example, a series of bytes in a file can represent a few letters, a group of small numbers, one big number, or part of the data stream for a graphic image. Unless you know what you are looking for, you won't find what you expect.

One form of almost-binary file that I have used with good effect is a *hybrid sequential file* — a text file with a little binary data mixed in. I insert a number that shows the length of a text record right at the beginning of the text (Figure 7-9). The next "size + text" record follows right after that, and so on throughout the file. To read the file — say, record number 12 — I read the first record length number and then skip that many bytes to the beginning of the next record. I skip from number to number through the file, without having to read through all the text, to get to the record I want.

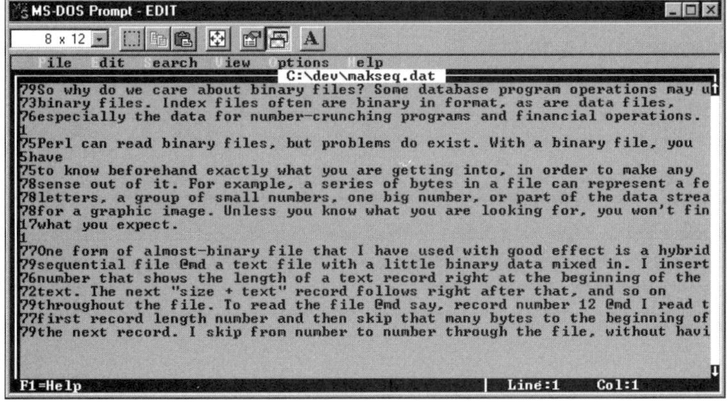


**Figure 7-9:** View into a hybrid sequential file, showing record length at the beginning of each record.

The skipping and hopping about requires the use of the seek function, one of the topics in this chapter's "PerlFacts" section.

## Memo files

Random-access database programs also can process variable-length text records with only a little cheating. The *memo field* in a random-access record doesn't actually hold the umpteen pages of text you type into the form. Rather, the text goes into a separate memo file, and the program uses the random-access file to store just the text's location in the memo file. When you ask to see the record in the random-access file, the program checks the memo field to fetch the address of the corresponding text in the memo file and then goes to the memo file to read the text.

The notion of memo files is one of the smartest, simplest concepts in text-oriented computing (Figure 7-10). It blends the speed and editing flexibility of random-access files with the processing and display flexibility of text files.

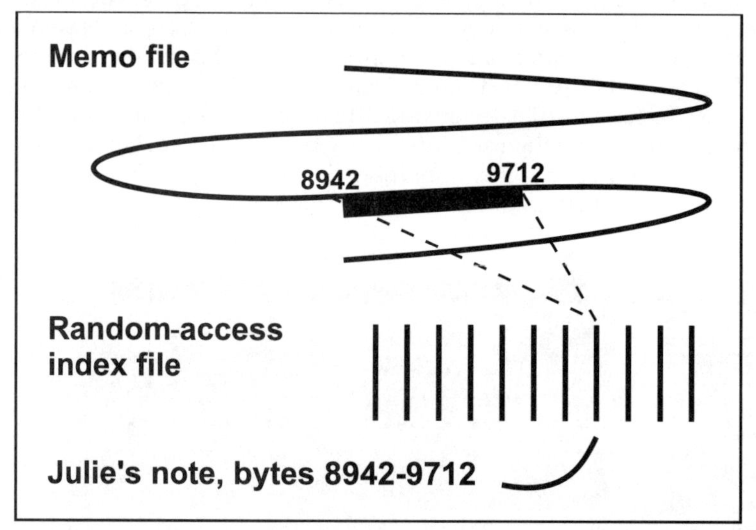


**Figure 7-10:** Memo files are usually separate sequential files referenced by random-access files.

# ISAM

*Indexed Sequential Access Method* (ISAM) files are a special class of half-binary, half-text files used by database management programs such as Microsoft Access (Figure 7-11). An ISAM file has a reserved block at the beginning that contains file structure and administration information. The rest of the file is made up of large, reserved blocks. These blocks hold records and indexes for the file. After a block is filled up with records, the system adds another large block to the file. Everything — the field descriptions and sizes, the indexes, and all the data — is stored in one large file.

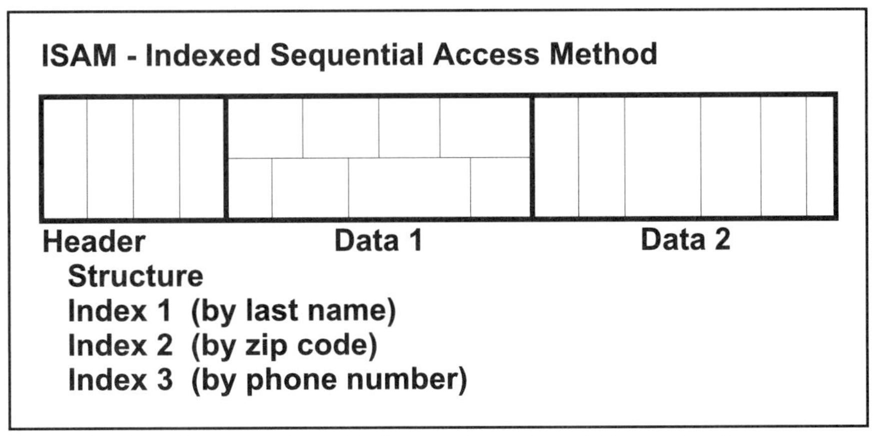


**Figure 7-11:** ISAM can be thought of as a series of files within one big file.

As a description, the Indexed Sequential Access Method means that the system retrieves records from a sequential file by using indexes to keep track of the location of records in the file and the length of each record. When you query the system for a record, ISAM checks for the location in an index and then uses the location information to skip to the right part of the file and read the right number of bytes. The difference between ISAM and random-access records is that ISAM records can be of any length, whereas the random-access records in a file all have to be the same length.

Another way to think of ISAM is as a random-access file with index files and memo files all rolled into one. It takes a powerhouse, specialized application to handle ISAM files, so I won't be throwing any Perl at them.

## Security issues

Your Web site involves you in remote computing, although twice removed. You upload files that run on a computer you don't control. Then a visitor, whom you also don't control, logs on to your Web page and runs your programs without your aid and assistance.

Exercising a bit of caution in regard to data files makes good sense. Don't put anything on a Web site that you don't want the public to see. If you are running response forms and remote CGI programs, monitor your site closely just to take care of business. If you have data files that can be updated without your knowledge, develop a reporting system that checks the data integrity and keeps you appraised of activity within those files.

Setting file-access rights and permissions becomes a bit awkward on a remote site. If your ISP has clear guidelines for file permissions (set with `chmod` and `chgrp` commands), follow the procedures exactly. You certainly don't need the hassle of living with programs that fail or merrily accept bogus data because the permissions are set wrong.

# PerlFacts: Random-Access Files

Random access is not all that random. You don't just go anywhere in a random-access file and grab something — you need a clear idea of where you're going and exactly how to get there. The main difference between random-access files and sequential files is the access method. The records in a random-access file all are the same size. That difference makes it possible to jump into a random-access file and change a specific record without tromping on another record's data — if you play by the rules.

## Advanced file operations review/preview

The following table describes the new functions covered in this chapter.

| Function | Description |
|---|---|
| `open (MYFILE, "+>filename.txt");` | Opens a file named `filename.txt` and assigns a filehandle called `MYFILE`. The plus-right-angle bracket operator sets the file to allow both read and write actions. This statement will create `filename.txt` if it does not exist. |

| `open (MYFILE, "+<filename.txt");` | Opens a file named `filename.txt` and assigns a filehandle called `MYFILE`. The plus-left-angle bracket operator sets the file to enable both read and write actions. This statement will fail if `filename.txt` does not exist. |
|---|---|
| `read(MYFILE, $data, 40);` | Reads into `$data` the next 40 characters from the current position in the file assigned to `MYFILE` . |
| `seek(MYFILE, $reclen, 0);` | Moves current position in the file, `MYFILE`, to `$reclen` bytes from the beginning of the file (`$reclen` must be positive or 0). |
| `seek(MYFILE, $reclen, 1);` | Moves current position in file `MYFILE` to `$reclen` bytes from the current position (`$reclen` may be positive or negative or 0). |
| `seek(MYFILE, $reclen, 2);` | Moves current position in the file, `MYFILE`, to `$reclen` bytes from the end of the file (`$reclen` must be negative or 0). |

# Accessing and updating random-access files

Typical operations for a random-access file require locating a record, reading it into memory, changing something in the record, and writing the changes back into the file. In other words, you have to open the file for reading and writing at the same time.

## Creating a random-access file

The trusty old `print` command writes anything to just about anywhere, including random-access files. Because newlines are not needed in a random-access file, just print without the `\n` newline option and keep every print object the same length. For example, Listing 7-1 shows a template program for producing a quick, 20-record test file of 32-character records.

**Listing 7-1 makeran.pl**

```
# makeran.pl -- makes 20-record random access file
$i = 11;
open(FTEST, ">rantest.dat");
while ($i <=40) {
  print FTEST "record $i                     XX";
  $i++;
}
close(FTEST);
# end of makeran.pl
```

I start at 11 for creating this demo file to make sure that each record has 32 characters — no format-wrecking, single- to double-digit shift exists that would be caused by going from "9" to "10." If I started counting at 1, the print statement would create a series of 31-character records until record number 10, because single-digit values of `$i` would only use a single character position. The result is records of different sizes, like this:

```
record 8                          XX
record 9                          XX
record 10                          XX
record 11                          XX
...
record 99                          XX
record 100                          XX
record 101                          XX
```

Much of the coding for random-access files is concerned with trimming and padding fields and records to exactly the right size. When you look at `rantest.dat` with an editor or the DOS `type` command, you'll see that all the records are the same length and simply are jammed together, one after another. It is a format that only a computer could love (Figure 7-12).

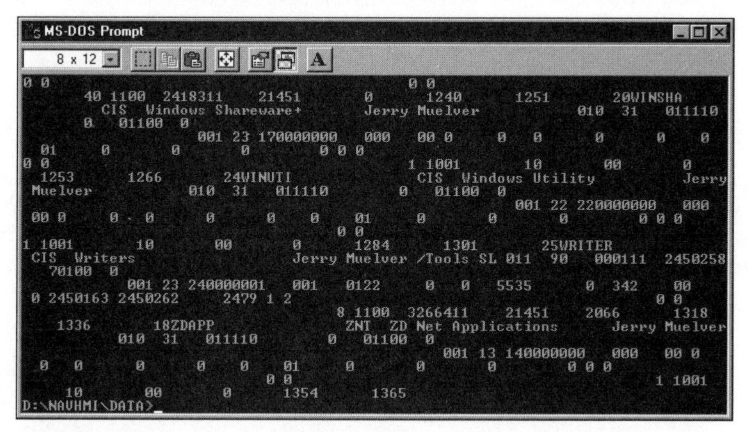


**Figure 7-12:** Random-access file revealed by a DOS `type` command.

## Opening for both read and write

You can't write to a file that is opened for reading and you can't read from a file that is opened for writing. One solution is to keep opening and closing a file, changing the access mode each time to keep in sync with reading and writing requirements. Perl's solution, however, is to enable simultaneous read and write access. The syntax for this is

```
open(FHANDLE, "+>myfile.dat");
```

where FHANDLE is a filehandle and myfile.dat is the filename. To write $data to the file, use the following command:

```
print FHANDLE $data;
```

If the file is formatted with one record per line (a newline at the end of each record), you read a record from the file with the familiar <FHANDLE> read operator (such as the following):

```
$line = <FHANDLE>;
```

To read data in chunks of a specific size, use the read function. The syntax is

```
read(FHANDLE, $chunk, size);
```

where FHANDLE is the filehandle that references the file opened earlier, $chunk is the scalar variable that receives the input from the file, and size is number of bytes (characters) to be read.

In some programs, you may see a variant of the read function that appends incoming data to the receiving variable rather than rewriting the value by loading the variable from scratch. The variant uses an additional parameter, skip, to determine how many characters in the receiving string it should skip before starting to append the new data. The syntax is

```
read(FHANDLE, $chunk, size, skip);
```

For instance, if $chunk starts out holding aaaaaaaa, you read six characters of a file full of bbbbbb, and then you skip the first four characters of $chunk, the read statement is as follows:

```
$chunk = "aaaaaaaa";
read(FHANDLE, $chunk, 6, 4);
          # $chunk now holds aaaabbbbbb
```

## Locating records with seek

A 16-character record length file may look like this (I marked record-ends with a vertical bar):

```
record.1.......|record.2.......|record.3.......|
```

Record #1 starts at the byte 0. Record #2 starts at byte 16. Record #3 starts at record #2 plus 16 bytes, or byte 32. The following example shows the record set stacked up, with the starting byte for each record posted at the beginning of the record:

```
0..............|
16.............|
32.............|
48.............|
```

To find the location of a record, subtract 1 from the record number and multiply the result by the record length. Record #101 starts at byte 1600. It's simple math, but repetitive. In other words, locating records in a computer file is a perfect job for computers.

The Perl tools needed for this task are (1) a tool to seek out the right record and (2) a tool to read the data. How about `seek` and `read` for appropriate function names?

The syntax for `seek` is

```
seek(FHANDLE, LEN, GOFROM);
```

where `FHANDLE` is the filehandle of an opened file, `LEN` is the number of characters (bytes) to move the current position, and `GOFROM` is the starting point for the move. The `GOFROM` value (0, 1, or 2) tells Perl from which point to calculate the move:

0 = Seek from beginning of file

1 = Seek from current position

2 = Seek from end of file

If GOFROM is not specified, the default is 0 (the beginning of the file). For instance, to get to record #4 of a file containing 16-character records, you can skip three records of 16 characters each, starting from the beginning of the file, by using this statement:

```
$reclen = 16;
seek(FHANDLE, $reclen * 3, 0);
```

The current position in the file — the number of the next byte to read or write — is 48. Another “seek the length of a record” action will put the current position at 48 + 16, as the following example shows:

```
$reclen = 16;
seek(FHANDLE, $reclen * 3, 0);      # byte 48
seek(FHANDLE, $reclen, 1);          # byte 64
seek(FHANDLE, 0, 1);                # no move, byte 64
seek(FHANDLE, -48, 2);              # byte 16
seek(FHANDLE, 0, 0);                # byte 0
```

Notice that the last seek put the current position at the beginning of the file, byte 0. Moves can be made in reverse as long as room is available to complete the action. To capture a return from seek, assign the function to a variable, such as in the following example:

```
$success = seek(RECFILE, $rec*120, 0);
```

When successful, seek returns a non-zero value. If the seek fails, usually because it ran out of room, seek returns 0. The return value can trigger flow-control decisions, as in the following example:

```
open(DATFILE,"+<phones.dat") ||         # fail if no file
   die "Can't open phones.dat";
$reclen = 32;
$recno = 127;
seek(DATFILE, $reclen*($recno-1), 0) ||
   die "Can't find $recno.";            # fail no nmbr 127
```

## Reporting position with `tell`

Abusing the power to skip around inside a file with one `seek` after another can leave you lost in the woods with no bread-crumb trail to find your way out. To check on the current position in a file, use `tell` with this syntax:

```
$curpos = tell(MYFILE);
```

where `$curpos` is the variable that holds the reported current position in the file, and `MYFILE` is the filehandle variable. For example

```
$reclen = 16;
seek(FHANDLE, $reclen * 3, 0);
$curpos = tell(FHANDLE);      # $curpos = 48
seek(FHANDLE, $reclen, 1);
$curpos = tell(FHANDLE);      # $curpos = 64
seek(FHANDLE, 0, 1);
$curpos = tell(FHANDLE);      # $curpos = 64
seek(FHANDLE, -48, 2);
$curpos = tell(FHANDLE);      # $curpos = 16
seek(FHANDLE, 0, 0);
$curpos = tell(FHANDLE);      # $curpos = 0
```

Knowing the current position in a file sometimes is a challenge. A series of operations involving record seeks, data retrieval from individual fields, and perhaps a data update or two — all handled by subroutines and `if-elsif` blocks — dazzles the mind. Finding out for certain where you are before making the next leap is common-sense good programming. `tell` is a memory action that does not involve disk access, so it is cheap and easy to use.

## Reading data

The familiar read-file `<>` and read-line `<FHANDLE>` operators work with random-access files only when the files are newline-delimited, with one record per line. As long as you remember to `chop` the line (to cut off the newline), you can search or seek to find the record, grab it with `<FHANDLE>` to read the entire line at once, and then be on your way with your data.

Files that use fixed-length records without newlines need to read an exact number of characters to keep from stealing data from the next record in the line. This is a job for the `read` function. The syntax is

```
read(MYFILE, $data, size);
```

where `MYFILE` is the filehandle, `$data` is the variable that receives the input, and `size` is the number of characters to read. For example

```
read(MYFILE, $data, 40);
```

reads the next 40 characters from the current position in the `MYFILE` file into `$data`. If the read is successful, `read` returns a non-zero value. If it fails, `read` returns 0.

Listing 7-2 shows one way to read the fifth record in a phonelist database containing 48-character records, which have a 36-character name field and a 12-character number field.

**Listing 7-2** **recread.pl**

```
# recread.pl -- fixed length record reading demo
$reclen = 48;
$recno = 5;
open(PHON, "+<phones.dat) ||
   die "Can't open phones.dat.\n";
$recpos = $reclen * ($recno -1);
seek(PHON, $recpos,0) ||
   die "Can't locate record $recno.\n";
read(PHON, $found, $reclen) ||
   die "Found record $recno, but can't read it.\n";
$name = substr($found, 0, 36);
$number = substr($found, 36);
print "$name --- $number\n";
$curpos = tell(PHON);        # $curpos = 240
print "position --- $curpos\n";
# end of recread.pl
```

To read the fields directly into appropriately named variables, use the variables in the `read` call with the matching field lengths:

```
seek(PHON, $reclen*($recno-1),0) ||
   die "Can't locate record $recno.\n";
read(PHON, $name, 36);
read(PHON, $number, 12);
```

**Exercise 7-1**

This exercise is like those puzzles in the Sunday paper. You have to remember that the first record in `makeran.dat` says "record 11" and do your calculations from that fact. Modify `recread.pl` to read `rantest.dat` and print the thirteenth 32-character record, which (because the file starts at 11 instead of 1) looks like this:

```
record 23                      XX
```

## Writing data with print and sprintf

To write data to a random-access file, start with strings exactly the right size to make up the record. Then find the beginning of the record and use `print`. For example, take a look at Listing 7-3.

**Listing 7-3** **recwrite.pl**

```
# rewrite.pl -- fixed record writing demo
$reclen = 48;
$recno = 3;
$name = "Calamity Jane                       ";
$number = "414-555-4321";
open(PHON, "+<phones.dat>) ||
   die "Can't open phones.dat.\n";
$recpos = $reclen * ($recno -1);
seek(PHON, $recpos,0) ||
   die "Can't locate record $recno.\n";
print PHON $name . $number;
$curpos = tell(PHON);       # $curpos = 144
print "position --- $curpos\n";
# end of recwrite.pl
```

The `$name` value (Calamity Jane) had to be padded to 36 characters so that the phone number starts printing at the correct position in the record. Typing the right number of spaces after the name is one (awkward) way of padding the value.

A much better way is to use the `sprintf` (string print format) function. This magic function uses a template string with formatting markers in it and a list of variables to feed the markers and then returns a string assembled from the pieces. I only show the `%s` marker for `"string"` in the following description, just to present a specific tool for a specific purpose. Markers for integers, floating-point numbers, and other object types also are available — I touch on a raft of options for `sprintf` later in this book. The syntax here is

```
$record = sprintf("%s", $var);
```

where `$record` receives the assembled string, `%s` is the format marker for a string, and `$var` is the value to be used in place of `%s` in the assembled string.

Take a look at this example:

```
$var = "Mabel";
$record = sprintf("%s", $var);
print $record;  # prints: Mabel
```

Big deal. You get back what you put in. The following example shows a fancier template that uses angle brackets to show the beginning and end of the resulting string:

```
$var = "Mabel";
$record = sprintf(">>%s<<", $var);
print $record;  # prints: >>Mabel<<
```

The next example shows "`Mabel`" after adding spaces to it:

```
$var = "Mabel";
$record = sprintf(">>%s     <<", $var);
print $record;  # prints: >>Mabel     <<
```

The next trick is to expand the string marker, `%s`, to include a string length value by inserting the desired string length between the `%` and the `'s'`. This trick pads the string with spaces to fill it to the required minimum length:

```
$var = "Mabel";
$record = sprintf(">>%10s<<", $var);  # min length of 10
print $record;  # prints: >>     Mabel<<
```

One more trick is to insert a minus sign before the length value to push the string to the left, so that the padding occurs toward the end of the string:

```
$var = "Mabel";
$record = sprintf(">>%-10s<<", $var);
print $record;  # prints: >>Mabel     <<
```

Almost perfect. I can set the length of the string to any length I want. But do I have to enter the actual numbers into the template? Or can I use a variable instead so that I can build a reusable subroutine? First, I tried this:

```
$var = "Mabel";
$len = 10;
$record = sprintf(">>%-$lens<<", $var);
print $record;  # prints: >>%-<<
```

Perl interpreted `$lens` as a new, empty variable rather than as the value from `$len` plus the `'s'` marker. After trying this, I was out of ideas, so I poured through reams of Perl documentation and discovered that the right way is to convert `$len` to `${len}`, using the following special format that `sprintf` knows how to interpret:

```
$var = "Mabel";
$len = 10;
$record = sprintf(">>%-${len}s<<", $var);
print $record;  # prints: >>Mabel     <<
```

The `${len}` operator extracts the value from `$len` and makes the template work again. Let me restate the expanded syntax for `sprintf` and summarize its components:

```
$record = sprintf("%-${len}s", $var);
```

The following table describes the parts and functions of this statement:

| | |
|---|---|
| `$record` | Receives the assembled string |
| `%` | Format marker |
| – | Means "push to the left" |
| `${len}` | Uses `${}` to extract the value from the variable `$len` and sets the minimum length of the assembled string |
| s | Marker for a string value |
| `$var` | Value to be used in place of 's' in the assembled string |

Anything that hard-won should be preserved. Listing 7-4 is a &pad subroutine that takes a string and a minimum length and returns the string in a field padded with spaces to the minimum length. Note that &pad also checks for any accidental newlines left on the string and cuts off the string if the original started out too long in the first place.

**Listing 7-4** **sub pad**

```
sub pad {
   # expects ($var, $len)
   local ($len, $var, $retval);
   ($var, $len) = @_;
   # look for newline, just in case
   chop($var) if ($var =~ /\n$/);
   $retval = sprintf("%-${len}s", $var);
   # cut if $var started out too long
   $retval = substr($retval,0,$len);
}
```

To use &pad, add it to the file-writing program, such as in Listing 7-5.

**Listing 7-5** **recwrite2.pl**

```
# rewrite2.pl -- fixed record writing with &pad
$namelen = 36;
$phonlen = 12;
$reclen = 48;
$recno = 3;
$name = &pad("Calamity Jane", $namelen);
$number = &pad("414-555-4321", $phonlen);  # just in case of a
short phone number
open(PHON, "+<phones.dat>) ||
   die "Can't open phones.dat.\n";
$recpos = $reclen * ($recno -1);
seek(PHON, $recpos,0) ||
   die "Can't locate record $recno.\n";
print PHON $name . $number;
$curpos = tell(PHON);        # $curpos = 144

sub pad {
   # expects ($var, $len)
```

*(continued)*

**Listing 7-5 *(continued)***

```
    local ($len, $var, $retval);
    ($var, $len) = @_;
    # look for newline, just in case
    chop($var) if ($var =~ /\n$/);
    $retval = sprintf("%-${len}s", $var);
    # cut if $var started out too long
    $retval = substr($retval,0,$len);
}
# end of recwrite2.pl
```

All that remains now is to build a project using some database readin', 'ritin', and 'rithmetic.

### Exercise 7-2

Modify `&pad` to make `&rpad`, which pushes the string to the right end of the padded field.

# PerlProject: Running a Guestbook

People like to receive compliments. Posting a guestbook entry shares compliments from your visitors with the rest of the world. It may seem like bragging, but ... well, okay, it is. The Karate Master won't brag about himself, of course, but if other people want to give him a pat on the back, he is not above turning slightly to make the gesture easier to accomplish.

The two schools of thought on guestbook processing are split on the basis of location: Do it all on the server or bring it back for home cooking.

Although the simplicity of processing a guestbook entirely on the server is attractive, some snags exist with this method:

- **File-access and permissions-adjustments hassle.** Once you get this hassle figured out with your ISP, however, the process runs smoothly.
- **The increased exposure to malicious misuse.** Anyone can post anything.

Bringing the postings home for merging into the guestbook requires more involvement (sometimes called "work") on your part because you have to juggle the mail and upload the revised guestbook yourself. In exchange for the extra effort, you gain control. Nothing goes up on your site that you haven't already seen and approved. The Karate Master, by his very nature, is a hard-working control freak, so he was happy with a system that monitored postings before adding them to the guestbook.

## Site layout

The Kombat Karate home page needs organizing. The Interest Survey that started the operation is still hanging around, even though it was just a demo. Much to the delight of the Karate Master, names and addresses are flooding in through the Visitor Info form. Some addresses are on the other side of the world, but that happens with Web sites. Adding a guestbook puts a couple more pages on the Kombat Karate site. I suspect that won't be the last of it, either. I've heard mention of a class schedule, a catalog, the history of the dojo. . . .

I proposed setting up the site with an index or menu page and dangling the other pages and programs from the menu. The Karate Master liked the idea so much that he added some pages of his own to the list:

```
index.html                  # menu page
    komsur04.html           # interest survey
        srt2mail.pl         # CGI form data mailer
    visinfo.html            # visitor info
        srt2mail.pl         # CGI form data mailer
        (mail2dat.pl)       # local mail data extractor
        (dat2phon.pl)       # local data to phone list convertor
    guestbk.html            # guest comment display
        signin.html         # guest comment collector
            srt2mail.pl     # CGI form data mailer
            (mail2gst.pl)   # guestbook comment inserter
    classes.html            # class schedule
    catalog.html            # equipment catalog
        srt2mail.pl         # CGI form data mailer
        (orders.pl)         # local order processor
    history.html            # dojo history treatise
    dojolink.html           # links to other dojo Web sites
```

Strange, isn't it, how Web sites just keep growing and growing?

## Sign-in form

The sign-in form extracts the name and a voluntary comment from the visitor. In keeping with the minimalist approach of the Karate Master, the code in Listing 7-6 is elegantly simple.

**Listing 7-6** **signin.html**

```
<HTML><HEAD>
<TITLE>Kombat Karate Guestbook Sign-in</TITLE>
</HEAD><BODY>
<H2>Kombat Karate Guestbook Sign-in</H2>
<HR>
We are honored to welcome you to our dojo.
Please leave your name a comment for our guestbook.
<FORM METHOD="POST"
ACTION="http:\\www.some.site/cgi-bin/srt2mail.pl">
<INPUT TYPE="HIDDEN" NAME="AAFormID" VALUE="KomSign">
<P>Your name:<BR>
<INPUT TYPE="TEXT" NAME="Guest" SIZE=40><BR>
Comment:<BR>
<TEXTAREA NAME="Posting"  ROWS=5 COLS=40>
</TEXTAREA><P>
<INPUT TYPE="SUBMIT" VALUE="Send">  
<INPUT TYPE="RESET" VALUE="Cancel">
</FORM>
<HR>
<A HREF="index.html">[ Return to Main Page ]</A>
<HR>
</BODY></HTML>
```

The sign-in form uses `srt2mail.pl` to return the comments via e-mail for merging into the guestbook page. Figure 7-13 shows the form in use.

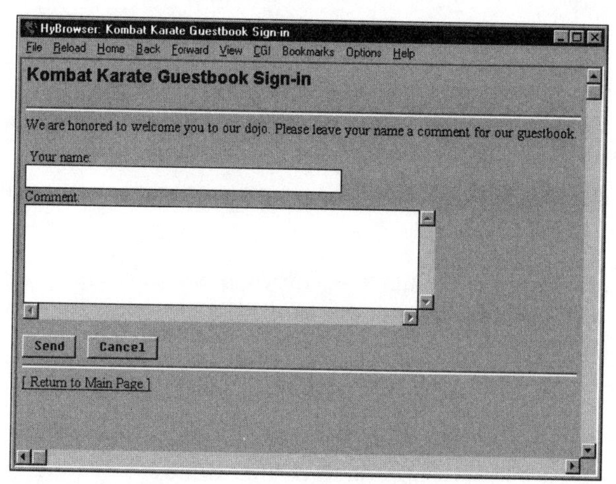


**Figure 7-13:** Browser view of sign-in form.

## Guestbook page

The guestbook page starts out simple but grows with each added comment (Listing 7-7).

**Listing 7-7** **guestbk.html**

```
<HTML><HEAD>
<TITLE>Kombat Karate Guestbook</TITLE>
</HEAD><BODY>
<H2>Kombat Karate Guestbook</H2>
<HR>
Previous visitors have honored us with the comments listed below.
 You may <A HREF="signin.html">add your comments</A> also, if you
wish.
<HR>
<DL>
<!-- newpost -->
</DL>
<HR>
<A HREF="index.html">[ Return to Main Page ]</A>
<HR>
</BODY></HTML>
```

The marker comment `<!-- newpost -->` is the target for the program that inserts new postings into the guestbook. Figure 7-14 shows how the guestbook looks after a couple of visitors sign in.

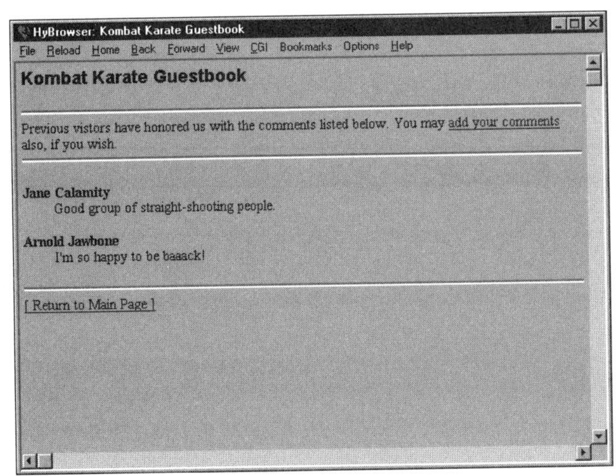


**Figure 7-14:** Browser view of guestbook.

## Guestbook processor

To process mail messages into the HTML code for the guestbook, the processor can rely on these facts about postings sent from `signin.hml`:

- `AAFormID:KomSign` marks the beginning of a relevant data section.
- `zzForm` marks the end of the data section.
- Between the beginning and the end of the data section, data records are formatted as name/value pairs, using one record per line, with the name and value separated by a colon.
- `Guest:` marks the visitor's name record, and `Posting:` marks the comment record. The comment record may run over several lines if the visitor pressed Enter while creating the comment.

The processor uses this information to find and extract the posting from e-mail. To merge the posting into the guestbook, the processor finds the `<!-- newpost -->` insertion marker and writes in the new posting at that point. In case more than one posting needs to be processed, Listing 7-8 stores new postings in an array until all of the e-mail has been processed.

**Listing 7-8** **mail2gbk.pl**

```
# mail2gbk.pl -- merge email data into guestbook page

# Loop though all *.msg files, load signin data into @signin

while ($filename = <*.msg>) {                              #1
   open (FHANDLE,$filename);
   while (<FHANDLE>) {
      if (/AAFormID:KomSign/) {                            #2
         ($head, $tail) = split(/:/, <FHANDLE>, 2);        #3
         push(@signin, $tail);                             #4
         ($head, $tail) = split(/:/, <FHANDLE>, 2);        #5
         $endMark = <FHANDLE>;                             #6
         while ($endMark !=~ /zzForm/) {                   #7
            $tail .= "<BR>\n" . $endMark;                  #8
            $endMark = <FHANDLE>;                          #9
         }
         push(@signin, $tail);                             #10
      }                                                    #11
   }
   close(FHANDLE)
```

```
}                                                   #12
push(@signin, "endsignin");                         #13

open (FHANDLE, "guestbk.html");                     #14
@gBook = <FHANDLE>;
close (FHANDLE);

# Make backup copy of guestbook.html
open (FHANDLE, ">guestbk.bak");                     #15
print FHANDLE "@gBook\n";
close (FHANDLE);

open (FHANDLE, ">guestbk.html");                    #16
# Find insertion point in array
foreach $htmLine (@gBook) {                         #17
  if ($htmLine =~ /<!-- newpost -->/) {             #18
     print FHANDLE "$htmLine\n";                    #19

     # For each new note, insert HTML text
     while($#signin > 0) {                          #20
        $gName = shift(@signin);                    #21
        $gPost = shift(@signin);
        print FHANDLE "<DT><B>$gName<\B>\n";        #22
        print FHANDLE "<DD>$gPost\n\n";
     }
  }
  else {
     print FHANDLE $htmLine;                        #23
  }
}                                                   #24

close (FHANDLE);
print "\nDone!\n\n";
# end of mail2gbk.pl
```

To help you understand how `mail2gbk.pl` works, I labeled the important parts of Listing 7-8 for your reference:

1. The `while (<*.msg>)` construct pulls in files with the `msg` extension one at a time.
2. Look for the start marker (`AAFormId:KomSign`) for guestbook data.

3. Pull another line from FHANDLE, split it into two pieces at the first colon, and then dump the first piece in $head and the second in $tail.
4. Add $tail to the end of the @signin array. This is the visitor's name.
5. Fetch and split another line to extract the comment.
6. Just in case the comment ran over more than one line, check whether the next line contains the record end marker, zzForm..
7. If zzForm does not appear yet, assume that the line is a continuation of the comment.
8. Add an HTML <BR> tag and newline to $tail and then tack on the current line to build on to the comment.
9. Fetch another line to check for zzForm.
10. I finally have zzForm in $endMark. The comment is complete. Push $tail onto the end of the @signin array.
11. Go back up to look for and process another guestbook posting from this file.
12. We're finished with this file. Go after the next one if any are left.
13. All files are finished. Add a dummy element to the array to use for testing the array-processing loop coming up.
14. Open guestbk.html, read it into array @gBook, and close the file.
15. Make a backup copy of guestbk.html, just in case a problem is encountered.
16. Open a new file for guestbk.html, to hold the updated page.
17. Cycle through @gbook, one element at a time, to copy existing HTML text or to add new lines into the new guestbk.html file.
18. Find the insertion marker.
19. Print the insertion marker line. All of the new postings will come after this marker, so new postings appear at the top of the comment list.
20. The while($#signin > 0) construct checks the subscript number of the highest-numbered element (returned by $#signin) for elements in the @signin array. When there is one element left, the $#signin returns 0.

21. Remove (`shift`) the first element in the array `@signin` and assign the value to `$gName`. Remove the next element and assign it to `$gPost`. As this loop runs, eventually only one element will remain: `$signin[0]`, which holds the dummy string `endsignin`. At that point, the loop fails, and the processing is finished.
22. Format the visitor's name as a definition term and the comment as a definition description.
23. Print any existing lines in the original `guestbk.html` file.
24. Go for another line.

Because all the required filenames are hardwired into the program, no command-line parameters are needed. Place `mail2gbk.pl` in the same directory with the message files and `guestbk.html`, and then run the program with the following command:

```
C:\dev\perl mail2gbk.pl
```

Upload the new `guestbk.html` to your server, and the job is done.

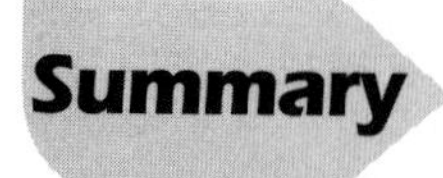


The following topics are covered in this chapter:

- *Random-access files* are files that provide random (direct) access by depending on fixed record and/or field length to allow in-place updating.

- Some random-access file formats use the beginning sections of a file to store file-structure information. These header sections have to be counted in the calculations determining record position so that seeks land in the right spot.

- Memos are variable-length text records, usually kept in a sequential file separate from the parent random-access file. The parent file fetches the memo by storing and using the memo's record length and position to find the record in the sequential file.

- The Perl `open` function uses flags to set the access mode of the opened file by prepending the appropriate flag (> write/create, < read if exists, >> append/create, +> read-write/create, +< read-write if exists) to the filename in the function call: `open(MYFILE, "+>filename")`.

- The `seek(FHANDLE, dist, gofrom)` function moves the pointer to the next access byte in a file, where `FHANDLE` is the filehandle, `dist` is the number of byte to move, and `gofrom` is the starting point (0 = start of file, 1 = current position, 2 = end of file).

- The `tell(FHANDLE)` function returns the current access-byte pointer position in the referenced file.

- The `sprintf("template",$var)` function returns a string formatted to `template`. If `template` contains a `%s` marker, `$var` is evaluated into the string to replace `%s`.

# Perl and Server Tasks

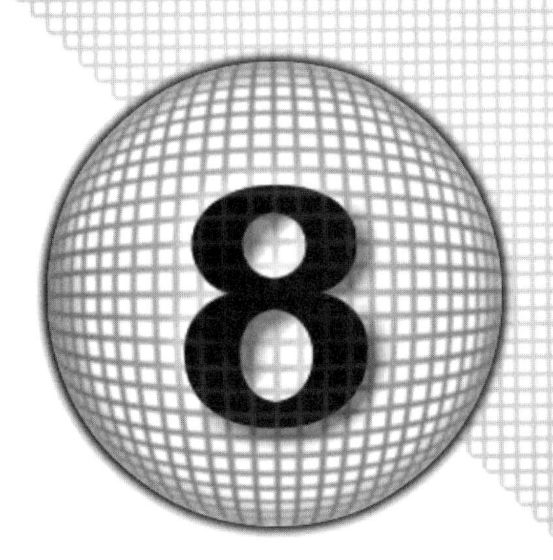


**Skill Targets**

Perl patterns for index-building

Manipulating strings to sort numbers correctly

Index file structures

Using `grep` to search indexes

The two preceding chapters' explorations into the wily ways of sequential and random-access files have established the background for excursions into the realm of *indexing*. Perl's approach to the task of sifting and winnowing through data files seems like cheating if you have spent much time with other computer languages. Pattern matching; associative arrays; and the slice-and-dice `grep`, `keys`, and `sort` array functions unleash programming power that you never knew you had.

To start off this chapter, I overview some of the championship-class Web sifters available to outline the possibilities that you can use. Then I unravel `sprintf` and `print` a bit more and finally help you build some data- and page-indexing tools with Perl.

## The World Wide Web as a Database

The current estimates for the number of pages accessible through the Web start at 60 million and go straight up from there. Yet given a URL, you can view a specific page just three or four seconds after dumping your document request into the Internet. Going to a specific page from a couple of keywords, a name, a book title, or a topic description takes a little longer. This delay is caused by the procedures used to find the URLs that match your needs. Imagine opening a 60-million page phonebook to find the number you want and discovering that the entries are not alphabetized.

Nothing gets found in a Web search unless it has been indexed somewhere.

## Indexing the entire Web

*Search engines* categorize Web pages along more lines than a zebra can show at a full gallop. Yahoo! groups and subdivides URLs by subject. Lycos indexes by page titles and content. Alta Vista indexes every word in every document it finds but pays special attention to information in `<META>` tags. Some search engines go after the text in headings, but some may only look at the first 250 characters following the `<BODY>` tag. In addition, some search engines take months to find and index a new Web site, whereas others locate and catalog new sites within a matter of days after the pages are first published. Standardization is the enemy, it seems.

The basic scheme for indexing Web documents is *key/value pairs*, where the key is a designated keyword and the value is a list of URLs where that word can be found. Thus, you ask for a keyword and receive a list of pertinent URLs. You can search on more than one word. Ask for key1 OR key2, and the search engine builds a list for key1 and another list for key2; then it merges the lists and throws out the duplicates. Ask for key1 AND key2 and the engine builds a list for key1 and another list for key2 — and then keeps only the URLs that appear on both lists.

Weighting algorithms also kick in to float certain URLs to the top of the list. When you search for the word "maxillary," a frequency-counting tool bumps a document that contains "maxillary" 12 times to a higher spot on the list than a document that mentions it only twice. For multi-word searches, the proximity of two words within a document may be the priority factor. Some engines enable you to exclude documents on the grounds of a "don't pick" list of non-keywords. I believe the academic field of Symbolic Logic was invented solely to give search-engine designers new universes of query-input formats to explore.

Search engines are fun! But they also are frustrating if you only have a rough idea of what to look for and no idea of how to describe it in a query. Fortunately, all search engines have Help files. Unfortunately, most people don't think to use them.

## Indexing a Web site

A Web site is like a holographic chunk of the Internet (Figure 8-1). The components of a particular site work just like all the components of the Internet, but you have fewer pieces to handle — usually, that is. I have visited sites reported to have more than 100,000 pages linked together, so even a single site can present some serious indexing problems.

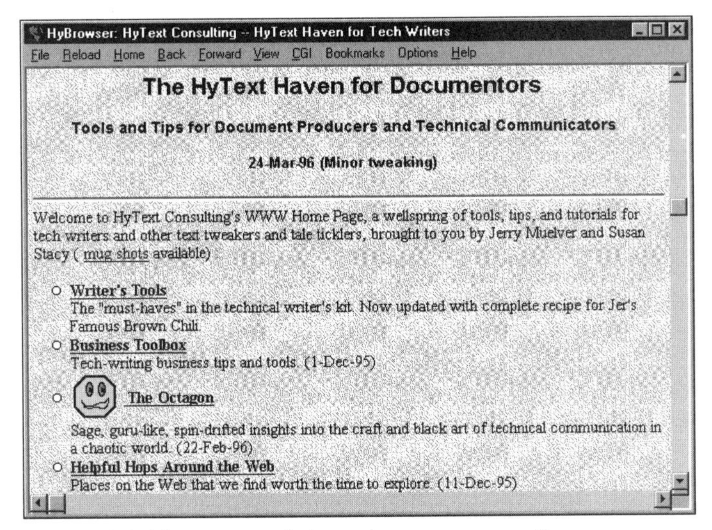


**Figure 8-1:** Home pages link to other pages on a site.

Tools for indexing Internet Web sites are readily available on the Internet. The tools I discuss next are most likely serious overkill for personal or small business needs, but you may see them mentioned in discussions on indexing. All of them are server-based tools — not the kind of thing you would have running on your own PC. (Forewarned is forearmed.)

## WAIS

WAIS (Wide Area Information Server) is the granddaddy and 800-lb. gorilla of indexing and search engines. Running as an information retrieval server within an Internet server, WAIS processes queries in either techie, database, Boolean-logic query format or in common language. The file formats that WAIS can index, catalog, and manipulate run the gamut of MIME types, from HTML to graphics, QuickTime movies, and spreadsheet and word-processing formats. Query matches come back from WAIS with priority ratings.

The original version of WAIS was created by a consortium that included Apple Computers, Thinking Machines, KPMG Peat Marwick, and Dow Jones. A public (meaning available on the Internet) version called *freeWAIS* is available from a number of sources. The main support is provided by Clearinghouse for Networked Information Discovery and Retrieval (CNIDR), with its information site at `http://cnidr.org/cnidr_projects/freewais.html`. WAIS, Inc., also offers a commercial version at `http://cnidr.org/`.

Perl gateway or interface scripts handle the input to WAIS and format the output into HTML pages. These scripts also come in commercial and free versions. Some of the tool sites that pop up in a search for WAIS gateways on the Web are

```
http://dewey.lib.ncsu.edu/staff/morgan/son-of-wais.html
http://ewshp2.csd.uiuc.edu/Source_table
http://ls6-www.informatik.uni-dortmund.de/SFgate/SFgate.html
http://server.wais.com/waisgate-announce.html
```

If your Internet Service Provider (ISP) has WAIS installed and running, you should be able to obtain instructions for plugging your pages into the system from your ISP.

## Glimpse

Glimpse is a text-only indexer with two components — an indexing engine and a query interface. The indexes built by Glimpse are smaller than WAIS-style indexes, which is important when space is at a premium. Like WAIS, Glimpse is a server-based rather than user-based system and requires expert handling for setup and maintenance. You can find more information at

```
http://glimpse.cs.arizona.edu:1994/
```

## SWISH

SWISH (Simple Web Indexing System for Humans) is simpler, smaller, easier to install, and generally more suitable for small Web-site operations than WAIS. For more information, aim your browser at

```
http://www.eit.com/software/swish/swish.html
```

## Harvest

Also not a beginner's tool, Harvest is a toolkit — a collection of programs that work together to access information on the Internet. Harvest can understand and use indexes compiled by other systems and will even catalog information stored in compressed archive files. Harvest is less of a Web site indexer and more of an integrated front end for other indexers. The latest information on Harvest is available at

```
http://harvest.cs.colorado.edu/
```

### Roll your own

No indexing system is available called "Roll your own." At least, not yet — but read on!

## PerlFacts: Indexing and Searching

Assuming that the object of the exercise is to return a filename or URL, the search process requires an engine to do the searching and something specific to find in a particular file. Creating an engine is easy to do in Perl. Some options for creating an engine are

- Convert the search query into a pattern and read source files madly to look for a match
- Convert the search query into a pattern and scan an array of index records in a sequential file with `grep`
- Convert the search query into a string and test an associative array for a key with that string
- Convert the search query to a database record key and look up the value in a random-access database file

In each case, the search engine returns a filename, a URL, or perhaps a list of them if the search is successful. The following discussions help you to warm up your mental muscles before using them to build a site index and query system.

### Menus and TOCs — the easy way out

Most Web builders start out with a small site using a topical organization. Such a site may not need a search engine because visitors can easily find the page of their choice through a menu or table-of-contents system. The mathematics of menus shows that a hierarchical system similar to the structure used by Yahoo! covers a great many pages in just a few layers of menus. Take a look at Figure 8-2 to see what you can do with just eight selections on each menu.

You may feel hard pressed to manage a 4,000-page site with just a four-level menu driving the entire structure. The point, though, is that your visitor can get to any of 4,000 pages with just three mouse-clicks and no Boolean syntax. So, if you don't need a search engine, don't use one.

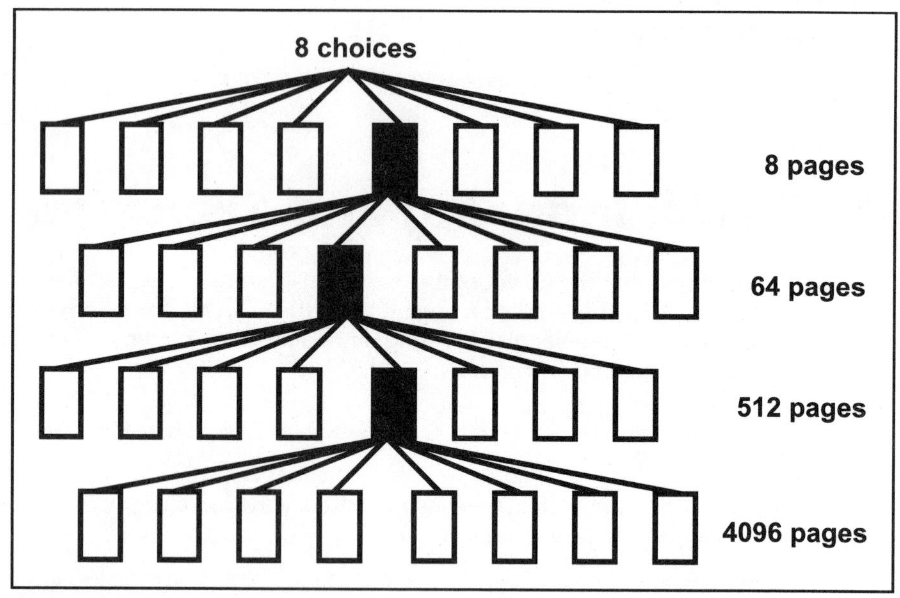


**Figure 8-2:** Menu math.

## Brute-force searching

The first method to consider is enabling a search of all files in a directory or specific list. This brute-force approach is suitable only for Web sites with just a few pages and a low likelihood of large numbers of simultaneous visitors. Disk thrashing on a server increases dramatically when a horde of visitors are scanning all files at the same time.

To test the concept of brute-force searching, try the quickie search engine provided by Listing 8-1 in a directory of HTML files. The procedure that `qwiksrch.pl` follows is to test each file for the requested pattern and then list the hits as links in a demo response page.

**Listing 8-1** **qwiksrch.pl**

```
# qwiksrch.pl -- search HTML files for pattern,
#   list hits in a linklist page
# usage: perl qwiksrch.pl "pattern" filedesc

$pattern = shift(@ARGV);          #1
while (<>) {
```

```
    if (/$pattern/i) {              #2
       push (@found,$ARGV);         #3
       close (ARGV);                #4
       next;                        #5
    }
}

open (FHANDLE, ">found.html");
print FHANDLE "<HTML><HEAD><TITLE>\n";
print FHANDLE "List of files with pattern</TITLE>\n";
print FHANDLE "</HEAD><BODY>\n";
print FHANDLE "<H2>Files with \"$pattern\"</H2>\n";

foreach $fFile (@found){            #6
   print FHANDLE "<P><A HREF=\"$fFile\">$fFile</A>\n";
}

print FHANDLE "</BODY></HTML>\n";
close (FHANDLE);
print "\nDone!\n\n";
```

The following steps outline how you set up `qwiksrch.pl` to enable brute-force searching:

1. Grab the first command-line argument after the program name — this is the quoted pattern to match. The `shift` function leaves `@ARGV` holding only a file description of a list of filenames, because `shift` removes the quoted pattern from the front of the array.
2. Note the `i` option that makes the search case-insensitive.
3. Add the current filename to the `@found` array if a pattern match occurs.
4. One match is enough — no need to keep looking. Close the file.
5. Go for the next file in the `@ARGV` list.
6. Print a link to the file in the response page.

Running `qwiksrch.pl` with the command

```
C:/dev> perl qwicksrch.pl "psyhol" *.html
```

returns a page of links to files that contain at least one reference to "psychology" or "psychologist," as shown in Figure 8-3:

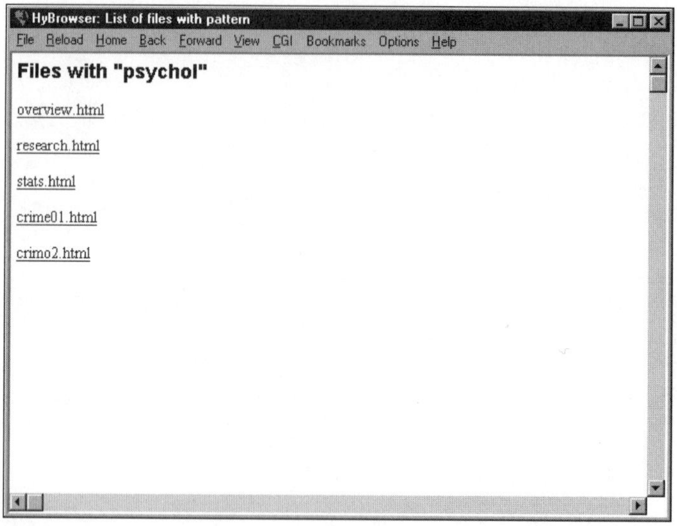

**Figure 8-3:** Response page with links to matched files.

You could use `qwiksrch.pl` as a nifty, organizational utility in the cache directory of your browser to break out a menu listing of recently-visited pages with a specific pattern. Note that the pattern "." catches every file that has at least one character in it, in case you want to create an instant-access HTML menu to all files in the directory. The enhanced version of `qwicksrch.pl` in the "PerlProjects" section of this chapter captures page titles for a more user-friendly approach to menu design (Figure 8-4).

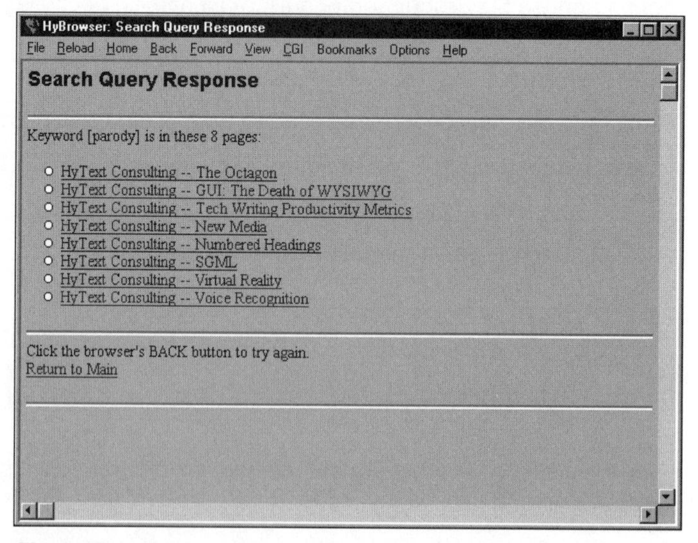


**Figure 8-4:** Response page using page titles to build a link menu.

**Exercise 8-1**

Compare qwiksrch.pl to Listing 2-9, grepfil.pl, paying particular attention to their respective handling of file input. Write grepfil2.pl so that it uses the techniques from qwiksrch.pl. for finding patterns in a directory of files.

# Indexing concepts

A better way for searching for information than reading every file in the house must be available. And one is — indexing.

The key to successful searching is a good indexing method. Here, *good* means matched to the task at hand. The various methods available are more or less suitable depending on the structure and purpose of your site. The basic approach for indexing is to mine the gold out of the files and let your visitors poke through a small bag of nuggets instead of a mountain of ore. In other words, collect the productive words and phrases from a set of files into an organized index file and then point searches into the index file.

## Designating keywords

If you don't care to restrict your visitor to a particular set of keywords, use the brute-force search method. Of course, if the visitor is looking for *syzygy,* and your files do not cover the topic of opposing points on the orbit of a heavenly body, you have to read every word of every file just to answer, "Sorry, not found." Using a fast-access index at least gets the bad news to the visitor as quickly as possible.

### Setting keywords with <META>

The HTML <META> tag flags information for special treatment by browsers and Web robots. The tag belongs in the <HEAD>...</HEAD> section of the page. It takes two attributes, NAME and CONTENT, whose contents are intended to be read as a name/value pair. The syntax is

```
<META NAME="keywords" CONTENT="apple fruit tree pie">
```

The contents of <META> tags do not appear on the displayed Web page. This invisible information is for administrative use only. For example, Alta Vista suggests using <META> tags to communicate indexing information to visiting search robots, such as in the following example:

```
<HTML><HEAD>
<META NAME="keywords" CONTENT="birds woodland nuthatch">
<META NAME="description"
CONTENT="Detailed descriptions of white-breasted,
rose-breasted, and brown nuthatches.">
```

The search robot checks <META> tags for `NAME` attributes labeled as `"description"` and `"keywords"`. The matching `CONTENT` values for `NAME="keywords"` work into the search engine's keyword index for that page. The `CONTENT` for the `NAME="description"` appears in the page's listing on the response for a successful query. Without the <META> information, the search engine is left to its own devices for both search parameters and page descriptions. If the first paragraphs on the page consist of a generic introduction to small, woodland birds, and that is all the search robot has to work with, the visitor won't be led to specific nuthatch identification secrets found on the page.

To use the <META> tag idea for your own indexing purposes, insert the tags on your pages and then scan all pages for <META> tag contents to build the index. If you want, you can use private labels for the `NAME` attributes to distract external search robots by setting `NAME` to `"myDesc"`, `"myKeys"`, or whatever label you prefer over `"keywords"`. You'll be the only one who knows what to look for when you scan the documents to build your private index. You can actually feed the robots a different line by also using the expected `"description"` and `"keywords"` entries, which allows for access tailored to the expected source of the request. Thus, visitors familiar with your site or topic would have a different search vocabulary for your local search engine from the search vocabulary used by newbies coming in from outside search sites.

## Keywords from page structures

In addition to <META> tags, some HTML structural components offer rich sources for keywords. The <TITLE> tag comes instantly to mind in this context, followed immediately by the heading tags <H1> through <H6>. In fact, these tags are the primary targets for most keyword searches. Using relevant descriptive terms in headings not only helps the visitor viewing the page, but also aids in building the index that points viewers to the page in the first place. A heading-collector also is a useful tool for generating automatic table-of-contents pages.

## Using a priority keyword list

The most useless indexing tool I ever used was a do-it-all, super-GUI desktop publishing package that indexed every word in the document. I couldn't choose phrases, "please don't pick these" lists, or any other helpful options with it. Clicking the index icon gave me an index listing at the end of the document that showed every word and all its locations in the document, come Hell, high water, or common sense.

The underlying concept missed by that early experiment in indexing is that common words appear in all documents, so using them in an index does nothing to narrow the search. A priority list of index-useful terms starts the indexing process on a productive path. You don't have to live with just any old words that turn up in a file for indexing.

Build a list of keywords as a separate file. For the index-scanning process, look at each word in the target document and compare the word against the list of allowable keywords. If the word is not on the list, go to the next one. If the word is on the list, add the filename to the hit list for that word. A search query makes a first stop at the priority list. If the keyword requested by the query is not on the list, it has no need to look any further — the visitor gets the bad news immediately.

## Building a word-frequency list

One way to generate a priority keyword list is by counting how often specific words occur in a document. Scan the document and tally the number of times each word appears. Sort the list by word frequency and throw out the 80 (or 90!) percent with the highest count. The survivors are good candidates for productive indexing. Listing 8-2, `wordfreq.pl`, is a starting point.

**Listing 8-2** **wordfreq.pl**

```
# wordfreq.pl -- word frequency counter
# usage: perl wordfreq.pl filedesc > outfile.dat

while (<>) {
   tr/A-Z/a-z/;                                   #1
   @wlist = split(/\W/);                          #2
   foreach $wd (@wlist) {                         #3
      if ($wd =~ /^[a-z_]+$/){                    #4
         $words{$wd}++ ;                          #5
      }
   }
}

while (($wd, $freq) = each (%words)){             #6
   push (@wordfreq, join (" ", $wd, $freq));      #7
   $freq = sprintf ("%4d", $freq);                #8
   push (@freqword, join (" ", $freq, $wd));      #9
}
@srtfreq = sort (@freqword);                      #10
```

*(continued)*

**Listing 8-2 *(continued)***

```
@srtword = sort (@wordfreq);
foreach $item (@srtfreq) {                              #11
   print "$item\n";
}
foreach $item (@srtword) {
   print "$item\n";
}
```

The steps that `wordfreq.pl` takes are described in the following list:

1. Bump to lowercase.
2. Split on non-alphanumerics — this delivers a "don" and a "t" out of "don't," but fixing that problem is a project for another day.
3. Work through the line, one word at a time.
4. Allow only letters and underlines.
5. Increment the count for that word in the associative array `%words`.
6. Loop through the `%words` array, breaking out each word and its matching frequency count.
7. Build a "word count" string, such as `banana 5`, and add it to the `%wordfreq` array. (This is a tutorial exercise, so it can be commented out or deleted later.)
8. Build a leading-space padded string from the frequency for sorting purpose, so that `"     2"` sorts ahead of `" 102"`.
9. Build a "count word " string such as `"     5 banana"` and add it to the `%freqword` array.
10. Sort the arrays.
11. Print the array sorted by frequency. The padded numbers sort properly.
12. Print the array sorted by word.

Steps 7 and 12 deal with sorting the word list alphabetically and are for informational or instructional purposes; so, you don't really need them for a word frequency list, but they are good for the inquisitive mind. Here's a sample run, showing some of the words that occur only once in the target file, then some of the high-frequency words:

```
1 additional
1 advice
1 again
```

```
1 allow
1 also
1 although
1 appear
1 appears
. . .
35 if
36 stream
37 data
39 for
39 size
43 length
47 this
50 bytes
55 and
55 file
```

**Exercise 8-2**

Want some more practice? Try these tasks:

**A.** Add a cut-off limit to `wordfreq.pl` so that only the words used three times or less appear in the final list.

**B.** Assume that queries will only be for words of five characters or more. Add a word-length cut-off to `wordfreq.pl`.

## The index file structure

At minimum, the index file holds a series of records, each containing a keyword paired with the name of file in which the keyword can be found. Variations on this theme are limited only by your imagination. The following table shows some samples, with arbitrary type names and comma-delimited templates:

| Type | Format |
|---|---|
| word/file | *word,file*<br>apple,fruit.html<br>apple,tree.html<br>banana,fruit.html |

*(continued)*

*(continued)*

| Type | Format |
|---|---|
| word/filelist | *word,file1,file2,file3*<br>apple,fruit.html,pie.html,tree.html<br>banana,fruit.html,tree.html,tropical.html |
| file/wordlist | *file,word1,word2,word3*<br>tree.html,apple,banana,elm,maple<br>pie.html,apple,banana,strawberry |
| weighted word | *word,file,frequency*<br>apple,fruit.html,5<br>apple,tree.html,2<br>banana,fruit.html,2<br>banana,joke.html,18 |
| file/weighted wordlist | *file,word1,freq1,word2,freq2,word3,freq3*<br>tree.html,apple,2,banana,1,elm,5,maple,8<br>pie.html,apple,7,banana,2,strawberry,6 |

Other arrangements are possible. You can see immediately that index files lend themselves to creative compression. Speed and economy of disk space motivate the desire for index compression. The two goals of speed and economy are sometimes in conflict, however. Having an index file larger than the total size of the files it represents is not unusual! A little ingenuity, however, can shrink file sizes drastically. For example, if every filename has `.html` on it, why not leave that extension off for the index file and tack it back on if you actually have to retrieve the file by name?

Because my purpose here is create a search method that is both workable and understandable, I'll avoid the really esoteric compression methods and stick with the word/filelist and file/wordlist formats for the basic index design.

## Index lookups

Conceptually, searching through an index is the same as searching through any file. The technique I favor for a small index file is to load the entire file into memory and do the searching in good, fast silicon. Large indexes offer large-file problems, however. A sequential file too large to be pulled into memory at once can be pulled in a piece at a time or even examined one line at a time. For really huge indexes, random-access files are the answer.

## Word/filelist

As explained a little earlier, a word/filelist index is organized like this:

```
apple,fruit.html,pie.html,tree.html
banana,fruit.html,tree.html,tropical.html
```

Loading a word/filelist index file into an associative array keyed on the search words is perfect for queries with multiple keywords (Listing 8-3). Simply ask for the value of the keyword. The result is either a list of files or failure.

**Listing 8-3** **wordex.pl**

```
# wordex.pl -- read word/filelist, search for query
# usage: perl wordex.pl "keyword"

open (IDX, "wdindex.dat");                    #1
while (<IDX>) {
   ($head, $tail) = split (/,/, $_, 2);       #2
   $widx{$head} = $tail;                      #3
}
close (IDX);
$query = $ARGV[0];                            #4
if (defined ($widx{$query})) {                #5
   %fileList = split (/,/, $widx{$query});    #6
} else {
   die "\n$query not found.", "\n";           #7
}
print "\n\"$query\" was found in the following files:\n";
foreach $fname (@fileList) {                  #8
   print "$fname\n";                          #9
}
```

The following list describes the steps that `wordex.pl` performs to create a word/filelist index:

1. Open the fictitious index file.
2. Split the word from the list of filenames.
3. Load the associative array `%widx` with a word for the key and the list of filenames for the value of the array element.
4. Grab the search word from the command line.

5. The `defined` function returns True if the key is in the array already or False if no such key exists. The advantage of using `defined` is that it won't create a key where one is not present, which is what would happen if you checked for the existence of a key with `if ($widx{$query} gt "")` or some other comparison that actually names the key. With the exception of `defined`, naming a key creates one.
6. Make a list of files from the value of the found key.
7. Quit if no elements appear in the "found" list.
8. Loop though the list of files that belong to the keyword in $query.
9. Ta-daa!

Running `wordex.pl` with a query for *peel* on an index file with an entry like this:

```
peel,apple.txt,banana.txt,orange.txt,sunburn.txt
```

generates this report:

```
peel was found in the following files:
apple.txt
banana.txt
orange.txt
sunburn.txt
```

## Filename/wordlist

A filename/wordlist index file uses a normal array for the initial loading. The file has one record per line, with a filename in the first record, followed by a list of keywords in that file separated by commas. Load each line of the file into an array element and then use `grep` to find matching keys. Listing 8-4 shows how to do so:

**Listing 8-4** **fildex.pl**

```
# fildex.pl -- read filename/wordlist, search for query
# usage: perl fildex.pl "keyword1"

open (IDX, "flindex.dat");
@flidx = <IDX>;                                        #1
close (IDX);
```

```
$query = $ARGV[0];                                      #2
@filelist = grep ($query, @flidx);                      #3
$nrHits = @filelist;                                    #4
if ($nrHits < 1 ) {
  die "\n$query not found.", "\n";
}
print "$query found in the following files:\n";
@srtlist = sort(@filelist);                             #5
foreach $fname (@srtlist) {
   ($head, $tail) = split (/,/, $fname, 2);             #6
   print "$head\n";
}
```

The following list describes the steps taken to create the `fildex.pl` program:

1. Load the entire index file into the normal array @flidx.
2. Grab the search word from the command line.
3. Use `grep` to break out a list of array elements that contain the search word.
4. See how many hits you have.
5. Add an elegant touch by sorting the list.
6. Break the filename out into `$head`.

The filelist/word format for indexing has much to recommend it:

- The index is easy to generate
- The query is easy to handle
- The file format is easy to read
- Searching an array with `grep` is very fast

Expect to see this procedure again — such as in the PerlProject.

## Big sites

For huge sites with a large, random-access index file, a binary search technique yields acceptable results. This topic is an excursion into the subject of huge indexes. This information is interesting and nice to know, but it is not required reading. I do not use binary searches in this book, but I want to prepare you for understanding them in case you encounter a binary search in a program somewhere else.

*Binary searching* is a divide-and-conquer process for tackling sorted lists and files. It works much like playing hide-and-seek with a coach telling you whether your tentative guess is hot or cold, or, alternatively, like the ancient game of 20 Questions. Each step toward a solution for the searching problem involves cutting the number of candidates in half. For a binary search, you start in the middle of the sorted list. If you don't find your target, your next decision is whether you have to go up or down the list to get closer to it, and then you jump halfway from your current location toward the far end of the next search area.

Figure 8-5 shows how this process works. Suppose that you have a list of 26 sorted items, inventively labeled A through Z. You want to find J but don't know exactly where it is. Start at the halfway point with element number 13, M. That's not J, but because J is less than M, you know it will be somewhere toward the front of the list. That means you can write off everything from numbers 13 to 26 and not bother with them anymore.

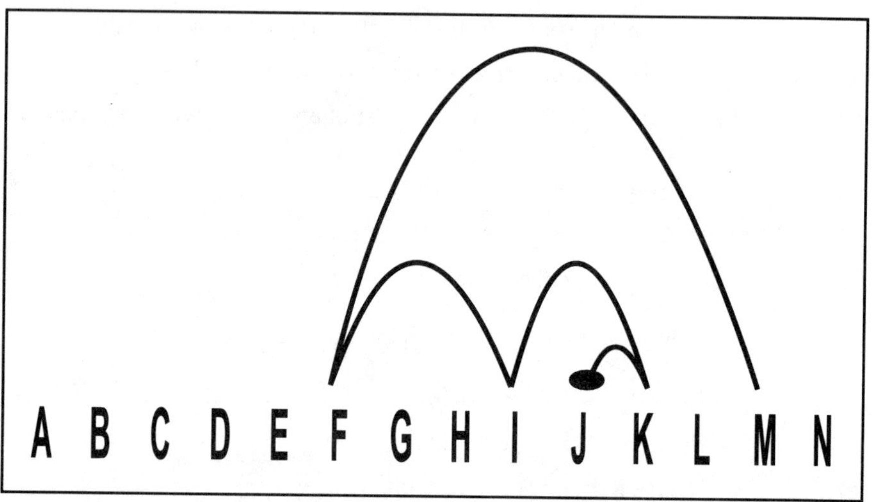


**Figure 8-5:** Binary search.

The next step is to jump halfway between 1 and 12, which (by computer math) is 6, or F. No hit, but now you can cut off everything from 1 to 6. The next step is to jump to halfway between 7 and 12, which computer math calculates to be 9, which holds letter I. No hit, but you've narrowed the field to a list of three remaining elements:10, 11, and 12. Binary-search computer math puts the next step at 11, or K. The next step is to the one element left that is less than 11.

At first, the process seems like a great deal of work — five accesses to find one record in a set of 26. But consider the economy of the binary search — every time you double the number of records, you add only one more access to find any of the records, as the following table shows:

| Number of Records | Max Accesses Required |
|---|---|
| 2–3 | 2 |
| 4–7 | 3 |
| 8–15 | 4 |
| 16–31 | 5 |
| 32–63 | 6 |

It only takes a little calculator work to determine that you can find one record from a million records with a maximum of 21 accesses. If the records were unsorted and you had to find your target by reading from the front of the file, on average you would have to read 500,000 records, instead of the 21 maximum, to succeed.

The downside to binary searching is that the records have to be sorted, and keeping a million or so records sorted is what computer science people call a "non-trivial" task. Some shortcuts are available, such as indexing the index itself or using a sorted list of keys to a file of unsorted records, but these options are even more non-trivial. If you're going to be indexing a million or more items, most likely you already have a crew of computer-science graduates on-hand. Any one of them will be happy to go through the algorithm with you and whip out a merge-sort and binary search program for your specific requirements. If your computer-science grad can't do that, someone should get a tuition refund.

# PerlProject: Searching Your Site

In keeping with my minimalist view of the world, the tools needed for implementing a site search capability are simple:

- Keywords in the HTML files, enclosed in `<META>` tags
- An index-building program in Perl that reads files and extracts keywords
- A query form in HTML
- A CGI program in Perl that processes the query and reports the results

## Building the index file

The index file-builder, called `bldidx.pl`, expects to find keywords in a <META> tag in each file it examines. To keep the process manageable, the <META> tag format should be as follows, all on one line:

```
<META NAME="keywords" CONTENT="word1,word2,word3">
```

The comma-delimited list of keywords enables you to use phrases that include spaces and hyphens, too. For example

```
<META NAME="keywords" CONTENT="living room,sofa,end table">
```

or

```
<META NAME="keywords" CONTENT="hammer,needle-nose pliers">
```

Keep in mind that if your visitor searches for `needle nose pliers`, you won't have a hit! Choosing useful keywords is a topic that deserves a book of its own. Because I'm using `grep`, selecting keywords that could contain findable subkeys is productive. For example, a search for `"connect"` finds such keywords as `connection`, `connected`, and `disconnected`. In some applications, a word or two of how-to-query advice, some helpful examples on the query page, or even a picklist of allowable keywords will be much appreciated by your visitors.

To fancy up the response page, I want to show the found pages by title instead of by ugly little URLs. This design feature adds another requirement: Each page must have a title ensconced in a <TITLE>...</TITLE> tag.

The index file now will be in a filename/title/wordlist format, as in the following examples:

```
chest.html,Chest Exercises,bench press,inclined press,butterfly
arms.html,Arm Exercises,biceps,triceps,curl,triceps extension
```

With such a simple file format, instead of generating the index file programmatically, you can just type one from scratch. Of course, it only takes one little typo to send your visitor looking for a file that never existed, but the option is still there.

Listing 8-5 shows `bldidx.pl` in action.

**Listing 8-5** **bldidx.pl**

```
# bldidx.pl -- build index file from HTML pages
#    using <META> and <TITLE> tag info
# usage: perl bldidx.pl filedesc

while (<>) {
   $line = $_;
   if ($line =~ /<META.*NAME=\"keywords\"/i) {     #1
      if ($line =~ /CONTENT=\"(.*)\"/i) {          #2
         $idxKeys = $1;                            #3
      }
   }
   if ($line =~ /<TITLE>(.*)<\/TITLE>/i) {         #4
      $idxTitle = $1;
      $idxTitle =~ s/^ *(.*) *$/$1/;               #5
      $idxTitle =~ s/,/\%\!/g;                     #6
   }
   if ($line =~ /<\/HEAD>/i) {                     #7
      $newRec = "$ARGV,$idxTitle,$idxKeys";        #8
      push(@idxRecs, $newRec);                     #9
      close (ARGV);                                #10
      $idxTitle = "";                              #11
      $idxKeys = "";
      next;
   }
}

open(FIDX, ">idxlist.dat");                        #12
foreach $recLine (@idxRecs) {
   print FIDX "$recLine\n";
}
close(FIDX);
```

The following list describes the step-by-step process that `bldidx.pl` takes you through to create an index:

1. Find the `<META>` tag and the `"keywords" NAME`.
2. Pick the keyword list out of its enclosing quotes. This program counts on the `<META>` tag and its information all being on one line, with nothing else on that line, to keep from falling into the leftmost-longest trap.
3. Hold on to the keywords.
4. Pick up and hold the title.
5. Strip leading and trailing spaces.
6. Convert commas to the unusual marker `%!` so that Perl won't confuse the embedded commas with the data-field delimiting commas.
7. `</HEAD>` is a clear signal that the data-picking for this file is done.
8. Build the index record for this file.
9. Add the record to the growing collection.
10. You're done with this file, so close it.
11. Perform the precautionary clean-up before reading the next file. Setting string variables to `""` assures that they won't be carrying left-over values into the next loop cycle.
12. Create the index file and fill it with records.

```
cheese.html,Cheesehead Page,cheese,local,tourist
chili.html,Jer's Brown Chili Recipe,chili,recipe
contract.html,Sample Tech Writer's Contract,contract
guest.html,Guest Book,guest,sign-in
hops.html,Helpful Hops,links
musthave.html,Writer's Tools,software,tools
o9000.html,Dealing with ISO-9000,ISO-9000,standards
ocertify.html,Tech Writer Certification,certify
octagon.html,The Octagon,humor,essay,menu
ogui.html,GUI: The Death of WYSIWYG,WYSIWYG,editors
ometrics.html,Tech Writing Productivity Metrics,metrics
onewmedi.html,New Media,sound,VRML
onumb.html,Numbered Headings,numbering,headings,format
osgml.html,SGML,SGML,ISO,format,standards
ovirtual.html,Virtual Reality,VRML,virtual,reality
ovoice.html,Voice Recognition,VR,voice,recognition
```

```
process.html,Process,process,methods,standards
schedule.html,Scheduling,scheduling,cost,analysis
survey.html,Visitor Survey,form,survey,visitor
toolbox.html,Tech Writing Business Toolbox,tools,editors
```

## Building the request form

The query form is short and sweet. Listing 8-6 shows all the HTML text, and Figure 8-6 shows the browser view of the form.

**Listing 8-6** **qform.html**

```
<HTML><HEAD><TITLE>Site Search Query Form
</TITLE></HEAD><BODY>
<H2>Site Search Query Form</H2>
<FORM METHOD="post" ACTION="/cgi-bin/sitesrch.pl">
<INPUT TYPE="HIDDEN" NAME="AAFormID" VALUE="Search">
Keyword: <INPUT TYPE="TEXT" NAME="Query" SIZE="20">
<INPUT TYPE="SUBMIT" VALUE="Submit"><P>
<INPUT TYPE="RESET" VALUE="Clear">
<A HREF="main.html">Return to Main</A>
</FORM></BODY></HTML>
```

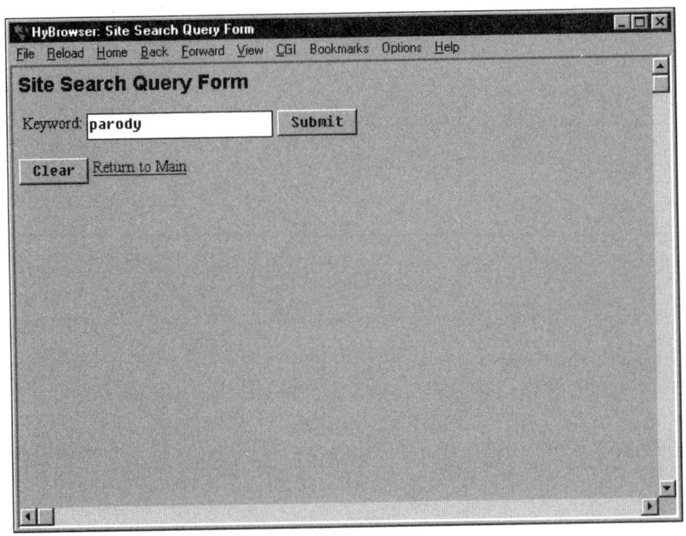


**Figure 8-6:** Browser view of qform.html.

## Searching and reporting

The `sitesrch.pl` program performs the searching and reporting operation on the server (Listing 8-7). This miniature search engine welcomes the query from the visitor, opens the data file, reads the data, finds matches with the keyword query, and finally composes the response page and returns it to the visitor.

**Listing 8-7** **`sitesrch.pl`**

```
#!/usr/local/bin/perl
# sitesrch.pl -- perform keyword search on index file

read(STDIN, $formdat, $ENV{'CONTENT_LENGTH'});          #1
@namevals = split(/&/,$formdat);                         #2
foreach $line (@namevals) {                              #3
   if ($line =~ /^Search/) {                             #4
      tr/+/ /;                                           #5
      ($head, $query) = split(/=/,$line);                #6
      $query =~ s/%(..)/pack("C",hex($1))/ge;            #7
      $query =~ s/\%\!/,/g;                              #8
   }
}

open(FIDX, "~/mydir/idxlist.dat") ||                     #9
   die "Problem opening idxlist.dat";
@idxRecs - <FIDX>;                                       #10
close(FIDX);

@goodList = grep($query, @idxRecs);                      #11
$nrHits = @goodList;                                     #12
print "Content-type: text/html\n\n";                     #13

print "<HTML><HEAD>\n";
print "<TITLE>Search Query Response</TITLE>\n";
print "</HEAD><BODY>\n";
print "<H2>Search Query Response</H2>\n";
print "<HR>\n";
print "Keyword \[$queryBR>\] is in these pages:\n";
if ($nrHits < 1 ) {                                      #14
   print "<P>None: keyword not found.\n";
}
```

```
else {
   print "<UL>\n";
   foreach $qRec (@goodList) {                         #15
      ($filname, $title, $kWords) = split(/,/, $qRec, 3);
      print "<LI><A HREF=\"$filname\">$title<\/A>\n";
   }
   print "<\/UL>\n";
}
print "<HR>\n
print "Click the browser's BACK button to try again.<BR>\n";
print "<A HREF="main.html">Return to Main<\/A>\n"/;
print "<P><HR>\n";
print "<\/BODY>\n<\/HTML>\n";
```

Here's how you set up `sitesrch.pl` to perform the operations:

1. Read the CGI variables to load the input from the form.
2. Set it up for parsing.
3. Only two name/value pairs will be used in this search.
4. The name/value pair you want here begins with `"Search."`
5. Perform the first step in parsing — replace `'+'` with space.
6. Split the name/value pair. Only the `VALUE` is interesting to you.
7. Complete the usual parsing.
8. Perform the unusual parsing to reinstate any commas that may have been part of the page's title.
9. Open the index file. The file address shown here is typical but may not be exact for your server. Your ISP can help you with the setup. If you keep the index file in the same directory as the HTML files, all the permissions should be working correctly.
10. Load the search array.
11. Perform a quick and easy search — `grep` returns all the lines that contain the query keyword. Note that titles are included in the `grep` search, free of charge.
12. Tally the number of hits.
13. Send out the beginning of the reply, the response header.

14. Test for success. I use `$nrHits < 1` instead of `$nrHits == 0` because it's too easy to mistype the double-equal. Then I have `$hrHits = 0`, which is an assignment operation that returns True as an operation success flag — not really what I want to see because I am looking for a False flag when `$nrHits` equals 0. Once bitten, twice learned.
15. Cycle through the list of hits, splitting each line into its component parts and using the filename and title to build links on the response page.

## Enhancement ideas

I wouldn't worry too much about Yahoo! or Alta Vista begging to license the technology of your `sitesrch.pl` engine. But maybe they would, with some enhancements and tweaking. The following are some suggestions you may want to mull over.

### Compound query

A compound (multiple, boolean) query simply requires another `grep`. Add another input field on the query form to accept a second keyword. In the search procedure, `grep` for the first word to load `@goodList`, then `grep ($query2, @goodList)` for the second query word to make `@finalList` for compiling the response page. Figure 8-7 shows the logic better than these frail words. The input form for a compound query might look like the screen in Figure 8-8.

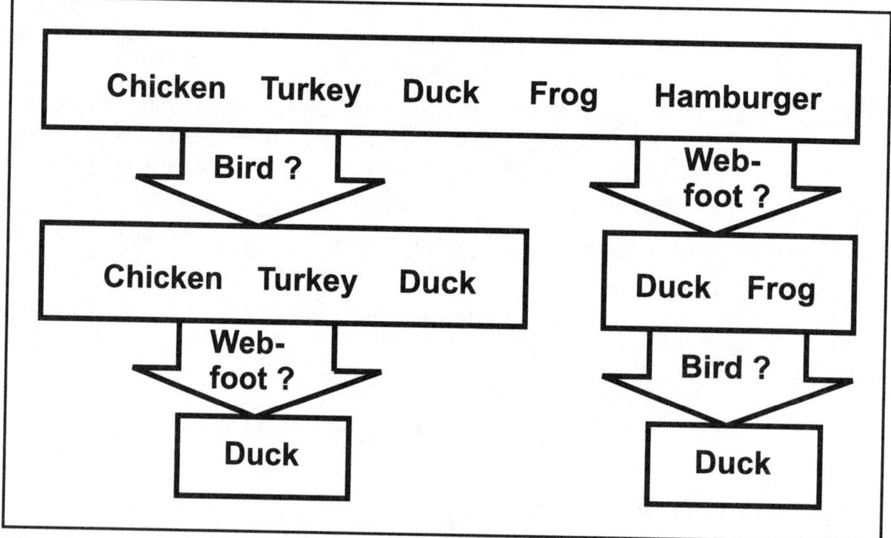


**Figure 8-7:** Block diagram showing a compound query.

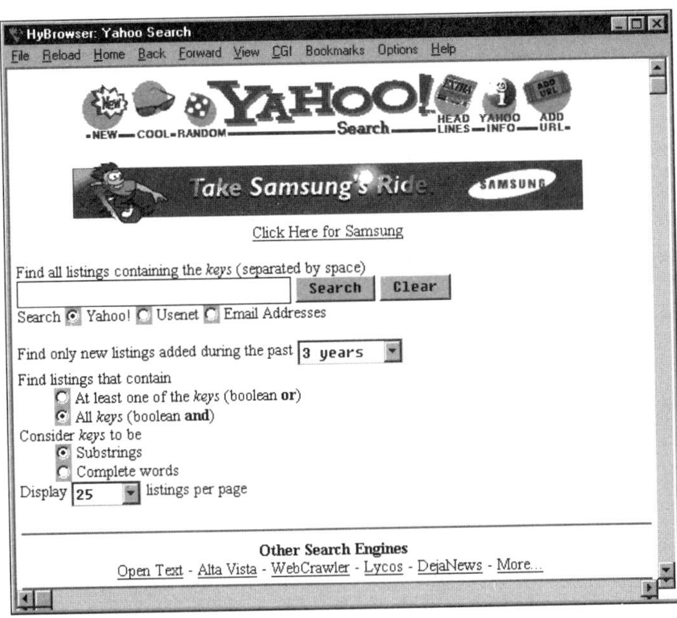


**Figure 8-8:** Input form for a compound query.

## Refined query

Faced with a long list of hits, visitors may give up the quest. You can offer an option to refine the list by accepting another search keyword on the response form. The first hitlist can be saved by embedding it as a series of hidden fields in the response form. The hidden fields on the response form go out with the new query and are parsed into the index array in place of `idxlist.dat`. You can make `sitesrch.pl` do the double duty by checking for the presence of your specially-named hidden fields. If no hidden fields exist in the URL string, the program uses `idxlist.dat`. Otherwise, the program builds the data from the hidden fields to produce a refined search on the first set of hits.

## Headings index

Instead of indexing keywords from a `<META>` tag, you could make a minor adjustment to the `<TITLE>` extraction statement to index the words in headings. The rest of the search procedure (the query page and the search processing) requires little change to accommodate a headings index.

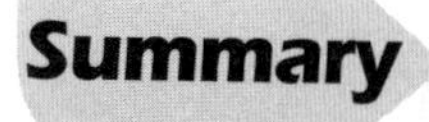


The following topics were covered in this chapter:

- The defined function tests whether a scalar variable or array element has a value assigned to it. When used for testing associative arrays, if(defined($array{$myKey}) does not create a new element, whereas a test such as if($array{$myKey} gt "") creates a new element with the key $myKey and a null value for performing the test.

- The <META> tag belongs in the <HEAD>...</HEAD> container of the HTML format. For indexing, <META> takes two attributes, NAME and CONTENT, which are used for data collection and management purposes.

- A header form of the <META> tag (<META HTTP-EQUIV="xxx">) can be used to create special-purpose HTTP headers.

- When sorting numbers as strings, the numbers need to be padded with blanks on the left so the numbers will sort in the right order: "  2" is less than "144". Unpadded, "144" sorts ahead of "2".

- Index file formats can be tailored to the needs of the application. At minimum, a Web site index record contains a filename and a keyword.

# Toolkit Construction with Perl

**Skill Targets**

- Accessing CGI (environmental) variables
- Flow control with `for(;;)`
- Operations with boolean (logic) functions
- Tricks with `print`, `printf`, and `sprintf`
- Advanced math functions
- Building a shopping cart for processing catalog orders

We started our journey with Perl by building little, single-task tools from a few lines of Perl. I love doing that. Perl is my first tool of choice for problems involving text and parsing — such as personal database reports, lists, file clean-ups, sorting and shuffling projects, and the like. I find keying in a read-file loop with a substitution pattern to run search-and-replace easier to do than having to learn Yet Another Word Processor's mysterious dialog boxes. Until standard desktop applications begin incorporating regular expressions and associative arrays, I believe Perl will be eternally useful — like a long-handled fork at a family reunion picnic.

In this chapter, after pointing you toward some do-it-yourself projects to stretch your imagination, I show you how to explore the murky world of CGI (environmental) variables and then wrap up loose ends by discussing boolean logic, printing preformatted text, and the magic of `printf` and `sprintf`. This frantic piling-on of Perl tricks will prepare you for using the many Perl programs and libraries that are now within your grasp. The final PerlProject explores the process of building a "shopping cart" program.

# Perl — Toolkit Extraordinaire

Programming skills are like all other skills — you need to exercise them to stay sharp. Perl is the kind of hammer that makes everything around you look like a nail. With Perl, you now have the skills to build a wide variety of handy tools. The following sections discuss some project ideas to keep you involved in programming and insulated from normal social activities. Some of these ideas have already appeared in rough prototypes and examples in this book. Becoming familiar with these ideas can ease you into creating more polished scripts.

## Perl at home

I know you're the kind of person who really wants to solve problems independently, instead of relying on some know-it-all from out of town to come in and throw his or her weight around. To foster that independent spirit, the following list briefly describes a number of handy household projects you are now fully capable of accomplishing on your own. Spread your wings and fly a little.

- **Grep files, list and count hits.** Accept a pattern and file descriptor on the command line and then produce a formatted report of the search results.
- **Search by weighted hit values (frequency, proximity, and so on).** Parse a query as a list of keywords and `grep` the target file for hits. Re-`grep` the hitlist for "must also have" keywords. For proximity finds, use `index` to find the keyword location in the text, use `index` again with the next word to find the added keyword location, and then compare the two results.
- **Address book.** Build an address, phone, and comment file with blank-line delimited records. Create an index file for the address book and an HTML version to display one page of records at a time.
- **Textbase operations.** Index a directory full of text files by filename and first line. Build the index into a Web page for access.
- **Financial records.** Start keeping your expenses in a comma-delimited sequential file. Write a report generator that accumulates expenses by the month and by the account name.

## Web project management

You can find programs and exercises in this book that perform the following useful duties:

- Extract URLs from files
- Compile list of URLs into HTML access page

- Map links in set of Web pages
- Generate mapped list of graphics

This list does not end the possiblities. Consider these ideas:

- **Build a list of Perl programs with comment lines.** Scan a directory for `*.pl` files, read the first line of each file, and list the files and first lines in a report.
- **Update filenames in a set of Web pages.** Find page URLs with `.htm` extensions and replace them with `.html` extensions.
- **Splice the current date into a Web page.** Embed a marker in a comment in HTML files, search the files for the marker, and insert the current date and time as text in the body of the page.
- **Format HTML file for pretty printing.** Parse HTML files and adjust their appearance to your liking. For example, all `<P>` symbols at the beginning of lines, all list elements indented appropriately, lowercase (or uppercase) for all HTML tags, double-spaced lines between list elements, and so on.
- **Convert HTML table to outline list.** Automatically generate a no-tables version of HTML tables by parsing the HTML file and converting tables into hierarchical lists.
- **Assemble Web pages from templates.** Insert keyword marker comments in skeletal HTML files and then parse the files to add template text at the keyword insertion points. Keep the templates in the files named to match the keywords.

The more I look at this list, the more I itch to dig in and start programming!

## Perl on the server: environmental variables

Environmental variables are everywhere in the computer world. Every operating system wraps itself in a protective coat of such variables. Perl peeks into the hidden pockets of the environmental trenchcoat with the `%ENV` associative array.

I confess to using the `%ENV` array to retrieve the `CONTENT_LENGTH` value from the CGI in programs earlier in this book without providing much explanation. Let me make amends.

### DOS environmental variables

The environmental variables on a DOS machine are the values created and loaded by the `SET` command in `AUTOEXEC.BAT` and sometimes on-the-fly by programs that need to communicate data to the system or other programs.

Perl knows how to to dig out these values. For example, Listing 9-1, envpeek.pl, tallies up the variables and values currently in the system and prints them out in a list.

**Listing 9-1 Looking at Environmental Variables with Perl**

```
# envpeek.pl -- look at environment variables
# usage: perl evnpeek.pl

while (($head,$tail) = each(%ENV)) {    #1
   $line = $head . "=" . $tail;         #2
   push(@envlist, $line);               #3
}
@srtenv = sort(@envlist);               #4
foreach $envar (@srtenv) {              #5
   print $envar, "\n";
}
```

The following list describes the steps you go through to create envpeek.pl:

1. Run through the %ENV array, placing key/value pairs in the variables $head and $tail.
2. Format $head and $tail into a "key=value" string.
3. Add the string to the @envlist array.
4. Sort the @envlist array into @srtenv.
5. Run through the sorted list of environmental variable strings and print each one to STDOUT.

As you can see in Figure 9-1, envpeek.pl reveals the inner secrets of my system's environmental variables.

## CGI variables

How would the %ENV associative array technique work on my ISP's server to examine CGI variables, I wonder? Quite well, in fact. Instead of crudely printing the variables to STDOUT, I'll format the information as a Web page to show you how the technique works. Listing 9-2 shows that the program env2html.pl starts out working the same as envpeek.pl but shifts gears in time to format the variables with HTML tags.

```
MS-DOS Prompt
8 x 12

C:\dev>perl envpeek.pl
BLASTER=A220 I5 D1 H5 P330 T6
CMDLINE=perl envpeek.pl
COMSPEC=C:\COMMAND.COM
INC=d:\perl5\lib
MIDI=SYNTH:1 MAP:E
MOUSE=C:\MSMOUSE
PATH=C:\WINDOWS;E:\WINDOWS;E:\WINDOWS\COMMAND;C:\;C:\DOS;C:\UTIL;E:\UTIL;D:\PERL
5;D:\PERL5\LIB;C:\STACKER;G:\VSW30\LIB;E:\IBOX\BIN;F:\IBLOCAL\BIN;F:\IDAPI;F:\MA
KER4\
PROMPT=$P$G
SOUND=E:\SB16
TEMP=D:\TEMP
TMP=d:\temp\tmp
TZ=EST5EDT
WINBOOTDIR=C:\WINDOWS
WINDIR=E:\WINDOWS

C:\dev>
```

**Figure 9-1:** DOS window showing how `envpeek.pl` sees the environmental variables.

**Listing 9-2 Report on CGI Variables from the Server**

```
#!/usr/local/bin/perl
# env2html.pl -- report CGI env variables from server

while (($head,$tail) = each(%ENV)) {
   $line = $head . "=" . $tail;
   push(@envlist, $line);
}
@srtenv = sort(@envlist);                                  #1
print "Content-type: text/html\n\n";                       #2
print "<HTML><HEAD>\n";
print "<TITLE>CGI Environmental Variables</TITLE>\n";
print "</HEAD><BODY>\n";
print " CGI Environmental Variables\n";
print "<HR>\n";
print "<PRE><B>\n";                                        #3
foreach $envar (@srtenv) {                                 #4
   print $envar, "\n";
}
print "</PRE></B><P><HR>\n";                               #5
print "</BODY>\n</HTML>\n";
```

Let's take a closer look at how `env2html.pl` works:

1. Except for the `!/user/local/bin.perl` comment, this program is the same as `envpeek.pl` from the beginning to this line.
2. Print the expected header, followed by a blank line and the requisite opening HTML tags.
3. Take the easy way out — use `<PRE>...</PRE>` to format the output. The `<B>` tag is a small concession to elegance.
4. This is the same printing loop used by `envpeek.pl`.
5. Wrap up the HTML text and quit.

After uploading and installing `env2html.pl` on my server, I can run the program by calling it up from my browser like any other URL:

```
http://some.site/some-cgi/env2html.pl
```

In just a couple of seconds, I get the report on my browser shown in Figure 9-2:

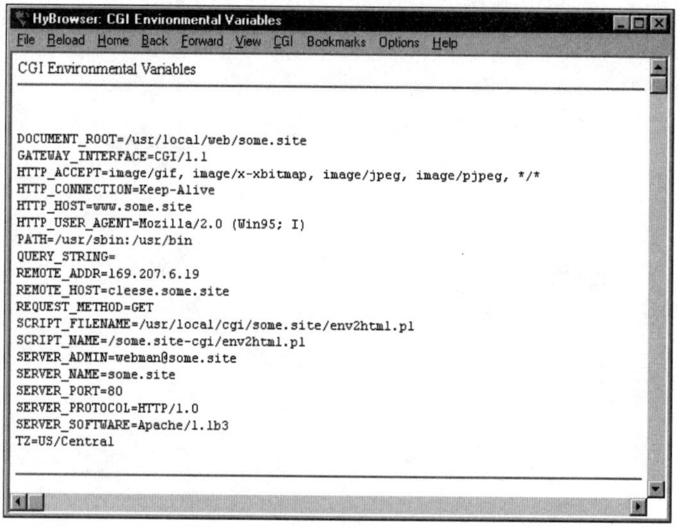

**Figure 9-2:** CGI variables reported by `env2html.pl`.

But look closely — no QUERY_STRING or CONTENT_LENGTH values appear in the report. That's because I didn't send a query with URL. I can add a query to my URL request to trigger the missing values, like this:

```
http://some.site/some-cgi/env2html.pl?cgi+vars+trigger
```

Now the report has the expected complement of variables (Figure 9-3).

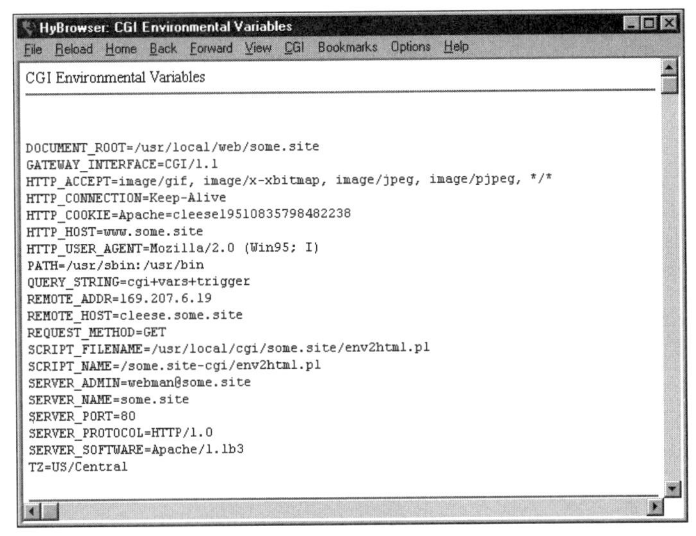


**Figure 9-3:** CGI variables include query information added to the URL.

Remember, the default method for a query is GET, as shown in the METHOD variable in Figure 9-3. The CONTENT_LENGTH variable is undefined because GET doesn't need it — all the data is in the QUERY_STRING variable.

To show what the CGI variables look like with a POST method, I'll change the ACTION in the Kombat Karate survey to call env2html.pl. Figure 9-4 shows the result of submitting the form.

The CGI variables you will worry about the most are REQUEST_METHOD and CONTENT_LENGTH, although QUERY_STRING is significant when you are using a GET method. Appendix B lists and explains all the CGI variables.

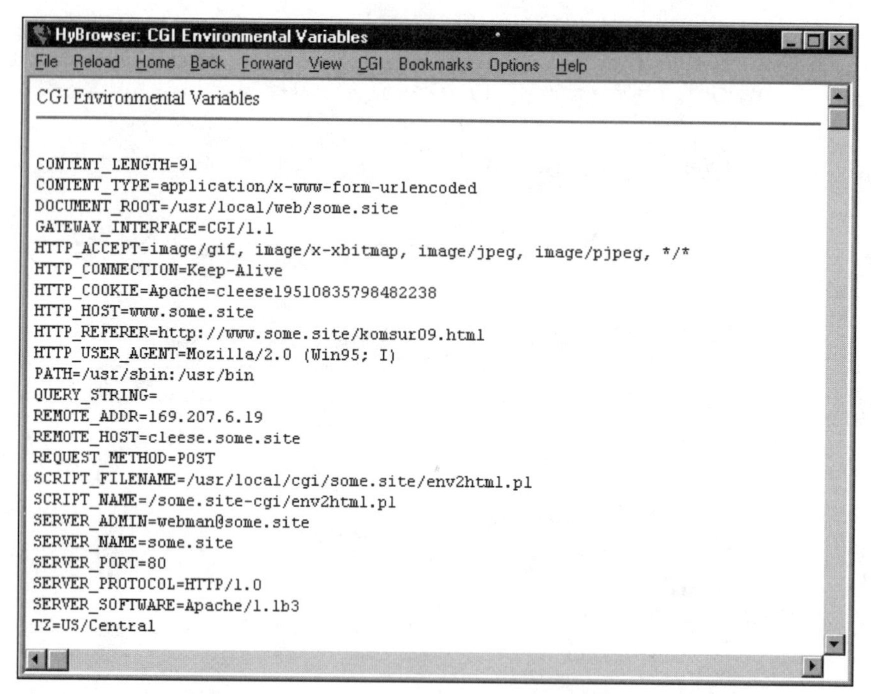


**Figure 9-4:** CGI variables with CONTENT_LENGTH loaded for a POST method.

# Perl on the Web — libraries

Perl libraries, modules, and archives of scripts are found everywhere on the Web. You can look for them through any of the major search engines — Yahoo! and Alta Vista both provide extensive listings of Perl-related URLs. Other resources and references are located in the Perl Resource page on the CD-ROM, with current updates available at this Web site:

```
http://www.hytext.com/coolperl
```

# PerlFacts: Advanced Topics, Loose Ends

By this point, you've learned Perl well enough to build useful, productive tools to support your Web pages with behind-the-scenes CGI programming. In the future, you will be scouring the Web for more Perl scripts and tricks to expand your capabilities. To that end, this edition of PerlFacts explains some (but not all!) of the features you may encounter in your growing collection of scripts.

Perl is grander and more complex than I make it seem in this book. You already may have discovered that fact by looking through the documentation files for the various versions of Perl. I don't believe in scaring people away with complexities of a language if the simplicities will do the progarmming task at hand. As your study of Perl deepens, you will be more comfortable with advanced topics, complex statements, and intricate functions.

## Flow control with `for(;;)`

The `while` loop has performed well in its role as a program flow controller. The `while` loop condition evaluation is flexible and powerful — you can compare counter values, strings values, and complex logical statements to determine whether the loop should run again or be terminated. For looping, `while` is really all you need, but another looping construct is available that you will often see used in Perl scripts — the `for(;;)` function.

The `for(;;)` function runs with a variable for the loop counter and takes three arguments — to set the starting value for the counter, to set the loop terminating value for the counter, and to set the size of the step by which the counter is incremented on each loop. The syntax, shown by the following example, is

```
for($i=1; $i<10; $i++)
```

where the following table describes the different parts of the function:

| | |
|---|---|
| `$i=1` | Sets starting value for counting variable `$i` to 1 |
| `$i<10` | Sets the conditional test to continuing looping as long as `$i` is less than 10 (terminate when `$i` = 10) |
| `$i++` | Sets counter to increment `$i` by 1 each time through the loop |

Listing 9-3 and Listing 9-4 show functionally equivalent code for printing lines of a file.

**Listing 9-3** **`while` loop to Print Lines 5-20 of a File**

```
$i = 5
while ($i <= 20) {
   $a = <STDIN>;
   print $a;
   $i++;
}
```

**Listing 9-4 `for` loop to Print Lines 5-20 of a File**

```
for ($i=5; $i<= 20; $i++) {
    $a = <STDIN>;
    print $a;
}
```

The `for(;;)` function typically appears in loops involving arrays, as shown in Listing 9-5.

**Listing 9-5 Using `for(;;)` to Step Through a Section of an Array**

```
@lines = <STDIN>;
for ($i=10; $i<=20; $i++){
    print $lines[$i];
}
```

The counter can run in reverse with `for(;;)` as well (Listing 9-6):

**Listing 9-6 Using `for(;;)` to Step Down Through a Section of an Array**

```
@lines = <STDIN>;
for ($i=20; $i>=10; $i--){
    print $lines[$i];
}
```

The `for(;;)` function is optimized for speed in Perl and is therefore a better choice than `while` in cases where a small, fast loop is required. Math functions, especially those involved in graphic composition and display, benefit from using `for(;;)`.

### Exercise 9-1

Try these steps with the `for` function to test your mettle with Perl:

**A.** Use `for(;;)` to write a program that reads files and prints the first five lines of each file.

B. Modify the program in the preceding step (A) to enable specifying on the command line the number of lines to print from each file.

# Booleans in `while` and `if` conditionals

George Boole (1815-1864) invented symbolic logic in his book *Laws of Thought* (1854) with little regard and no mention whatsoever for its application for Web-page development and CGI programming. Boole's system of two-valued logic (True and False, or 1 and 0 respectively) with the operators AND, OR, and NOT is today called *boolean logic,* in lowercase honor of his creation. The three operators are accordingly called boolean operators or logical operators. Any system that only has two numbers and three operators in it has to be simple, right?

## AND, OR, NOT

The laws of boolean logic are simple, as shown in this table where 1=True and 0=False. This type of table, showing the statement and the values for each of the statement's components, is called a *truth table:*

```
Statement  A=?  B=?  Result
A AND B     1    1     1    True if both are true
            1    0     0
            0    1     0
            0    0     0

A OR B      1    1     1    True if either is true
            1    0     1
            0    1     1
            0    0     0

NOT A       1          0    False if A is true
            0          1    True if A is false
```

Everyone seems to know these basic structures already. A two-part AND statement is true only if both parts are true, and an OR statement is false only if both parts are false. A NOT statement is a toggle changing true to false or false to true. The logic behind these statements is trickier, however, when the statements are more complex.

## Complex boolean logic

Just tacking NOT onto the front of a boolean statement complicates matters, as you can see from these examples:

```
Statement        A=?  B=?  Result
NOT (A AND B)    1    1      0
                 1    0      1
                 0    1      1
                 0    0      1

NOT (A OR B)     1    1      0
                 1    0      0
                 0    1      0
                 0    0      1

(NOT A) AND B    1    1      0
                 1    0      0
                 0    1      1
                 0    0      0
```

To unscramble complex boolean statements, start with the innermost parentheses, determine the truth of that one small part, and work your way out into the whole statement. For example, `A AND B` is true only when both A and B are true, so `NOT (A AND B)` is false only when both A and B are true. Otherwise (either A or B false), the parentheses contain a false statement, and the NOT reverses the statement to true.

## Boolean operators in Perl

You need to know how booleans work because they are at the core of the conditional tests in functions such as `while` and `if` and `elsif`. A conditional statement such as

```
if ($min > 10) {
```

is easy to understand. Suppose that you want the test to work as long as `$min` is greater than 10 and, simultaneously, as long as `$max` is less than 100. In other words, if A is the truth of the `$min` test, and B is the truth of the `$max` test, you want a statement that will work as long as both A and B are true. That would be a boolean `A AND B`.

Perl uses boolean expressions but replaces the boolean AND, OR, and NOT operators with symbols. The following example shows the symbols and examples of their use:

```
Boolean  Perl  Example
  AND     &&    if (($min > 10) && ($max <100)) {
```

```
OR      ||   if (($min > 10) || ($max <100)) {
NOT      !   if (!($min > 10)) {
```

The combinations are endless and thoroughly entertaining. The following, for example, is a `while` statement using boolean logic:

```
while (($min > 10) && !($max < 100)) {
```

### Exercise 9-2

What will the following program snippet print? (The answer in Appendix A unravels the logic step-by-step.)

```
$A = 1;
$B = 0;
if (!$A || (($A && $B) && ($A || $B))) {
   print "True\n";
} else {
   print "False\n";
}
```

## Block printing with `print <<label`

CGI programs often call for printing blocks of preformatted text. For instance, `echo2htm.pl` in Chapter 4 prints the opening lines of HTML code for a response form like this (Listing 9-7):

**Listing 9-7 Printing a Block of Formatted Text**

```
print "<HTML><HEAD>\n";
print "<TITLE>Form Data Echo</TITLE>\n";
print "</HEAD><BODY>\n";
print "Form Data Echo\n";
print "<HR>\n";
```

Perl offers a better way to handle block printing than the monotonous series of print statements you see in the preceding listing. The `print <<` command works much like HTML's `<PRE>...</PRE>` tag, with a start command at the beginning of a block of text and a stop label at the end of the text. The syntax for this command is

```
print <<label;
  Multiline formatted
  text to print
label
```

Perl prints everything between `<<label` and the following `label` (on a line by itself) exactly as the text is written.

Listing 9-8 shows an example that generates the same result as the code in Listing 9-7.

**Listing 9-8 Printing a Block of Formatted Text with `print <<`**

```
# prtblock.pl -- print block of text using print <<
print <<EOPRT;
<HTML><HEAD>
<TITLE>Form Data Echo</TITLE>
</HEAD><BODY>
Form Data Echo
<HR>
EOPRT
```

Running `prtblock.pl` from the command line gives the results shown in Figure 9-5.

**Figure 9-5:** Formatted output from `prtblock.pl`.

While coding with `print <<` , you need to follow these six rules:

1. Do not put space between << and the stop-printing label. `print <<myLabel;` works fine, but `print << myLabel;` won't work.
2. Newline `\n` is not required in the text to be printed. The linebreaks in the text are preserved by Perl in the printed output. If you add `\n` to a line, you will force an extra blank line in the output.
3. Variables and special characters such as `\n` are evaluated as if they were in a quoted print command. If you assign a value to `$a` before the print block and then use `$a` in the print block, the value of `$a` appears in the output:

```
$a = "<BODY>";
print <<endText;
   </HEAD>$a
   Body text here.
endText
```

   prints

```
   </HEAD><BODY>
   Body text here.
```

4. Nothing extra goes on the `print <<` line except the semicolon. You may someday see Perl code for `print <<` that does not have a semicolon after it, but don't imitate that style — it relies on a bug in Perl to work if the block print procedure is the last executable code in the program. Perl enables you to skip the semicolon statement-terminator for the last statement of a block of code, which would be `print <<` if you are close enough to the end of the program. That little twist cost me two days of frantic bug-chasing and knuckle-gnawing to figure out, and I am indebted to Gary Johnson for pointing the way.
5. Nothing extra goes on the line with the stop label at the end of the text to be printed. The label appears at the far left column of the script and stands alone on its line.
6. A blank line is the default stop label, which kicks in if you use the statement

```
print <<
```

with no specified stop label. In other words, the statement `print <<` with no label following the << operator means "print all the following text as it is printed here and stop printing at the first blank line."

As long as you follow these rules, you'll be the master of cut-and-paste Perl programming!

**Exercise 9-3**

Convert `frm2mail.pl` (see Chapter 5) to use the `print <<` block statement.

# String formatting with printf and sprintf

The string-formatting function `sprintf` first appeared in Chapter 7. The output-formatting complement, `printf`, has not appeared at all. As Lewis Carroll's Walrus might have said in the midst of his Perl oyster-munching, "It's time to speak of many things, like cabbages and `printf` strings."

## Relating print, printf, and sprintf

The lineage of the `print`, `printf`, and `sprintf` functions is direct, as I show here in preparation for more detailed explanation:

- `print` sends a list of objects to `STDOUT` or another filehandle. The syntax is

```
print FHANDLE obj1, obj2 ...
```

- `printf` uses a template and a list of arguments to send a string to `STDOUT` or another filehandle. The syntax is

```
printf FHANDLE ("template", arg1, arg2, ...)
```

- `sprintf` uses the same templates as `printf`, but returns the formatted string instead of sending it out. The syntax is

```
$var = sprintf ("template", arg1, arg2, ...)
```

The only difference in behavior between `printf` and `sprintf` is that `sprintf` creates a formatted string and needs a variable to receive it, whereas `printf` sends its output to a filehandle (optional — `STDOUT` is assumed). Both statements use templates and agruments the same way, so the following discussion deals with `printf` but applies to `sprintf` as well.

## Specifier tokens in templates

In the `printf` statement, `"template"` is a string with formatting information in the form of embedded tokens (or *specifiers*) marked by a percent sign `%`. For each token in the template, there must be an appropriate argument in the list following the template. By *appropriate,* I mean an object of the type called for by the token. If the token calls for an integer, the matching object must provide an integer (or something that can be interpreted as an integer).

Some of the template tokens available for `printf` and `sprintf` are listed alphabetically in the following table (examples follow in another table in the next section):

| Token | Object Formatted |
|---|---|
| `%c` | Character, just one |
| `%d` | Integer in whole-number format |
| `%e` | Floating-point in scientific notation |
| `%f` | Floating-point in decimal format |
| `%g` | Floating-point in either `%e` or `%f` format, whichever is shorter, with leading and trailing non-significant zeros trimmed off |
| `%s` | String |
| `%x` | Integer in hexadecimal format (lowercase letters, such as `af`) |
| `%X` | Integer in hexadecimal format (uppercase letters, such as `AF`) |

## Template tweaking — size, decimals, left placement

Template tokens for `printf` and `sprintf` accept modifiers (numbers, decimal point, and the minus sign) between the percent sign `%` and the token letter, as follows:

| Type | Example | Usage | Result |
|---|---|---|---|
| Size | 5 | %5d | Integer pushed to the right edge of five character places (two-digit integer would have three leading spaces) |

| Type | Example | Usage | Result |
|---|---|---|---|
| Decimal | 3.2 | %3.2f | Floating-point number with 3 character places to the left of the decimal, and two places to the right (trailing zeroes preserved) |
| Left | – | %–10s | String placed to the left end of ten character places (string is padded wtih spaces on the right side) |

## Literals and special characters in templates

In addition to the formatting tokens, the template in `printf` accepts literals (specific characters) and Perl's famous special characters. The literals are printed as-is, and the special characters are evaluated before printing. The most common special characters used in `printf` statements are newline `\n` and tab `\t`.

## Clarifying examples

The following snippet (Listing 9-9) shows the `printf` function hard at work. I show the results of each `printf` statement right after the comment hash `#`.

**Listing 9-9 Sample printf Statements**

```
$dec = 14;
$flt = 45.78;
$str = "Cardassian";
printf ("%d\n", $dec);                    #14
printf ("   %d\n", $dec);                 #   14
printf ("|%5d|\n", $dec);                 #|   14|
printf ("|%-5d|\n", $dec);                #|14   |
printf ("|%5d|\n", $flt);                 #|   45|
printf ("|%5d|\n", $str);                 #|    0|
printf ("%e\n", $flt);                    #4.578000e+001
printf ("%e\n", $dec);                    #1.400000e+001
printf ("%6.3f\n", $flt);                 #45.780
printf ("%g\n", $flt);                    #45.78
printf ("%1.1g\n", $flt);                 #5e+001
printf ("%6.3g\n", $flt);                 #45.8
printf ("exactly %d puppies\n", $dec); #exactly 14 puppies
printf ("%s\n", $str);                    #Cardassian
printf ("%d %s ears\n", $dec, $str);   #14 Cardassian ears
```

```
printf ("%d %s ears\n", $str, $dec);     #0 14 ears
printf ("%2.2f toes\n", $dec);            #14.00 toes
printf ("|%12s|\n", $str);                #|  Cardassian|
printf ("|%-12s|\n", $str);               #|Cardassian  |
printf ("|%5s|\n", $str);                 #|Cardassian|
```

As you study these examples, notice that

- Numerical values fit into string tokens (`%s`), but string values do not play well at all in numerical tokens.
- Floating-point values constrained by too little space for decimal places convert to misleading scientific notation (see `"%1.1g\n", $flt)`.
- Decimal values placed in floating point tokens acquire zeros if they have to.
- String values play out to their full length in string tokens, even if the token has a length modifier shorter than the length of the string value.

## Formatting data with `printf`

The program in Listing 9-10, `ascii.pl`, shows an extreme case of formatting with `printf`. This program generates a table of ASCII characters along with the decimal and hexadecimal values for each character. I used it to create the Dec/Hex/ASCII table in Appendix A. Notice how cleverly the program draws upon the hot topics in this chapter — the `for(;;)` function, boolean operators in the `if` condition, and a very dense `printf` statement. I provide an exploratory analysis of the different parts of the program after the listing.

**Listing 9-10** **Generating a Formatted dec/hex/ascii Table**

```
# ascii.pl -- prints dec and hex for ascii characters

for ($i=0;$i<=63;$i++) {                                   #1
  if ($i == 8 || $i == 9 || $i == 10 || $i == 13) {       #2
     printf ("%3d%3X%3s     ",$i,$i," ");                  #3
  } else {
     printf ("%3d%3X%3s     ",$i,$i,pack("C",$i));         #4
  }
  printf ("%3d%3X%3s     ",$i+64,$i+64,pack("C",$i+64));
  printf ("%3d%3X%3s     ",$i+128,$i+128,pack("C",$i+128));
  printf ("%3d%3X%3s\n",$i+192,$i+192,pack("C",$i+192));
}
```

Let's now look at this program and its parts in a little more detail:

1. The `for(;;)` function starts at 0, runs up to 63, and increments each step by 1. The program will print four sets of data across the page, using the value in `$i` for the first data set, then cumulatively adding 64 to `$i` for each additional data set. This row-at-a-time method is easier than juggling the positions for 256 individual characters in rows and columns and is a common technique for column-based reports.
2. ASCII characters 7 (bell), 8 (backspace), 9 (tab), 10 (linefeed), and 13 (carriage return) are troublesome in a formatted table. Printing any of these characters actuates its formatting power and messes up the table design. This `if`-block traps any of these bad actors for special handling (replacing the character with a space).
3. This step labels the prototype `printf` statement for the data set. The template `"%3d%3X%3s"` means "print a decimal value in three spaces padded on the left, then a hexadecimal value also in three spaces padded on the left (the capital X prints the letters A-F in uppercase when they appear in the hex number), then a string in three spaces padded left, then five blank spaces." Notice that `$i` is used for both the decimal and hexadecimal numerical values, relying on the `printf` specifier tokens `%d` and `%X` to perform the necessary conversions. The trouble characters are trapped and replaced by a quoted space for the `%s` token.
4. Non-trouble characters use the value of `$i` for the `%s` token in the template. First, `$i` has to be converted by pack into a printable character. For each subsequent data set in the `printf` statements immediately following, `$i` is bumped up another 64 units before it is fed to the template.

A few lines from the output of `ascii.pl` show how the formatting works:

```
 38 26  &      102 66  f      166 A6  |      230 E6  æ
 39 27  '      103 67  g      167 A7  §      231 E7  ç
 40 28  (      104 68  h      168 A8  ¨      232 E8  è
 41 29  )      105 69  i      169 A9  ©      233 E9  é
 42 2A  *      106 6A  j      170 AA  ª      234 EA  ê
```

The whole table is in on the CD-ROM. The characters actually printed depend upon the font selected.

### Exercise 9-4

To enhance your learning of Perl, now try these tasks:

A. ASCII 12 is a formfeed character and will mess up the character table with a page break on some systems. Assume that ASCII character 11 is also expendable and rewrite the if-block conditional to trap characters 8 through 13.

B. I use the string token `%s` in `ascii.pl` for printing a character as a very short string. What is another way of printing the character in this template?

## Math functions

There are three kinds of people in the world — those who understand math, and those who don't. (Get it?)

If you're a math fan, you'll be delighted to know that Perl has a full complement of math functions that go by the common names of `int`, `sqrt`, `exp`, `log`, `sin`, `cos`, `atan2`, `rand`, and `srand`. If you're not a math fan, you'll appreciate the brevity of my treatment of these functions. In Table 9-1, *val* may be a numeric value, a variable, or an expression that evaluates to a numeric value.

**Table 9-1 Math Functions**

| Name | Usage | Value Returned |
|---|---|---|
| `int` | `$var = int(val)` | Integer portion of floating-point *val* (2.7 returns 2) |
| `sqrt` | `$var = sqrt(val)` | Square root of *val* |
| `exp` | `$var = exp(val)` | Natural log *e* raised to the power of *val* |
| `log` | `$var = log(val)` | Natural log *e* of *val* |
| `sin` | `$var = sin(val)` | Sine of *val*, expressed in radians |
| `cos` | `$va4 = cos(val)` | Cosine of *val*, expressed in radians |
| `atan2` | `$var = atan2(val1, val2)` | Arctangent of *val1* divided by *val2*. Math people use this function for conversions, such as expressing degrees as radians. I am told that such conversions are legitimate and useful. |

**Table 9-1 Math Functions**

| Name | Usage | Value Returned |
|---|---|---|
| `rand` | `$var = rand(val)` | Floating-point number between 0 and the integer *val* |
| `srand` | `srand(val)` | Seeds (assigns a starting value for) the random-number generator used by rand. Using the same number for *val* in two runs of rand will generate identical "random" number sequences. That means you have a handy tool for replicating data sets when you need them for testing. That also means that random number generators are only approximately random. If you use `srand` as a statement with no arguments, srand will grab numbers from the current time on the computer clock to seed the generator, which usually provides a random-enough start on a unique sequence for most non-critical applications. |

A typical sequence of statements for selecting a random number is

```
srand;
$random = int(rand(101));
```

The `srand` statement provides the random-number generator with values from the system clock, and the `rand` assignment delivers a number between 0 and 100 to `$random`. The `int` function cuts off the fractional component of floating-point numbers rather than rounding the numbers up (2.7 becomes 2, not 3), so to include the possibility of the number 100 as one of the random numbers you have use 101 for the argument for `rand`.

For those of you who think I know anything about math, here's a nice surprise — there'll be no exercises today, class.

# Perl Project: Shopping Cart

A "shopping cart" on the Web is an order-picking, catalog-cruising, boutique-browsing program that displays a site's wares and takes orders from the eagerly buying public. The analogy is to the wire-frame cart you push up and down the supermarket aisle as you take one of this and two of that to toss into the cart's open, hungry maw. The analogy falls apart immediately, however. On the Web, you have to get a new, empty cart for every aisle and then another new, empty cart to push up to the cashier's counter. It's a strange way to do business.

## Web transactions are discontinuous

As I've pointed out before, the visitor's connection with a Web site is a transitory event. A normal connection is like tracking the ball possession times during a game of catch. The browser tosses a request to the server, the server tosses a page back to the browser, and both ends go to sleep (or take care of other business) while the visitor reads the page. The next request from the browser is, for all practical purposes, a new transaction, completely unconnected with any previous transactions. Think of an outfielder playing catch with 10,000 people in the bleachers, and you'll have a good idea of a Web server's view of the world.

This discontinuity means that the server doesn't remember faces. I can select all the items I want from a Web catalog page and send the order along its merry way with my name firmly attached, as long as only one form and one page are involved. If I flip to another page to add more items to my shopping cart, the cart disappears, and I get a new one to fill. With standard forms, no method is available for putting my name on the cart to make sure that I get the same cart back that I just sent out.

## Temps, cookies, and hidden fields

Three favored techniques are available for providing a Web server with a sense of continuity, however — temporary files, cookies, and hidden fields.

### Temporary files

Temporary files seem workable at first. Ask the visitor for some identification, store the identification in a temporary file along with the list of purchased items, and read the data back out after the transaction is completed or when it needs modification — right? But how do you know which temporary file belongs to which visitor?

Well, ask the visitor for some identification, look for a matching temp file, and — hold on, here. You don't gain much by having to ask the visitor for a valid ID on each page, except for an awful lot of temporary files sloshing around on a busy site.

## Cookies

The *cookie,* a kind of "Hello, My Name is . . ." party-badge for browsers, was invented by Netscape to solve the awkwardness of repeatedly asking for an ID. To use cookies, the CGI program checks the environmental variables to determine whether the requesting (or form-submitting) browser can handle cookies. If the answer is yes, the program makes up a magic number (for instance, from the system clock) and adds an expiration timestamp and its own domain name, and then folds these identifying teeth marks into a Set Cookie response header. The browser accepts the cookie and automatically builds it into each new request header going back to the server. In other words, the cookie gets passed back and forth between the browser and the server.

The browser has the job of remembering the cookie and passing it along, and the server simply reads the cookie to get the ID of the sender. Any time the visitor accesses a page on that particular server, the cookie goes along with the request. The visitor can even log off for a few hours or days and come back to continue an interrupted transaction, because the cookie is valid and functional any time up to its built-in expiration date. Now the shopping carts can be personalized — "Pardon me, sir, but wasn't that your cookie I saw in the other aisle?"

## Hidden fields

Cookies are marvelous but not universally recognized by all browsers. That leaves the third option — *hidden fields.* I introduced hidden fields in the first complete form in this book. The hidden field with the name `AAFormID` provides information to the CGI programs accepting the form, much like a minicookie. I like to use the `AAFormID` name/value pair to pick data out of e-mail files or to tailor a generic CGI program for a special case. For example, the form ID could trigger an alternate e-mail address so that Survey A goes to analyst A and Survey B goes to analyst B.

Hidden fields in a static form are fairly innocuous, but if you start using them in forms generated on-the-fly by CGI programs, you'll see them flexing their muscles. The basic concept is to take a name/value pair from an incoming form, rework the data, and embed the name/value pair as a hidden field in an outgoing form. After that form comes back, find the hidden fields again, rework the data — well, you get the idea. Instant cookie!

After the first "Tell me your name," no ID requests are needed — and no temp files, either. Because all the real work is done on the server, the hidden fields data-passing method works with any browser. The Kombat Karate Chop Shop uses hidden fields for its shopping cart.

## Kombat Karate Chop Shop main screen

The main screen for the Kombat Karate Chop Shop (and knuckle boutique) is clean and simple, as shown in Figure 9-6.

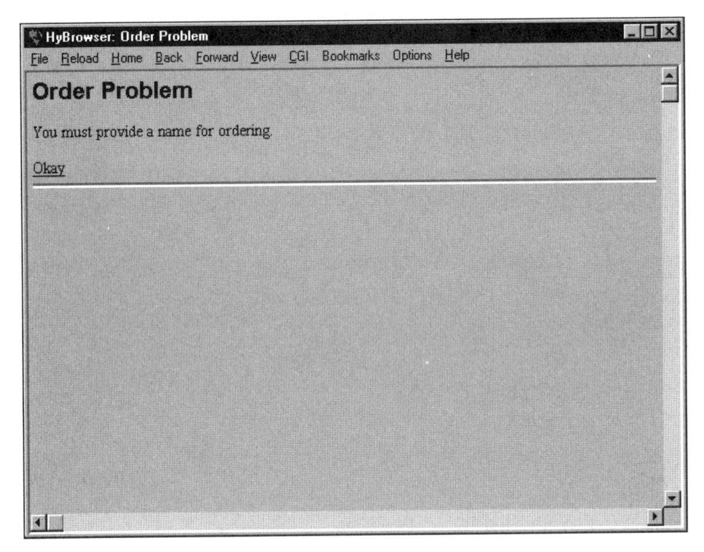


**Figure 9-6:** Main catalog screen for Kombat Karate Chop Shop.

The price for each item is listed next to the item. The visitor enters a name, makes selections, and clicks on the View Order button. The HTML tags for the screen is shown in Listing 9-11, which is on the CD-ROM as shopmenu.htm.

**Listing 9-11 HTML Code for Main Screen**

```
<HTML><HEAD>
<TITLE>Kombat Karate Chop Shop</TITLE>
</HEAD><BODY>
<H1>Kombat Karate Chop Shop</H1>
<FORM ACTION="http://some.site/cgi/korder.pl" METHOD="POST">
<INPUT NAME="AAFormID" TYPE="hidden" VALUE="shopmenu">
   
```

*(continued)*

**Listing 9-11** ***(continued)***

```
Ordered by (name): <INPUT NAME="Ordered By" TYPE="text" SIZE=30
 MAXLENGTH=80><HR>
<TABLE>
<TR><TH>Uniforms</TH><TH>ea    </
TH><TH>Weapons</TH><TH>ea    </TH><TH>Gear</
TH><TH></TH></TR>
<TR><TD>
<INPUT NAME="Small" TYPE="checkbox" VALUE="1"> Small </TD>
<TD>30</TD>
<TD><INPUT NAME="Knife" TYPE="checkbox" VALUE="1"> Knife</
TD><TD>35</
TD>
<TD><INPUT NAME="Helmet" TYPE="checkbox" VALUE="1"> Helmet<BR></
TD><TD>85</TD></TR>
<TR><TD><INPUT NAME="Medium" TYPE="checkbox" VALUE="1"> Medium</
TD><TD>35</TD>
<TD><INPUT NAME="Sword" TYPE="checkbox" VALUE="1"> Sword</
TD><TD>90</
TD>
<TD><INPUT NAME="Gloves" TYPE="checkbox" VALUE="1"> Gloves<BR></
TD><TD>75</TD></TR>
<TR><TD><INPUT NAME="Large" TYPE="checkbox" VALUE="1"> Large</
TD><TD>40</TD>
<TD><INPUT NAME="Staff" TYPE="checkbox" VALUE="1"> Staff</
TD><TD>25</
TD>
<TD><INPUT NAME="Cup" TYPE="checkbox" VALUE="1"> Cup<BR></
TD><TD>10</
TD></TR>
</TABLE>
   
<INPUT NAME="Order" TYPE="submit" VALUE="View Order">
   
<INPUT NAME="Cancel" TYPE="submit" VALUE="Cancel">
   
</FORM><HR></BODY></HTML>
```

The ` ` notations are non-breaking spaces. I use them in the table heads for column spacing and again for spacing the Submit buttons. Notice that the Cancel button is input type *submit*. The only hidden field here is `AAFormID` with a value `shopmenu`. This form calls `korder.pl` for the `ACTION` attribute.

# Viewing the order with korder.pl

I discuss korder.pl in sequential pieces. The program is about 150 lines — too much to take all in one gulp.

## Parsing the form data

The form-data parsing routine at the beginning of korder.pl is shown in Listing 9-12. There are no mysteries here — you've seen it all before.

**Listing 9-12 Form-Data Parsing**

```
#!/usr/local/bin/perl
# korder.pl -- shopping cart order viewer

read(STDIN, $formdat, $ENV{'CONTENT_LENGTH'});

@namevals = split(/&/,$formdat);
foreach (@namevals) {
    tr/+/ /;
    s/=/=/;
    s/%(..)/pack("C",hex($1))/ge;
    ($head, $tail) = split(/=/,$_,2);
    $order{$head} = $tail;
}

$ordname = $order{"Ordered By"};
```

The parsing routine ends with the assignment to `$ordname` of the visitor's name in the hidden field `Ordered By` from `shopmenu.htm`. This line is our mini-cookie to be passed along as an ID marker from one screen to the next.

## Trapping for an improper name

I make a dirt-simple test for an acceptable visitor name — is it longer than two characters? A more sophisticated check would be to look up the name in a database of registered Kombat Karate members, but I want to paint in broad brush strokes in this PerlProject to get the general principles down without fretting over details.

Notice in Listing 9-13 that a too-short name causes an error screen to be printed to `STDOUT` for response to the visitor. Using the block `print <<` statement here enables workable HTML code to be cut and pasted from my Perl editor to my HTML editor (for preview) and back again without hassle.

**Listing 9-13 Creating the Error Message for a Too-Short Name**

```
if (length($ordname) < 2) {
   print <<eopage;
Content-type: text/html

<HTML><HEAD><TITLE>Order Problem</TITLE></HEAD>
<BODY><H1>Order Problem</H1>
You must provide a name for ordering.<P>
<A HREF="http://some.site/shopmenu.html">Okay</A>
<HR></BODY></HTML>
eopage
}
```

The resulting page, shown in Figure 9-7, links the visitor back to the main screen for another try.

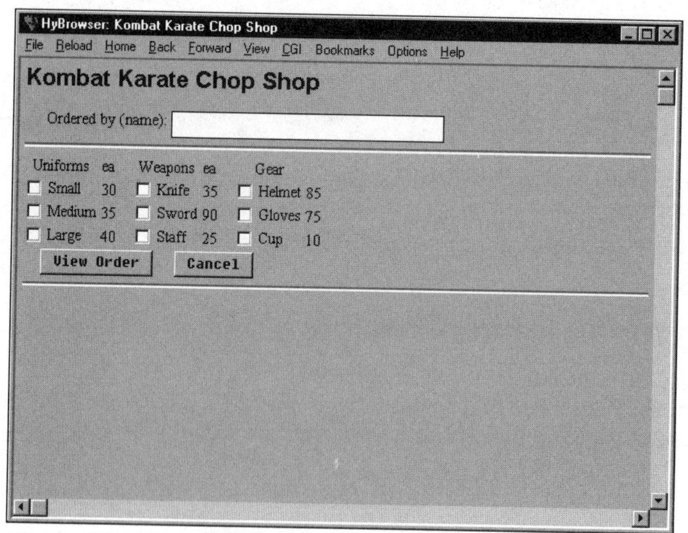


**Figure 9-7:** An unacceptable name routes the visitor back to the main screen.

## Handling a cancelled session

If the visitor selected Cancel on the main screen, `korder.pl` finds the name/value pair `Cancel=Cancel` in the form data. Selecting the other choice places the name/value pair `Order=View Order` in the form data instead. The cancel request triggers the code in Listing 9-14 to generate the page shown in Figure 9-8.

**Listing 9-14 Confirmation of a Cancelled Order**

```
elsif ($order{"Cancel"} eq "Cancel") {
   if (length($ordname) < 2) {
       $ordname = "visitor";
   }
   print <<eopage;
Content-type: text/html

<HTML><HEAD><TITLE>Order Cancelled</TITLE></HEAD>
<BODY><H1>Order Cancelled</H1>
Order for $ordname has been cancelled.<P>
<A HREF="http://some.site/index.html">
Return to Main Page</A>
<HR></BODY></HTML>
eopage
}
```

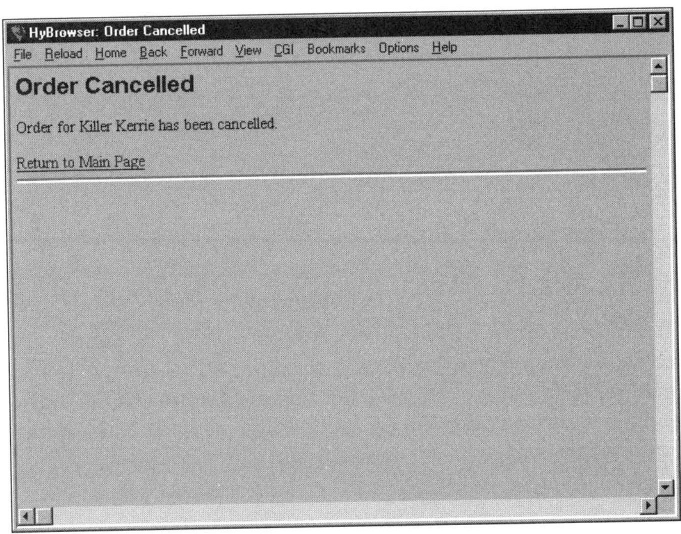


**Figure 9-8:** Response page for cancelled order.

## Submitting an approved order

When the order is to the visitor's liking (within the budget), the visitor clicks the Submit button with the value `Send Order`, which inserts the name/value pair `Submit=Send Order` into the data stream parsed by `korder.pl`. Listing 9-15 shows the code for responding to the `Send Order` instruction. After responding to the visitor with the page shown in Figure 9-9, the program sends the order information via e-mail.

**Listing 9-15 Generating the Send Order Response Page and E-mail**

```
elsif ($order{"Submit"} eq "Send Order") {
   print <<eopage;
Content-type: text/html

<HTML><HEAD><TITLE>Order Sent</TITLE></HEAD>
<BODY><H1>Order Sent</H1>
Your order has been sent.
<A HREF="http://some.site/index.html">
Return to Main Page</A>
<HR></BODY></HTML>
eopage

   $efmail = "order\@some.site";
   open (MAILOUT, "| mail $email") ||
      die "Cannot start mail program.";
   foreach $line (sort(keys(%order))) {
      print MAILOUT "$line = $order{$line}\n";
   }
   close (MAILOUT);
}
```

## Setting up arrays to show current selections

If the visitor's name passed validation, the order was not canceled, and the order also was not sent for processing, `korder.pl` displays the visitor's current selections. The setup for the order display requires totalling the charges. Listing 9-16 shows how to build an associative array of catalog items with the price of each item.

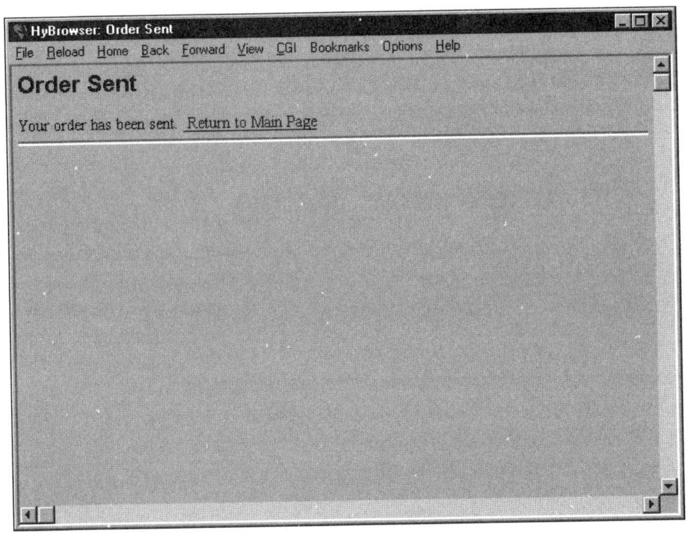


**Figure 9-9:** Confirmation page for completed order.

**Listing 9-16 Building Arrays for Catalog Items Selected**

```
else {
$price{"Small"} = 30;
$price{"Medium"} = 35;
$price{"Large"} = 40;
$price{"Knife"} = 35;
$price{"Sword"} = 90;
$price{"Staff"} = 25;
$price{"Helmet"} = 85;
$price{"Gloves"} = 75;
$price{"Cup"} = 10;

@ordkeys = keys(%order);
foreach $try (@ordkeys) {
    if (defined $price{$try}) {
        push (@curkeys, $try);
    }
}
$nritems = @curkeys;
```

The `foreach` block uses `defined` to test each catalog item in the price list against the array of selected items parsed from the incoming data stream and collects the list of selected items in the `@curkeys` array. I use `defined` for the test because with associative arrays, looking for an element with an explicit call, like if `$price{$try} gt ""` will create the element if it doesn't exist, and will assign the value "" to the new creation. The critical test here is for existence — only incoming elements belong in the `$curkeys[]` array.

## Displaying the current order status

To display the current order, `korder.pl` builds a response page as shown in Listing 9-17. The visitor's name and the list of selected items and charges appear in the body of the page, where they can't be changed. The `foreach` block uses `sprintf` to assemble each line of the order and then tallies the total charges with an assignment to `$totbucks`.

**Listing 9-17 Showing the List of Selected Items**

```
print <<eopage;
Content-type: text/html

<HTML><HEAD>
<TITLE>Kombat Karate Chop Shop Order</TITLE>
</HEAD><BODY>
<H1>Kombat Karate<BR>Chop Shop Order</H1>
eopage
print "<B>Order for $ordname:</B><HR>\n";
print "Items currently ordered:<BR>\n";

if ($nritems > 0) {
    foreach $pick (@curkeys) {
        $bucks = sprintf("%-3d",$price{$pick});
        $totbucks += $bucks;
        print " \; \; $pick \(\$$bucks\)<BR>\n";
    }
    print "<P><B>Total order: \$$totbucks</B><HR>\n";
}
```

## Assembling the catalog as checkbox fields

The original catalog listing is in `shopmenu.htm`. No method is available for changing the HTML for that page, so `korder.pl` recreates the catalog and shows which items have already been selected. All items are displayed in checkbox fields. The code for each field is assembled in the associative array `%item`, as shown in Listing 9-18. The `defined` function again picks out which items should have the `CHECKED` attribute built into their input field description:

**Listing 9-18 Setting Up the Catalog Display**

```
@catlist = keys(%price);

foreach $cat (@catlist) {
    $item{$cat} = "INPUT NAME=\"$cat\"";
    $item{$cat} .= " TYPE=\"checkbox\" VALUE=\"1\"";
    if (defined ($order{$cat})) {
        $item{$cat} .= " CHECKED";
    }
}
```

## Redisplaying the catalog with selected items marked

The catalog appears on the order page to enable the visitor to modify the original order. The format is the same as the original catalog in `shopmenu.htm` — a table of checkboxes. The checkbox field for each article is displayed in position by using the value from `%item` with the article as the key (see Listing 9-19). The form calls `korder.pl` reflexively (that is, calls itself) until the order is sent or canceled.

**Listing 9-19 Displaying the Catalog with Selected Items Checked**

```
print <<eopage;
<FORM ACTION="http://some.site/cgi/korder.pl" METHOD="POST">
<INPUT NAME="AAFormID" TYPE="hidden" VALUE="korder">
<INPUT NAME="Ordered By" TYPE="hidden" VALUE="$ordname">
Please make selections, then choose Update, Send, or Cancel.<BR>
<TABLE>
<TR><TH>Uniforms</TH><TH>ea    </
TH><TH>Weapons</
TH><TH>ea    </TH><TH>Gear</TH><TH></TH></TR>
<TR><TD>
<$item{"Small"}> Small </TD><TD>30</TD>
<TD><$item{"Knife"}> Knife</TD><TD>35</TD>
<TD><$item{"Helmet"}> Helmet<BR></TD><TD>85</TD></TR>
<TR><TD><$item{"Medium"}> Medium</TD><TD>35</TD>
<TD><$item{"Sword"}> Sword</TD><TD>90</TD>
<TD><$item{"Gloves"}> Gloves<BR></TD><TD>75</TD></TR>
<TR><TD><$item{"Large"}> Large</TD><TD>40</TD>
<TD><$item{"Staff"}> Staff</TD><TD>25</TD>
```

*(continued)*

*(continued)*

```
<TD><$item{"Cup"}> Cup<BR></TD><TD>10</TD></TR>
</TABLE>
   
<INPUT NAME="Order" TYPE="submit" VALUE="Update Order">
   
<INPUT NAME="Submit" TYPE="submit" VALUE="Send Order">
   
<INPUT NAME="Cancel" TYPE="submit" VALUE="Cancel">
   
<HR></FORM></BODY></HTML>
eopage
}
```

Figure 9-10 shows the displayed page. The visitor now selects or deselects catalog items, sends the order in, cancels the order, or redisplays the order to show the current selections and charges.

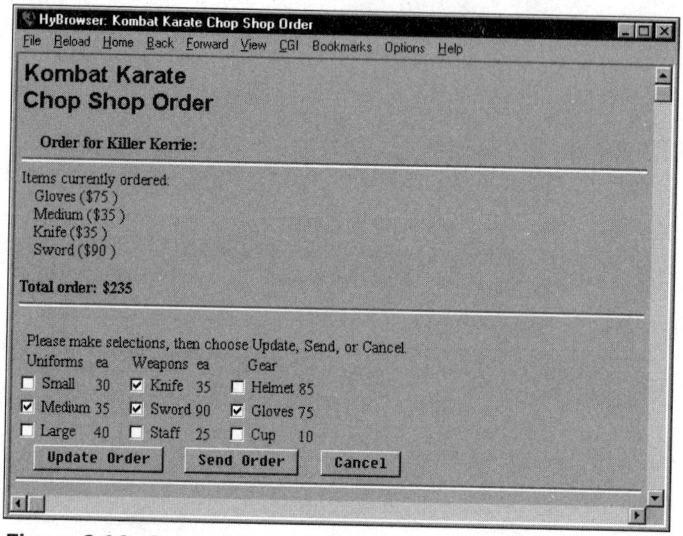

**Figure 9-10:** Order recap and catalog view.

# That's it!

Let a out a big sigh — we're done! I took you through the whole process of learning enough Perl to raise your Web pages a notch above millions of show-and-tell pages by using CGI to involve your visitors with two-way interaction. I even showed you the stumbles and stubbed toes I suffered when I went through that process before you.

Perl has a richness and depth that will continue to surprise and delight you as you pull yourself beyond this introductory level to develop your own applications and expand your knowledge of programming techniques. You will be using subroutines, libraries, and the special tricks with objects that Perl 5 can perform. I hope you will pour through the Perl documentation — the manpages and HTML help files — to experiment with new functions and expressions.

Programming with Perl doesn't *have* to be fun — it just *is!*

## Summary

This chapter covered the following:

- Accessing and listing CGI(environmental) variables
- Using `for(;;)` as an alternative to `while` for flow control
- Operations with boolean (logic) functions, including Boolean AND, OR, and NOT expressed as `&&`, `||`, and `!` in Perl and using truth tables to unscramble complex logic
- Block printing pre-formatted text with `print <<`, which causes all spaces and line breaks to print as-is, and variables and special characters to be evaluated before printing
- Formating strings with `printf` and `sprintf`
- Performing advanced math functions
- Some design considerations for building a shopping cart for catalog orders, including using hidden fields to pass data from one form to another, block printing with `print <<` to duplicate complicated Web page designs, and trapping and processing error conditions and special actions

# Exercise Answers

One of Perl's most endearing charms is that there is rarely just one correct way to program a solution to a problem. The answers given here for the exercises sprinkled throughout the book are not the only correct answers — they are the answers I came up with while thinking of the level of Perl at your command at each point in this book. When given the choice of economy (also known as syntactical elegance) versus clarity (known as clarity), I have chosen clarity every time.

## Exercise 1-1

Experiments with single and double quotes:

```
C:\dev>perl -e "print 'Hello, World!';"
Hello, World!
C:\dev>perl -e 'print "Hello, World!";'
Can't find string terminator "'" anywhere before EOF at -e line
1.
C:\dev>perl -e "print "Hello, World!";"
No comma allowed after filehandle at -e line 1.
C:\dev>perl -e 'print 'Hello, World!';'
Can't find string terminator "'" anywhere before EOF at -e line 1.
```

## Exercise 1-2

### A.

```
C:\dev>perl -e "print 'Hello, Anybody!';" >> hello.txt
C:\dev>perl -e "print 'Hello, Anybody!';" >> hello.txt
C:\dev>perl -e "print 'Hello, Anybody!';" >> hello.txt
C:\dev>type hello.txt
Hello, Anybody!Hello, Anybody!Hello, Anybody!
```

### B.

```
Hello, Anybody!Hello, Anybody!Hello, Anybody!Goodbye, Everybody!
```

### C.

```
Hello, Anybody!Hello, Anybody!Hello, Anybody!Goodbye, Everybody!

This is perl, version 4.0

$RCSfile: perl.c,v $$Revision: 4.0.1.8 $$Date: 1993/02/05
19:39:30 $
Patch level: 36

Copyright (c) 1989, 1990, 1991, Larry Wall
```

(and so forth, at some length)

## Exercise 1-3

### A.

```
C:\dev>perl -ne "print" citymile.dat >> citymile.txt
```

### B.

```
C:\dev>perl -v >> citymile.txt
```

C.

```
C:\dev>perl -en "print" citymile.dat
```

doesn't work, because `'n'` is evaluated, and it doesn't mean anything.

```
C:\dev>perl -n e "print" citymile.dat
Can't open perl script "e": No such file or directory
```

## Exercise 1-4

A.

```
C:\dev>perl -ne "print if /C/" citymile.dat
Boston, MA, Chicago, IL, 963
Chicago, IL, Cairo, IL, 375
Cairo, IL, St. Louis, MO, 153
St. Louis, MO, Cincinnati, OH, 340
Cincinnati, OH, Cleveland, OH, 244
Cleveland, OH, Dallas, TX, 1159
```

B.

```
C:\dev>perl -ne "print if /OH/" citymile.dat
St. Louis, MO, Cincinnati, OH, 340
Cincinnati, OH, Cleveland, OH, 244
Cleveland, OH, Dallas, TX, 1159
```

C.

```
C:\dev>perl -ne "print if /1159/" citymile.dat
Cleveland, OH, Dallas, TX, 1159
```

## Exercise 1-5

```
C:\dev>perl -ne "print if /C.*.o/" citymile.dat
Boston, MA, Chicago, IL, 963
```

*(continued)*

*(continued)*

```
Chicago, IL, Cairo, IL, 375
Cairo, IL, St. Louis, MO, 153

C:\dev>perl -ne "print if /Ci*/" citymile.dat
Boston, MA, Chicago, IL, 963
Chicago, IL, Cairo, IL, 375
Cairo, IL, St. Louis, MO, 153
St. Louis, MO, Cincinnati, OH, 340
Cincinnati, OH, Cleveland, OH, 244
Cleveland, OH, Dallas, TX, 1159

C:\dev>perl -ne "print if /C.*i/" citymile.dat
Boston, MA, Chicago, IL, 963
Chicago, IL, Cairo, IL, 375
Cairo, IL, St. Louis, MO, 153
St. Louis, MO, Cincinnati, OH, 340
Cincinnati, OH, Cleveland, OH, 244

C:\dev>perl -ne "print if /3/" citymile.dat
Atlanta, GA, Boston, MA, 1037
Boston, MA, Chicago, IL, 963
Chicago, IL, Cairo, IL, 375
Cairo, IL, St. Louis, MO, 153
St. Louis, MO, Cincinnati, OH, 340

C:\dev>perl -ne "print if /3.*5/" citymile.dat
Chicago, IL, Cairo, IL, 375

C:\dev>perl -ne "print if /5.*3/" citymile.dat
Cairo, IL, St. Louis, MO, 153
```

## Exercise 1-6

```
C:\dev>perl -ne "print if /B/" citymile.dat
Atlanta, GA, Boston, MA, 1037
Boston, MA, Chicago, IL, 963

C:\dev>perl -ne "print if /^B/" citymile.dat
Boston, MA, Chicago, IL, 963
```

```
C:\dev>perl -ne "print if /^C/" citymile.dat
Chicago, IL, Cairo, IL, 375
Cairo, IL, St. Louis, MO, 153
Cincinnati, OH, Cleveland, OH, 244
Cleveland, OH, Dallas, TX, 1159

C:\dev>perl -ne "print if /3/" citymile.dat
Atlanta, GA, Boston, MA, 1037
Boston, MA, Chicago, IL, 963
Chicago, IL, Cairo, IL, 375
Cairo, IL, St. Louis, MO, 153
St. Louis, MO, Cincinnati, OH, 340

C:\dev>perl -ne "print if /3$/" citymile.dat
Boston, MA, Chicago, IL, 963
Cairo, IL, St. Louis, MO, 153
```

## Exercise 1-7

### A.

```
/Price: \$12.56$/;
```

### B.

```
/myfile.\*/;
```

### C.

```
/^Me, crazy\?/;
```

### D.

```
/mc\^2\/3/;
```

## Exercise 1-8

Spaces, any punctuation except the underscore, and variable names beginning with a digit (right after the $) won't work.

## Exercise 1-9

One way to insert a space between array elements as-printed is to add it to the end of each element. Another way is to wrap the array in quotes when printing. Try this enhanced version — note the treatment of the array in the last line:

```
# addarray.pl -- add elements to an array

@my = ("one", 2, "three", 4);  # start small
print @my, "\n";    # show the array so far
$my[4] = "five";    # put "five" at a new subscript
print @my, "\n";    # show the expanded array
push(@my, 6);       # push a value onto the end of array
print @my, "\n";    # show the expanded array
print "@my\n";      # show the expanded array
# end of addarray.pl
```

The program produces this output:

```
one2three4
one2three4five
one2three4five6
one 2 three 4 five 6
```

## Exercise 1-10

### A.

```
# revline3.pl -- read three lines into array, print in order

$one = <STDIN>;
$two = <STDIN>;
$three = <STDIN>;
@lines = ($one, $two, $three);
print @lines;
# end of revline3.pl
```

### B.

```
# revline4.pl -- read four lines into array, print in order

$one = <STDIN>;
$two = <STDIN>;
$three = <STDIN>;
$four = <STDIN>;
@lines = ($one, $two, $three, $four);
print @lines;
# end of revline4.pl
```

## Exercise 1-11

### A.

```
# prtafile.pl -- print from FHANDLE until the file is done

open (FHANDLE, "citymile.txt");
while (<FHANDLE>) {
  print;
}
```

### B.

```
# prtafile.pl -- print from FHANDLE until the file is done

open (ANYTHING, "citymile.dat");
while (<ANYTHING>) {
  print;
}
```

It's customary to use all-caps for filehandles — because no Perl functions have all-caps names, you'll avoid possible conflicts.

## Exercise 1-12

These are exploratory "try it yourself" exercises.

## Exercise 1-13

Again, this is an exploratory exercise.

## Exercise 2-1

### A.

```
/[0-9]{3}\.txt/;
```

### B.

```
/ [A-Za-z][a-z]{5} /;  # tricky -- allowing for initial CAP
```

### C.

```
/^[A-Za-z][a-z]{4}ing/;
```

## Exercise 2-2

### A.

```
/4[0-9]{2}-[0-9]{3}-[0-9]{4}/;
```

### B.

```
/ [a-z0-9]{3,8}\.pl/;
```

### C.

```
/[A-Z][0-9]{3,9}x?/;
```

## Exercise 2-3

### A.

```
/either\/or|and\/or/;
```

### B.

```
/800-[A-Z0-9]{3}-[A-Z0-9]{4}/;
```

### C.

```
/(jr|Jr|JR)\./;
```

## Exercise 2-4

### A.

```
/\(\d\d\d\) \d\d\d-\d\d\d\d/;
```

### B.

```
/\shttp:.*\s/;
```

### C.

```
/\d{5}(-\d{4})?$/;
```

## Exercise 2-5

### A.

```
$n9 = 9; $n10 = 10;
$res = $n9 <=> $n10;  # $res is -1: 9 is less than 10
```

### B.

```
$res = $n9 cmp $n10;  # $res is 1: "9" sorts after "10"
```

## Exercise 2-6

### A.

```
if ($sales > 25000) {
   $salary *= 1.1;
} elsif ($sales < 5000) {
   $salary *= 0.9;
}
```

### B.

```
if ($first gt $last) {
   print $last, " ", $first; # or print "$last, $first";
} elsif ($first lt $last) {
   print $first, " ", $last; # or print "$first, $last";
}
```

## Exercise 2-7

### A.

```
# findtex2.pl -- use command-line argument for pattern search

$pattern = $ARGV[0];
open (FINDFILE, $ARGV[1]);
while (<FINDFILE>) {
    if (/$pattern/) {
       print;
    }
}
# end of findtex2.pl
```

### B.

```
# findtex3.pl -- use command-line argument for pattern search

$pattern = $ARGV[0];
open (FINDFILE, $ARGV[1]);
```

```
while (<FINDFILE>) {
    if (/$pattern/) {
       print;
    } else {
       print "Nope\n";
    }
}
# end of findtex3.pl
```

```
C:\dev>perl findtext3.pl "Chicago" citymile.dat
Nope
Boston, MA, Chicago, IL, 963
Chicago, IL, Cairo, IL, 375
Nope
Nope
Nope
Nope
```

### C.

Deleting the closing curly brace for `else` ....

```
C:\dev>perl findtext4.pl "Chicago" citymile.dat
Missing right bracket at findtext4.pl line 12, at end of line
syntax error at findtext4.pl line 12, at EOF
Execution of findtext4.pl aborted due to compilation errors.
```

## Exercise 2-8

```
# gold5.pl -- find gold in the treasure, count lines
while (<STDIN>) {
    $i++;
    if (/treasure/) {
        print "Maybe ";
        if (/gold/) {
            print "Dig here! ";
            print "Line $i has gold!\n";  # new line
            last;
        }
```

*(continued)*

*(continued)*

```
    }
    print "Line $i\n";
}
print "Done.\n";
# end of gold5.pl
```

## Exercise 2-9

Exploratory — what did you find out?

## Exercise 2-10

```
# grepfil2.pl -- read files listed on command line to find
pattern
# usage: perl grepfil2.pl "pattern" file1 file2 file3 ...

$i = 1;
$parnum = @ARGV;
$pattern = $ARGV[0]
while ($i < $parnum) {
    $theFile = $ARGV[$i];     # new line
    open (FHANDLE, $ARGV[$i]);
    while (<FHANDLE>) {       # new line follows:
        print "$theFile:\n   $_" if /$pattern/;
    }
    close (FHANDLE);
    $i++;
}
# end of grepfil2.pl
```

## Exercise 3-1

### A.

```
while (<>) {
  s/IL/Illinois/g;
  print;
}
```

**B.**

```
s/(Chicago,IL,Cairo,IL/Chicago,Illinois,Cairo,Illinois/;
```

**C.**

```
s/<form>/<FORM>/;
s/<\/form>/<\/FORM>/;
s/form>/Form>;
```

## Exercise 3-2

```
tr/\+&/ \n/;
```

## Exercise 3-3

```
%favorite = ("color","burgandy","pie","apple","ice cream",
"chocolate almond","fruit","banana","pasta","linguini");
@mykeys = keys(%favorite);
foreach $k (@mykeys) {
   print "$k\n";
}
```

## Exercise 3-4

**A.**

```
$line = "name=Mary+Jones&address=123+Main+Street&city=Rome";
@urls = split(/&/, $line);
```

**B.**

```
foreach $pair (@urls) {
   ($nam, $valu) = split(/=/, $pair);
}
```

C.

```
foreach $pair (@urls) {
   ($nam, $valu) = split(/=/, $pair);
   $pairlist{$nam} = $valu;
}
```

## Exercise 3-5

This is an exploratory exercise.

## Exercise 4-1

Checkboxes placed in a table — note the code for non-breaking space added after the "Newspaper" prompt to force a wider column, and <BR> tags to make the table readable for non-table browsers:

```
<P>How did you hear about us? Check as many as apply:<BR>
<TABLE BORDER="0">
<TR><TD><INPUT TYPE="checkbox" NAME="Friend" VALUE="Yes">
Friend</TD>
<TD><INPUT TYPE="checkbox" NAME="Word" VALUE="Yes"> Word of
mouth<BR></TD></TR>


<TR><TD><INPUT TYPE="checkbox" NAME="Magazine" VALUE="Yes">
Magazine</TD>
<TD><INPUT TYPE="checkbox" NAME="Bully" VALUE="Yes"> Bothered by
bully<BR></TD></TR>


<TR><TD><INPUT TYPE="checkbox" NAME="Paper" VALUE="Yes"> Newspa-
per     </TD>
<TD><INPUT TYPE="checkbox" NAME="Hospital" VALUE="Yes"> Hospital
reports<BR></TD></TR>
<TR><TD><INPUT TYPE="checkbox" NAME="Radio" VALUE="Yes"> Radio
</TD><TD></TD></TR>
</TABLE>
```

Radio buttons arranged with <PRE>. . .</PRE> tags — the extra line between each row is just to show that the row should be written all on one (wrapping) line. The extra line should be removed in actual use, because the <PRE> tag will preserve the space and make the format too airy:

```
<P>What belt rank have you achieved in karate?<BR><pre>

<INPUT TYPE="radio" NAME="Belt" VALUE="None" CHECKED> None
<INPUT TYPE="radio" NAME="Belt" VALUE="Blue"> Blue

<INPUT TYPE="radio" NAME="Belt" VALUE="White"> White    <INPUT
TYPE="radio" NAME="Belt" VALUE="Purple"> Purple

<INPUT TYPE="radio" NAME="Belt" VALUE="Yellow"> Yellow   <INPUT
TYPE="radio" NAME="Belt" VALUE="Brown"> Brown

<INPUT TYPE="radio" NAME="Belt" VALUE="Orange"> Orange   <INPUT
TYPE="radio" NAME="Belt" VALUE="Black"> Black

<INPUT TYPE="radio" NAME="Belt" VALUE="Green"> Green
</pre>
```

## Exercise 4-2

```
$_ = "His theory is more theatrical than useful.";
$found = s/the/the/g;
print "Found \"the\" $found times.\n";
```

Assigning the result of `s///` to a scalar variable captures the number of substitutions made. The `g` option on `s///g` forces all possible substitutions in the target.

## Exercise 4-3

### A.

```
# x0403a.pl
$mystring= "Once upon a time, in a faraway land";
@words = split(/\W+/,$mystring);
foreach $word (@words) {
   print "$word=", length($word), "\n";
}
```

Results:

```
once=4
upon=4
a=1
time=4
in=2
a=1
faraway=7
land=4
```

**B.**

```
# x0403b.pl
while ($line = <STDIN>) {
   @words = split(/\W+/,$line);
   foreach $word (@words) {
      $wdlist[$i++] = $word;
      print "$word=", length($word), "\n";
   }
}
```

**C.**

```
# x0403c.pl
while ($line = <STDIN>) {
   @words = split(/\W+/,$line);
   foreach $word (@words) {
      $wordlist{$word} = length($word);
   }
}
while (($head, $tail) = each (%wordlist)) {
   print "$head=$tail\n";
}
```

## Exercise 4-4

```
# x0404.pl
@myList = ("a01\n","b02\n","c03\n","d04\n");
```

```
print @myList, "\n";  # prints: column of values
chop(@myList);        # cut the newline off each element
print @myList;        # prints: a01b02c03d04
```

## Exercise 4-5

```
# x0405.ol
%fruit = ("Banana",5,"Apple",2,"Pear",4,"Kiwi",8);
print %fruit, "\n"; # prints: Pear4Banana5Apple2Kiwi8
@basket = sort(keys(%fruit));  # sort and assign
print @basket, "\n"; # prints: AppleBananaKiwiPear
foreach $item (sort(keys(%fruit))){
   print "$item $fruit{$item}\n";
}
```

## Exercise 4-6

```
#!/usr/local/bin/perl
# x0406.pl -- echo decoded URL string back to requester
#    with <PRE> formatting

print "Content-type: text/html\n\n";

read(STDIN, $formdat, $ENV{'CONTENT_LENGTH'});

print "<HTML><HEAD>\n";
print "<TITLE>Form Data Echo</TITLE>\n";
print "</HEAD><BODY>\n";
print "Form Data Echo\n";
print "<HR>\n";
print "<PRE>\n";                # new line

@namevals = split(/&/,$formdat);
foreach (@namevals) {
   tr/+/ /;
   s/=/ = /;
   s/%(..)/pack("C",hex($1))/ge;
   print "        $_\n";        # changed line
}
print "</PRE><P><HR>\n";        # changed line
print "</BODY>\n</HTML>\n";
```

## Exercise 5-1

### A.

```
<!--#CONFIG TIMEFMT="%A, %B %d, at %i %p sharp" -->
```

### B.

```
<!--#CONFIG TIMEFMT="%Y/%b/%d" -->
```

## Exercise 5-2

```
print &revname("Leonardo", "da Vinci"), "\n";

# revname.pl -- sub to return lastname, firstname
sub revname {
   local ($firstname, $lastname ) = @_;
   $lastname = $lastname . ", " . $firstname;
}
```

Prints: da Vinci, Leonardo

## Exercise 6-1

### A.

```
while ($line =~ /href=\"(.*?)\">/i) {
      $a = $1;
      if ($a =~ /http/i) {   # remove the ! from if()
         print "$ARGV, $a\n";
      }
      $line = substr($line,index($line,$a)+length($a));
}
```

Of course, if same-site references are made with full pathnames (`http://`, etc.), then they too will be picked up. You could add another level of verification, and check for the absence of the current DNS in the reference call before deciding that the URL really was external.

**B.**

```
while ($line =~ /<img src=\"(.*?)\"/i) {
        $a = $1;
        print "$ARGV, $a\n";
        $line = substr($line,index($line,$a)+length($a));
}
```

**C.**

```
# x0601c.pl -- print list of IMG calls, show all
#   files that call each image.
#   Perl 5 version
# usage: perl x0601c.pl *.htm > imgurl.dat

while (<>) {
   $line = $_;
   while ($line =~ /<img src=\"(.*?)\"/i) {
      $a = "$1,$ARGV";
      $imglist{$a} = 1;
      $line = substr($line,index($line,$a)+length($a));
   }
}
while (($head, $tail) = each (%imglist)) {
   push(@imgfile, $head);
}
@srtimg = sort (@imgfile);
foreach $rec (@srtimg) {
   print $rec;
}
# end of x0601c.pl
```

## Exercise 7-1

```
# x0701.pl -- modified fixed length record reading demo
$reclen = 32;
$recno = 13;
open(MRAN, "+<makeran.dat>) ||
   die "Can't open makeran.dat.\n";
$recpos = $reclen * ($recno -1);
```

*(continued)*

*(continued)*

```
seek(MRAN, $reclen * ($recno-1),0) ||
   die "Can't locate record $recno.\n";
read(MRAN, $found, $reclen) ||
   die "Found record $recno, but can't read it.\n";
print "$found]n";
# end of x0701.pl
```

## Exercise 7-2

```
sub rpad {
   # expects ($var, $len)
   local ($len, $var, $retval);
   ($var, $len) = @_;
   # look for newline, just in case
   chop($var) if ($var =~ /\n$/);
   $retval = sprintf("%${len}s", $var);
   # cut if $var started out too long
   $retval = substr($retval,0,$len);
}
```

## Exercise 8-1

```
# grepfil2.pl -- read files listed on command line to find
pattern
# usage: perl grepfil2.pl "pattern" filedesc ... > outfile

$pattern = shift(@ARGV);
while (<>) {
   if (/$pattern/i) {
      print "$ARGV\n";
      close (ARGV);
      next;
   }
}
# end of grepfil2.pl
```

## Exercise 8-2

### A.

```
# wordfrq2.pl -- word freq counter, keeps if freq =< 3
# usage: perl wordfrq2.pl filedesc > outfile.dat

while (<>) {
   tr/A-Z/a-z/;
   @wlist = split(/\W/);
   foreach $wd (@wlist) {
      if ($wd =~ /^[a-z_]*$/){
         $words{$wd}++ ;
      }
   }
}

while (($wd, $freq) = each (%words)){
   if ($freq < 4) {                    # add if-block
      push (@wordfreq, join (" ", $wd, $freq));
      $freq = sprintf ("%4d", $freq);
      push (@freqword, join (" ", $freq, $wd));
   }
}
@srtfreq = sort (@freqword);
@srtword = sort (@wordfreq);
foreach $item (@srtfreq) {
   print "$item\n";
}
foreach $item (@srtword) {
   print "$item\n";
}
# end of wordfrq2.pl
```

### B.

```
# wordfrq3.pl -- word freq counter, keeps if freq =< 4
#    and word length => 5
# usage: perl wordfrq3.pl filedesc > outfile.dat
```

*(continued)*

*(continued)*

```
while (<>) {
   tr/A-Z/a-z/;
   @wlist = split(/\W/);
   foreach $wd (@wlist) {
      if ($wd =~ /^[a-z_]*$/){
         $words{$wd}++ ;
      }
   }
}

while (($wd, $freq) = each (%words)){
   if ($freq < 4) {             # add if-block for =< 3
      if (length($wd) > 4) {  # add if-block for >= 5
         push (@wordfreq, join (" ", $wd, $freq));
         $freq = sprintf ("%4d", $freq);
         push (@freqword, join (" ", $freq, $wd));
      }
   }
}
@srtfreq = sort (@freqword);
@srtword = sort (@wordfreq);
foreach $item (@srtfreq) {
   print "$item\n";
}
foreach $item (@srtword) {
   print "$item\n";
}
# end of wordfrq3.pl
```

The two if-blocks after `while (($wd, $freq)...` may also be written combined with a logical AND (`&&`):

```
if (($freq =< 3) && (length($wd) > 4)) {
```

## Exercise 9-1

### A.

```
# print5.pl -- print first five lines of each
#     file in the file descriptor
# usage: perl print5.pl filedesc
#     (for instance, print5.pl *.pl)

while (<>) {
   for ($i=1; $i<6; $i++){
      $line = <ARGV>;
     print $line;
   }
   print "------------------------\n";
   close (ARGV);
}
```

### B.

```
# printhd.pl -- print designated number of lines of each
#     file in the file descriptor
# usage: perl printhd.pl nmbr filedesc
#        (for instance, printhd.pl 3 *.pl)

$nbr =shift (@ARGV);
while (<>) {
   for ($i = 1; $i <= $nbr; $i++){
      $line = <ARGV>;
     print $line;
   }
   print "------------------------\n";
   close (ARGV);
}
```

## Exercise 9-2

```
$A = 1;
$B = 0;
if (!$A || (($A && $B) && ($A || $B))) {
   print "True\n";
} else {
   print "False\n";
}
```

Prints: False

Why? Because:

($A || $B) = True OR False = True

($A && $B) = True AND False = False

($A && $B) && ($A || $B) = True AND False = False

!$A = NOT True = False

!$A || (($A && $B) && ($A || $B)) = False OR False = False

## Exercise 9-3

Convert `frm2mail.pl` (see Chapter 5) to use the `print <<` block statement.

```
#!/usr/local/bin/perl
# frm2mal2.pl -- return form data via email

# your email address goes here -- be sure to
# escape the @ with a backslash -- \@
$email = "me\@mymail.com
read(STDIN, $formdat, $ENV{'CONTENT_LENGTH'});
open(MAILOUT, "| mail $email") ||
   die "Can't start mail program.";

@namevals = split(/&/,$formdat);
foreach (@namevals) {
   tr/+/ /;
```

```
    s/=/ = /;
    s/%(..)/pack("C",hex($1))/ge;
    print MAILOUT "$_\n";
}
close(MAILOUT);

print >>EOPRT;
Content-type: text/html

<HTML><HEAD>
<TITLE>Form Data Sent</TITLE>
</HEAD><BODY>
<H3>Form Data Sent</H3>
<HR>;
Your completed form was delivered.<BR>
Click the browser's BACK button to return.
<P><HR>
</BODY>
</HTML>
EOPRT
```

Note: Make sure there are no trailing spaces after the string terminator `EOPRT` — the string terminator has to be on a line *all by itself.*

## Exercise 9-4

### A.

```
# ascii2.pl -- prints dec and hex for ascii characters
```

### B.

Here is a variation on the `printf` template

```
printf ("%3d%3X%3s     ",$i,$i,pack("C",$i));
```

to print the single character with three spaces to its left:

```
printf ("%3d%3X   %c     ",$i,$i,pack("C",$i));
```

# CD-ROM Guide

The programs and reference files on the CD-ROM for this book are the tools I use for creating Web pages and CGI programs. I hope they will be as valuable and useful to you as they are to me. Update notices and additional references are posted on my Cool Perl support site:

```
http://www.hytext.com/coolperl
```

The Cool Perl page also is the place to go for FAQs (Frequently Asked Questions) about this book and its programs, corrections and enhancements to programs and text, programs submitted by readers, links to Perl-related Web sites, and feedback comments to me about the book.

## Reference Files in \REFDOCS

The `\REFDOCS` directory on the CD-ROM holds HTML references. Perl reference materials are included in the compressed Perl program files.

### *Bare Bones HTML Guide* by Kevin Werbach

`BAREBONE.TXT` is the text file version of Kevin Werbach's famous *Bare Bones HTML Guide*. The format is a condensed, no-nonsense listing of HTML tags and syntax that I use as a memory-jogger. Open the file in Notepad and keep it handy while you are building a Web page. Kevin also has HTML and HTML-Tables versions of the *Bare Bones HTML Guide* at his Web site:

```
http://werbach.com/barebones/
```

## HTML Windows Help Files by Stephen Le Hunte

HTMLHD3X (for Windows 3.*x*) and HTMLHP95 (for Windows 95) are the file sets for Stephen Le Hunte's richly detailed Help files for HTML — the *HTML Reference Library*. To install the files, choose the appropriate directory for your system, and copy it into a fresh, new directory on your hard drive. Then run the SETUP.EXE program in the directory to decompress and install the support files. Open the HLP file (run HELP in Windows 3.*x* Program Manager File⇨Run menu and select the file, or, in Win95, double-click on the HLP file) to access Stephen's remarkably useful organization of details, explanations, and examples on HTML. Updates for the HTML Reference Library are at

```
http://subnet.virtual-pc.com/~le387818/
```

# Windows 95 Tools in \TOOLSW95

Sometimes Notepad just isn't enough to satisfy my desire for text-editing muscle. That is when I use TextPad for Perl code and WebEdit for writing HTML. When the files are written and ready to go, I use WS_FTP to load the whole works up to my Web site. The editors come in 32-bit (for Windows 95) and 16-bit (for Windows 3.*x*) flavors.

## TextPad by Helios Software Solutions

TextPad is the file set for the 32-bit version of the delightful shareware, do-all, text editor TextPad. The list of features is so long that you would be better off living in TextPad's Help file for a while than having me try to summarize them for you. My favorite features include regular expression search and replace, Save As UNIX file, and programmer-friendly macro capability CD-ROM.

To install TextPad, create a new temporary directory and copy the folder's contents into the temporary directory. Then create a new, separate directory for TextPad. Run SETUP.EXE in the temporary directory, aiming the installation at the separate TextPad directory.

You can receive updates and other information about TextPad through e-mail at

```
textpad@heliosof.demon.co.uk
```

## WebEdit by Kenn Nesbitt

`WE2STD32.ZIP` is the file set for the shareware, 32-bit flavor of WebEdit Version 2.0 Standard — my favorite HTML editor. This one is for people who like to roll up their sleeves and dig into a page of tags. Although WebEdit is not all-graphics WYSIWYG, it has a page previewer that gives you a good idea of what the HTML looks like in a browser, a browser-link that displays the HTML in your very own browser, tag-insertion shortcuts, WYSIWYG table and image-map builders, incredible Help files with even a special SSI section and HTML version flags to mark browser-specific and HTML version-specific tags, and a user-support philosophy that's the best I've ever seen.

Kenn has an extra-cost Professional version (to be released just before this book is published) that adds such goodies as HTML tag syntax checking, WYSIWYG Frame wizard, WYSIWYG form designer, FTP upload facility, Link Validation wizard, Table of Contents wizard, and many other features for advanced, big-site Web page production.

Install WebEdit by creating a temporary directory, copying the WebEdit folder's contents into the temporary directory, and running `SETUP.EXE`. Information and updates are at

```
http://www.nesbitt.com
```

## WS_ftp by John Junod

`WS_FTP32.ZIP` holds John Junod's freeware FTP (File Transfer Protocol) client. This program handles FTP transactions across the Internet and brings click-and-drag file management to the world of the Web. WS_ftp is such a nifty little program and so good-looking that I sometimes fire it up just to watch it work, whether or not I've got files to transfer. Please note that this is not a program for Internet beginners — you will have to learn about FTP on your own before you can use WS_ftp.

Install WS_ftp by copying the contents of the `WS_FTP` folder into the final destination directory of your choice. The `README.TXT` file has installation details. As John points out in the instructions, the operation of the program is obvious, but only if you understand what FTP is all about. For information on the commercial use of WS_ftp, contact Ipswitch, Inc., e-mail at

```
info@ipswitch.com
```

# Windows 3.*x* Tools in \TOOLSW3X

In spite of the impression left by advertising and magazaine articles, not everybody has Windows 95. This directory has 16-bit versions of WebEdit and TextPad for people who are quite happy with their Windows 3.*x* environment.

## WE2STD16.ZIP

`WE2STD16.ZIP` contains the 16-bit version of Kenn Nesbitt's WebEdit for Windows 3.*x*. For description and installation, see my preceding notes for the 32-bit version, `WE2STD32.ZIP`.

## TPAD16.ZIP

`TPAD16.ZIP` contains the 16-bit version of TextPad by Helios Software Solutions for Windows 3.*x*. For a description and installation instructions, see my notes for the 32-bit version, `TPAD32.ZIP`.

# Perl for Windows 95 in \PERLW95

`108-I86.ZIP` has the files for Perl 5 ported to Win32 (Windows 95 and Windows NT) by Hip Communications, Inc. This version has the Perl manpages (documentation) in HTML format — a goldmine of official, detailed Perl 5 facts at your beck and call.

Install Perl 5 for Win95 by creating a `/perl` directory in the root of the hard drive, then unZIP `108-I86.ZIP` into the `/perl` directory. **READ THE TEXT FILES AND STUDY THE BAT FILES** so you know what to expect. Now go to the command line in a DOS window. Navigate to the newly stuffed `/perl` directory, and run the installation script: `INSTALL.BAT`. This file will generate new directories and fill them with the appropriate files.

Additional information and updates are at

```
http://info.hip.com/
```

# Perl 4 in \WINPERL

Two sets of freeware Perl files by Maxwell Nairn Andrews are available in the /winperl directory:

| | |
|---|---|
| PERL4003 | Alpha versions of Maxwell's port of Perl 4 for DOS, for Windows 3.11, and for Windows 95 (and NT). |
| PERL4100 | Beta versions of the same triple-threat (DOS, Win 3.*x*, Win95) programs, built with a new compiler. |

The Beta version (PERL4100) includes four Perls:

- PERL386 (16-bit DOS 386 CPU and above)
- PERL32 (32-bit DOS Perl GUI Development 386 CPU and above)
- EASYPERL (32-bit Win32 for Win95/NT WinPERL without the GUI)
- WINPERL (32-bit Win32 Perl GUI Development for Win95/NT)

I asked Maxwell for both versions to give you a choice. I got used to the alpha programs and found the user interface comfortable and much to my personal liking. You may prefer the beta version, which is functionally and graphically enhanced.

The installation instructions are in each file set's PERLTECH.TXT file. Create a directory to hold the files, and unZIP your choice of versions into the directory.

The DOS alpha version requires the files PERL32.EXE, DPMI32VM.OVL, 32RTM.EXE, and GLOB32.EXE to run Perl.

The Win 3.*x* version needs the files PERL32.EXE, GLOB32.EXE, and WINDPMI.386 to run.

The Win95 version uses just PERL32.EXE and GLOB32.EXE because the memory managers required by the other setups are built into Win95.

In his installation instructions, Maxwell points out that this program suite is designed for someone who knows DOS, Windows, and Perl from the get-go, so he doesn't provide any tutorial guides or basic "how to" procedures. You only have to make the files accessible throughout the DOS search path, then run the appropriate Perl EXE. Maxwell's installation instructions are terse, but adequate — they work.

I used WinPerl's Win95 GUI setup throughout the writing of this book to check Perl code snippets without having to build and save complete scripts when I only needed to see how a few lines would work. It's a perfect "I wonder what this will do" test platform. I also made comparisons of Perl 4 and Perl 5 behavior by running full programs in WinPerl from the command-line to check the Perl 4 operation.

Updates are available by FTP from

```
ftp.demon.co.uk
```

in the directory `pub/perl/msdos`.

# Perl for DOS in \PERLDOS

The DOS versions of Perl included in the `/perldos` directory are available from CPAN (Comprehensive Perl Archive Network), a collection of archives in mirrored (duplicated) sites located around the world. You can gain access to CPAN and a number of other useful Perl resources via Yahoo! at

```
http://www.yahoo.com/Computers_and_Internet/Languages/Perl/
```

There are two versions of Perl 4 from CPAN — a small DOS Perl for a minimum-hassle setup, and a big (huge) DOS Perl with everything there is to know about Perl 4.036.

## Perl 4 in \PERLDOS\SMALLDOS

To run Perl with a minimum configuration, you need `perl.exe` and `perlglob.exe` from the set of files compiled by Eelco van Asperen in `BIN4036.ZIP`. Place the two EXE files in the DOS search path (I simply copy them into the \DOS directory).

## Perl 4 in \PERLDOS\BIGDOS

The Perl 4.036 in the `\BIGDOS` directory has everything you need to compile Perl with your very own C compiler — all the source code, all the header files, all the make files, everything. The binary files (EXE) are in `Perl4036`. Of these, you need `perl.exe` and `perlglob.exe` in the DOS search path to run Perl with this set of files. To install the entire programming file and directory structure with all the source code and other heavy duty goodies, create a directory called `\perl` to hold everything, and unZIP the four files into the directory with the `-d` option to preserve directory paths. This is a very educational set of files!

# Listings in \BOOKCODE

The `\BOOKCODE` directory has a batch of subdirectories, one for each chapter of this book. Each subdirectory has the Perl code, data files, and HTML text for the listings in that chapter. The answers for the chapter's exercises are also included.

# HyBrowser in \HYBROW

HyBrowser is my answer to the problem of testing HTML forms locally, without having to hook up to the Internet. HyBrowser is a simple Web browser with a few small tricks built into it. When you click on the Submit button for forms with the `ACTION` parameter set to `"hybrowser"`, this program will print the URL-encoded data string into a local file for your examination and testing.

The version of HyBrowser on the CD-ROM is for Windows 95. To install HyBroswer, run `SETUP.EXE` in the CD-ROM `\HYBROW` directory, and follow the installation prompts.

A 16-bit version of HyBrowser for Windows 3.*x* is in the works. The latest versions of HyBrowser and updated Help files in HTML format are available at

```
http://www.hytext.com/coolperl
```

## Symbols & Numbers

C

# IDG BOOKS WORLDWIDE, INC.
# END-USER LICENSE AGREEMENT

Read This. You should carefully read these terms and conditions before opening the software packet(s) included with this book ("Book"). This is a license agreement ("Agreement") between you and IDG Books Worldwide, Inc. ("IDGB"). By opening the accompanying software packet(s), you acknowledge that you have read and accept the following terms and conditions. If you do not agree and do not want to be bound by such terms and conditions, promptly return the Book and the unopened software packet(s) to the place you obtained them for a full refund.

**1. License Grant.** IDGB grants to you (either an individual or entity) a nonexclusive license to use one copy of the enclosed software program(s) (collectively, the "Software") solely for your own personal or business purposes on a single computer (whether a standard computer or a workstation component of a multiuser network). The Software is in use on a computer when it is loaded into temporary memory (i.e., RAM) or installed into permanent memory (e.g., hard disk, CD-ROM, or other storage device). IDGB reserves all rights not expressly granted herein.

**2. Ownership.** IDGB is the owner of all right, title, and interest, including copyright, in and to the compilation of the Software recorded on the disk(s)/CD-ROM. Copyright to the individual programs on the disk(s)/CD-ROM is owned by the author or other authorized copyright owner of each program. Ownership of the Software and all proprietary rights relating thereto remain with IDGB and its licensors.

**3. Restrictions on Use and Transfer.**

(a) You may only (i) make one copy of the Software for backup or archival purposes, or (ii) transfer the Software to a single hard disk, provided that you keep the original for backup or archival purposes. You may not (i) rent or lease the Software, (ii) copy or reproduce the Software through a LAN or other network system or through any computer subscriber system or bulletin-board system, or (iii) modify, adapt, or create derivative works based on the Software.

(b) You may not reverse engineer, decompile, or disassemble the Software. You may transfer the Software and user documentation on a permanent basis, provided that the transferee agrees to accept the terms and conditions of this Agreement and you retain no copies. If the Software is an update or has been updated, any transfer must include the most recent update and all prior versions.

**4. Restrictions on Use of Individual Programs.** You must follow the individual requirements and restrictions detailed for each individual program on the "Disc Installation Instructions" page of this Book. These limitations are contained in the individual license agreements recorded on the disk(s)/CD-ROM. These restrictions may include a requirement that after using the program for the period of time specified in its text, the user must pay a registration fee or discontinue use. By opening the Software packet(s), you will be agreeing to abide by the licenses and restrictions for these individual programs. None of the material on this disk(s) or listed in this Book may ever be distributed, in original or modified form, for commercial purposes.

**5. Limited Warranty.**

(a) IDGB warrants that the Software and disk(s)/CD-ROM are free from defects in materials and workmanship under normal use for a period of sixty (60) days from the date of purchase of this Book. If IDGB receives notification within the warranty period of defects in materials or workmanship, IDGB will replace the defective disk(s)/CD-ROM.

**(b) IDGB AND THE AUTHOR OF THE BOOK DISCLAIM ALL OTHER WARRANTIES, EXPRESSED OR IMPLIED, INCLUDING WITHOUT LIMITATION IMPLIED WARRANTIES OF MERCHANTABILITY AND FITNESS FOR A PARTICULAR PURPOSE, WITH RESPECT TO THE SOFTWARE, THE PROGRAMS, THE SOURCE CODE CONTAINED THEREIN, AND/OR THE TECHNIQUES DESCRIBED IN THIS BOOK. IDGB DOES NOT WARRANT THAT THE FUNCTIONS CONTAINED IN THE SOFTWARE WILL MEET YOUR REQUIREMENTS OR THAT THE OPERATION OF THE SOFTWARE WILL BE ERROR FREE.**

(c) This limited warranty gives you specific legal rights, and you may have other rights which vary from jurisdiction to jurisdiction.

**6. Remedies.**

(a) IDGB's entire liability and your exclusive remedy for defects in materials and workmanship shall be limited to replacement of the Software, which may be returned to IDGB with a copy of your receipt at the following address: Disk Fulfillment Department, Attn: *Creating Cool Web Pages with Perl,* IDG Books Worldwide, Inc., 7260 Shadeland Station, Ste. 100, Indianapolis, IN 46256, or call 1-800-762-2974. Please allow 3-4 weeks for delivery. This Limited Warranty is void if failure of the Software has resulted from accident, abuse, or misapplication. Any replacement Software will be warranted for the remainder of the original warranty period or thirty (30) days, whichever is longer.

(b) In no event shall IDGB or the author be liable for any damages whatsoever (including without limitation damages for loss of business profits, business interruption, loss of business information, or any other pecuniary loss) arising from the use of or inability to use the Book or the Software, even if IDGB has been advised of the possibility of such damages.

(c) Because some jurisdictions do not allow the exclusion or limitation of liability for consequential or incidental damages, the above limitation or exclusion may not apply to you.

**7. U.S. Government Restricted Rights.** Use, duplication, or disclosure of the Software by the U.S. Government is subject to restrictions stated in paragraph (c) (1) (ii) of the Rights in Technical Data and Computer Software clause of DFARS 252.227-7013, and in subparagraphs (a) through (d) of the Commercial Computer—Restricted Rights clause at FAR 52.227-19, and in similar clauses in the NASA FAR supplement, when applicable.

**8. General.** This Agreement constitutes the entire understanding of the parties and revokes and supersedes all prior agreements, oral or written, between them and may not be modified or amended except in writing signed by both parties hereto which specifically refers to this Agreement. This Agreement shall take precedence over any other documents that may be in conflict herewith. If any one or more provisions contained in this Agreement are held by any court or tribunal to be invalid, illegal, or otherwise unenforceable, each and every other provision shall remain in full force and effect.